3d Edition

Comparative Economic Systems

Martin C. Schnitzer
Professor of Management
College of Business
Virginia Polytechnic Institute and State University

James W. Nordyke
Professor of Economics
College of Business Administration and Economics
New Mexico State University

Published by

H77 **SOUTH-WESTERN PUBLISHING CO.**

CINCINNATI   WEST CHICAGO, ILL.   DALLAS   PELHAM MANOR, N.Y.   PALO ALTO, CALIF.

Copyright © 1983
by South-Western Publishing Co.
Cincinnati, Ohio

ISBN: 0-538-08770-6
Library of Congress Catalog Card Number: 81-85864

1 2 3 4 5 6 7 8 D 9 8 7 6 5 4 3 2
Printed in the United States of America

PREFACE

The purpose of this book is to present a concise account of existing economic systems so that the student may secure an intelligent understanding of how they operate. To facilitate this understanding, the book is organized to include separate chapters on the economies of a number of important industrial nations. The economic systems of these countries are treated in a similar organizational manner so that a common frame of reference runs throughout the book.

However, it is necessary to point out that the advanced industrial countries of today do not fall into a rigid ideological system or classification labeled capitalism, communism, or socialism. It is more useful instead to think of a spectrum of systems ranging from those that rely heavily upon market mechanisms to allocate resources to those that rely on central command or planning for resource allocation. The United States lies near the market end of the spectrum. In the realm of economies, great faith has been traditionally placed in the efficacy of individual initiative, private ownership of property, production for profit, competition, and a minimum of interference by government in business. But there has developed a quite substantial element of governmental control of the economy. Japan and the countries of Western Europe lie near the center of the spectrum. Although resource allocation is achieved primarily through the market mechanism, there is some government ownership of industry and extensive participation by government in the economy. Even in those countries that have command economies, market arrangements are used to some degree to supplement central planning. The degree varies from one country to the other.

The book proceeds through the spectrum. Part 1 explains the functioning of capitalism, socialism, and communism. Part 2 describes the operation of the United States, taking into consideration the governmental and other arrangements that have been superimposed on the market system. Part 3 presents the mixed economic systems of four highly advanced industrial democracies: France, Japan, West Germany, and the United Kingdom. Part 4 pertains to countries which have economies of modified central command. Four nations—the Soviet Union, China, Yugoslavia, and Poland—are examined. Part 5 summarizes the performance of the economic systems in the early 1980s.

Thanks and appreciation are expressed to individuals at the War College, the Central Intelligence Agency, and the U.S. Department of Commerce for providing data; to Dr. Harrison Fox and Senator John Warner for their assistance in providing classified materials; and Dr. Sumer Aggarwal of Pennsylvania State University for the use of his chart on the Russian distribution system. Dr. Schnitzer also wishes to thank his graduate assistant, Susan Monroe, for her help in data collection, and his wife, Joan, for typing the manuscript. Jane and Danuta, two friends from Poland, were invaluable in providing first-hand information on the events preceding the military crackdown in December 1981.

CONTENTS

PART 1
INTRODUCTION TO ECONOMIC SYSTEMS

1

Market Mechanisms and Capitalism

INTRODUCTION

A fundamental dilemma of any economic system is a scarcity of resources relative to wants. Decisions are necessary to determine how a given volume of resources is to be allocated to production and how the income derived from production is to be distributed to the various agents—capital, labor, and land—that are responsible for it. Human wants, if not unlimited, are at least indefinitely expansible, but the commodities and services which can satisfy these wants are not, and neither are the productive agents which can produce the desired goods and services. The various grades and types of these productive factors usually have alternative uses; that is, they can be used in the production of a number of different goods and services. There is the necessity of allocating limited productive resources, which have alternative uses, to the satisfaction of great and growing human wants.

Large amounts of capital will not be available for use in production unless there is a process of saving and capital formation. This process is fundamentally the same in all types of economic systems. It cannot operate unless the available productive resources are somewhat more than adequate to provide a bare living for the people of a system. When it is able to operate, the process involves, in a money sense, spending part of the money income of an economy, directly or indirectly, for capital goods rather than for consumer goods. In a nonmonetary sense, saving and capital formation require the allocation of a part of the productive resources of a country to the turning out of capital goods rather than consumer goods. The cost of obtaining capital goods is the same in all economic systems. It is found in the necessity of going without at present the quantities of consumer goods and services which could have been produced by the agents of production.

In general, societies have endless ways of organizing and performing their production and distribution functions. In economic and political terms, the possible range is from laissez-faire capitalism through totalitarian communism. The economy of the United States today by no means represents a pure laissez-faire capitalist system. It is rather a mixed economic system, since there are public enterprises, considerable government regulation and control and various other elements that hinder the unrestrained functioning of market forces. However, to understand how a capitalist system works, it is necessary to know something about its institutional arrangement. For practical purposes, an *institutional arrangement* is a practice, convention, or custom which is a material and persistent element in the life or culture of an organized group. *Economic institutions* are ways of reacting, in certain economic situations and with respect to certain economic and social phenomena, some of which rest on custom, while others are formally recognized through legislative enactment.

CAPITALISM AS AN ECONOMIC SYSTEM

There are a number of institutional arrangements that characterize a capitalist economic system. These arrangements provide a set of basic beliefs that define how a society should be organized and how goods and services should be produced and income distributed. These beliefs are incorporated into the institutional arrangements that so typify a capitalist system—private property, the profit motive, the price system, freedom of enterprise, competition, individualism, consumer sovereignty, the work ethic, and limited government. Each of these institutions will be discussed in some detail.

Private Property

Under capitalism there is private ownership of the agents of production—land, labor, and capital. There is also the existence of certain rights of persons who own property. An individual has the right to acquire property, to consume or control it, to buy or sell it, to give it away as a gift, and to bequeath it at death. Private property ownership is supposed to encourage thrift and accumulation and to serve as a stimulus to individual initiative and industry, both of which are considered essential to economic progress.

However, private property ownership is subject to certain limitations. In practice, even under capitalism, property rights are often restricted by the actions of larger or smaller social groups or government units. Also, a good deal of the private wealth of capitalist systems, such as the United States, is not owned by individuals, but rather by corporations. There is actually a good deal of public property within a capitalistic system. Where public property exists, the exclusive control of wealth is exercised by a group of individuals through some governmental unit.

The Profit Motive

The kinds of goods produced in a capitalist or market economy that relies on market arrangements is determined in the first instance by managers of business firms or by individual entrepreneurs. They are directly responsible for converting resources into products and determining what these products will be, guided, of course, by the actions of consumers in the marketplace. The profit motive is the lodestar that draws managers to produce goods that can be sold at prices that are higher than the costs of production. In private enterprise, profit is necessary for survival; anybody who produces things that do not, directly or indirectly, yield a profit will sooner or later go bankrupt, lose his or her ownership of the means of production, and so cease to be an independent producer. There can be no other way. Capitalism, in other words, uses profitability as the test of whether any given item should or should not be produced, and if it should, how much of it should be produced.

The Price System

Individuals and business firms under capitalism are supposed to make most types of economic decisions on the basis of prices, price relationships, and price changes. The function of prices is to provide a coordinating mechanism for millions of decentralized private production and distribution units. The prices that prevail in the marketplace in the main determine what kinds and quantities of goods and services shall be produced and how they shall be distributed. Price changes are supposed to adjust the quantities of these goods and services available for the market.

It is through the mechanism of prices, rather than a comprehensive national economic plan, that scarce resources are allocated to various uses. The interaction between the price system and the pursuit of profits is supposed to keep economic mistakes down to a reasonable level. Profits, which depend upon the selling price of goods and the cost of making them, indicate to business firms what people are buying. A product that commands high prices draws business firms into that industry; low prices check production by causing business firms to drop out.

In general, the conditions of supply and demand determine prices and guide production. Demand originates with the consumer. It implies a desire for a good or service that can be expressed through a willingness to pay money for it in the marketplace. A small supply relative to demand raises prices; a large supply relative to demand lowers prices. Conversely, a large demand relative to supply raises prices, and a small demand relative to supply lowers prices.

The forces of supply and demand acting through the price mechanism can send effective signals to the marketplace. Resource allocation responds to shifts in supply and demand. For example, an increase in demand means that buyers will be willing to purchase more at each of a series of prices than they were formerly. An increase in demand, with supply remaining constant, would result in both an increase in price and quantity; a decrease in demand would have the opposite effect.

Freedom of Enterprise

Freedom of enterprise is another basic institution of capitalism. It refers to the general right which each individual has to engage in any line of economic activity which appeals to him or her. As far as the government is concerned, the individual is free to move to any part of the country, select any occupation that pleases him or her, and find and operate a business unit in virtually any field of economic activity. By comparing market indicators, namely prices and costs, the individual is supposed to be able to select a field of activity which promises to be remunerative. The institution of private property furnishes the social sanctions necessary for the use and control of the agents of production vital to the chosen field of activity. The theory which is used to justify the existence of freedom of enterprise is quite simply one of social welfare. That is, the individual, in choosing the field of economic activity in which he or she will be the most productive and useful from the point of view of private gain, will also be selecting the field in which he or she will be most productive.

Competition

The attempts of individuals to further their economic self-interest, given the institutions of private property and freedom of enterprise, and with the guidance of the price system, result in competition. Competition is an indispensable part of a free enterprise system. In economic life, self-reliant individuals must struggle and compete for economic rewards—good jobs, high pay, promotions, desirable goods and services, and security in old age. There is the element of social Darwinism in competition—life is a competitive struggle in which only the fittest get to the top, winners in a race where victory goes to the swift and resourceful.

Certainly, *competition* is one of the "good" words in the American vocabulary. From a very early age, schoolchildren are told that the distinguishing characteristic of the historically successful U.S. economic system is competition, and that other economic systems have inefficiencies because, in some degree, they lack that magic ingredient in the particular and unique context in which it exists in our economy. It is, therefore, not surprising that by statute and at common law our legal system has been actively concerned with the maintenance of a competitive system.

Certain benefits are thought to be derived from the inherent characteristics of competition in the marketplace. These benefits are as follows:

1. A competitive market will allow the price mechanism to reflect actual demand and cost and thus maximize efficiency in the use of capital and other resources.
2. A competitive market will encourage product innovation and long-run cost reduction.
3. A competitive market will result in the equitable diffusion of real income.
4. A competitive market will provide consumers with a wide variety of alternative sources of supply.

Individualism

Individualism is linked to a set of related institutional values of capitalism. For one thing there is social Darwinism—life is a competitive struggle where the fit survive and those who are unfit do not. Individualism also involves competition, which, when combined with social Darwinism, is supposed to provide some guarantee of progress through the inexorable process of evolution. Individualism is also related to equality of opportunity—the right of each person to succeed or fail on his or her own merit or lack of it.

The institution of private property rights and individualism are related from two standpoints. First, private property ownership provides the spur for individual initiative, a reward to be gained through competition and hard work. Second, it provides some guarantee of individual rights against the encroachments of the state. It follows that a necessary requisite for individualism is a limited state role. The individual would have preference over the state, for the latter is a fictitious body composed of individual persons who are considered to represent its members. The idea of individualism can therefore be a safeguard against the tyranny of the state.

To some extent individualism is linked to the philosophical roots of capitalism. The idea itself is a distinctive achievement of human consciousness—a mark of high civilization. It is consistent with the principles of a libertarian society in that it carries with it the concept of freedom to live and work as one prefers. There is a sense of privacy in individualism, privacy as something sacred in its own right. Under classical liberalism the individual is the center of society—the fulcrum that makes a free enterprise system work. Through energy applied to the fulfillment of personal needs, the individual pushes society forward. This will not result from charitable motives, but from the inexorable logic of the system—Adam Smith's "invisible hand." Stated simply, if all people are motivated to work at full capacity—whether they work as laborers, artisans, or executives—the net supply of goods and services available for consumption by all will be increased.

Consumer Sovereignty

In a capitalistic market economy, consumer sovereignty is an important institution because consumption is supposed to be the basic rationale of economic activity. As Adam Smith said, "Consumption is the sole end and purpose of all production; and the interest of the producer ought to be attended to only as far as it is necessary for promoting that of the consumer."[1] Consumer sovereignty assumes, of course, that there is a competitive market economy in which consumers are able to vote with their money by offering more of it for products that are in greater demand and less of it for products that are not in demand. Shifts in supply and demand will occur in response to the way in which consumers spend their money.

In competing for consumers' dollars, producers will produce more of those products that are in demand, for the price will be higher, and less of those products that are not in demand, for the price will be lower. Production is the means; consumption is the end. Those producers that effectively satisfy the wants of consumers are encouraged by large monetary returns, which enable them in turn to purchase the goods and services they require in their operations. On the other hand, those producers that do not respond to the wants of consumers will not remain in business very long.

Freedom of choice is linked to consumer sovereignty. In fact, one defense of the market mechanism is the freedom of choice it provides

---

[1]Adam Smith, *The Wealth of Nations* (New York: Random House, 1937), p. 336.

consumers in a capitalistic economy. Consumers are free to accept or reject whatever is produced in the marketplace. Thus, the consumer is king, since production ultimately is oriented toward meeting the wants of consumers. Freedom of choice is consistent with a laissez-faire economy. It is assumed that consumers are capable of making rational decisions, and in an economy dominated by a large number of buyers and sellers this assumption has some merit. Since the role of the government is minimal, the principle of caveat emptor, "let the buyer beware," governs consumer decisions to buy.

The Protestant Work Ethic

The Protestant ethic is an ideological principle which stems from the Protestant Reformation of the 16th century[2] and is associated with the religious reformer John Calvin, who preached a doctrine of salvation that later proved to be consistent with the principles of a capitalist system. According to Calvin and the Puritan ministers in early New England, hard work, diligence, and thrift were earthly signs that individuals were using fully the talents given to them by God for His overall purposes. Salvation was associated with achievement on this earth. Work and economic gain came to have a moral value. It was good for the soul to work, rewards on this earth would go to those who achieved the most, and salvation in the world to come was a reward that was in direct proportion to the deceased person's contribution during his or her life.

The Calvinist doctrine of work and salvation became in integral part of the ideology of capitalism. The hard work of merchants and traders often produced profits, and their thrift led to saving and investment. Saving is the heart of the Protestant ethic.[3] With Adam Smith's idea of parsimony or frugality, and Nassau Senior's idea of abstinence, it was established that saving multiplied future products and earned its own reward through interest. Carried into American society in the 19th century, the Protestant ethic came to mean rewards for those who were economically competent and punishment for those who were incompetent or unambitious. Work was put at the center of American life. Most of the industrial capitalists of the last century belonged to fundamentalist Protestant churches. John D. Rockefeller, who became the then richest man in the world, attributed his success to the "glory of God." Skeptics, however, attributed his success to much more mundane factors than God's beneficence.

---

[2]Max Weber, *The Protestant Ethic and the Spirit of Capitalism* (New York: Scribner, 1930).

[3]It has been said with a considerable degree of truth that charge accounts destroyed the Protestant ethic.

Limited Government

For many years, the idea prevailed that the government in a capitalist system, however it might be organized, should follow a policy of *laissez-faire* with respect to economic activity. That is, activities of the government should be limited to the performance of a few general functions for the good of all citizens, and government should not attempt to control or interfere with the economic activities of private individuals. Laissez-faire assumes that each individual is a rational being and a better judge of his or her own interests than any government could possibly be.[4] The interests of individuals are closely identified with those of society as a whole. It is only necessary for government to provide a setting or environment in which these institutions can operate in a free fashion. This the government was supposed to do by performing only those functions that individuals could not do for themselves: provide for national defense, maintain law and order, carry on diplomatic relations with other countries, and construct roads, schools, and public works.

It has been pointed out that in a free enterprise market economy competition is regarded as a virtue rather than a vice, particularly when business is concerned. The proper use of resources in a free enterprise system is assured by the fact that if a firm does not use resources efficiently, it goes broke. If the market is to function effectively, there can be no other way. If there is intervention in any form, then there is no effective mechanism for the weeding out of inefficient enterprises. Nevertheless, government has always participated to some extent in business activity of capitalist countries. From the beginning of the United States as a republic in 1787, the federal government has been interested in the promotion of manufacturing, and it passed tariff laws very early to protect American business interests. Subsidies were used to promote the development of canals, roads, and railroads. Business was a direct beneficiary of those subsidies.

INCOME DISTRIBUTION IN A CAPITALIST ECONOMY

Once the production of goods and services has taken place, the next important problem in any economic system concerns the manner in

---

[4]The term *laissez-faire* originated in France, possibly as early as the first half of the 18th century, and was later developed by Adam Smith as a rule of practical economic conduct. In particular, see Adam Smith, *The Wealth of Nations* (London: Nelson, 1891), Book IV, especially p. 286. Laissez-faire was a reaction to the stringent government restrictions imposed on all phases of economic activity by mercantilism. Under mercantilism, the state controlled all businesses, and one could engage in a particular activity only by receiving a monopoly from the state.

which these goods and services are to be divided or apportioned among the individual consumers of the economy. The distribution of income does not refer to the processes by which physical goods are brought from producers to consumers, but rather it refers to the distribution of the national income, first in money and then in goods and services, among the owners of the productive agents—land, labor, and capital.

As long as the productive agents of an economy are incapable of producing an adequate volume of goods and services for consumption, the question of income distribution is likely to remain in the background, while attention is focused on the problem of increasing production. But as the productive capacity of an economy increases, income distribution becomes progressively more important. In a vital sense, the distribution of income has been a key issue that had pervaded Western society since the beginning of capitalism.

Income distribution in a market economy is based on institutional arrangements, such as the pricing process, that are associated with this type of system. High prices are set on scarce agents of production and low prices on plentiful agents. In terms of rewards to labor, those persons whose skills are scarce relative to demand enjoy a high level of income, while those persons whose skills are not scarce do not. The implication is that persons whose productivity in value terms is low will earn little, regardless of whether the low productivity is attributable to lack of effort, lack of skill, or low demand for the skill.

Income in a market economy emanates from two sources: (1) earned income from wages and salaries or self-employment and (2) property income. Property may be regarded as a stock of claims on the value of wealth, including natural resources, capital, and consumer durable goods. The structure of property claims in a capitalist economy is complex; the claims on wealth owned by corporations, for example, may be represented by common or preferred stock, by corporate bonds, and by notes and mortgages. In national income accounting, labor income consists of wages, salaries, and entrepreneurial income, while property income takes the form of rent, interest, and profit. Thus there is a fundamental dichotomy between labor and nonlabor income.

The most basic theory underlying income distribution in a market economy involves the marginal productivity concept. This concept can be applied to the distribution of both labor and property incomes. Under competitive conditions, the income received by the worker tends to be determined by supply and demand, so that the income received equals the marginal contribution that the worker is able to make to the exchange value of goods and services. The same reasoning is also applied to the distribution of property income. Resource owners tend to be remunerated according to the marginal revenue products of the resources they own.

The marginal productivity concept is based on the law of diminishing returns, which holds that an increased amount of a resource applied to a fixed quantity of other resources will yield a diminished marginal product. Thus if employers were to take on a number of workers so large that the marginal revenue product was not worth the wage that had to be paid, they would soon find that number excessive. The number of workers that any employer would prefer to take on is that number that maximizes his or her profit, and that number is given by the equality of wages to the marginal revenue product of the last worker employed. Below this point an employer would be reducing his revenues more than his costs, and so diminish his profit. Above this point, profit is not being maximized because labor costs are increasing faster than revenues.

The marginal productivity theory of income distribution, however, is subject to much criticism. First of all, the assumptions upon which it is based are open to question. For one thing, it is assumed that a truly competitive economy exists and that all units of an economic resource are basically alike, so that they may be interchanged in production and may contribute to the production of a number of goods and services with different exchange values. Without these assumptions, there is no close correlation between the income received by resource owners and the value of the marginal revenue products of the resources they provide.

In a complicated modern economy, it is inconceivable that marginal productivity analysis is sufficient in itself to explain the distribution of income. This does not, however, deny the validity of the concept. It can be said that decisions made by individuals (or groups, such as trade unions, government, or large-scale enterprises), within the framework of demand and supply, determine income distribution. Generally, the demand for an economic resource is derived from the goals of production (either maximum profit or the volume of production) as determined by institutional considerations. The supply of an economic resource is based upon numerous and varying economic and sociological factors that represent a composite of quantity and quality variables, such as education.

SAVING AND CAPITAL FORMATION UNDER CAPITALISM

In a capitalistic system, large amounts of savings are made by individuals on the basis of the relationship between interest rates and other prices. The necessary condition for such savings is that the interest rate be sufficient to overcome the time preference of the savers—their desire to consume their incomes in the present as opposed to some time in the future. However, a certain amount of savings is independent of the interest rate. In this class, savings are made to provide for certain financial emergencies or to obtain the power which an accumulation of income can bring. Persons with very large incomes may save almost automatically because of the difficulties involved in finding enough consumption uses for their incomes.[5] Other savings, such as those that result when corporations retain their earnings instead of paying dividends to stock-holders, do not depend on the voluntary decisions of those individuals (stockholders) whose earnings are being saved. Finally, there may be forced savings in the form of taxes that government may use directly or indirectly for capital purposes.

The use of capital goods in production clearly involves the existence of savings. Savings are translated into investment in a capitalist system through the market mechanism of supply and demand, with interest rates performing an allocative function. In order to be able to afford to pay interest on a loan and ultimately to repay the principal, the borrower must be able to put the funds to good use. This tends to exclude the less productive uses and thus ration savings for more productive uses.

Under capitalism, saving and investment, in large part, are carried out by different sets of people for different reasons. Investment is the pur-chase of capital goods and as such is largely undertaken by business firms. The act of saving is undertaken by both individuals and business firms. With large numbers of scattered savers and borrowers desirous of obtain-ing funds for investment purposes, there is clearly a need for some type of intermediary or go-between to bring the savers and borrowers together. This function is performed to a large extent by commercial and invest-ment banks which are privately owned and operated for a profit. They underwrite securities issues for governmental units as well as business firms. The investment bankers bring together the business and govern-ment units which desire short- and long-term funds and the individuals and institutions which have these funds to invest.

THE HISTORICAL DEVELOPMENT OF CAPITALISM

The roots of capitalism lie far back in the Middle Ages, where the seeking of profit was already becoming the dominant motive in the lives of many, especially the merchants of the Italian city-states of Genoa and Venice.[6] In fact, the discovery of America in 1492 can be attributed to the search for new markets. The Church and other molders of public opinion came to accept the concept of profit, in part because they too found good use for money. Earlier Church thought held that money was sterile in

---

[5]However, man's psychology, as pictured by Hobbes, is an appetitive drive which drives him ferociously to achieve his desires. In a modern society, the engine of appetite is an increased standard of living, with an emphasis on display. Thorstein Veblen makes a similar point when he contended that men are driven by an impulse for status. See Thomas Hobbes, *Leviathan* (Oxford: Blackwell, 1946); also Thorstein Veblen, *The Theory of the Leisure Class* (Boston: Houghton Mifflin, 1973).

[6]The merchants of the Italian city-states invented almost all of the commercial devices that made a profit-seeking society possible. One such device was double-entry bookkeeping, which showed merchants that they were supposed to show a balance on the right side of the ledger.

that it did not reproduce itself. It was not morally feasible to lend money at interest. However, there was nothing wrong in using money to buy something. But when it was seen that, if invested in productive enterprises, it could indeed make more money for the benefit of all, and that payment for the use of money (interest) would alone persuade the owners of money to invest it, the earlier concept was abandoned. Thereafter only the practice of lending money at interest for purposes of consumption was condemned. In due course, even this practice came to be condoned.

No pronounced break can be discerned between the growing capitalistic practices of the later Middle Ages and those of modern times. The influx of gold and silver from the New World entailed major political and economic consequences in Europe, contributing to the rise of the nation-states. The new wealthy classes, who engaged in trade everywhere, needed a stable national government to guarantee commerce, protect sea routes, and assure the arrival of merchant ships. Monarchs, who needed the financial support of the wealthy merchants to pay for their wars, were expected to support home commerce. One method of supporting home commerce was by ensuring that only ships of the home country could be used in transporting goods from, and sometimes even to, home ports.

Mercantilism

It became accepted theory during the 16 to 18th centuries that a country was wealthy when it had a large amount of gold and silver bullion. To obtain this result the country had to have what was known as a favorable balance of trade, gained by exporting more than was imported. Thus, it was in the country's own interest to support home industry to enable it to export as many products as possible. This policy of supporting home industry came to be called *mercantilism.* It meant government intervention everywhere, but particularly in foreign trade. In the domestic field, it meant regulation of industry and domestic trade; in external affairs, it meant regulation of commercial relations between the mother country and her colonies. This meant that the colonies existed to furnish the mother country with goods that could not be produced at home. The colonies were also expected to furnish the mother country with a favorable balance of trade, as represented by an inflow of precious metals into the country. It was against the colonial policy of mercantilism that the 13 colonies of North America arose and fought for their independence.

The Industrial Revolution

The Industrial Revolution changed national attitudes from the policy of mercantilism to a policy of laissez-faire. Scientific breakthroughs, inventions, and the factory system encouraged specialization and the concentration of production. This encouraged a movement from state self-sufficiency to a doctrine of free trade, which was supported by the classical economists such as Adam Smith and David Ricardo and the philosopher John Locke. During the 19th century, world trade turnover increased rapidly while the pattern of world trade also changed.

The Industrial Revolution consisted mainly of the application of machinery to manufacturing, mining, transportation, communication, and agriculture, and of the changes in economic organization that attended these applications.[7] Fundamental in the new industrial order was the development of a cheap, portable source of power. James Watt's invention of the condenser and of a practical method of converting the reciprocating motion of the piston into rotary motion made the steam engine a practical prime mover for all kinds of machinery.

The Industrial Revolution probably represented the hallmark of capitalism. With the development of machinery, the old method of small-scale production in the home with one's own tools could not meet the competition of machine production, and the cost of machinery was prohibitive to individual workers. Hence, the factory system arose, with large-scale production in factories using machinery owned by the employer. The factory system stimulated the growth of division of labor and mass production through the standardization of processes and parts. Old industries began to produce on a much larger scale than previously, and new industries developed, offering new goods to satisfy mass wants.

Industrial capitalists were created, and it was they who shaped the course of future industrialization by reinvesting their gains in new enterprises. The Industrial Revolution also enormously accentuated the movement toward international economic interdependence that had begun in the previous centuries. As the population of Europe became more and more engaged in urban industry, they raised less food on their farms and became heavy importers of wheat, meat, and other food products. In exchange for food, Europe exported manufactured goods, and the entire world became a marketplace.

The doctrine of laissez-faire fit in with the development of capitalism. It carried with it a sense of independence, personal initiative, and self-responsibility. If individual initiative is respected, it gives free play to entrepreneurs to create those products that are responsive to those who want them and will pay for them. A necessary requisite for individualism was a limited state role. The individual should have preference over the state, for the latter is a fictitious body composed of individual persons who are considered to be its members. The ideas of individualism and

---

[7]The Industrial Revolution began in England between 1770 and 1825 and in continental Europe after 1815. Some scholars contend that we are in a new period of post-industrial development. See, for example, Daniel Bell, *The Coming of Post-Industrial Society* (New York: Basic Books, 1976).

laissez-faire were therefore regarded by Adam Smith and others as a safe-guard against the tyranny of the state.

Finance Capitalism

A constant growth in the use of machinery, and especially mass production, made it increasingly necessary for individual entrepreneurs to raise large amounts of capital. As this became more difficult, the control of industry passed more and more into the hands of a few large investment banking houses. This system became known as *finance capitalism*. Banks became professional accumulators of capital. Corporations, which by the latter part of the 19th century had become the dominant form of business unit, were able to obtain large quantities of long-term capital funds by selling their securities with the assistance of investment banks. The banks underwrote and distributed the securities, eventually getting them in the hands of insurance companies, banks, investment trusts, and individual investors. These banking houses were able to acquire an inordinate amount of economic power through the ownership of securities and through the interlocking directorate device.

MODIFICATIONS OF CAPITALISM

Various elements have conspired over time to transform pure market capitalism to more of what can be called state-guided capitalism. In fact, the term *mixed economic system* is used in later chapters to describe countries which were at one time purely capitalistic. Part of this transformation has been the development of the welfare state, which resulted from the extremely unequal distribution of income that developed during the Industrial Revolution. A growing concentration of economic power in the hands of a few persons created extremes of wealth and poverty. In the United States, for example, during the 1890s the department store magnate Marshall Field had an income calculated at $600 an hour; his shop-girls, earning salaries of $3 to $5 a week, had to work three to five years to earn that amount.[8] Working conditions for the mass of workers in the Western industrial world were deplorable: the 12-hour work day and 7-day work week were not uncommon. There were no child labor laws; children of eight and even less worked in the coal mines and textile mills in the United States and England.

---

[8]Cited in Otto Bettman, *The Good Old Days—They Were Terrible* (New York: Random House, 1974), p. 67.

The Decline of the Protestant Ethic

There were other factors influencing the transformation of capitalism. Thrift, which at one time was a linchpin of the Protestant work ethic, began to decline. Traditional morality, as represented by Puritanism, was challenged by the automobile, movies, and credit cards. A mass production society could not tolerate thrift. Why save when you could buy an automobile on credit? Since the 1920s credit has become the passport to instant gratification. American culture was no longer concerned with how to work and achieve, but with how to spend and enjoy.

The Decline of Individualism

Another capitalist institution that has been transformed is individualism. The idea of rugged individualism had always been a greatly romanticized part of the American frontier spirit. This individualism, as epitomized by John Wayne in the movie *True Grit*, carried with it a sense of independence, personal initiative, and self-responsibility.[9] Life was a series of constant challenges to be met head on, as did John Wayne when, at the end of *True Grit*, he went charging into the four bad men, reins in teeth and guns blazing. It was the individual rather than the state who did the punishing, and moralizing was left to the preachers. There was in individualism the idea of a "just meritocracy."[10] Individuals should be left free to achieve what they can through their own abilities and efforts. Naturally, there will be winners and losers, but this is the inevitable end result in a libertarian society.

To some extent, individualism in the Western world has been superceded by egalitarianism. The decline of individualism is largely a concomitant of urban industrialized life. Individual desires often clash with the wishes of groups. Often there is disharmony, as the individual pulls in one direction while the group wants to go in the other direction. Claims on a community have come to be decided on the basis of group membership rather than individual attributes.[11] Social life has increasingly become organized on a group basis.

Egalitarianism has meant different things at different time periods. In the United States, the Jeffersonian concept of equality was an equality of the elect (those eligible to vote).[12] The Jacksonian idea of equality was

---

9Henry Hathaway, director, *True Grit*, with John Wayne, Glenn Campbell, and Kim Darby, Paramount Pictures, 1969.

10Daniel Bell, "On Meritocracy and Equality," *The Public Interest*, Fall 1972, pp. 18–32.

11Daniel Bell, *The Cultural Contradictions of Capitalism* (New York: Basic Books, 1976), pp. 141–145.

12To Jefferson, equality meant giving each person an equal opportunity, before the law

somewhat simpler. In essence it was that any man was just as good as the next one. Equality has come to be defined in terms of equity; hence the emphasis on equality of result which is defined as a group right rather than an individual right. This equality is not to be achieved through upward mobility or merit, but through government action. The rules of the game are changed so as to reduce the rewards of competition and the cost of failure. Or as the Dodo said to Alice in Wonderland in explaining the results of the Caucus race, "Everybody has won and all must have prizes."[13]

Government and the Decline of Laissez-Faire

Government has always played some role in Western society even during the zenith of capitalism. In the historical development of the United States, government policy was primarily a mixture of measures that provided equality of opportunity for the comman man, such as public education, and generous favors for those who knew how to help themselves, such as railroad and canal builders. Tariffs were enacted to protect American business firms from foreign competition. In France, where state participation in the economy had always been important, much of the railroad system was state-owned by the 1850s, and the state also had a monopoly over the sale of such products as alcohol, tobacco, and tea. State ownership of certain industries also existed in Prussia.

The Depression of the 1930s was probably the catalyst as far as increasing the role of government is concerned. On the basis of experience during the Depression, organized labor, farmers, business firms, and consumer groups turned to government for assistance in improving their incomes and economic security. The satisfaction of these demands made for a new concept of government. An increase in the power of the state has become the central fact about modern Western society. Crucial decisions about production and distribution have come to be made through the political process rather than through the marketplace.

Restrictions on Competition

Competition is one of the basic institutions of capitalism. Its justification, like that of the other institutions, is found in the notion that it

---

and under God. He said, "There is a natural aristocracy among men. The grounds of this are virtue and talents. . . . The natural aristocracy I consider as the most precious gift of nature." See Thomas Jefferson, *Notes on the State of Virginia*, ed. Thomas Abernethy, (New York: Harper & Row, 1964), pp. 1–10.

[13]Lewis Carroll, *Alice's Adventures in Wonderland* and *Through the Looking Glass* (New York: Airmont, 1965), p. 27.

contributes to the social welfare. It is a regulator of economic activity and is thought to maximize productivity, prevent excessive concentration of economic power, and provide for effectuation of consumer interests. *Competition* may be used to describe the economic structure of a nation, applicable to all economic units—individuals, farmers, and business firms. Economic success goes to those firms that are efficiently operated, and failure eliminates those firms that are inefficiently and wastefully operated. The impersonal qualities of a market system avoid the locking in of products or skills that have become obsolete and therefore nonproductive.

But competition is a hard taskmaster, for there are losers as well as winners. Since losers don't think they should lose, they take action to prevent losing and thus the rules of the game are altered. The market system has been changed in many ways by government action to prevent or cushion the effects of losing. Through subsidies and restraints on foreign competition, uneconomic production and job skills have been maintained by governmental intervention.

Business firms have formed into various forms of combinations, cartels, trusts, and holding companies to prevent competition. Workers have joined labor unions to avoid individual competition, and obsolete job skills have been preserved. In the Unites States obsolete jobs have been preserved in the construction industry and elsewhere through federal building codes, and inefficient firms, such as Chrysler, have received financial support from the government when otherwise they would have been eliminated by the forces of competition.

SUMMARY

Capitalism is an economic system which is characterized by a set of institutional arrangements. The centerpiece of capitalism is a freely competitive market where buyers satisfy their wants and sellers supply those wants in order to make a profit. The price mechanism determines resource allocation, and freedom of enterprise and private property ownership provide incentives to save and produce. Individualism is also at the core of the capitalist or free market ideology. It was assumed by Adam Smith and others that people were rational and would try at all times to promote their own personal welfare. The individual, in promoting his or her self-interest, works in the interest of society.

Competition is an indispensable part of a free enterprise system. In economic life, self-reliant individuals must compete for economic rewards (good jobs, high pay, and promotions) and business must compete for consumer incomes. The Protestant work ethic stressed rewards in this life, not in the hereafter. Hard work included thrift, which could provide the savings necessary for investment. The role of government is minimal in a capitalist economy.

The advanced capitalist countries of today have modified the institutions of capitalism. In the operation of capitalist economies, problems have arisen that seemed impossible for private individuals to solve and whose impact upon their lives brought a demand for government intervention. As a result, government intervention and regulation is a very common feature of life under capitalism. Consumers are not left to depend solely on competition to furnish them with foods and drugs of acceptable quality and purity; there are laws that provide certain standards in these matters. Capitalistic societies have never been willing to extend complete freedom of enterprise to any individual. That is, it has always been recognized that an individual, in selecting the field of activity that would be most profitable to him or her, might well choose something that would be clearly antisocial. In such cases, government has not hesitated to step in with restrictions. But government has also altered the economic institutions of capitalism through, for example, subsidies to farmers and protection of inefficient business firms from competition.

REVIEW QUESTIONS

1. What is meant by the term *institutions* as applied to an economic system?
2. Explain the concept of economic scarcity. Are there things which are not scarce?
3. Apply the concept of scarcity to life in the United States today. Is scarcity still present in the United States? How does scarcity affect an American's life?
4. What are the three agents of production? Why do economists classify resources in this way?
5. What is the function of profit in a market economy?
6. What is the function of the price mechanism in a market system?
7. How are incomes distributed in a market economy?
8. What are some of the factors responsible for the breakdown of a true market economy?
9. The United States economy has diverged from pure market capitalism. Why has this divergence occurred?

RECOMMENDED READINGS

Bell, Daniel. *The Coming of the Post-Industrial Society.* New York: Basic Books, 1976.

Hacker, Louis M. *The Triumph of American Capitalism.* New York: Simon and Schuster, 1940.

Heilbroner, Robert L. *The Making of Economic Society,* 4th ed. Englewood Cliffs, N.J.: Prentice-Hall, 1962.

Hofstadler, Richard. *Social Darwinism in American Thought,* rev. ed. Boston: Beacon Press, 1955.

Polanyi, Karl. *The Great Transformation.* New York: Rinehart, 1944.

Smith, Adam. *The Wealth of Nations,* ed. Edwin Canaan. New York: Random House, 1937.

Tawney, R. H. *Religion and the Rise of Capitalism.* New York: Harcourt, Brace and World, 1926.

Toynbee, Arnold. *The Industrial Revolution.* Boston: Beacon Press, 1956.

Weber, Max. *The Protestant Ethic and the Spirit of Capitalism.* New York: Scribner, 1930.

2
Nonmarket Mechanisms: Socialism and Communism

INTRODUCTION

Differences in economic and political institutions are one way to compare economic systems. Capitalism is an economic-cultural system, organized economically around the institutions of private property and the production of goods for profit, and based culturally on the idea that the individual is the center of society. Other economic systems can be defined in terms of the modifications they would make in these institutions. For example, in a capitalist economy the agents of production—land, labor, and capital—are privately owned. In a socialist system, the agents of production are owned by a public authority and operated, not with a view of profit by sale to other people, but for direct service of those whom the authority represents.

However, a caveat is in order. There are many definitions of socialism, and it is necessary to differentiate between socialism as the concept is applied to the governments of France and Greece and socialism which is used as a self-description of the countries controlled by Communist parties—the Soviet Union, China, the Eastern European countries, Cuba, North Korea, and Vietnam. To the West these countries are Communist.

To avoid confusion, in Marxist terminology there are two stages of communism. The first stage, or *socialism*, is a transitional stage during which some elements of capitalism are retained. The second stage, or *communism*, is a higher stage to be marked by an age of plenty, distribution according to needs, the absence of money and the market mechanism, the disappearance of the last vestiges of capitalism, and the withering away of the state. The Soviet Union calls itself a socialist country (Union of Soviet Socialist Republics—USSR). It is a state-directed society which has sought to fuse all realms into a single monolith and to impose a common direction, from economics to politics to culture, through a single institution, the Communist Party. Bureaucratic collectivism characterizes the Soviet economy. Thus, when the Soviet Union is discussed in the latter part of this book, the term *communism* will be used.

In a non-Marxist form, socialism is an economic system which would modify, but not eliminate, many of the institutions of capitalism. The extent of modification is something that has never been answered by socialists because there are many variations of socialism. Some socialists favor the complete elimination of private property with replacement by public property ownership. Other socialists favor placing maximum reliance on the market mechanism while supplementing it with government direction and planning in order to achieve desired economic and social objectives.

Socialism today has come to be more associated with the concept of a welfare state, where the state through a wide variety of transfer payments assumes responsibility for protecting its citizens against all of the vicissitudes of life. Private ownership of the agents of production is permitted, with state ownership existing in those areas of production and distribution considered vital to the interests of society. In reality Western society has incorporated many of the principles of both capitalism and socialism.

HISTORICAL DEVELOPMENT OF SOCIALISM

The words *socialist* and *socialism* are relatively new concepts. They first came into use in England and France in the early part of the last century, and were applied to the doctrines of certain writers who were seeking a transformation of the economic and moral basis of society by the substitution of social for individual control of life and work.[1] The word *socialism* was popularized as the antithesis of *individualism*. However, precursors of socialism can be found among the medieval writers and even going back to Plato. For example, Saint Thomas Aquinas be-

---

[1]Socialist seems to have been used first in England to describe the followers of Robert Owen. The word *socialism* was used in France to describe the writings of Saint Simon and Fourier.

lieved that property ownership should be private, but that the use of goods should be in common. Whatever goods a man possessed should be shared with the poor. He considered poverty undesirable because it led to sin, and he proposed that both church and state should help poor persons to bring healthy children into the world.

The Renaissance Utopias

During the Renaissance a number of scholars turned their attention to the construction of imaginary communities or utopias in which society was so organized as to remove all of the evils of the day. These utopias were primarily economic and social, rather than religious. For the most part, they formed a definite pattern, the authors placing a group of regenerated people on an isolated land area where they could be free from contamination by the rest of the world. Rigid conditions would then be set up by means of which an ideal state would be attained. For example, in Sir Thomas More's *Utopia*, everything is owned in common and there is no money.[2] In the middle of each city is a marketplace to which each family takes the things it produces, and from these central marketplaces products are distributed to central warehouses from which each family draws what it needs. Women and men have equal rights, and the households are so arranged that the women are relieved of some of their most time-consuming domestic duties.

French Utopian Socialists

French utopian socialism was associated with the French Revolution and later with the Industrial Revolution. The French Revolution created a great economic and political upheaval the impact of which was felt all over Europe. In France every political and social division became rooted in the alignment of the revolution. Commercial business interests, as represented by a merchant class, replaced the aristocracy who had gone to the guillotine. A large urban class of workers who had helped make a revolution found that their living conditions were largely unchanged. The fact that a great political revolution had taken place in France and that socially the results of this revolution were largely unsatisfactory set the stage for a new group of reformers, the French utopian socialists.

In general, the ideas of the utopian socialists were based on the theory that nature had ordained all things to serve the happiness of humankind and that every man had natural rights due him at birth.[3] Furthermore, it

---

[2]Lewis Mumford, *The Stories of Utopias* (New York: Boni and Liveright, 1922), pp. 23–37.

[3]Richard T. Fly, *French and German Socialists in Modern Times* (New York: Harper, 1883), pp. 37–51.

was believed that man was perfect in his original state. However, at various times in the past men had tampered with the natural order of things by establishing customs and institutions which ran contrary to it. As a result man in his existing state was not happy, enjoyed few if any rights, and certainly was far from being perfect. Having discovered the cause of man's difficulties, the utopian socialists proceeded to the obvious solution of the problem of social regeneration. If man had been rendered bad by unnatural customs and institutions, the thing to do was to discover the nature of man's original state of goodness and then reorganize society so as to give nature's forces full play, unhampered by the conventions and institutions of the existing social environment.

However, the French utopian socialists could not agree on how to reorganize society. Some advocated the elimination of private property, considering it the main reason for man's degeneracy. Others favored complete income equality. Babeuf proposed that production be carried out in common, distribution be shared in common, and children be brought up in such a way as to prevent the growth of individual differences. Saint-Simon, one of the better known of the early French utopian socialists, rejected the whole idea of equality, arguing instead that men were naturally unequal and that any attempt to make them equal would involve greater injustices than actually existed at the time. However, differences were to be based on talent, rather than the inheritance of wealth. Saint-Simon favored an economic mechanism which would require each person to labor according to his capacity and would reward him on the basis of service. Charles Fourier worked out a plan for cooperative living in small communities, which he hoped would lead to a transformation of society. These communities were called *phalanxes,* and each phalanx was to be self-sufficient. The highest pay would go to those performing the most necessary work as determined by the members of the phalanx.

Socialism and the Industrial Revolution

The Industrial Revolution in due course was to revolutionize the economic life of the whole Western world. The availability of new technology encouraged the formation of real capital with which the technology might be put into widespread use. The availability of resources for use in capital formation encouraged the search for new technology which, once discovered, could be embodied in the real capital. The new technology enabled gross national product to be large enough to provide sufficient consumer goods to satisfy the minimum subsistence needs of the population and still have some resources left over. The population growth provided labor to use the enlarged amounts of real capital to increase total national output.

However, there was a darker side to the Industrial Revolution. Working conditions in the factories were unpleasant. The equipment was sometimes dangerous and caused workers to have serious accidents. Average wages were low for industrial workers, largely because the rapid expansion of population provided a large number of workers for the labor force. These workers concentrated in the industrial cities and competed with each other for jobs.

The cities which grew up or expanded to house the workers were unattractive and unpleasant. Many of them consisted of slums with houses of poor quality when constructed and in a constant state of disrepair thereafter. Charles Dickens, that great chronicler of English society in the last century, has a rather graphic description of the squalor of the London slums in his book *Bleak House*.

> Jo lives—that is to say that Jo has not yet died—in a ruinous place known to the like of him by the name of Tom-all-Alone's. It is a black, dilapidated street, avoided by all decent people, where the crazy houses were seized upon, when their decay was far advanced, by some bold vagrants who after establishing their own possession took to letting them out in lodgings. Now, these tumbling tenements contain by night, a swarm of misery. As on the ruined human wretch vermin parasites appear, so these ruinous shelters have bred a crowd of foul existence that crawls in and out of gaps in walls and boards; and rocks itself to sleep in maggot numbers, where the rain drips in; and comes and goes, fetching and carrying fever and sowing more evil in its every footprint.[4]

Modern Socialism

Modern socialism, as opposed to utopian socialism, had its genesis during the Industrial Revolution. Socialism developed as more of a social reform movement to protest the seamy side of the Industrial Revolution. Robert Owen, an early English socialist, was considered a utopian socialist in that he developed a scheme for social regeneration: change society, you change the person. He believed that true happiness is found in making others happy.[5] Owen, unlike many other social reformers, had the money to carry out his plan of social regeneration by creating a textile mill at New Lanark in Scotland in 1800. He reduced the hours of work to 10½ hours per day, raised wages, and did not employ children under the age of 10.[6] Education was provided for the children of mill workers, and playgrounds were provided. The experiment made money, and Owen was able to get a factory reform bill introduced in Parliament. Other mill owners were not willing to adopt measures similar to those used by Owen. Subsequent experiments by Owen were unsuccessful. He came to

---

[4]Charles Dickens, *Bleak House* (New York: Signet Press, 1964), pp. 232–233.

[5]Or in the words of Paul: ". . . remember the words of the Lord Jesus, how He said, it is more blessed to give than to receive." Acts 20:35.

[6]By the standards of those days, these provisions were not harsh.

the United States and created a community, called New Harmony, in Indiana. His attempts to create a perfect community failed.

Socialism coalesced into a political movement in England around the middle of the last century. A contributing factor in the development of socialism was mass unemployment created by business recessions. One of the basic defects of capitalism was the constant recurrence of recessions. In England and in other countries, unemployment and labor unrest began to occur more frequently, and a working class movement developed in these countries.

The movement found its support in labor unions and in intellectuals who were not of the working class but who felt that the political and economic structure of society had to be reformed for the benefit of the workers. A split developed between Marxist and non-Marxist socialists, with the former preaching class revolution and the overthrow of the existing political and social order, and the latter believing in the attainment of economic, political, and social reforms by working within the existing system. Political parties representing both the Marxist and non-Marxist points of view had been formed in France and Germany before 1900.

INSTITUTIONS OF SOCIALISM

Socialism, as mentioned above, developed into a viable political force in Western Europe around the latter part of the last century. The Social Democratic Party now controls the West German government. Socialist parties captured control of the government of France and Greece in elections held in 1981. Socialism is a political force which is important today, but socialism, like capitalism, has lost much of its original meaning. There are certain institutional arrangements that set socialism apart from capitalism and communism. These arrangements represent a modification of most of the institutions of capitalism, since socialism developed in opposition to some of the worst abuses of capitalism.

Private Property

Under ideal socialism, the rights of private property would be limited to consumption goods; productive wealth, land, and capital would in general be owned by society as a whole. The socialists today say that the social ownership of the means of production would be limited to the land and capital used in large-scale production. For example, the socialist government of François Mitterand proposed the nationalization of some French banks (the more important ones have already been nationalized) and some key industries, such as aluminum. In France, one car company (Renault) is state-owned, but another car company (Peugeot) is not.

Most socialists would permit private individuals to own and operate small farms, stores, and repair shops. Sometimes it is even contended that certain industries, which operate satisfactorily under private ownership and which are not suited to government ownership and operation, be left alone to function in the hands of individuals. Modern socialists thus do not adhere to ideal socialism when it comes to the right of private property ownership.

The Price System

According to many socialists, the ideal socialist system would retain money and the price system, but it would not rely on price movements and price relationships in making important economic decisions to nearly as great an extent as does a capitalist system. Decisions as to the kinds and quantities of goods, particularly public goods, would be made by the government. A major socialist criticism of the price mechanism in a market economy is that prices do not reflect nonmarket wants of the people, such as the desire for economic security. Nor can negative wants be expressed through the price mechanism.[7] Also, individuals with large sums of money can express their wants through prices, and thus alter the allocation of resources into areas of production for goods that the mass of consumers cannot afford. Socialism would divert productive resources to satisfy basic wants of all of the people before the relatively less important wants of the few with large incomes are satisfied.

Socialism and Government

Perhaps because various noncapitalistic economic systems have so often operated under dictatorial governments, there is a tendency in popular discussion to link capitalism with democracy and to link socialism and communism with dictatorship. However, this is not the case with socialism. European social democratic parties have operated within the framework of democracy. The 1981 elections of socialist governments in France and Greece illustrate the point.

By the early 1960s, many of the European social democratic parties severed completely whatever remaining ideological ties they had with Marx and communism.[8] They abandoned their traditional opposition to

---

[7]For example, there may be a number of people whose total of satisfactions would be much increased if they could prevent the publication and sale of pornographic books or the production and sale of cigarettes. They may well be glad to pay a price to obtain such satisfaction of their negative preferences if any opportunity could be given them to do so. But there seems to be no way, short of government edict, in which the market mechanism can take these negative preferences into account.

[8]The staunchest European supporter of President Reagan's attempts to attain military parity with the Soviet Union is the socialist president of France, François Mitterand. Even

private property and their goal of social ownership, and turned their attention to improving the public mix of total goods and services. Thus, what have developed in Western Europe are mixed capitalist-socialist economies. When socialists come into power, the tilt is toward socialism; there is still reliance on a market economy, but also heavy government direction and planning in order to achieve desired social and economic objectives.

COMMUNISM

Early vestiges of communism can be found in Plato's *Republic*.[9] Plato's criticisms of the economic and social structure of his time led to his proposal for an ideal state. The state described in the *Republic* is a city-state, a type of political organization quite common in Greece at the time of Plato (431–351 B.C.). Among other things, Plato's ideal republic is a communist society in which all things are held in common, at least as far as the upper classes are concerned. The upper classes, or guardians of the state, eat in common dining rooms and live in common quarters, receiving their support from contributions made by the citizens at large.[10] Members of this group never consider their own personal interests but always work for the good of the whole state. To insure their disinterest, Plato does not have any private interest, not even a private family life. However, Plato's communism was not for the masses who were excluded from political life in his republic. Instead, it was communism of the select.

Karl Marx and *Das Kapital*

Both modern communism and socialism began in England and were reactions against capitalism. As mentioned previously, unequal incomes, squalor, and poverty were characteristic of industrial life in England. The winds of revolution that had blown in from France had died away, and in England rank and privilege were firmly entrenched. This class was all-powerful over a tenantry for the most part unenfranchised.

---

though he has communists in his government, Mitterand is in opposition to the Soviet Union, regarding it as a threat to the security of Western Europe. It is interesting to note, that massive anti-nuclear missile demonstrations against U.S. policy were held in Holland, the United Kingdom and other European countries, but not in France. In fact, the French were busy with their construction of nuclear warheads.

[9]Irwin Edman, ed., *The Works of Plato* (New York: Modern Library, 1956), pp. 397–481.

[10]In Plato's republic there are three classes, the rulers or guardians, the auxiliary guardians, and the artisans. The ruling class is selected from the auxiliary class and is composed of philosophers who have been selected after a long course of study. The artisans comprise the largest group in the republic, but have little status.

Flattered, adulated, deferred to, the English aristocracy reigned supreme, with incomes enormously increased by the Industrial Revolution and as yet untaxed. The aristocracy was subject to no ordinary laws and held the government firmly in its hands. However, an entrepreneurial class had begun to emerge as a result of the Industrial Revolution, and a conflict between the two classes over government control occurred. This conflict did very little to ameliorate the working conditions of the industrial masses.

This was the general economic and social milieu within which Karl Marx wrote *Das Kapital*. It is necessary to remember that he was a product of his time, and it is also important to remember that the activities of other persons in England, as well as in other counties, had attracted widespread attention to the existence of poverty. Marx is important for the reason that in *Das Kaptial* he presented a dynamic theory of economics which still serves as the basis of much of Communist dogma. The most important elements of the theory are summarized as follows.

The Marxist Theory of Income Distribution

At any given time, according to Marx, the way in which people make a living is conditioned by the nature of the existing productive forces. There are three productive forces: natural resources, capital equipment, and human resources. Since people must make use of these productive forces in the process of making a living, some sort of relationship between people and the productive forces is necessary. Specifically, the property relation is involved. People may own certain productive forces individually, as in a capitalist society; or they may own them collectively, as in a socialist society. Under capitalism, there were those who owned property or capital, and there were those who owned only their own labor. Marx called the former the capitalists or the *bourgeoisie* and the latter the *proletariat* or the workers.

The Labor Theory of Value. Many economists of the 18th and 19th centuries, including Adam Smith and David Ricardo, believed that labor supplied the common denominator of value.[11] Karl Marx adopted this idea and made it the basis for his own theory of income distribution. Marx stated that the one thing common to all commodities is labor and that the value of a commodity is determined by the amount of socially necessary labor required for its production. Socially necessary labor, as defined by Marx, is the amount of time necessary to produce a given product under existing average conditions of production and with the

---

[11]*Value* may be defined as the worth of a commodity or service as measured by its ability to command other goods and services in return. It is, in short, exchange value, which is the power to command exchange in the market.

average degree of skill and intensity of labor.[12] The relative prices of two products will be in the same proportion as the amount of socially necessary labor required to produce them. If 2 hours of labor are required to make a pair of shoes and 5 hours of labor are required to build a cart, the price of shoes in the market will be two-fifths that of the cart.

The price of labor is the wage rate. The wage rate determines the income of those who own their own labor. Marx asserted that the wage rate itself is determined by the labor theory of value. How much a worker shall receive in income in return for working for an employer depends on how many labor hours are required to produce the necessities of life for a worker. If the necessities can be produced with 5 hours of labor per day, a worker can produce and be available to the employer for work if 5 hours' wages are paid to the worker each day. Even if the worker actually works 12 hours each day for an employer, the pay will only be for 5 hours because that is all it takes to sustain the worker. That is all the pay can be, under a labor theory of value. In effect, Marx believed in a subsistence theory of wages in a system of market capitalism.

Theory of Surplus Value. Although all value is created by the workers, it is expropriated by employers in the form of *surplus value,* which can be defined as the difference between the value created by the workers and the value of their labor power. When a worker sells labor power to an employer, the worker gives up all title and claim to the products of that labor. Income in the Marxist schema is divided into two categories— surplus value, which is the source of all profit, and labor income. Value in the Marxist rubric can be expressed in the formula $C + V + S$, where C represents raw materials and capital consumption, V represents various outlays on wages, and S represents surplus value in the form of rent, interest, and profit. The C component, raw materials and capital, although clearly not labor, is explained away by Marx, who regarded it as stored-up labor from past periods. Thus the remainder, $V + S$, represents net output, which consists of the two basic income shares, wages and profit.

How much a worker gets as a wage is based on the amount of labor time socially necessary to produce subsistence or maintenance for the worker and the worker's family. Assume that this subsistence only requires 5 hours of socially necessary labor time for its production. If the worker only worked 5 hours for the employer, the worker would be fully paid and there would be no surplus value. However, it is the employer's right to set the length of the working day, and it will normally be set at a number of hours greater than that required to produce the worker's subsistence. The difference between the actual hours worked and the labor time needed for subsistence is surplus value.

---

[12]Karl Marx, *Das Kapital* (New York: Modern Library, 1906), pp. 198–331.

The Dynamic Weaknesses of Market Capitalism. The market distribution of income between workers and property owners was bound, according to Marx, to be a source of increasing difficulty for capitalist
economies.

Crisis and Depressions. For one thing, it would sometimes be difficult to sell the output being produced. The workers received money income enough to buy only part of the total output. This part would necessarily take the form of subsistence or consumer goods. The capitalists
received the rest, an amount sufficient to buy the remainder of the output
of goods and services. But would they buy it? Of course they would buy
some of it to satisfy their own consumption desires. The rest they might
purchase in the form of capital goods with which to carry on production
and to expand productive capacity if they found such purchase profitable.
From time to time there would be periods of months or of a year or two
when they would not find it profitable. These would be periods of crisis
and depression. During these times there would be sharply increased
financial losses for business, unsold output, business bankruptcies, falling prices, and unemployment.

Worsening Trends. Marx suggested that these crises and depressions
would become increasingly severe. In each successive crisis, the weakest
firms would disappear, being absorbed or replaced by a fewer number of
larger firms. In the long run the number of firms and the number of
capitalists would decline both absolutely and relative to the size of the
economy and of the population. The proletariat would be absolutely and
relatively enlarged.

The capitalist employers would be impelled by competition among
themselves to substitute machinery or capital for labor, even though it
was labor which provided surplus value and profits. The capitalists would
be impelled to discover and introduce into use new technology. They
would do so because such technology would reduce the cost of subsistence needs for labor and thereby enlarge the amount of surplus value and
profit. The increasingly severe crises, the substitution of capital for labor,
and the introduction of new technology would create a larger and larger
volume of unemployment among the workers. There would be an ever
increasing *industrial reserve army* of the unemployed.

Marx felt that the rate of profit on capital would fall continually
lower. The fall would occur primarily because of the replacement of
laborers with machines. The laborers were the source of all surplus and
hence of all profits. Machines produced no surplus and, therefore, did not
contribute to profits. The capitalists, desperately seeking to sustain profits, would seek ways to increase the surplus value by greater exploitation
of the workers. They would resort to longer working hours, more intense
work, and the employment of children.

There would be more and more severe crises, fewer and fewer capitalists, larger and larger unemployment, lower and lower profit rates, bigger and bigger amounts of unsold goods, and ever more outrageous exploitation of the workers by the capitalists. These trends would lead, in the Marxist view, ultimately to the end of market capitalism. It would be replaced with a new economic system, or rather, with a whole new society. In Marx's view, economic arrangements were causally determinant of all else in society, and capitalism's inevitable demise would mean a complete change of all else in society.[13]

Economically Determined History. To reiterate, Marx contended that economic conditions were the basic causal forces shaping the nature of society. All other aspects of society—political, religious, and philosophical—were dependent upon the economic system of the society.

Materialism. For example, in a primitive nomad society where horses might be of peculiar importance in enabling the people to gather food and to exist in general, the ownership of horses would also be important to the people. Those persons who owned the horses would be able to control the others. That is, those who possessed the principal means of production would also possess the ability to rule. The religion and philosophy of the nomad society would center about horses and those who owned them. The patterns of marriage and inheritance would be heavily influenced by considerations regarding the use and ownership of horses.

In a society which had amassed considerable real capital and technology, the capital would be the principal means of production. The society would be organized around the existence, ownership, control, and use of the capital. Political power would reside with the owners and controllers of capital, the capitalists. Religion and philosophy would sanctify the ownership and rationalize the social dominance of the owners.

In some advanced societies with great real capital, all ownership and control might be exercised by the government. It would act on behalf of all the people. Political power would rest with all the people. A philosophy of altruism would develop among them.

In the most advanced society, so much capital and such advanced technology would exist that there could be produced goods and services great enough that the desires of everyone could be more than completely satisfied. The ownership of the means of production would cease to matter. Political control over others cease to have significance. Interpersonal animosity, based on the covetousness of each for the material goods and services of others, would disappear. Government, no longer necessary as

---

[13]A clear, entertaining, and brief explanation of Marx's theories appears in Sir Alexander Gray, *The Development of Economic Doctrine: An Introductory Survey* (New York: Wiley, 1931), Chapter 11. A more technically difficult account, which assumes more knowledge of economic analysis, can be found in Mark Blaug, *Economic Theory in Retrospect*, rev. ed. (Homewood, Ill.: Irwin, 1968), Chapter 7.

the instrument by which some controlled others or by which some were protected from others, would gradually wither away.

Marx felt that the character of a society wholly depended upon its economic system. Hence, his philosophy is labeled one of *materialism.*

The Dialectic. Marx's view of philosophy and history was also *dialectic.* From the philosopher Hegel, Marx adopted the notion that what happened in the world could be explained by the clash of opposites. Hegel claimed that a proper understanding of the world could be achieved if all change were viewed as the result of clashing ideas. First, there is an idea, such as scarcity. Then there emerges an opposite idea, such as abundance. Finally the two opposing ideas are combined into a new and superior idea, such as *economy,* which is a means to achieve abundance out of scarcity.

Marx adopted the notion of the clashing of opposites to produce a successor synthesis. However, he rejected the view that this clashing and synthesis took place basically and most significantly in the realm of ideas. Rather, according to Marx, the essentially basic and casual conflict and synthesis took place, as his philosophy of materialism suggests, in the real world of economic events, economic classes, and economic systems.

Dialectical Materialism. Marx welded together his views of the primacy of economic arrangements and of history as progressive conflict into the doctrine of *dialectical materialism.*

A society, such as that of the European Middle Ages, is based on an economic system, such as manorial agriculture. A political structure, such as feudalism, and a philosophical and religious structure, such as medieval Catholicism, grow up in harmony with the economic base. There exist several socioeconomic classes: landed nobility, clergy, and serfs. The economic system is successful in filling the material needs of the people. In fact, it is too successful for its own permanence.

The increasing productive ability of manorialism makes it possible for some persons to leave agriculture and became traders or town craftsmen. Others have sufficient time to make discoveries and innovations of an economically useful sort. Gradually the techniques of production and the other economic arrangements change. Local economic self-sufficiency decreases as trading increases. First guilds and then factory workers carry on production in place of the manorial serfs or craftsmen. There begins to grow up a new socioeconomic class made up of the shopkeeping proprietors, the factory managers and owners, and the merchant traders.

In the meantime, the political power remains, in an increasingly outmoded way, with the hereditary landed aristocracy. The religious rules grow more and more inappropriate for the economic system. For example, the doctrines against usury and in favor of just prices become obsolete. Finally, the economic system and the seat of real power have changed enough that the new class, the bourgeoisie, is able to wrest political power from the landed nobility. They do so either by forceful revolution, by new laws, or by influence with the sovereign. They also reshape the religious code, perhaps by replacing Catholicism with Protestantism.

Capitalism thereby replaces feudalism. Then, because of its inherent nature, capitalism under the bourgeoisie unintentionally promotes its own replacement. Capitalism brings together the working proletariat and infuses in them a unity born of misery and exploitation. The class conflict between the proletariat and the bourgeoisie sharpens with conditions increasingly favorable to a proletarian victory. The political superstructure of government is in the hands of the bourgeoisie. They have used it as an instrument for the perpetuation of their power. However, it fails to reflect the underlying economic reality of bourgeoisie weakness and proletarian strength. Religion has been used as a device for cowing the workers, for justifying their exploitation, and for drugging them with visions of heaven so that they will accept their earthly misery. However, religion becomes more and more obviously a sham.

Eventually, the workers topple the bourgeoisie government, seize the means of production, abolish private property, and set up a socialist state under the dictatorship of the proletariat. The economic system is thus converted to socialism. Then, because all else follows from economic change, the society becomes ultimately a communist one, with neither government, scarcity, conflict, nor classes.[14]

The Weakness of Marxism

What is wrong with Marx's views? Each of Marx's main ideas can be attacked on a number of grounds.

The Labor Theory of Value. The labor theory of value, as an explanation of what determines relative prices of goods and services, is extremely vulnerable to criticism. Marx anticipated some of the vulnerabilities and tried to deal with them.

Exceptions to the Theory. A piece of fertile, virgin land may exist and command a high price without any human labor at all having been expended on its creation. Such nonreproducible goods, Marx would say, fall in a special category. The prices or values of this category are determined without reference to amounts of labor. Then what of a durable good which was produced some time ago and for whose production a technological improvement has been discovered in the meantime? The value

---

[14]A readable but biased account of world history, including the Industrial Revolution, as seen by a modern Marxist is Leo Huberman, *Man's Worldly Goods: The Story of the Wealth of Nations* (New York: Monthly Review Press, 1952).

of such a good will fall, Marx would say, in the meantime. It is not the amount of original labor expended but the amount necessary to replace a good that is the determining variable.

What of a unit of a good much like many other units of the same good except that it embodies a much greater amount of labor because it was turned out by a very slow, inept worker? Will it on that account be much more valuable than the other units? No, it will not, because it is not the actual amount of *socially necessary* labor that determines values and prices, Marx would answer. What of a good, like a hideous piece of sculpture, on the production of which a great amount of labor has been expended but which cannot be sold for any price because no one wants it? Can it, all in all, be said to be of great value? No, Marx might answer, because labor expended on a useless product is not socially necessary labor. What of a good produced by a monopolist and sold at a high price? Is its price in proportion to the labor in it? Admittedly it is not, for monopoly may distort prices from true values.

The Problem of Diverse Kinds of Labor. What of two goods, one of which embodies 4 hours of unskilled labor and the other of which embodies 4 hours of skilled? Will the two goods sell at the same price? Do they have equal value? No, in creating and determining value, 1 hour of skilled labor counts for more than 1 hour of unskilled. To compute value, one must convert skilled labor into unskilled labor by multiplying the number of hours of skilled labor by an appropriate conversion number. How can the appropriate number be known? It is determined, in part, by the number of hours of labor socially necessary to produce the goods and services needed to sustain the skilled laborer through the period of training. It is also determined, in part, by the number of hours required for every laborer, skilled or unskilled, to produce the goods needed to rear that person from infancy and for subsistence during working years.

Too many qualifications and exceptions spoil the attractiveness of a generalization. There is little left of the labor theory of value after all of the obviously necessary modifications are taken into account. Furthermore, the modifications suggested in the preceding paragraphs are incomplete. In the last qualification, for example, the number of labor hours necessary to sustain a worker consists itself of some hours of unskilled labor and some of skilled. To add the two together, a conversion number must be available. Of course, it is not available, for it is precisely what the whole procedure is set up to find.

Alternative Modern Theory. Modern economic theory, developed since Marx, explains values or relative prices in terms of degrees of scarcity. According to this theory, the value of a thing in exchange for something else depends on how scarce it is. Its scarcity in turn depends on the state of its supply and the state of demand for it. Behind supply and demand lie a great many interdependent determinants. The scarcity theory is a complicated one, but it provides a more satisfactory explanation than the labor theory of value. The scarcity theory treats not only labor but also capital and natural resources as productive and value-creating.

Marx's labor theory of value is weak. His use of it as a basis for attacking the capitalistic market society's distribution of income makes that attack weak. One might still condemn market capitalism or market capitalism's distribution of income. However, one would probably do so for some reason other than because one believed that only labor had the power to create value and all value was in proportion to labor used.

The Subsistence Theory of Wages. Another element in Marx's theory of market capitalism was a subsistence theory of wages. There are for this theory two alternative meanings between which Marx vacillated. One is that the wage rate will tend to fall until workers receive only enough income to provide a minimum physical existence for themselves. The other is that the wage rate will tend to fall until workers receive only enough to provide a psychologically or culturally determined minimum level of living for themselves. The latter minimum might change with time as attitudes changed. It might vary from place to place, depending upon what attitudes prevailed in the society of each place. Marx did not give a satisfactory causal explanation of why the wage rate under market capitalism tended toward a subsistence minimum, however defined.

The Malthusian Explanation. Marx rejected the explanation offered by such persons as Thomas Malthus. Malthus had argued that any wage higher than subsistence would reduce the death rate or raise the birth rate. These changes would cause the population and the supply of labor to increase. The increase would depress the market for labor and force the wage rate down. Perhaps Marx rejected the Malthusian explanation because it seemed to place the blame on the workers or to suggest that any economic system, not just market capitalism, would produce the same undesirable result.

Lopsided Bargaining Power. Marx did contend that the bargaining power of each individual worker would be small relative to that of a capitalist employer in the negotiations on wage rates. A worker sometimes has no real alternative, other than unemployment, to accepting a job from one accessible employer. On the other hand, most employers either can offer work to any one of a number of different workers who are competing with each other for jobs or can withhold work entirely by shutting down operations.

Critics of Marx have pointed out that, at least sometimes, workers have considerable bargaining power. Their power arises because of their unusual skills, because they band together in labor unions, because there is competition among employers for their services, or because without their labor real capital is unprofitable. Even with weak bargaining power, there is no proof that the wage rate will fall to the subsistence level.

The Reserve Army of the Unemployed. Marx also contended that there usually would be substantial numbers of unemployed workers. They would always be ready to compete with those who had jobs. They would also furnish an inexhaustible supply of labor at a minimum subsistence wage rate, no matter how strong the demand for labor.

Critics of this argument emphasize that Marx never really convincingly demonstrated that capitalism creates unemployment. Indeed, if Marx was right that only labor creates surplus value and profits, capitalist employers would seek out and employ every available worker because, by so doing, profits could be maximized. Actually, real wage rates in countries heavily dependent upon market capitalism have risen substantially in the long run. A Marxist may choose to dismiss this evidence by claiming that it merely reflects a rising psychological minimum subsistence level. But one can reasonably rejoin that capitalism is performing well, not badly, in this respect. It has raised both aspirations and the means to fulfill them.

The Theory of Surplus Value. The theory of surplus value asserts that workers usually produce more goods and services than are needed for their subsistence. This assertion seems acceptable. It is probably equally acceptable, however, to assert that land is capable of producing more crop than that needed to reseed the land adequately in the next growing season. Likewise, a labor-saving machine may spare more labor hours than were required to make it. As the basis for an attack on market capitalism, the theory of surplus value is no attack at all unless supplemented by a labor theory of value and a subsistence theory of wages. If these latter two ideas are invalid, the theory of surplus value loses its sting for market capitalism.

Actually, land, labor, and capital cooperate in most production activities, regardless of the economic system. The complete removal of any one of these three factors would cause production to cease almost entirely. So long as they do cooperate, the productive output is usually more than enough to replace the worn equipment, maintain the natural resources, and provide for the subsistence needs of the workers. The excess may take the form either of suprasubsistence consumer goods or of capital goods which increase the society's stock of real capital.

The Theory of Crises and Trends. Another element in Marx's attack on market capitalism is the crisis or business cycle. These do occur in many forms of capitalistic economic systems. They had been the object of economists' inquiries and theories before Marx, and they continued to be afterward. Marx's explanation of them was incomplete and faulty. A complete understanding of them has not been achieved. However, most economists believe that, as a result of economic studies undertaken since the Great Depression, mixed economic systems can avoid severe crises and cycles. They can be avoided if rather modest government economic intervention to counteract the cycles is accepted. In any case, crises and cycles have not yet forced the complete collapse of market capitalism and its replacement with Marxist socialism or communism.

Many of the trends which Marx predicted would carry capitalism to its doom have not been corroborated by history subsequent to Marx. Most striking has been the failure of the capitalist owners to become a smaller and smaller percentage of the population and the proletariat a larger and larger percentage. An increasingly greater portion of the people of Western Europe and North America possess property in the form of savings accounts, shares of corporate stock, government bonds, houses, automobiles, and durable consumer goods. The proletarian proportion of the populace has diminished as skilled white-collar and service workers have come to outnumber unskilled, manual workers.

The percentage of the labor force unemployed has not increased in the long run, as Marx predicted it would. The quality of life of the majority of the population has not become increasingly miserable. Working conditions have improved, not deteriorated, on the average at least. In the long run the rate of profit on capital has not fallen as much as Marx predicted. Technological and social changes have provided new, profitable opportunities for the use of machinery and other capital goods. The governments of most capitalist countries have not resolutely blocked every attempt by the majority of the people to obtain legislation to improve their lot. It would be laughable to contend that for most non-communist, developed countries the government is used as the instrument by which an increasingly small number of capitalists keep subjugated an ever more preponderant working class.

The Theory of Economic Determinism and Dialectical Materialism. Marx's emphasis upon the economic system of a society as determinant of all else about society is also easily criticized.

Economics as Only One of Many Interdependent Forces. The economic system is as much a result as a cause of the general character of society. Religion and philosophy, for example, help to determine economic organization. A people's religion may emphasize the evil of the accumulation of material goods and the virtue of asceticism. In consequence, the economic system is likely to remain a traditional one, and economic growth will not occur. Alternatively, religion may lay stress upon individual responsibility and upon working hard, saving much, and investing productively. As a result, the economic system is likely to become a market one with rapid change. A people's philosophy may accord great prestige to those who are very successful in military, spiritual, or governmental affairs and little prestige to those who are economically successful. Then the economic system of the people is likely to remain organized around the principle of tradition, and what modern Westerners regard as economic progress will probably be absent.

The political system of a society may place and keep in power those who wish to maintain the status quo. Then economic change will probably occur only slowly. The cultural heritage of a people may include a great accumulated stock of technological knowledge. The economic system of that people will probably be very different from that of a people with little such knowledge. The physical environment of a people is likely to shape their economic system. The tropics may offer no challenge to traditional economic organization, which remains primitive. The arctic may offer too great a challenge, which prevents economic organization from being anything but traditional and primitive.

Monocausal Theories of History. It is implausible to view human history simply as a sequence of economic changes which bring about other changes. Such a theory of history probably deserves the same derision as every other monocausal explanation of history. One other such theory is the *hero theory*, which claims that the shape of history is the result of the occurrence from time to time of extremely influential people such as Plato, Jesus, Caesar, Charlemagne, Columbus, Luther, Marx, and Lenin. Another is the *idea theory*, which stresses the great historical influence of ideas such as monotheism, asceticism, altruism, capitalism, democracy, and communism. Another is the *war theory*, which claims that conflicts of arms provide the key to the understanding of history. There is also the *political theory*, which claims that history is the sequence of governments.[15]

Marx's selection of struggles between economic classes as the vehicle of historical progress is also not convincing. People generally have not thought of themselves primarily as members of an economic class, but as members of a family, an occupation, a tribe, a race, a district, or a nation, or simply as individuals. A theory of history which explains behavior as arising out of a loyalty which people do not have does not explain much.

The Merits of Marx

Marx was not totally without merit. He did indicate some of the weaknesses of the market capitalism of his time and place. The in-

---

[15]A brief elaboration of this kind of criticism of Marx can be found in William Ebenstein, *Today's Isms: Communism, Fascism, Capitalism, and Socialism,* 7th ed. (Englewood Cliffs, N.J.: Prentice-Hall, 1973), Chapter 1.

equality of income, wealth, and power of 19th-century European capitalism was too great. It was too great to be permanently tolerated by the populace and too great by 20th-century, Western standards. Marx correctly predicted some of the trends in market capitalism. Recurrent and sometimes severe business fluctuations have taken place. Unemployment has been a persistent problem. Inordinate political and social power has accrued to the economically most successful. Control, if not ownership, has been concentrated in the hands of those who guide the great private corporations.

Marx was perhaps the first to try to explain why history had occurred as it had rather than merely to describe what had occurred. He attempted to integrate economic theory with history. He was undoubtedly one of the few of his time to do so.

Perhaps Marx's greatest achievement was as a propagandist or as an inspiration for revolution and reform. It is ironical that Marx denied the influence of ideas on history and claimed instead the ascendancy of events. His own ideas have inspired and provoked people ever since he propounded them. Perhaps half the earth's population either are led by or desire to be led by those who proclaim their allegiance to Marxism. This is not to say, of course, that the world today is markedly different than it would be had Marx never lived. It is entirely possible that events subsequent to Marx's time, such as the Russian and Chinese communist revolutions, would have taken place whether or not Marx had ever existed. People Like Lenin and Mao, bent on seizing power and on changing society, are likely to pluck from the pages of previous history one name if not another to sanctify their actions and increase the probability of their success. Historical speculation aside, however, it is easy to claim for Marx that no other person did so much as he to besmirch the reputation of market capitalism.

INSTITUTIONS OF COMMUNISM

Communism, in Marxist ideology, is supposed to be the final stage of historical development. It is the end result of a classless society with the withering away of the state, and production from each according to his ability and distribution to each according to his need. However, modern communism is far removed from ideal or pure communism; neither can it be considered a transitory stage through which a country passes on its way to pure communism. There are variations in communism, ranging from the bureaucratic collectivism of the Soviet Union to a supplementary market economy in Yugoslavia. All communist countries subscribe, or at least pay lip service, to Marxism-Leninism, which provides an ideological guideline for various institutional arrangements that distinguish modern communism from other economic systems.

Economic Planning

The role of economic planning in the communist countries is to allocate resources through the setting of economic targets by a central planning agency. It is the state, as represented by the planning agency, rather than the market mechanism that determines both output and its distribution. A rationale for central planning is the elimination of the wasteful use of resources that often occurs in a capitalist system. This waste is exemplified by planned product obsolescence, the duplication of goods and services, unnecessary product differentiation, and conspicuous consumption. Since the state has control over resource allocation in a communist system, presumably planning can make better use of these resources.

The primacy of social over private preference is ensured by planning. The state, through the mechanism of the plan, is supposed to be in a better position to study social costs and benefits of resource allocation, which the market mechanism in a capitalist system cannot do. However, a weakness of planning is that prices, which are an integral part of the market mechanism under capitalism, have never been integrated into planning and do not perform a rational allocative function. This makes decision making under economic planning highly arbitrary.

Social Ownership of Property

Most property is owned by the state under communism. Included under property is land and capital. Labor is in a somewhat different position from land and capital. It is supposed to be the only factor of production capable of creating value. As the means of production are owned by the state, owners and workers are supposed to be the same people, so there should be no antagonism between the employer (the state) and the employees (the workers).[16]

The purpose for state ownership of property is simple. Of all of the capitalist institutions, private property ownership was regarded as being the one institution most responsible for the evils of capitalism. It was responsible for the division of society into two opposing classes—the bourgeoisie and the proletariat. The bourgeoisie controlled land and capital and exploited the workers by appropriating their surplus value. Property inheritance contributed to a widening income division between rich and poor and provided the former with unearned income. Interest and dividend payments accrued only to those few persons who had a claim on the ownership of capital.

---

[16]This would make it impossible for workers to strike against the state, because they would be striking against themselves. The strikes by labor in Poland have put an end to this fiction.

Concentration of Power in the Communist Party

The Communist Party is supposed to represent the interests of the working class. It is the sole repositor of political power and is involved in all phases of economic activity. For example, the election of trade union officials is usually arranged by the Communist Party, and higher union positions are mostly occupied by Party members. In all factories, collective farms, military units, or organizations, the Communist Party maintains local units or cells. Under the supervision of higher Party organizations, they attempt to improve the discipline and political education of the workers and spur them on to the fulfillment of planned economic goals.

In spite of the democratic façade which some communist countries maintain (the German Democratic Republic), the government is a complete dictatorship, with the leaders of the Communist Party in complete control. The Communist Party controls the armed forces and the electoral process. All candidates for office must have the approval of the Party if they hope to be successful. The Communist Party maintains Party officials and agencies to match the various officials and agencies of government. For all practical purposes Party and state are one and the same.

Cooperation

Individualism, which is one of the basic institutions of capitalism, is replaced by cooperation. Individualism is supposed to foster acquisitive ambitions, which is contrary to the ideal of the "communist man" free of such antisocial instincts. In a communist country, the interests of the individual are subordinate to those of society. Communism has the conception of regenerated man in a regenerated society, acting in tandem with their fellow human beings rather than in competition against them. This cooperation is supposed to lead to the development of the perfect society or, as the placards say in the various May Day parades in communist countries, "We are building for socialism." Competition is directed toward the attainment of political and social goals. In the Olympic Games, the communist countries do quite well because success in sports is one way to tout the superiority of the communist system.

SUMMARY

Although the philosophical roots of socialism and communism go back thousands of years, modern socialism and communism are products of the Industrial Revolution. The Industrial Revolution, although it produced many benefits, also had its seamy side: squalor, poor working conditions, low wages, and income insecurity. Both socialism and communism promised a new economic and social order, but differed in degree as to how the new order would be achieved. The socialists believed in the attainment of a new society through an evolutionary process; the communists believed in class revolution, with the ultimate dictatorship of the proletariat. Socialism in the latter part of the 20th century has come to be equated with the democratic process as socialist parties have won major elections in France and Greece. The socialists advocate nationalization of certain key industries and increased welfare measures, but leave such capitalist institution as private property and the price mechanism pretty much intact. Communism has come to mean bureaucratic collectivism, with the state, as represented by the Communist Party, making the decisions concerning production and distribution of goods and services.

REVIEW QUESTIONS

1. What role did market conditions have in creating the bad conditions for the working classes of Britain in the last century?
2. What was utopian socialism?
3. Marx is said to have had an interpretation of history and explanation of social existence in his "dialectical materialism." What is "dialectical materialism"?
4. In the Marxist framework, what is the difference between socialism and communism?
5. What was Marx's labor theory of value? How can this theory be criticized?
6. What was Marx's theory of surplus value? Is it a valid theory?
7. What were the causes and consequences, according to Marx, of the distribution of income under market capitalism? What was Marx's theory of income distribution?
8. What are some of the institutions of modern socialism?
9. What was the difference between socialism in France and socialism in England in the 18th and 19th centuries?

RECOMMENDED READINGS

Balinsky, Alexander. *Marx's Economics: Origin and Development*. Lexington, Mass.: Heath, 1970.
Dickens, Charles. *Hard Times*. New York: Signet, 1962. (A novel protesting working conditions and education in 19th-century England.)
Gray, Alexander. *The Development of Economic Doctrine: An Introductory Survey*. New York: Wiley, 1931.
Hammond, John L., and Barbara Hammond. *The Rise of Modern Industry*. New York: Harper & Row, 1969.
Harrington, Michael. *Socialism*. New York: Saturday Review Press, 1972.
Hill, Christopher. *Reformation to Industrial Revolution*. Baltimore: Penguin, 1969.
Marx, Karl. *Das Kapital*. New York: Modern Library, 1906.
Taylor, Philip A. M., ed. *The Industrial Revolution in Britain: Triumph or Disaster?* Rev. ed. Boston: Heath, 1970.
Toynbee, Arnold. *The Industrial Revolution*. Boston: Beacon Press, 1956.
Tucker, Robert C. *The Marxian Revolutionary Idea*. New York: Norton, 1969.

3

Market Mechanisms and the Less Developed Countries

INTRODUCTION

A majority of the world's population live in *less developed* countries. Most of the nations of Latin America, Africa, and Asia are in this category. Until very recently the economies of most of these nations have been organized predominantly on the basis of tradition. However, in the last few decades social, political, and economic changes have come to these countries, and they have begun to acquire new economic systems. They are continuing to struggle in order to convert themselves from underdeveloped poverty to developing wealth. Will heavy reliance upon market mechanisms alone be likely to produce good solutions for the problems which these countries are encountering in their struggles? Many economists and many of the leaders of these countries believe not. In this chapter the apparent suitability of market arrangements for these countries is explored.

The less developed countries are by no means all alike. There is a vast difference between, say, the situation of a typical slum dweller of Mexico City and that of an average Vietnamese peasant. Nevertheless, the less developed countries do seem to have many common features, and a brief summary of some of these is useful at this point.

Typical Economic Conditions

Whether a country should be classed as less developed is sometimes determined by its gross national product (GNP) per capita. Per capita GNP is a rough measure of the goods and services produced and available on the average to each person. Among the poorest countries in the world are Haiti, Bolivia, Somalia, Yemen, Pakistan, India, China, and Indonesia. For these countries the GNP per capita is less than 5 percent of the annual United States figure, which was about $12,500 in 1981. The poverty which this low percentage figure represents shows up in a tangible way in nutritionally inadequate diets, primitive and crowded housing, ragged clothes, an absence of medical services, and an unavailability of schools. Disease, emaciated bodies, short lives, and illiteracy are other symptoms.

Most of the output of the less developed countries is consumer goods, primarily food. Capital goods are usually a very small part of the GNP. The techniques of production are predominantly primitive. There is very little equipment or other real capital. Labor provides most of the energy. Knowledge of more efficient techniques is lacking.

The vast majority of people are farmers and live in rural areas. They tend to have rather high death rates but even higher birth rates, so that the population size keeps increasing. The age structure of the population is heavily weighted with children. One result is that each person in the economically productive age groups has a greater average number of dependents than is the case for advanced countries.

In some less developed areas the arable land is fragmented into very small, individually owned and managed plots. Elsewhere it is organized into large estates or plantations with most of the labor force as wage laborers or sharecroppers. A typical condition on these lands is supposed by many observers to be *underemployment*. This is a state of affairs in which there are so many laborers per acre that some of them could be removed without a reduction in the size of the output of product. Much of the rural populace gets along by barter or near self-sufficiency. Money transactions are rare.

Typical Social and Political Conditions

Social conditions differ in most less developed countries from those in advanced countries. In many of the poor countries there is an elite class which is wealthy and educated. The families of this class own most of the property and possess most of the political power. This class constitutes a small minority of the total population, the vast majority of whom are, of course, very poor. The middle classes are small or nonexistent.

The rich and powerful elite have, to a considerable extent, adopted European culture as a style of life for themselves. The poor majority remain bound in native tradition. The striking differences between the two major classes have led some people to call the society *dualistic.*

Among the majority there exist such traditions as the *extended family.* This is an arrangement in which all the aunts, uncles, grandparents, grandchildren, nieces, and nephews either by blood or by marriage are regarded as entitled to share in the income earned by their productive relatives. The tradition of *tribalism* survives in many African countries and makes a feeling of national unity difficult.

The governments of most of these countries tend to be autocratic. More than a few are military dictatorships. Some are quite politically unstable with abrupt and sometimes violent changes in leadership occurring rather frequently. Some governments which succeed in staying in power attempt to maintain the status quo in economics. Others press vigorously for some kind of enforced economic change, sometimes including alteration of the economic system.

International Relations

Many of the less developed countries, especially those in Asia and Africa, were colonial possessions of advanced countries until after World War II. Since independence, there has remained a lingering mistrust of foreigners. This mistrust is a result of earlier political domination and frequent economic exploitation of native peoples by the Europeans.

The heritage of mistrust continues to manifest itself in various ways. One manifestation is the existence in many poor countries of a vigorous spirit of *nationalism.* Nationalism is a feeling of the importance, merit, superiority, and priority of one's national group and the belief that one's own nation must be made to triumph whenever it is challenged by any other nation. Another manifestation is the resentment felt by the peoples of the less developed nations in their continuing economic relations with the advanced nations. By and large, the less developed nations specialize in the production for export of agricultural and mineral raw materials. They rely upon imports from the advanced nations for manufactured goods, including capital equipment, and for technical services. This is the same trade pattern which existed before independence. Its continuation gives the impression to the less developed peoples that economic independence has not yet been achieved.

In matters of international investment and foreign aid, too, resentment arises. Typically, international investment has been undertaken by private businesses with headquarters in advanced countries and with ownership vested with Europeans or Americans. These businesses have established production facilities in less developed countries. Such facilities have consisted mainly of plantations for products like bananas and rubber, mines for the extraction of metallic ores, and petroleum fields. The products of these operations are usually exported to the advanced countries. The ownership and control of these activities have usually remained with the Western foreign investors, and to the less developed peoples the arrangements smack too much of continued colonialism. The grants, loans, and technical assistance which have been extended by the governments of advanced countries to the less developed ones have been resented in the recipient countries because of the sometimes justified suspicion that the assistance is given for the purpose of undermining the political and economic independence of the recipients.

Typical Values and Attitudes

The strong resentment felt toward foreigners is only one of the values and attitudes which distinguish the people of the less developed nations from more economically advanced peoples. Typically there is an unquestioning acceptance of the already established modes of production. Change in these matters is seldom considered as an alternative to tradition.

There is also an acceptance by parents of whatever number of children that chance happens to bring or even a positive desire for as many children as possible. There is an expectation that one born of a poor family will remain poor and will give birth to children who will remain poor. Similarly, there is an expectation that the children of the present elite will be the elite of the next generation. There is a presumption that one must share one's material means with one's relatives of the extended family. There is in some nations a strong feeling of loyalty to and dependence upon the tribe.

In some less developed countries there is a cynicism about the government's ability to be anything other than autocratic. There may even exist a failure to imagine that there is any other way for a government to be. There is an apparent inability among many of both the governors and the governed to understand that the government can be used as an instrument for society's improvement rather than as an instrument of personal aggrandizement for those who happen to hold power. There is a failure to comprehend that those who hold power could ever voluntarily relinquish it or that those who are not in power might voluntarily and actively cooperate with those who govern.

In recent decades the people of most less developed countries have become aware that there are other peoples whose material existence is significantly better than their own. The less developed peoples are believed to have adopted the desire to exist at least as well. The process by which this adoption has taken place is sometimes called the *revolution of rising expectations.* Among the devices by which the awareness was transmitted and the desire created were colonialism, missionary activities, World War II, and Hollywood movies. In these ways Western individuals, or their likenesses, with habits of high material consumption came among the less developed peoples. Though the desire was thus implanted among them, an understanding of the means by which the desire could be satisfied has not yet fully occurred to them. A gap exists between their economic aspirations and their actual economic achievement. In an attempt to narrow the gap, they have considered and are considering the appropriateness of various economic systems. One of these is, of course, the market system.

MARKET MECHANISMS AS POSITIVE FORCES FOR ECONOMIC DEVELOPMENT

Market mechanisms can play a large role in the conversion of a less developed country into a developed one. The ideas of how they can do so have been formulated from the British experience and from that of other developed nations such as the United States, Japan, and those of Western Continental Europe. One of the most famous and controversial theories of economic development based on these experiences was that of Karl Marx. Another and more recent theory, also highly controversial, is that of Walt Whitman Rostow.[1]

Rostow's Theory of the Stages of Economic Development

According to Rostow, in the process of economic development nations pass through several stages.

The Traditional Society. In the first stage the nation's society is a traditional one. All societies before the Renaissance were traditional societies. These societies have many of the attributes described in the introduction of this chapter. A crucial attribute is the absence of any cumulative, self-reenforcing process of material improvement. Change may occur, but it is not in the form of a systematic trend.

The Prerequisites for Change. In the second stage, as Rostow describes it, there is the establishment of the prerequisites for sustained and systematic change, though such change does not itself begin yet. Chief among the prerequisites is an abandonment, by at least some of the population, of a philosophy of fatalism and determinism. In its place there arises a

---

[1]Walt Whitman Rostow, *The Stages of Economic Growth: A Non-Communist Manifesto*, 2d ed. (New York: Cambridge University Press, 1971).

belief in rationality (a belief in an ordered universe whose laws are discoverable and advantageous to those who understand them).

Other changes of attitudes and philosophical values also take place. Individuals come to be respected, not because of inherited states, but because of economic efficiency. The maximum number of babies physically possible ceases to be the optimum number as viewed by parents and society. Somehow income above subsistence needs must cease to be distributed to those who use it merely for ceremonial ostentation and instead must begin to be distributed to those who use it for the formation of real capital.

These prerequisites were established in Western Europe by the long process the beginning of which can be traced to the ancient civilizations of the Near East. In countries outside Western Europe and in today's less developed countries, these prerequisites have been established by contact with Europeans.

The Takeoff. The third stage is described by Rostow as a takeoff, which suggests that the pace of social and economic change suddenly accelerates. An important part of this acceleration is the increase in the percentage of the gross national product which is saved and which takes the form of capital goods. Another is the establishment of manufacturing activities. There is also continued alteration in such things as the customs of the people, the governmental forms and practices, and the kinds of economic units in existence. Rostow conceives of the takeoff as some stimulating event. The event may be a war, a revolution, or a sudden change in international trading relationships. The event reacts back upon the already established prerequisites in such a way as to set off the accelerated changes named above.

Later Stages. The fourth of Rostow's stages is a period of self-sustaining increases in gross national product both in total and per capita. These increases eventually bring the nation to the fifth stage, one of high mass consumption. There may possibly follow further developments which are worthy of being classed as additional stages but whose character can only be guessed since no nation as yet progressed so far.

Criticisms. Rostow's *theory of the stages of economic growth* has been criticized on a number of counts. Included among these is the charge that it fails to fit with historical fact. There are also assertions that it fails to specify what makes each of the stages peculiarly distinctive relative to each of the others. It is further criticized for its failure to include forces which may be important in causing growth.[2] However, Rostow's termi-

---

[2]A summary of criticism of Rostow's theory and a useful bibliography on the subject appear in Gerald M. Meier, *Leading Issues in Development Economics: Studies in International Poverty,* 3rd ed. (New York: Oxford University Press, 1976), pp. 59–120.

nology has been widely adopted by other writers, and his theory does convey much of the vision which many economic historians have regarding the process of economic development.

The Role of the Market in Economic Growth

What role does the market play in a Rostow-like growth process? In the traditional societies, market mechanisms are only peripherally present since economic coordination is achieved mainly by tradition. In fact, what seems to distinguish the traditional society from societies of the later stages is the small degree to which market mechanisms are relied upon in the former.

Changes in Religion and Philosophy. In the establishment of the prerequisites for takeoff, the market may play a role both as a cause and as an effect. For example, the growth of the practices of specialization in producing, buying, and selling things for money may undermine the traditional religious rules against profit making. When the religious authorities attempt to enforce these religious rules, their prestige and that of their deterministic philosophy may be at stake. If they fail in the enforcement, the philosophy may be discredited, and the way opened for a rational skepticism to replace the determinism. Market mechanisms may thus help to establish what Rostow regards as the crucially important prerequisite to growth.

On the other hand, if determinism has already been replaced with rationalism, the rationality may deliberately lead individuals to engage in specialization in production and concomitant buying and selling. These activities will be undertaken because they prove to be the most rational means by which individuals and groups can achieve their material desires.

Changes in Birth Rates. A further illustration of the role which the market can play in the establishment of the preconditions and the takeoff is provided by a study of what sometimes happens to the birth rate during the stages or process of development. In traditional societies the birth rates are high. It is probably appropriate that they be so, for the death rates are also high.

Typically in most of today's less developed countries, however, the stage involving the establishment of prerequisites to takeoff has included the rapid and drastic reduction of death rates. This reduction has occurred as contact with Westerners and Western medical technology, public health measures, and transportation techniques have brought about the eradication of epidemic diseases and regional famines. Meanwhile, the birth rates have remained high and, in combination with the lowered death rates, have created the population explosion. This explosion has had some disadvantageous results for most less developed countries. There are already too many people crowded on the land. There is too little capital equipment for each worker, and the extra mouths to feed leave less output for capital formation.

However, many demographic experts foresee an optimistic outcome, which will be achieved through the operation of market forces. It is this: The changes already occurring in less developed countries are causing a shift in population from rural pursuits to urban ones. In a farm situation large numbers of children in a family are regarded by the parents as assets since they can be put to work at an early age. Hence rural parents choose to have large numbers of children, and the birth rates are high. In an urban situation, however, children are often economic liabilities to their parents. They cannot work until they are almost adults, and they require expensive training and sustenance in the meantime. Moreover, either the mother or the father frequently is prevented from obtaining available work away from the home because child care is necessary.

Circumstances such as these of a market economy suggest to the parents that a rational choice is to have fewer children. So if urban industrialization is occurring and if most parents act in the way just suggested, the population explosion will be ended. It will be ended not by governmental command or by tradition, but by individual decisions representing rational responses to the economic forces of the market.[3]

The Takeoff. The stimulus of which Rostow conceives as the heart of the takeoff stage may also originate in market forces. For example, a business cycle expansion in an advanced country may increase market demand for the raw material exports of a less developed country. In response, that activity or industry which produces the material in the less developed country may reap unusual profits and may expand. Such expansion may increase the demand for labor and other supplies there so that the whole economy of the less developed country begins to grow faster than before the takeoff occurred.

Even a sudden decline in the demand for a less developed country's principal raw material export may act as a stimulus to takeoff. For example, suppose a recession occurs in an advanced country so that import purchases of a raw material from a less developed country dramatically decline. The shock in the less developed country may cause the raw material producers there to begin to process and to try to sell their output to their own nationals. This activity may be the real beginning of manufacturing operations in the less developed country.

---

[3]Frank W. Notestein, Dudley Kirk, and Sheldon Segal, "The Problem of Population Control," in *The Population Dilemma*, ed. Philip M. Hauser, 2d ed. (Englewood Cliffs, N.J.: Prentice-Hall, 1969); and Kingsley Davis, "Population," *Scientific American*, Vol. 209, No. 3 (September 1963), pp. 62–71.

Cumulative Growth. The market can provide the mechanism by which growth becomes self-sustaining once something like a takeoff occurs. According to Rostow, the growth of one industry is likely to lead to the establishment and growth of others, all through market forces.[4] As one industry grows, it requires and demands increasing amounts of supplies, which are themselves the products of other industries. These other industries can therefore be expected to expand in size, thus creating demand for the products of still other industries, which also then expand. The increased incomes earned by workers in the initially expanding industries provide the demand for products from other consumer goods industries, which then expand. The profits from the initially expanding industries are available and are likely to be used to finance the increase in the productive capacity of these industries. Such expansion probably will create a demand for capital goods so that industries producing capital goods may be established.

In this way it is plausible to argue that market mechanisms can be a vehicle by which economic development can occur.

THE OBSTACLES TO DEVELOPMENT

The fact is, however, that economic development has been occurring very slowly or not at all for the majority of less developed nations. GNP per capita is not only low, it is not increasing very much. It is probably even true that there are periods in which the GNP per capita has been falling in some countries. It turns out that economic development is an extremely elusive objective. The obstacles to its achievement are many.[5] The task of converting backward, poor peoples into progressive, rich ones is not easy.

Inadequate Natural Resources

One might claim that the major obstacle to economic development is lack of natural resources. There are certainly some less developed countries that seem to lack climate, soil, minerals, waterpower, and most other features of a rich, natural endowment. Yeman, Chad, Malawi, New Guinea, and India are but a few of these. Then, too, some countries are so small in size as measured in total natural wealth that they seem by themselves economically unviable. Some examples are Guatemala, Mauretania, Oman, Singapore, Trinidad, and Lesotho.

The fact is, however, that these kinds of obstacles can be overcome.

---

[4]Rostow, *op cit.*

[5]For another summary and critical account of the obstacles to economic development in less developed countries, see Walter Elkan, *An Introduction to Development Economics* (Baltimore: Penguin, 1973), Chapter 2.

Japan is an example of a nation which, with an extremely poor endowment of natural resources, was able to pursue the development process successfully. Libya is an example of a nation which once seemed hopelessly poor in natural resources, level of living, and prospects. It suddenly discovered in the late 1950s that there was located beneath it one of the world's largest natural petroleum reservoirs, which will probably prove the means to its development. Kuwait, too, is an example of an extremely small desert nation whose path to wealth was through petroleum. One of the most prosperous nations in the world is also the smallest with a population of only about one-third million people: Luxembourg has been able through specialization and trade with other countries to overcome the diseconomies of small national size.

Finally, there are nations with low, stagnant average levels of living which seem to be rather amply endowed with natural resources. Bolivia, Zaire, and Indonesia are among these. It seems that one could conclude that excellent natural resources and large national size are neither necessary nor sufficient to assure development.

Inadequate Real Capital

Inadequate amounts of real capital and inability to increase the amounts are obstacles to economic development. It is sometimes said that poor countries are, in this regard, caught in a vicious circle. Because the capital stock of each of these countries is small, the real gross national product of each is small. Because its GNP is small, almost all of the GNP must take the form of consumer subsistence goods such as food, or else the people would starve. But if most of the output must take the form of consumer goods, little can take the form of capital goods. The capital stock remains low as do output or GNP, the level of living, and the rate of economic development. The less developed country is locked in a vicious circle of poverty.

Yet it is well to remind oneself, in assessing this argument, that the advanced countries of today were once in much this same situation. They somehow managed, nonetheless, to develop in the meantime.

Overpopulation

Perhaps the chief obstacle to economic development is people themselves—their numbers, their abilities as producers, their attitudes and values, and the arrangements to which they have become accustomed in their contacts with each other.[6] If one thinks of people as providers of the

---

[6]A broad and original treatment of the roles of human values and social institutions in economic development occurs in W. Arthur Lewis, *The Theory of Economic Development* (Homewood, Ill.: Irwin, 1955).

most important factor of production, labor, one might conclude that the more people, the more labor, the greater the GNP, and the better off the country. For some countries with small populations and access to large natural resources and stocks of real capital, this is appropriate reasoning. Countries such as the United States in the 19th century and Australia or Canada today are in this category.

It is well to remember, however, that for most countries more people mean not only more labor and output but also more consumers among whom to share the output. The more people there are, the less will be the real capital and natural resources per capita. Suppose a country is already large enough to take full advantage of economies of mass production and other advantages of large scale. Suppose that the goal is maximum output per person rather than maximum total output. Then more people are a disadvantage, not an advantage. These suppositions are true for most less developed countries. That is why there is so much concern among so many social scientists and public officials about the population explosion and overpopulation among less developed people.

Unproductive Labor

The majority of people in most less developed countries are workers of only low quality. Whatever may be their virtues as people, as workers they are of little productivity. They are unskilled, uneducated, and untrained. Few of them are capable of acting as business managers with any success. Still fewer of them are able to recognize the opportunities for reorganizing a productive activity in a new way so as to increase output without increasing inputs or to decrease inputs without decreasing output. Few of them are able to put into practice such reorganization even when the opportunity to do so is recognized.

Here again one can explain the predicament in terms of a vicious circle. Without skilled workers, adroit management, and imaginative entrepreneurship, the less developed countries conduct their economic activities in ways which do not require these inputs. Activities are conducted instead with unskilled workers, on a small scale which can dispense with much management, and with a reliance upon tradition rather than upon the imaginative innovations of good entrepreneurship. With activities conducted in this way, there is very little opportunity for workers through practice to develop skills and become trained. Similarly, opportunities are lacking for managers to develop their skills through practice and for a tradition of entrepreneurship to become established. So the less developed countries may be locked in a vicious circle of a low average quality of human resources and backward techniques of production.

Another vicious circle is not unlike that, described several paragraphs ago, between lack of capital and low GNP. This vicious circle has to do with the reenforcing action between untrained labor and low GNP. Because labor is untrained, total output is low. Because output is low, little output can be spared from consumer goods to take the form of training services. Because labor cannot be trained, output remains low.

Values and Attitudes

Behind the large number of peoples and the poor economic quality of human resources lie, partly as causal forces, attitudes and values which are prevalent among the less developed peoples.

Family Size. The attitudes toward births and family size are instructive in this respect. These attitudes were formed during the pre-1900 millennia when death rates were high. Then the chances of a newborn baby's surviving until its first birthday were less than one out of two. The chances of children's surviving into adulthood were almost as low. Many babies would be necessary to have as many as two of them survive to adulthood, when as adults they might be needed to care for aged parents and to perpetuate the family line. Not all parents deliberately and consciously reasoned this argument through, of course; perhaps very few did. Yet the survival not only of the family line but also of the larger society of which the family was a part depended upon high birth rates.

By the dawn of the industrial and technological age, most societies of the world contained the tradition of high birth rates. The approved mode of behavior among their people was to strive for many babies and large families. This attitude was, at least by this time, predominantly a traditional one rather than a reasoned one. When there became available technological knowledge which permitted death rates to decline, the attitude was outmoded and inappropriate. It persisted, nonetheless, to the economic detriment of the peoples.

Economic Effort. The attitudes and values toward occupational self-improvement of individuals were likewise appropriate to a traditional society. They have persisted into an era which is one of a growing and changing society. They are incompatible with the new society, and they stand as obstacles against it.

In a traditional society one accepted the occupation conventionally reserved for one's family. One's rewards depended upon such acceptance, and the cohesiveness of society depended upon it, too. Individuals were not encouraged by public opinion to seek material gain for themselves through violation of tradition; it was quite the contrary.

Now that the time for change has come, the attitudinal mechanism for the achievement of change is absent. Individuals desire economic improvement for themselves, but there is too little recognition among them of the causal link which can exist between hard work and a higher standard of living. They do not understand that disciplining themselves to an industrial routine is necessary to make available steel mills and cars. They do not see that honesty in observing contracts is prerequisite to greater income and output. They fail to comprehend that saving and training will lead to economic improvement over time.

Success as an entrepreneur is accorded less prestige than success as a military leader, a religious zealot, a civil servant, or a learned scholar. Tolerance of and apathy toward inept, corrupt government prevents the best economic decisions from being made and carried out. Determination by the ruling oligarchy that it shall remain in political and economic power frustrates economic change. Willingness of the popular majority to believe in and follow the demagogic appeals of the latest military leader or rabble-rousing politician provides an atmosphere of insecurity in which good economic decisions are unlikely to be made.

MARKET MECHANISMS AS OBSTACLES TO DEVELOPMENT

In the kind of environment just suggested as typical of less developed countries, it seems unlikely that market mechanisms alone will achieve rapid economic development for these countries. Essentially, market mechanisms consist of permitting individual owners, buyers, and sellers to make economic decisions for themselves and of letting things be as they are or as they will be. In the cases of many less developed countries, this means letting things be as they traditionally have been or letting them be in chaos as they are. This usually will not suffice. The argument against exclusive reliance upon market mechanisms can be given detail as follows.

The Inhibition of Investment

Productive investment induced through market forces is inhibited by several conditions of underdeveloped nations.

Political Insecurity. In many less developed countries the wealthiest portion of the population live considerably above the subsistence minimum and save sizable parts of their incomes. These savings could be spent by them on real capital formation or be loaned to others for the same purpose. In this way the vicious circle of lack of capital and low output might be broken. Unfortunately, the political atmosphere in many of these countries is one of great insecurity. The possibility of revolution or confiscation of capital is quite real. So the savers prefer to buy property outside the country, to purchase land, jewelry, or precious metals within the country, or to invest in quickly saleable merchandise inventories. The corrupt, inept governmental administrators inadvertently encourage the same behavior by the wealthy savers. Consequently, the countries remain without equipment and other real capital and lack economic development.

Lack of Complementary Industries. In order to be profitable to the owners, some types of productive operations, such as factories, require the prior existence of public utilities such as railways, highways, and water, sewage, and electric power facilities. However, these things do not exist, and so investment in factories is not undertaken. The profitable investment in factories may also require the prior existence of a trained labor force, of industries to supply inputs and services, or of a market with buyers who have purchasing power with which to buy the factories' products. Usually one, some, or all of these prerequisites are missing so that there is no investment and no development. Here development by way of market mechanisms is caught up and held back within a vicious circle of lack of complementary industries, each being a prerequisite for the others.[7]

The Inhibition of Enterprise

There may exist among the population of less developed countries individuals with entrepreneurial talents and inclinations. These people may have a sharp sense of what is profitable. Yet the same factors which channel savings and investments into the relatively less productive forms, such as merchandise inventories, land, and foreign property, are likely to direct the entrepreneurial talents into these same lines. Moreover, the entrepreneurs may lack a tradition of honesty in dealings and of a sense of obligation to fulfill contracts. They may aim mainly to devise ways to cheat those with whom they deal. In such cases they are more likely to be an obstacle than an aid to economic development.

The Inhibition of Labor

The reaction of workers on the market for labor may also be a deterrent to economic development. Suppose that as economic development begins, the first increases in real and money wages occur. The reaction of

---

[7]It seems likely that some of the conditions prerequisite for investment in private productive facilities must be provided by governmental action. When prerequisites such as transportation, electric power, and education are lacking, it is usually a government which must create them. Government expenditures to create them are said to constitute either public investment in *social overhead capital* or public provision of an *infrastructure*. Specific discussion of the infrastructure and of social overhead capital appears in Everett E. Hagen, *The Economics of Development*, rev. ed. (Homewood, Ill.: Irwin, 1975), pp. 170–176. The infrastructure of agriculture is discussed in Clifton R. Wharton, "The Infrastructure for Agricultural Growth," Chapter 4 of Herman M. Southworth and Bruce F. Johnston, eds., *Agricultural Development and Economic Growth* (Ithaca, N.Y.: Cornell University Press, 1967), pp. 107–146. Additional general discussion of the accumulation and use of real capital can be found in Meier, *op cit.*, pp. 165–250.

the workers may be to decide that they now need to work as many hours as before the wage increase. They may react in this way because fewer hours of work now provide as much income as before. If they do react in this way, the economic development which made possible the increased wages may grind to a halt for lack of an adequate supply of the right kinds of labor.[8]

This reaction to market forces may be especially likely in countries with a tradition of the extended family. There any extra income earned is likely not to seem worth the extra effort. This is so since the income, but not the effort, must be shared by the worker with so many relatives.

In other cases, the market may encourage partially inappropriate decisions with regard to the purchase by a worker of training or exertion of effort to improve skills. The market may fail to induce the worker to take into account all the benefits which occur from such training and effort. The market inducement to the worker, of course, occurs mainly in the form of higher income which can be earned through increased training or improved productive ability. The worker makes the decision by weighing the improvement's cost against the higher income to be earned. In some instances the worker rationally decides against undertaking the training when, from society's viewpoint, the decision should be in favor of the training. The worker's decision is socially inappropriate because there are benefits which accrue to society from the training in addition to and apart from the direct benefits of greater output and higher income which accrue to the worker.

The additional social benefits include the better citizen the worker is likely to be because of the training. They also include the knowledge that associates absorb, gratis, from the worker because of that trained status. There is, in addition, the increased probability that through additional training the worker will discover production improvements for which there is no personal compensation but which, nevertheless, raise the productive capacity of the society of which the worker is a part.

Reliance exclusively upon market forces to determine the amounts of training, education, and other improvements in labor quality produces too little of these. This may be a crucially important defect of the market system for less developed countries.

SUCCESSES IN DEVELOPMENT

The latter portions of this chapter have dwelt upon possible weaknesses of market mechanisms as devices for achieving economic develop-

---

[8]The economic phenomenon in which the amount of labor supplied may decrease when the wage rate rises is called by economists *the backward-bending supply curve of labor*. One brief criticism of it occurs in Elkan, *op. cit.*, pp. 37–39. The supply curve of labor is probably more likely to be backward-bending when there are few additional attractive goods available to be purchased by workers than when many such goods are available.

ment. One should keep in mind, however, that market mechanisms can, in combination with the right government policies, sometimes be positive forces in promoting economic development. Indeed, there are numerous instances in which market mechanisms have obviously contributed to economic development in less developed countries. Some of the empirical evidence of these instances is summarized in this section.

Mexico

Mexico has achieved considerable economic progress in recent decades. Real gross national product, both per capita and in total, has risen at high rates. This achievement has occurred while the Mexican economic system has consisted of a unique and interesting combination of market and governmental arrangements.

Over 90 percent of all production in Mexico is conducted by privately owned and operated enterprises. Much of the new investment is financed from privately generated savings channeled through private financial institutions. Private foreign investment has been important in promoting growth. Much of the agricultural sector is organized as private commercial farms. The transactions conducted by all of these economic units are basically motivated by the desire for maximizing profits and income, in response to market forces. Rewards in income and wealth have gone in great measure to those who act efficiently in response to market opportunities. For the most part, comprehensive detailed central planning of the economy by the government has been absent.

On the other hand, the Mexican government has exercised pervasive influence in the economy. It has not hesitated to take over the ownership and control of a few entire industries such as petroleum production. It has established government enterprises in competition with private ones in the same industry, such as in the case of steel production. It has exercised considerable control over access to financial credit through government financial institutions and through regulation of private financial firms. It has constructed social overhead facilities, such as ports and roads, with a clear intention of influencing the geographical location and other characteristics of new private real investment. It has controlled access to imported goods and to foreign sources of capital.

It is impossible to indicate exactly the extent to which Mexico owes its economic development to private market forces as opposed to governmental direction. What does seem clear is that Mexico's combination of the two has at least not impeded fairly successful economic development. The particular combination of the two probably is an effective one and has been an important force in Mexico's economic success.[9]

---

[9]A basic long-run description and assessment of the Mexican economic system can be found in Raymond Vernon, *The Dilemma of Mexico's Development* (Cambridge: Harvard

Less Developed Countries as a Group

All less developed countries are like Mexico in the sense that they combine market arrangements with governmental policy. Economic growth results from both. A crucial question is to what extent the market arrangements rather than the governmental policies are the cause of growth. No very accurate answer to the question can be given. However, one respected scholar of economic development has made relevant estimates.

Angus Maddison studied the growth rate in 22 less developed countries for the period 1950–1965. He concluded that on the average "autonomous growth influences" accounted for almost two-thirds of the growth, while governmental policy accounted for the remaining one-third. Autonomous growth influences refer mostly to market forces but also include some economic aid from foreign governments.

Maddison's study cannot be regarded as decisive, but it does suggest that market mechanisms have played an important role in achieving development in less developed countries in recent decades. Some of the countries where market forces seem to have been the cause of much growth in real gross national product in the period 1950–1965 are Israel, Venezuela, Taiwan, Greece, and South Korea. Some of the countries where market forces were probably very important as causes of growth, *relative to* government policies as causes of growth, are Venezuela, Israel, Argentina, and Chile.

On the other hand, Maddison's study indicated that countries where government policy seemed to have been a cause of much growth are Yugoslavia, Spain, Taiwan, and Thailand. Countries where government policies were unusually important as causes of growth, *relative to* market forces as causes of growth, are Yugoslavia, Peru, Sri Lanka, and Thailand.[10]

SUMMARY

A majority of the world's people live in less developed countries where per capita output and income are very low. The people in these countries aspire to be affluent. Perhaps they will become so by following a process of development similar to that already experienced by Western nations. In the West, market forces played a significant role in development. These forces may be equally useful for the less developed countries. The profit motive may encourage investment and innovation, for example, and the desire for economic self-improvement among individuals may

University Press, 1963). A more recent brief summary of Mexico's economic status is Robert Looney, *Mexico's Economy* (Boulder, Colo.: Westview Press, 1978).

[10]Angus Maddison, *Economic Progress and Policy in Developing Countries* (New York: Norton, 1971).

induce them to work hard and to make decisions which cause themselves and their countries to advance economically.

However, there are many obstacles to development for today's poorer countries. Inadequate natural resources, too little capital, overpopulation, backward attitudes, and inefficient governments all interact to constitute a self-perpetuating set of mutually reenforcing impediments to economic growth. In such a set of circumstances, market arrangements may work poorly as a mechanism for development. Investment may be inhibited or induced to take perverse forms because of political insecurity. Entrepreneurial effort may not be forthcoming because little social prestige is attached to economic success. Social institutions such as the extended family may stifle market incentives to work.

Market mechanisms have been considerably less than a perfect means for achieving economic development for poor countries. This evidence of the inadequacy of market mechanisms alone to achieve economic goals can be added to similar evidence drawn from the experience of the United States, Britain, and the other advanced nations. The basis can thus be provided for a generalized exposition of the need for market mechanisms to be supplemented and partially replaced by other arrangements. Such an exposition is the subject of the next chapter.

REVIEW QUESTIONS

1. What are the typical economic features and class structure of less developed countries?
2. What kinds of feelings exist among many citizens of less developed countries toward Westerners? Why do these feelings exist?
3. What is Rostow's theory of the stages of economic growth? What role do market forces play in each stage?
4. In traditional societies, what is the typical attitude toward family size? Why does this attitude exist? How can market forces induce a beneficial change in this attitude as economic development occurs?
5. What do you regard as the paramount and overwhelming obstacle to economic development in less developed countries? Why?
6. What is the vicious cycle of small real capital and low income in less developed countries?
7. What are some examples of social customs which block economic development? What are some examples of the values or attitudes which block economic development?
8. How can market mechanisms, in combination with other circumstances, impede investment, enterprise, and labor effort in less developed countries?

RECOMMENDED READINGS

Albin, Peter S. *Progress without Poverty: Socially Responsible Economic Growth.* New York: Basic Books, 1978.
Hagen, Everett E. *Economic Development.* 3rd ed. Homewood, Ill.: Irwin, 1980.
Heilbroner, Robert L. *The Making of Economic Society.* 6th ed. Englewood Cliffs, N.J.: Prentice-Hall, 1980.

Kemp, Tom. *Historical Patterns of Industrialization*. London: Longman, 1978.

Kindleberger, Charles P. *Economic Development*. 3rd ed. New York: McGraw-Hill, 1977.

Leontief, Wassily W. *The Future of the World Economy*. New York: Oxford University Press, 1977.

McCutcheon, Robert. *Limits of a Modern World*. London: Butterworth, 1979.

Meier, Gerald M. *International Economics*. New York: Oxford University Press, 1980.

Pitt, David. *The Social Dynamics of Development*. New York: Pergamon Press, 1976.

Rostow, Walt Whitman. *Why the Poor Get Richer and the Rich Slow Down*. Austin: University of Texas Press, 1980.

4

Market Mechanisms, Economic Problems, and the Need for Governmental Policy

INTRODUCTION

The United States, Britain, and other countries, primarily those of European culture, have had several centuries of experience with market arrangements. More recently the less developed nations have had such experience, too. All this experience provides the empirical basis for generalizations about the kinds of problems which seem likely to arise in an economy heavily reliant upon market mechanisms. Such generalizations are the essence of this chapter.

It is useful to divide these generalizations into two groups. The first group involves the prerequisite conditions within which market mechanisms operate most effectively. The absence of these conditions usually necessitates governmental action to create them. The second group involves the problems which seem to arise as results of the effective operation of market forces and which usually require governmental actions as correctives for those results.

This chapter deals with the prerequisites and the problems. Most of the remaining chapters deal with the kinds of corrective governmental actions which have been tried in various countries. The successes and failures of these actions and the new problems which these actions have in turn created are also treated in later chapters. In the real world it is not always possible to know whether a given problem arises from the operation of market forces or from governmental actions. However, in this chapter the emphasis is placed upon market forces as possible sources of trouble. In later chapters governmental policies are subjected to similar analysis.

PREREQUISITES OF A MARKET SYSTEM

In order to work well, a market system requires that the people of the society in which it is to operate have certain personal qualities, including entrepreneurship. A minimum degree of political stability must exist, and it is necessary for the government to provide a framework of law and order within which the market can operate. There should be at least some degree of competition and of price flexibility. In general, a market system works well if the cultural heritage is appropriate for market forces.

Personal Qualities

Market mechanisms widely diffuse among individuals the power to make economic decisions. It is therefore important that the individuals be able to make good decisions. To do so, they must be informed, prudent, honest, and willing to adjust to changing conditions.

Knowledgeableness. Lack of information has been a basic source of the economic troubles in societies relying heavily on market mechanisms. The Great Depression occurred in the United States in the 1930s partly because the managers of individual American firms had been poorly informed of prospective demand for their products and of each other's expansion activities. Once the depression began, these business people had no accurate information about how long it might last or how deep it might become. This uncertainty probably caused the depression to be deeper and longer than it otherwise would have been.

Lack of information contributes to the monopoly problem, too. Both consumers and purchasers of inputs for businesses are open to exploitation by monopolistic sellers because of lack of knowledge. The buyers may lack knowledge of other sellers who may exist, of the existence of other products which may serve as close substitutes, or of techniques which would make the use of such substitutes possible. Resource owners, such as 20th-century American farmers or 19th-century British factory workers, experience difficulties partly because they are poorly informed of alternative uses for their land, labor, or capital. Millions of citizens of less developed countries are caught in their poverty partly because they are not informed of new productive techniques which they might employ, new skills which they might acquire, and new products which they might produce.

Just as individuals need to be informed if they are to function efficiently within a market system, they must also be able to use the information prudently on their own behalf. They must be able to select from all the information available that which is relevant for their situation. They need to understand the causal relationships between their actions and the consequences. Business people may expand their production facilities when they already are informed of a prospective decline in the demand for their product. Workers may move into a region which they already know is one of surplus labor supply. Consumers may choose to purchase a durable appliance even though they realize it is technically obsolete. All these people create problems for themselves and others.

Honesty. To a minimum degree at least, commercial honesty seems also to be a requisite for a populace relying upon market mechanisms. Suppose that an overriding propensity existed among a people to strive to cheat each other in exchanges. The employer would spend so much time and effort checking on the suspicious activities of thieving employees that there would exist little opportunity to work out new, more efficient productive arrangements. The consumer would become so wary of deceitful sellers that exchange and specialization would tend to decline. Considerable resources of the society might have to be devoted to police activities. Market mechanisms, which depend upon the exercise of economic decision-making power by many individuals, become ineffective when that power is used primarily and consciously to deceive.

Adaptability. Individual willingness to adjust to changing conditions is necessary for the effective working of a market system. A great many of the historical difficulties of market-oriented societies seem to have occurred partly because of the people's unwillingness to adjust. Some American farmers have been unwilling to adapt to the relative decline of agriculture. They have helped to create the problem of rural poverty by their reluctance to move off the farms. Business firms, too, have disliked having to adjust to changing forces of the competitive market and have striven for monopolistic arrangements by which to insulate themselves. Workers have refused to accept lower wages when declining demand for or increasing supply of their type of labor called for such a decline. Unemployment for some of them has resulted.

Entrepreneurship

To work at their best, market mechanisms require that some of the market participants possess at least a minimum degree of entrepreneurial inclination and ability. An *entrepreneur* is one who is willing and able to supervise production, to organize workers, materials, and machinery to produce a product, and to strive to achieve efficiency in production. An entrepreneur is eager to experiment with new techniques to increase efficiency and to risk loss for the sake of such experimentation.

Entrepreneurs are essential to a market system. Achievement of productive efficiency and economic growth to provide a high and rising average level of living for the population of a market system depends upon their presence. It is they who make consumer sovereignty work by discovering what consumers want and by producing it. It is they who provide the opportunities for the efficient employment of each unit of land, labor, and capital. It is they who diligently seek ways to increase the output size without increasing the volume of resources used. It is they who break constraining traditions with the result that there emerge new products, new ways of producing old products, new sources of natural resources, and new ways of conveying products to users.

Political Conditions

A market system frequently is regarded as the antithesis of a governmentally directed economy. Although in a market system the government does not assume total directive activity, it is impossible to conceive of a market system's working well in the complete absence of an effective government. Without government there is anarchy, and a market system could not function within anarchy.

Therefore, it is concluded that a stable government is necessary to supply a framework of law and order within which a market system works. Government, with its nonmarket power to punish offenders, provides a means of protecting property from destruction or seizure. As a result, owners have an incentive to accumulate and productively use their property, as their preferences and market forces direct. Government enforces agreements or contracts between private transactors in markets and thereby encourages market transactions to take place. Government provides a population with the means of preventing hostile incursions by foreign peoples. Thus it permits market transactions to continue uninterrupted.

When governments become so weak that they cease to perform these requisite functions, market systems become less effective. In early medieval Europe, because there was no effective central government, a market system could not have existed as an important coordinator of inter-manorial economic affairs. Today in some less developed countries with weak and unstable governments, market systems have failed to develop or have disintegrated and produced perverse results.

Competition and Price Flexibility

For a market system to work well and to provide for adjustments to changing conditions, it is necessary that the prices of specific goods, services, and resources be able to rise and fall. Changes in these prices are the means by which independent consumers, producers, and resource owners are induced to make adjustments beneficial to others.

Product Price Changes. Thus, if consumer preferences change in favor of some good, its price rises as a result, and the higher price induces pro-ducers to supply more of the good. Sometimes a price is not permitted to rise because there are legal *price ceilings*. In other cases political pressure is brought to bear upon the suppliers not to raise a price. There may also be social and moral pressure against price increases. In these instances the inducement to the producers to increase the quantity supplied is reduced or eliminated, and consumer sovereignty is frustrated.

For example, in a large city, increased population or increased in-comes may lead people to desire more apartments. However, apartment rent rates may be prevented from rising by city or state law. Then market mechanisms will be prevented from responding to the changing con-sumer needs. The number of apartments being built will not rise because the return to capitalists on their property as apartments is not allowed to increase.

Resource Price Changes. Changes, including decreases, in the prices of resources are often necessary if a market system is to work well. If a technological innovation reduces the demand for a given type of labor, a fall in the relevant wage rate is called for. Such a fall would encourage employers to reemploy some of the labor. They would substitute it for other factors, and they would use it to produce more of the product. More of the product could now be sold because the labor costs of production would be lower. Lower production costs would permit lower prices for the product, increasing the quantity demanded of the product.

A decrease in the wage rate would also encourage some of the work-ers to cease to offer the skill for sale and to offer themselves, instead, in other occupations. However, the power of labor unions, the humanitarianism of employers, or minimum wage legislation may pre-vent the wage rate from falling. Then those thrown out of work by the technological innovation are likely to remain jobless and constitute an unemployment problem. Flexible wages and prices are necessary prerequisites for markets to work well.

The Cultural Heritage

There have been many societies in which the prerequisites discussed above were absent. Therefore, it must be conceded that heavy reliance upon market mechanisms cannot be a universal prescription for all societies, at all times, in all places. The recent difficulties of the less developed countries suggest as much. There exists no ubiquitous human nature such that, if just allowed to do so, all persons will always pursue profits, income, and satisfaction, and will always benefit each other in the process. The pursuit of profits, income, and satisfaction is learned behavior, and it is not innately present in humans. It is acquired by some from their environments and it is not acquired by others at all. It is socially beneficial only when the environment is appropriate, and the environment is not always appropriate.

Values and Behavior Patterns. The *environment* in this context refers primarily to the social traditions which make up the cultural heritage of the people of a society. There are social traditions in the nature of mental attitudes, philosophical values, or moral principles which are possessed by the people of a society. These they pass on from one generation to the next, and, according to these values, they make decisions or choices which result in their behavior in one way or another. Other social traditions are in the nature of behavior patterns themselves, patterns common to most or all of the people of a society. The values help to determine the behavior patterns, and behavior patterns help to shape the values. An individual who is born into a society learns to accept most of its values and soon learns to repeat its behavior patterns.

Uncertainty about Basic Causes. What causes the cultural heritage of one society to contain most of the prerequisites of a successful market system and that of another to contain few of these prerequisites? Economists generally do not know and are not particularly equipped to discover the answer. Such matters would seem most appropriately to lie within the provinces of sociologists, historians, cultural anthropologists, and social psychologists. These specialists have not thus far been able to provide adequate explanations.[1] It is really not known, for example, why

---

[1]One famous example of an attempt by a psychologist to discern the origins of entrepreneurial spirit is David C. McClelland, *The Achieving Society* (New York: Free Press, 1967). See also, as a kind of sequel, David C. McClelland and David G. Winter, *Motivating Economic Achievement* (New York: Free Press, 1971).

one nation has political revolutions frequently while another has none. Consequently, there remains ignorance about the deeper determinants of the suitability of a market system for a society. There is, however, more knowledge about the immediate requisite social conditions for the proper working of a market system. In other words, it is not possible deliberately to shape a society so that a market system will work well for it. Nevertheless, it is possible to predict with some accuracy whether, for any given society, a market system has a good immediate chance of working well for it.

COMMON PROBLEMS UNDER MARKET SYSTEMS

The cultural heritage of some societies seems to contain all or most of the necessary requisites for the effective operation of a market system. Even for these societies, excessive reliance upon the market, to the exclusion of tradition, command, and altruism, seems to produce some undesirable results.[2] Each of these troublesome results will be taken up in turn in the following sections.

Unequal Distribution of Income and Wealth

A market system tends to distribute income among the participating households in proportion to their contribution to production. Large shares in the national income go to those persons who work hard, who own resources in great demand or in small supply, who are discerning enough to make wise choices for themselves, and who are willing to be mobile in the use of their resources. Small shares go to those who have opposite traits. It is almost a certainty that the distribution of these attributes among the population will be such as to cause income to be distributed unequally to households.

The Argument That Inequality in Incomes Is Unjust. If it is conceded that a market system is likely to distribute incomes unequally, there are some people who would judge the inequality to be unjustified. Their arguments can be summarized as follows.

First, they argue that at least some of those people who work hard enjoy work. Consequently, they should not be rewarded with large incomes just for working hard.

---

[2]General surveys of the strengths and weaknesses of a market system appear in these: Gregory Grossman, *Economic Systems,* 2nd ed. (Englewood Cliffs, N.J.: Prentice-Hall, 1974), pp. 49–55; Heinz Köhler, *Welfare and Planning: An Analysis of Capitalism versus Socialism,* 2nd ed. (Melbourne, Fla.: Krieger, 1979), Chapter 5; William N. Loucks and William G. Whitney, *Comparative Economic Systems,* 9th ed. (New York: Harper & Row, 1973); and Gary M. Pickersgill and Joyce E. Pickersgill, *Contemporary Economic Systems: A Comparative View* (Englewood Cliffs, N.J.: Prentice-Hall, 1974).

They also assert that, in many cases, those who happen to own the scarcest and highest-paying resources may have come into the ownership through no effort or choice of their own. For example, they may have inherited the resources they own. Therefore, they do not deserve large rewards for such ownership since the income which the market system accords them is a matter of chance.

Some who adjudge income inequality to be unjust contend that persons who own large quantities of property do not necessarily merit large incomes simply for allowing that property to be used in production. They may passively allow compound interest and, in the case of land, increased population to provide them with ever-enlarging wealth and income.

Critics of the way in which the market system distributes income also argue that persons who make wise choices for themselves regarding such matters as what jobs to take or what use to make of their property are not necessarily meritorious. Some of them simply were lucky to be born in a society that contained a cultural heritage of wisdom. Their parents transmitted great intelligence to them genetically and provided a home environment in which a process of wise decision making was constantly carried on. The process became deeply etched into the impressionable minds of the children as a behavior pattern to follow.

Finally, those who contend that unequal income distribution is unjust say that persons who are willing to shift their resources from one use to another derive adequate satisfaction from the spirit of adventure which is associated with such change. Additional reward for such mobility in the form of large incomes is unwarranted.

Most people living in market system countries do not feel that unequal distribution of income is necessarily unjust. Many feel that absolute equality of income is undesirable since this could only be attained by the suppression of individual freedoms which would result in the destruction of existing social and legal institutions.

The Interaction of Wealth and Income. Inequality of income interacts with and mutually reinforces inequality of wealth. Those with large incomes have a greater ability to save part of their income and accumulate it in the form of wealth or property than do those with small incomes. A family with a low income will probably expend its entire income in essential consumption goods. A family with a high income has extra income after expenditures on essentials; this extra income may be saved.

A family which possesses property or wealth derives more income than just its labor income in wages and salaries. It receives, in addition, rent, dividends, interest, and profits. It tends, therefore, to be a family with a high income.

A family with a large income and with considerable wealth can afford to take risky ventures in choosing its occupations and in the use of its wealth. If these ventures are successful, they will augment the wealth and income further. A poor family is usually without a cushion of wealth or *discretionary* income on which to rely in case a risky venture fails. That family cannot undertake the risky venture for fear of jeopardizing income which is essential to them. So it is that in a market system inequality of wealth and income may be cumulatively self-reinforcing.[3]

Unemployment

The spectre of large numbers of people who are capable and desirous of working but who are unable to find a job has haunted market economies for two centuries. The severity of the problem has varied with time. During the Great Depression of the 1930s, it was the foremost problem in the United States, but it disappeared during World War II. There is no complete agreement about why unemployment occurs in a market system, but modern economic analysis emphasizes two important types of unemployment, classified by cause. These are unemployment caused by too little total spending in the economy and structural unemployment.

Unemployment Caused by Too Little Total Spending. The theory of unemployment caused by too little total spending was developed primarily by the foremost economist of the 20th century thus far, John Maynard Keynes. This Englishman, writing in his *General Theory of Employment, Interest, and Money*[4] in the 1930s, sought to explain the Great Depression.

Keynesian Determinants of Employment. According to Keynes the volume of employment in the economy is determined by the volume of production of goods and services by business. This volume of production in turn depends upon the volume of sales of goods and services by business—in other words, upon how much businesses are able to sell. Sales depend upon how much spending is being done to buy the products. If spending is large, employment will be large, but if spending is small, there will be much unemployment.

Total spending to buy final products is called *gross national product spending.* GNP spending has three main components. (1) There is *con-*

---

[3]Discussions of economic inequality in a market economy are included in George N. Halm, *Economic Systems: A Comparative Analysis,* 3rd ed. (New York: Holt, Rinehart & Winston, 1968), Chapter 5; and Carl Landauer, *Contemporary Economic Systems: A Comparative Analysis* (Philadelphia: Lippincott, 1964), Chapter 7.

[4]John Maynard Keynes, *The General Theory of Employment, Interest, and Money* (New York: Harcourt, Brace & World, 1936). This is a classic but very difficult work, and one might best use one of the standard guides to it: Dudley Dillard, *The Economics of John Maynard Keynes: The Theory of a Monetary Economy* (Englewood Cliffs, N.J.: Prentice-Hall, 1948); Alvin H. Hansen, *A Guide to Keynes* (New York: McGraw-Hill, 1953). Keynes and his ideas are presented in a more elementary and entertaining style in Robert L. Heilbroner, *The Worldly Philosophers: The Lives, Times, and Ideas of the Great Economic Thinkers,* 5th ed. (New York: Simon & Schuster, 1980), Chapter 9.

sumer spending. This is spending by households to buy newly produced consumer goods and services. (2) There is *business investment spending.* This is spending by businesses to buy newly produced capital goods in the forms of plant, equipment, and additional inventories. (3) There is *government spending* for newly produced goods and services. When these three types of spending are too small in total, unemployment will occur.

Keynesian Determinants of Spending. What determines these three types of spending? Consumer spending is determined mainly by two variables. One is the size of consumer income. This is directly and closely related to the size of total spending or the GNP. The other is the willingness of consumers to spend their income. Business investment spending is determined by business expectations regarding the profitability in the future of additional plant, equipment, and inventories created now. Such expectations are influenced by the interest rates prevailing on funds borrowed to undertake this investment spending, by the extent of idle plant and equipment, and by the current size of GNP and sales of products. Government spending is determined by the need for publicly provided goods and services and by the felt need to minimize government deficits and debt.

There are a number of reasons why GNP spending may be too low and why unemployment caused by too little total spending may thus exist. Consumers may be too unwilling to spend out of their incomes. Business expectations regarding the future profitability of additional plant, equipment, and inventory may be too low. The interest rate may be too high. The amount of idle equipment may be too great. Product sales may be too low. The willingness of governments to engage in *deficit spending* may be too small. That is, governments may be too unwilling to have their own spending exceed tax receipts.

This is Keynes's explanation for unemployment. It is still largely accepted today among economists as an explanation for one of the two important types of unemployment in a market system.

Structural Unemployment. The second kind of unemployment is structural unemployment. *Structural unemployment* is unemployment caused by changes in the structure of the labor market. These are changes in the demands and supplies of various specific types of labor. Adjustment to these changes is slow and imperfect.[5]

Changes in Demand. Structural changes may originate on the demand side of the labor market. For example, there may be a shift in consumers' preferences from coal as a residential heating fuel to natural

---

[5]One good discussion of structural unemployment occurs in this governmental publication: *Economic Report of the President: January, 1964* (Washington: U.S. Government Printing Office, 1964), pp. 166–183.

gas. There will then be a decrease in the demand for the labor of coal miners. A delayed and incomplete transfer of enough workers from mining to other occupations may then cause unemployment for some of the miners. As another example, geographical shifts of economic activity may decrease the demand for labor in the locality which the activity is leaving. This was the case during much of the last century as the American textile industry shifted from New England to the South. New England textile workers were, for a time, structurally unemployed. If a technological advance such as automation occurs, the new methods may decrease the demand for certain types of workers, who may then become unemployed. If it becomes the practice for employers to provide large pensions to their employees, the demand for older workers may decrease since they involve large pension costs relative to the length of time worked. Older workers may then experience unemployment.

Changes in Supply. Structural changes may also originate on the supply side of the labor market. One cause might be a large increase in the birth rate, such as occurred in the United States in the 1940s. Fifteen or twenty years later there will be an increase in the supply of teenage labor, some of which may go unemployed. Another cause might be an increase in the average length of life so that the supply of labor from older people increases. Then some of these people may go unemployed because the quantity of labor demanded of them fails to increase rapidly enough to employ all of them.

The Possibility of Unemployment in a Market System. Is a market system likely to feature unemployment? The answer appears to be yes, at least sometimes. There appears to be no automatic mechanism to assure that total spending will always be sufficient to avoid unemployment caused by too little total spending. Suppose that consumers wish to save more and spend less. Apparently there is no market force which will assure that business investment spending will increase enough to offset the decreased consumer spending and thereby avoid unemployment.

It was once thought that decreases in the interest rate and in the general level of money wages would, in such a case, keep total spending adequate to avoid unemployment. However, now most economists agree that changes in interest rates have rather little influence on the volume of investment spending. Changes in interest rates are too weak to increase investment spending sufficiently to offset decreases in consumer spending. Furthermore, it is now recognized that decreases in wage rates are likely to have as many effects which reduce employment as they have which increase it. Finally, there is a strong resistance to decreases in money wages, in any case.

History also suggests that structural unemployment may be rather common in a market system. Ignorance of employment opportunities, unwillingness to make adjustments in occupations or location, and failure to realize or admit that any alternatives to previous jobs exist seem sometimes to characterize workers thrown out of work by change. Sometimes, too, employers appear to be unable to discover ways of attracting, retraining, and utilizing unemployed workers.

Inflation and Deflation

Inflation is an increase in the average prices of goods and services, a rise in the general level of prices.[6] *Deflation* is a fall in the general level of prices. Both are regarded as serious socioeconomic problems because both have undesirable consequences.

Redistribution of Income and Wealth through Inflation. Inflation tends to hurt those people who receive fixed money incomes. Examples are pensioners, earners of interest income, and civil servants. These people are hurt because during inflation the prices of the goods and services they buy tend to rise faster than their money incomes. Thus the real purchasing power of their incomes decreases; i.e., their real incomes decline.

Inflation also tends to hurt those who are owners of fixed price assets, such as bonds, savings accounts, and demand deposits at banks. The prices of these assets remain the same while the prices of other goods and services rise. In this way the real purchasing power and the real wealth of the owners of these assets decline.

Inflation is, of course, advantageous to some groups of people. During inflation the real burden of debt declines so that debtors have an easier task of repaying their debts. Owners of some businesses may find the prices of their products rising faster than their costs of doing business so that their profits grow.

Since inflation harms some people and helps others, one might assert that the net effect is not undesirable because the harm is offset by the help. However, this is probably an unwarranted conclusion for two reasons. First, the redistribution of income, wealth, and advantage from those who are hurt to those who are helped is not judged as just by many. Those who are hurt do not particularly deserve to be hurt nor do those who are helped deserve the help. Second, inflation may have other effects which are harmful to all of society.

Other Disadvantages of Inflation. What are these other harmful effects of inflation? First, inflation diverts the attention of entrepreneurs from the attainment of efficiency in production to the attainment of specula-

---

[6]Two useful volumes on inflation are George Leland Bach, *The New Inflation: Causes, Effects, Cures* (Hanover, N.H.: University Press of New England, 1974); and Robert Lekachman, *Inflation: The Permanent Problem of Boom and Bust* (New York: Random House, 1973).

tive gains from price increases. Society depends upon productive efficiency for a high level of living. Society therefore suffers as business managers and others become absorbed in the speculative purchase and sale of real estate, shares of corporate stock, and inventories of goods from which extraordinary gains can be made in a time of inflation.

Second, prices of various goods and services rise at different rates during inflation, and prices cease to be as good guides to production and consumption decisions as they should be. Consumers make fewer wise decisions for themselves when confronted by a crazy quilt of rising prices. Business people become confused as to what the truly lowest-cost production choices are.

Third, inflation may cause social unrest. People look upon their wage and salary increases as long-delayed, highly justified, richly deserved, and finally received recognition of their true merit. At the same time, they resent increases in the prices of things they must buy as unjustified exploitation. Of course, both the wage and salary increases and the price increases are really parts of a single inflationary process, but people do not realize this. Consequently, they become dissatisfied.

Finally, inflation of moderate amounts might be acceptable because it involves only moderate disadvantages. However, it can be argued that moderate inflation tends to give way to inflation of quite immoderate intensity with great disadvantages. If prices rise slowly for a time, people may begin to expect them to continue to rise. These people will then accelerate their purchases before prices rise further. This very acceleration will constitute increased demand, which will drive prices up further and faster.

Deflation. Deflation has analogous disadvantages. An unjustified redistribution of income, wealth, and advantage may occur with deflation. Consumption and production decisions are likely to be disturbed in the confusion of differentially falling sets of prices. Social unrest is likely. Particularly, deflation is likely to be accompanied by unemployment since purchases of products are likely to be delayed in anticipation of lower prices to come, and lowered purchases and sales induce lower employment.

Market and Nonmarket Causes of Inflation. Inflation and deflation, particularly inflation, have occurred frequently in societies which have relied heavily on a market system. There is, however, substantial evidence that much of these changes in the general price levels have been the result, not of the market system, but of governmental activities of a nonmarket sort. This is so since the size of the money supply, which is the most important determinant of the general level of prices, has usually been under the control of the government rather than having been left to market forces. This governmental control of the money supply has existed even in those societies otherwise heavily reliant upon markets.

There are, nevertheless, strong logical reasons and some historical evidence that a market system without government control of the money supply would produce undesirable results including inflation and deflation. In a system where any enterprising private person can print up currency, mint coins, or create money in the highly abstract form of book credits, there is strong inducement to do so almost without limit. Such money creation is a very profitable method for paying for real goods purchased by the money creator or for earning interest on loans made with created money.

Money creation may be limited by several circumstances. Tradition and the attitude of the populace may require that money be based on some real commodity such as gold. If the real commodity is itself limited in amount, so also will be the money. If a political authority decrees a legal limit, then the money will be limited. Fear that the money will decline in purchasing power may limit acceptance of the money. Then its creation may be limited as a result. If none of these conditions is present in sufficient degree, excessive quantities of money are likely to be created. Inflation will be the consequence.

Indeed, it seems likely that several issuers of money would exist in a market system. Each is likely to issue a different kind of money, and the price of each kind is likely to fluctuate in terms of each of the others. A probable consequence is a chaos of prices and price changes. There will be a price of each money in terms of every other, and a price of each good and service in terms of each money. In such circumstances a revulsion against money may occur, and there will be a resort to barter with all its economic disadvantages.

Changes in the Velocity of Money. Even if the quantity of money is fixed in some way, market forces may cause inflation and deflation through changes in the velocity with which money is spent. Suppose that, for some reason, people's expectations change in the direction of higher prices or greater shortages of goods in the future. Then people will begin to spend money faster, and inflation probably will occur. If lower prices or increased supplies of goods are expected, people will spend the existing money more slowly, prices will fall, and deflation will occur.

Recurrent Instability: Business Fluctuations

Experience with market systems suggests that, without nonmarket controls, these systems tend to produce recurrent periods of prosperity alternating with periods of depression. A period of prosperity and the period of depression following it are together called a *business fluctuation*. Each fluctuation has been unique in terms of the actual historical sequence of prosperity and depression. The duration, intensity, amplitude, and other characteristics of each fluctuation are peculiar to it.

There are several phases to a typical fluctuation. First there is a period of prosperity or *expansion*, which may last from a few months to several years and which is characterized by increasing employment, incomes, prices, and gross national product. The expansion inevitably ends at a point of time called a *peak* or *upper turning point*. There follows a period of depression, recession, or *contraction*, which may last from a few months to several years and which is characterized by declining employment, incomes, prices, and GNP. There is something about a contraction which causes it, at a point of time called a *trough* or *lower turning point*, to end and to become reversed, initiating the next expansion phase.

Causes of Business Fluctuations. Business fluctuations are supposed to be self-generating in a market system. One of the most intriguing problems of economics is to explain why this should be so. Why does an expansion continue and intensify for a time? Why must it end? Why should it not continue indefinitely? Why, if it does end, must a contraction, rather than a plateau, follow? What is it about the expansion which necessitates an ensuing contraction?[7]

The modern, generally accepted explanation for business fluctuations in a market system is an eclectic one. It draws upon and weaves together older, monocausal theories into a rather untidy and still incompletely resolved synthesis. It is admitted that forces quite outside the economic system may initiate or end a contraction or an expansion or may modify one already underway. Such forces include a reason of good or bad weather and good or bad harvests, a war or war's end, an international diplomatic crisis, a revolution, an election outcome, and an invention or discovery.

Psychological Factors. Psychological factors may play an important and real role in business fluctuations. For example, once an expansion has begun, the higher incomes, employment, profits, and sales may cause both consumers and business people to become optimistic about the economic future. Their optimism causes them to increase both consumer spending and business investment spending. The increased spending stimulates the expansion, causing further optimism, and so on, with behavior and outlook interacting in a mutually reenforcing manner. Sim-

---

[7]If one wishes to pursue the subject of business fluctuations in a market economy, one might look at some of the standard texts in that field: Carl A. Dauten and Lloyd M. Valentine, *Business Cycles and Forecasting*, 6th ed. (Cincinnati: South-Western Publishing Co., 1982), especially Chapters 2–7 and 12–13; and Maurice M. Lee, *Macroeconomics: Fluctuations, Growth, and Stability*, 5th ed. (Homewood, Ill.: Irwin, 1971). A readable survey of business cycle theory appears in Gottfried Haberler, *Prosperity and Depression: A Theoretical Analysis of Cyclical Movements*, 4th ed. (Cambridge: Harvard University Press, 1964).

ilarly, waves of decreased spending and pessimism may cause a contraction to become cumulatively more severe.

Differential Rates of Reaction. Differential rates of adjustment to change among various economic magnitudes in a market system may be partially responsible for business fluctuations. For example, suppose that an expansion is just underway. An increased demand for products occurs as a part of the expansion. In combination with market conditions such as flexible prices, the increased demand causes a rise in the prices of products. There is also at the same time likely to be an increase in the demand for labor and other resources, but the prices of these may be prevented from rising for a time by contractual arrangements. Therefore, salary increases must await the expiration of employment contracts. Rental increases must await the expiration of leases. Interest rate increases must await the expiration of loans. In the meantime, the prices of the products businesses sell increase, and the prices of the inputs businesses buy remain the same. Profits, which are the difference between businesses' gross incomes and total costs, increase. The increased profits provide both the inducement and the means for businesses to increase real investment spending. The result is that the expansion is further stimulated.

As the expansion reaches its later stages, however, the prices of labor and other resources do at last begin to rise because the contractual arrangements expire and are renewed on new terms. Business costs rise, and profits are squeezed. The decrease in profits prompts businesses to decrease their investment spending, and this causes total spending to decrease. The decline in total spending constitutes the upper turning point and the beginning of the contraction. During the early stages of the contraction, product prices fall rapidly, but resource prices remain high. Profits decline further or give way to losses. Investment spending is depressed further, and the contraction becomes more severe. Later, however, resource prices fall, allowing an end to the contraction.

General Appraisal. There is worthy of note one aspect which is present in most of the various explanations of business fluctuations in a market economy. The fluctuations occur because the power to make economic decisions is diffused among many independent businesses which are imperfectly informed and coordinated by the market mechanism. The individual businesses have inadequate understanding of what their competitors are doing. They do not fully understand what the aggregate effect of their own decisions, together with those of their competitors, will be. Furthermore, there is no means by which an individual business can commit itself to certain courses of future action on condition that many other firms simultaneously commit themselves. The consequence is that heavy reliance upon a market system is likely to result in fluctuations which are troublesome to virtually all of the market participants.

Economic Insecurity

A market system features instability in the aggregate levels of employment and prices. There are also constant changes in prices, quantities produced and sold, techniques of production, and particular resources used in the production of specific goods and services. These changes produce a feeling of insecurity for the people of the society using the system. *Economic insecurity* is the fear that there will occur in the future changes which are not entirely foreseeable and which will require painful and undesired adjustments.

Causes of Insecurity. These adjustments may be made necessary by a wide variety of events. Most business cycle contractions occur rather unexpectedly. Workers never know when they may suddenly be without work. Similarly, owners never know when their income from profits may suddenly shrink. The timing, duration, and intensity of the expansions of business fluctuations with their accompanying inflation cannot be accurately forecast. Consequently, owners of fixed-price assets and recipients of fixed money incomes stand in almost perpetual fear that the real value of their income and wealth may be greatly reduced.

There is always a possibility of the introduction of new technology. A constant threat is thus posed that workers may lose their old jobs, may have to undergo expensive and psychologically distressing retraining and relocation, and then may find that their new jobs and locations are less rewarding both monetarily and psychically than their old ones. Consumer preferences may erratically shift away from some product, whose producers then experience a drastic reduction in the value of machinery which produces the product and into which they as owners have already invested their wealth.

Market Mitigation of Insecurity. It should be pointed out that not all changes create pain and disadvantages. Furthermore, not everyone is troubled by insecurity. There are those venturesome individuals who enjoy the excitement of not knowing what the future has in store for them and who welcome the challenge of adjustment.

It should also be noted that a market system provides some opportunities of self-protection for individuals who dislike having to make unexpected adjustments and who tend to suffer from insecurity. An individual who fears unemployment can, when selecting a job or an occupation, choose those which experience shows are the steadiest and most likely to endure. Someone who is afraid of the loss of income which occurs when unemployment comes can build up savings while employed. A person who fears the possibility that residential property may fall in value may rent a house rather than buy one. One who fears that inflation may wipe out the value of fixed price assets may place personal wealth instead in real estate or common stocks. Someone who is afraid that the ability to earn income may be unexpectedly eliminated through death or illness may buy insurance. A person who dreads a pauperous old age can buy an annuity or take a job with a company which has a program of large pensions. One who fears that all personal wealth will be destroyed in some single catastrophe can make diversified investments. That person can have some real property and some financial, some fixed-price assets and some variable, and some in one industry and some in another.

Nevertheless, it must be admitted that some insecurity will remain in a market system. There are some risks that remain uninsurable, and the elimination of one kind of risk often means the introduction of another.

Inadequate Economic Growth

Economic growth refers to increases through time in either the per capita or the total GNP. Among the chief immediate causes of growth are enlargement of the stock of real capital through the processes of saving and investment, improvement in the quality of the people as workers and entrepreneurs through education and training, and advances in technology. There may be a tendency for a market system to produce a growth rate which is too low.

It is useful to recall the process by which growth is brought about in a market economy. The basic decisions regarding growth are made by individual households and firms. Each of these separate units decides such things as how much to save, how much to invest, how much education to purchase, and how much research and exploration to undertake on the basis of a comparison of the benefits and costs to itself of the activities. If the benefits to itself exceed the costs to itself, the activity is undertaken. If the benefits to itself are less than the costs, the activity is not undertaken.

Saving. For example, consider a family trying to decide whether to save some of its income. What is the principal cost of this saving to the family? It is the sacrifice now of the goods and services which the family could buy and enjoy if it did not save. The principal benefit to the family from saving is the goods and services which the family will be able to buy and enjoy some time in the future, when the savings are finally spent. If the family decides that goods in the present are less satisfying than goods in the future, combined with interest income earned in the meantime, it will save.

In an *ideal* market economy this decision to save should lead to increased economic growth. The money savings are transmitted through financial institutions and loaned to businesses. The businesses use the borrowed funds to purchase the use of resources which have been released by the saving from the production of consumer goods. The businesses now use these resources to create capital goods. The capital goods so created make possible thereafter a larger real GNP.

However, in a *real* market economy the process might work differently. The attempt to save, which constitutes a decrease in spending for consumer goods, may discourage businesses. There may be no increase or perhaps even a decrease in borrowing and the creation of capital goods by businesses. With decreased consumer spending and no increase in business investment spending to create capital goods, unemployment is likely to result.

The unemployment can be a cost of the attempted saving. It is a cost, not to the family making the decision to save, but to society. The family does not take this cost into account in making its decision. There is no reason for it to do so since the unemployment resulting from its own decision is extremely unlikely to affect its own members. However, if many families, acting in this way, decide to save, the consequent unemployment is likely to be quite large. Furthermore, the unemployment and the failure of the capital formation will probably result in a rate of growth lower than appropriate.

Education. Something similar happens when a family determines whether to buy education for its members. In a market economy a family buys the education if the education's cost to the family is less than the education's benefits to the family. The main real cost to the family is the other goods and services whose purchase and use is foregone by the family because it buys the education. The main benefits to the family are the increased income which the education, once received, enables the family to earn and the increased enjoyment of life which the education makes possible for the family. Comparing the costs and benefits, the family makes a decision. In many cases, a family will decide not to buy the education because the cost to it exceeds the benefits to it.

However, in many of these cases, the education should have occurred. There are additional benefits to people other than the family itself when the family is educated. These additional benefits cause the total benefits to exceed the cost of the education. What are these additional benefits which accrue to people other than the family? An educated person is more likely to respect the property of others than an uneducated one. All property owners are benefited when education occurs. An educated person is more likely to make a technological discovery, which increases the real GNP and causes economic growth. An educated person is more likely to vote intelligently and adopt wise views on political issues, all to the benefit of other people.

Education is a major source of economic growth. Inadequate amounts of education could be chosen by people acting in a strictly market framework. Hence, a market system may produce a rate of economic growth which is too small.

Research and Development. A major means of achieving technological progress is research. In a market system each business firm decides for itself the amount of research it will undertake. It does so on the basis of the cost and benefits of itself of the research. The main cost is the expense of undertaking the research. The main benefit is the greater profit from reduced costs, which, through an advantage over competitors, enable the firm's profits to be larger.

However, often when an individual firm's research is successful, it is difficult or impossible to prevent the resulting knowledge from being diffused among rival firms. These rival firms benefit from the expensive research undertaken by the researching firm, whose competitive advantage is then lost. Because of this prospective loss of advantage, many firms do not undertake the research in the first place. The private profits to one firm do not justify the research, even though the benefits to society in the form of economic growth and a higher level of living clearly do justify the research.

A Nonoptimal Commodity Composition of Gross National Product

A market economy, unless modified by at least a little government intervention, may produce relatively too few of some goods and services and relatively too many of others.

External Benefits. The preceding section on economic growth indicated that a market system may produce too few capital goods, too little educational services, and too little research. It may do so because the individual decision makers take into account only the benefits to themselves and ignore benefits to others. When there are *external benefits*, too little of some goods and services may be produced and used.[8]

External Costs in Production. When there are *external costs*, too much of some goods and services may be produced and used. An example is steel. One of the costs external to the steel firms but quite real to society is the pollution of the air and water. This pollution is inherent in the production of steel in a market society with the techniques known in the 20th century.

---

[8]One of the classics on the effect which the existence of external costs and benefits has in creating imperfections in the results of a market system is William J. Baumol, *Welfare Economics and the Theory of the State*, 2d ed. (Cambridge: Harvard University Press, 1965). See also Richard L. Carson, *Comparative Economic Systems* (New York: Macmillan, 1973), Chapter 15.

Suppose a steel firm is declining whether to establish and operate a steel mill. The firm adds up the expected revenues from selling the product and subtracts therefrom the costs of production, including the cost of labor, raw materials, and machinery and buildings. To the steel producer there is no cost in sending smoke into the air to blacken the drying clothes in neighborhood yards. To it there is no cost in raising the temperature and the noxious chemical content of the local river, even though fish are killed and the potability of water downstream is decreased. These are costs to society, but they are costs which are external to the steel producer. In a market economy without enforceable and established property rights in the air and water, these costs are not taken into account.

If these external costs were taken into account, there would be at least some instances in which the total costs, internal and external, would exceed the benefits. As a result, some of the steel mills would not be established and less steel would be produced. The GNP would then consist of less steel and more of other things. In that sense, a market system may produce relatively too much of some goods, such as steel. The commodity composition of the GNP may then be other than optimal.

External Costs in Consumption. For some products the external cost exists in connection with their consumption rather than their production. Liquor is an example. A purchaser and consumer of bourbon decides how much of it to buy and thus helps to determine how much of it will be produced. This consumer makes a decision on the basis of the costs and benefits of the liquor. The costs which are external to the consumer, but very real to others, are ignored. These external costs occur when the consumer shouts loudly at a party so that neighbors cannot sleep or drives drunkenly into a pedestrian. Consequently, more bourbon, relative to some other product, may be produced in a market system than is best.

The case of bourbon is but one example. The reader is invited to consider in this connection the cases of such other products or activities as pornographic literature, violence on television, opium, billboards, redwood lumbering, prostitution, strip mining, and gambling.

Other Causes. There are several reasons other than the existence of external costs and benefits for believing that a strictly market system produces a nonoptimal GNP. Some goods and services seem to be incapable of division so as to be sold to individual buyers on the market. National defense is usually cited as the prime example of such an indivisible good, much needed but not supplied by a market system. Other goods and services require excessively costly arrangements for the market collection of the fees for their use. Even though their benefits are large relative to their costs exclusive of collection fees, little of them would be produced in a market economy. Examples of these goods are highways, sidewalks, and parks.

Unattractive Personal Qualities

Some critics of market systems argue that such systems tend to encourage the development of unattractive personalities and characters for those people who participate in the markets. Their argument, shorn of modifications and expressed in vivid terms, could be stated that to work well, a market system requires people to be adaptable, competitive, and enterprising. It accords wealth and power to those who are most so. However, people who are adaptable can also be said to be rootless, unprincipled, and unsteady. Those who are competitive may be aggressive, hostile, and unscrupulous. Those who are enterprising may be domineering, materialistic, and callous. In a market system it may be, indeed, that the race is to the swiftest and good guys finish last. In a market system, children may arrive at adolescence with certain impressions, never to be altered. They may believe that a person's worth is to be measured by the number of subordinates commanded on the job, the number of bathrooms in a house, or the number and intensity of a person's ulcers. They may believe that if anything is worth striving for, it is money, because almost all else worthwhile and subject to one's control follows from it.

There is no way of proving that a market system produces these qualities among its people to a greater degree than does any feasible alternative system. Furthermore, there is no scientific way of demonstrating that these qualities are really bad ones. However, the suspicion remains among critics of the market system that both may be the case.[9]

SUMMARY

When the appropriate prerequisites are present, a market system functions at its best. Even then, however, some of the results may be imperfect and necessitate governmental actions as correctives.

In a market system the distribution of income and wealth can become quite unequal and, in the judgment of some persons, inequitable. Unemployment may persist or recur. The general level of prices may rise or fall with harmful results to groups in society and to society as a whole. Business fluctuations may take place. In consequence of this instability and for other reasons, the people may feel economically insecure. Economic growth may be lower than the people really desire. The commodity composition of GNP may be other than optimal. A market system may cause people to acquire unattractive characteristics.

The above description should not be allowed to suggest that a market system produces nothing but undesirable results. Market mechanisms can be extremely effective means for achieving economic coordination and for producing good results. In addition, it would be incorrect to infer from the contents of this chapter that

---

[9]For an attack on the personal qualities that a market system seems to encourage, see R. H. Tawney, *The Acquisitive Society* (New York: Harcourt, Brace & World, 1955).

nonmarket arrangements do not also produce many defective results. The inference would be incorrect whether the arrangements took the form of governmental intervention in an otherwise predominantly market economy like that of the United States or the form of a governmentally directed, centrally commanded economy like that of the Soviet Union.

All in all, however, there is ample cause for a people of a society not to seek to retain an economic system based strictly and exclusively on markets. There is sufficient reason for them to modify their economy in one way or another, so as to try to alter at least some of the results of market mechanisms. The American experiment in modification, primarily through governmental action, is the subject of the next chapter.

REVIEW QUESTIONS

1. Have you yourself, living within a predominantly market economy, ever made poor decisions for yourself as to what consumption goods you should buy, what job you should take, or what investment you should make? Why did you make them? It could be argued that such poorly made decisions have adverse effects, not only on the person making them and upon that person's family, but on others as well. How is this so?

2. Suppose that everyone in the United States suddenly began to behave dishonestly in their buying and selling relations with others. What might happen as a result to the average degree of economic well-being in the United States? Why?

3. Imagine two countries, both with predominantly market-oriented economic systems. In country A the level of entrepreneurship is high, in B, low. In which country would the average level of living be likely to be the higher? Why? In which would the economic growth rate be higher? Why? Now consider carefully the following question: In which country would the people be likely to be happier?

4. "A truly market economy implies little government intervention in the economy, that is, a weak government." Comment on the validity of this statement.

5. Can you think of some realistic examples in the United States—other than those described in the text of this chapter—in which price rigidity has prevented the market from working well? Carefully describe the causal relationship between the price rigidity and the poor results in your examples.

6. The cultural heritage of a nation is supposed to have something to do with how well a system of markets might work in a nation. Consider a foreign nation whose cultural heritage you know differs from that of the United States. In the light of the differences in the cultural heritages of the two nations, would markets be expected to work better in the United States or in the other nation?

7. Suppose a market economy was in operation without taxation or spending by government. Why would you expect inequality in the distribution of income? Now suppose someone proposed to impose taxes upon the people with high incomes and to give the tax proceeds to those with low incomes? Would you agree or disagree with the proposal? Why? What do you suppose would be the most convincing arguments of those who took the side opposite your own?

8. What is the difference between unemployment caused by too little total spending

in the economy and structural unemployment? Are both likely to occur in a market economy? Why? What use do you think there is in distinguishing between the two kinds of unemployment?

9. "Market forces, not governmental actions, are primarily responsible for most of the inflation that has occurred in nations with market systems." Comment.

10. What is meant by economic insecurity? Do you personally welcome uncertainty about your economic future or do you find it worrisome? Do you think most people share your view? Try to suggest some of the things which government intervention in the economy can do to reduce the economic insecurity.

11. What does it mean to say that "external" benefits unrecognized in a market economy may cause inadequate economic growth?

RECOMMENDED READINGS

Bach, George Leland. *The New Inflation: Causes, Effects, Cures*. Hanover, N.H.: University Press of New England, 1974.

Dauten, Carl A., and Lloyd M. Valentine. *Business Cycles and Forecasting*. 6th ed. Cincinnati: South-Western Publishing Co., 1982.

Dillard, Dudley. *The Economics of John Maynard Keynes: The Theory of a Monetary Economy*. Englewood Cliffs, N.J.: Prentice-Hall, 1948.

Grossman, Gregory. *Economic Systems*. 2d ed. Englewood Cliffs, N.J.: Prentice-Hall, 1974.

Heilbroner, Robert L. *The Worldly Philosopher: The Lives, Times and Ideas of the Great Economic Thinkers*. 5th ed. New York: Simon and Schuster, 1980.

Keynes, John Maynard. *The General Theory of Employment, Interest, and Money*. New York: Harcourt, Brace & World, 1936.

Köhler, Heinz. *Welfare and Planning: An Analysis of Capitalism versus Socialism*. 2d ed. Melborne, Fla.: Krieger, 1979.

Lee, Maurice W. *Macroeconomics: Fluctuations, Growth, and Stability*. 5th ed. Homewood, Ill.: Irwin, 1971.

Lekachman, Robert. *Inflation: The Permanent Problem of Boom and Bust*. New York: Random House, 1973.

_____. *The Age of Keynes*. New York: McGraw-Hill, 1975.

McClelland, David C. *The Achieving Society*. New York: Free Press, 1967.

_____, and David G. Winter. *Motivating Economic Achievement*. New York: Free Press, 1971.

Mermelstein, David, ed. *Economics: Mainstream Readings and Radical Critiques*. 2d ed. New York: Random House, 1973.

Tawney, R. H. *The Acquisitive Society*. New York: Harcourt, Brace & World, 1955.

PART 2
THE MODIFIED MARKET ECONOMY
OF THE UNITED STATES

5

The Economic System of the United States

INTRODUCTION

The American economic system is dominated by three major institutions—business, labor, and government. Although there is reliance upon the market mechanism to allocate resources, it cannot be said that the United States conforms to the model of a pure free enterprise market economy. Instead, the "rules of the game" have been modified over time as various groups or individuals have sought protection against the results that a free market economy implies. Farmers seek protection against the vagaries of supply and demand by demanding subsidies. In a free market economy, there are winners and losers, and losers are supposed to lose and not call on government to help as have Chrysler and others. Many changes have occurred over time to supplement and modify the effects of the market mechanism so that the consequences are other than they would be with a market system. Thus, it is more appropriate to call the United States a modified market economy in which the role of government is of considerable importance.

One institutional arrangement is the large corporation. The original impetus for the emergence of the large corporation was partly technologi-

cal—economies of scale become available with bigness—and partly monopolistic—bigness provides control over markets and over rivals. These
large corporations helped to modify the market system. Moreover, large
corporations have also been in part responsible for the development of
two other institutions that have also served to modify the market mechanism—labor unions and big government. Both of these have become major features of the economic system in the United States and in other
countries still relying heavily on the market system. Both have become
major means for counteracting some of the undesirable results of large
business firms and for mitigating some of the undesirable effects of a pure
market system.

Of the two, government is by far the most important institution. It
has intervened in the U.S. economy in several ways: to redistribute income between groups through taxes and transfer payments; to manage
the economy through fiscal and monetary policy; and to protect various
special interest groups against such things as discrimination and foreign
competition.

LARGE CORPORATIONS

The concentration of industry in the hands of a few firms is a fact of
life in the United States and other major industrial countries, regardless
of their political ideology. The trend toward industrial concentration in
the United States began in the last century, when many industries came
to be dominated by a few relatively large firms or even by only one firm.
In the 1920s largeness was stimulated by changes that were occurring in
the economy as a whole, in particular the mass production of the automobile and the development of the electrical appliance and broadcasting
industries. General Motors became the leader in the automobile industry
through a series of mergers with other auto firms. Size came to have an
advantage from the standpoint of using modern marketing and production methods.

World War II contributed to the trend toward largeness. The industrial might of the United States was probably the decisive factor in contributing to the Allied victory over the Axis powers. Large corporations
produced the airplanes and tanks used by the United States and its allies
in the war.[1] During the 1960s and 1970s the trend toward largeness was
facilitated by the development of a new type of merger called the conglomerate merger, which represents a union of disparate companies.

---

[1]The author saw some old destroyed Sherman tanks rusting on a farm in Poland. They
represented part of the thousands of tanks sent by the United States to the Soviet Union in
World War II.

Concentration by Firm Size

Table 5-1 presents a division of firms based on number of employees, payrolls, value added by manufacturing, and capital expenditures. The data are for 1976. Firms employing 1,000 workers or more accounted for 1.5 percent of all manufacturing firms, but accounted for 27.8 percent of total employment in manufacturing, 35.5 percent of total value of payrolls, 34.8 percent of value added by manufacturing, and 36.0 percent of new capital expenditures. However, these percentages show a decline when compared to earlier statistics for 1967. The respective percentages for 1967 were as follows: employment in manufacturing, 32.8 percent; total value of payrolls, 39.1 percent; value added by manufacturing, 38.0 percent; and new capital expenditures, 38.3 percent. However, it can be said that approximately 4 percent of all industrial firms in the United States produced about half of the value added by manufacturing and of all new capital expenditures for 1977. These figures appear to hold for at least up to 1980.

TABLE 5-1
DISTRIBUTION OF INDUSTRY IN THE UNITED STATES
BY CLASS SIZE FOR 1977
(establishments and employees in thousands;
money figures in millions of dollars)

Item	Total	Class of Establishment in Employee Size				
		Under 20	20–99	100–249	250–999	1,000 and over
Establishments	351	237	78	22	12	2
Employees	18,515	1,206	3,489	3,336	5,393	5,191
Payroll	242,032	13,713	38,693	37,772	66,248	85,609
Value added by manufacturing	585,166	30,081	89,829	92,232	172,607	200,417
Capital expenditures	47,459	1,377	4,280	7,812	13,337	17,001

Source: U.S. Bureau of the Census, *1977 Census of Manufacture,* General Summary Report (Washington: U.S. Government Printing Office, 1981).

The Extent of Concentration by Industry

The extent of concentration in the United States varies considerably by industry. In some industries, one large firm is clearly dominant, in that it contributes 50 percent or more of total output. General Motors, with over 60 percent of U.S. domestic output of automobiles, is an example. In other industries, a few firms may account for the bulk of sales, with no one firm clearly dominant over the others. The tobacco industry, with Reynolds Industries, Philip Morris, and American Brands, is a case in point. There are some industries that have little or no concentration, and thus approximate the market situation called pure competition in which no seller produces more than a negligible share of market supply. The shoe and clothing industries afford examples. The degree of concentration by industry is shown in Table 5-2, which compares the output of the four largest firms in a number of high- and low-concentration industries. However, a high degree of concentration alone does not necessarily mean there is a monopoly or a general lack of competition.

TABLE 5-2
THE EXTENT OF CONCENTRATION BY INDUSTRY
IN THE UNITED STATES
(output measured by value of shipment)

High Concentration	Shipment Percentage of Four Largest Firms
Motor vehicles	93
Cereal breakfast foods	87
Cigarettes	82
Sewing machines	80
Metal cans	79
Tires	72
Soap	70
Aircraft	65
Low Concentration	
Oil refining	30
Meat packing	24
Machine tools	21
Book publishers	18
Concrete products	10
Women's dresses	9
Fur goods	8

Source: U.S. Department of Commerce, Bureau of the Census, *Concentration Ratios in Manufacturing: 1977 Census of Manufactures* (Washington: U.S. Government Printing Office, 1981), Table 7, pp. 12–65.

The Issues Involving Industrial Concentration

In a number of industries, a certain amount of industrial concentration is apparently inevitable. Some types of business organizations lend themselves to large-scale production. For example, there are industries in which the product itself is highly complex and can be constructed only by a large and diversified organization. Automobiles and computers are a case in point. There are industries in which the product is large in size, requiring complex equipment for construction and large capital investments—for example, shipbuilding and locomotives. Then there are industries that require a large capital investment, particularly in plant and equipment. For example, there are many good reasons for conducting the manufacture of iron and steel on a large scale. One of the most important is the tremendous outlay necessary to secure blast furnaces, steel furnaces, and other equipment. Finally, there are industries in which a natural resource is required and in which the natural resource is available only in limited amounts and in specific geographic locations. Examples of this are the lead and petroleum industries.

Moreover, industrial concentration may well be an inevitable result of advancing technology in all major industrial countries, regardless of their ideologies. Data show that for the same industries, concentration ratios are generally higher in other Western countries than in the United States; foreign industries in which concentration is high are generally the same as those in which concentration is high in the United States; and industries that are not highly concentrated in foreign countries are generally unconcentrated industries in the United States also. In West Germany, three chemical companies produce 87 percent of all chemical products, and each company is larger than DuPont, the leading American chemical company.[2] The West German electrical equipment company Siemens produces 58 percent of all West German electrical equipment. The French aluminum firm Pechiney Ugine Kuhlmann produces 90 percent of French aluminum products, specialty steels, and nonferrous metals such as titanium and zirconium.[3] In Japan two automobile companies account for 85 percent of all Japanese automobile production.[4] These data strongly suggest that fundamental technological and economic factors determine to some extent the degree of concentration of industries in all market economies.

The extent of industrial concentration is even higher in the advanced Communist countries than in the United States.[5] To some extent the

---

[2]Statistisches Bundesant, *Statistisches Jahrbuch für die Bundesrepublik Deutschland, 1980* (Wiesbaden: Kohlhammer, 1980), p. 315.

[3]Ministerie de l'Economie et des Finances, *Statistiques Français 1979* (Paris, 1979). The greatest degree of industrial concentration in all capitalist countries may exist in France. This also holds true in banking.

[4]Bureau of Statistics, *Japan Statistical Yearbook, 1979* (Tokyo: Office of the Prime Minister, 1979), p. 47.

[5]Frederick L. Pryor, "An International Comparison of Concentration Ratios," *Review of Economics and Statistics*, Vol. 54 (May 1972), pp. 130–140.

centralized planning characteristic of Communist states necessitates the concentration of output into large production units. The organization of industry has to be considered a basic part of the economic and political organization of the state. There is a constant effort to combine industrial and agricultural enterprises into larger units to increase output to supply the population and to export to world markets. In the German Democratic Republic (East Germany), one of the Communist superpowers, the largest 100 industrial enterprises, or about 1 percent of all enterprises, produced 45 percent of total industrial output in 1979.[6] In Poland the tractor combine URSUS produced 100 percent of all tractors made in the country, and in Hungary the combine RABA produces all the heavy-duty trucks, tractors, and railroad equipment made in Hungary.[7] The high degree of concentration in centrally planned economies may be used as evidence that large-scale operations and the concentration that accompany them do yield economies of scale.

Industrial concentration also can transcend national boundaries. Large American firms acquire foreign firms and large foreign firms acquire American firms. As competition becomes global, additional economies of scale may be effected. A *Business Week* article suggests that it is conceivable that by the end of the 1980s, only five automobile companies will be left in the world—two American, one Japanese, one French, and one German. Perhaps this is the final extension of an evolutionary process that began with the creation of the automobile industry when there were literally hundreds of firms turning out autos for the populace who could afford them. This world trend may be irreversible, regardless of the product; and laws, antitrust and otherwise, will have to be restructured within a global frame of reference.

Advantages of Concentration. There are certain advantages to large-scale production. An expansion in the production units of a firm often permits greater specialization in the use of both labor and capital equipment. Overhead costs can be spread over a larger output, which results in a lower unit cost. Economies can result from new combinations of the factors of production (land, labor, and capital) which result in lower minimum costs. Economies of scale result when more of all factors are used, and the total output increases at a rate greater than the increase in the production factors. Specialized labor and capital equipment frequently can be added to a production unit only in large, indivisible amounts and therefore cannot be used profitably in small-scale operations. In fact, smaller business units may well result in higher unit costs in many

---

[6]Staatliche Zentralverwaltung für Statistik, *Statistisches Jahrbuch der Deutschen Demokratischen Republik, 1979* (East Berlin: Staatsverlag der DDR, 1979), pp. 125–135.

[7]Martin Schnitzer, *U.S. Business Involvement in Eastern Europe* (New York: Praeger, 1980), pp. 81, p. 103.

industries, and therefore the best answer to the problems of concentration may not necessarily be found by breaking up large firms. Market power can be based on underlying economies of scale and technological or managerial leadership. In some cases large firms are the price of efficiency and innovation.[8]

Problems of Concentration. However, industrial concentration also carries with it certain problems. In a competitive market economy, the interest of producers and consumers coincide because the way to larger profits for the producers is through greater efficiency, price reductions, and increased volume of sales, all of which naturally benefit the consumers, too. In a monopolistic market, or one approaching this state, profits may be maximized at the expense of the consumer by selling a smaller quantity of goods at a higher price than under competitive conditions. The existence of monopoly power also means that the spur to efficiency and technical progress that competition provides is often lacking.

There is evidence to indicate that small or medium-sized firms are often more innovative than large firms. For example, in the steel industry, the oxygen converter was introduced in this country by McLough Steel, one of the smallest steel producers. Many of the innovative developments in the automobile industry were made by small companies who were eventually absorbed by other companies. Packard developed the automobile air conditioner; Pierce-Arrow, power brakes; Studebaker, the power-operated windshield wiper; Hudson, the sedan-type body; Reo, the gear shift on the dash; Nash, a pressured fresh-air heating system; and Duesenberg, four-wheel brakes, both mechanical and hydraulic.

Small firms are often put in the position of having to innovate in order to survive. From this comes a willingness to take risks. Big firms, like big government, can be so encrusted with bureaucracy that there is more of a desire to maintain the status quo than to be experimental. Besides, experimentation usually requires approval from someone in the hierarchy of the organization. This can be disturbing, for often no one in the hierarchy wants to be held responsible in the event of failure. Often it is much easier to go out and absorb a smaller company that has already made the innovation and has survived the risk of failure.

Top management of a large firm cannot know all the details of the business and must rely upon the reports of subordinates. Finally, large firms in certain situations can exercise discretionary power over prices and entry into markets. It is the power to engage in restrictive practices that provides one of the bases of American antitrust policy.

---

[8]In a case involving Alcoa, the Supreme Court was unwilling to split up the company for fear of losing substantial economies of scale in production and in research and development.

Industrial Concentration and Competition

Though comparatively few American industries operate under strict textbook competitive conditions, we should not jump to the conclusion that there is no competition at all. Competition can exist in a number of forms. Firms in an industry compete with each other on the basis of quality and product differentiation. They compete for customers with firms in industries that produce other products intended for the satisfaction of the same general consumer want. They compete with firms in completely unrelated industries for the limited incomes of consumers in general.

Competitors in any industry compete with each other and with firms in all other industries for the scarce agents of production. The firms in any given industry also compete on the basis of technology. That is, they continually try to develop improved machines and production methods that will both lower their own costs of production and render obsolete the machines and methods of competitors. Even large firms, which do not have to face much competition within their own industries, must compete with firms in other industries for the limited money of consumers and for supplies of the scarce agents of production.

Then there is the matter of international competition, for many U.S. firms compete globally. The plight of Chrysler in particular and the automobile and steel industries in general indicates that there is plenty of competition in the world, particularly from the Japanese. The American automobile industry, an oligopoly if there ever was one, lost $4 billion in 1981, with most of that loss resulting from increased imports of cars from the Japanese auto industry, also very much an oligopoly. There is obviously competition, with the Japanese firms winning and the U.S. auto makers losing enough to want U.S. government protection against the Japanese.

Large companies, such as Chrysler and U.S. Steel, have to compete as ferociously as many small firms to survive in markets that are now international in nature, against competitors from countries which have different attitudes toward bigness and competition. In Japan competition is fierce, but it is a "survival of the fittest" type of competition, with no help for the losers. If the winners become larger in the process of winning, there is no government objection.

The number of American business firms, large and small, is rising both absolutely and in proportion to population. For example, in 1910 there were 2,923 corporations per million people; in 1968 the number was 7,936 per million people. In 1976 there were 9,800 corporations per million people.[9] The number of business enterprises in the United States

---

[9]U.S. Bureau of the Census, *Statistical Abstract of the United States, 1981* (Washington: U.S. Government Printing Office, 1981), p. 553.

grew from 3,114,000 in 1945 (1 per 46 persons) to 7,950,000 in 1976 (1 per 39 persons). Individuals with self-employment income went from 7,377,000 (1 per 19 persons) in 1945 to 14,700,000 (1 per 15 persons) in 1977.[10] This reflects the fact that the American economy is becoming less oriented toward manufacturing and more toward service, with the result that overall opportunity for the independent entrepreneur is growing. The proportion of manufacturing employment relative to total employment declined from 34 percent in 1967 to 30 percent in 1976.[11]

LABOR UNIONS

The workers of many capitalistic countries (and of the United States in particular) have not been content to rely entirely on government intervention for the improvement of their economic status. Instead, they have banded themselves together into labor unions for the purpose of bargaining collectively with employers. The individual worker is usually at a disadvantage in bargaining with an employer; lack of financial resources requires an earned income. On the other hand, while an employer must have employees, one worker more or less doesn't mean much. Under collective bargaining, the worker's disadvantage is greatly reduced. The worker's need for a job is not reduced, but the question facing the employer becomes one of having or not having a complete labor force rather than one of having or not having a particular worker. The workers, gathered together in a union and delegating the task of bargaining with the employer to an official or agent of the union, can often obtain much better terms of employment than the individual workers could obtain for themselves.

Development of Labor Unions

Labor unions are a product of the last century. Early labor unions which existed before the Civil War were generally impermanent bodies, established to redress certain grievances, and dissolved shortly when either successful or defeated. In 1828 the Workingman's party was formed in Philadelphia and spread to at least 15 other states. The labor movement accelerated after the Civil War. The development of large impersonal business units seemed to many workers to place them at the mercy of employers. In 1869 the first major U.S. labor union, the Knights of Labor, was organized in Philadelphia. The union did not last long, in part because of poor leadership. In 1881 the American Federation of Labor (AFL) was created. As a federation of craft unions, the AFL made no effort for

---

[10]*Ibid.*, p. 279.
[11]U.S. Bureau of the Census, "General Summary Report," in *1977 Census of Manufactures* (Washington: U.S. Government Printing Office, April 20, 1981).

many years to enroll unskilled labor. The AFL, under Samuel Gompers, adopted a policy of political neutrality. Its main thrust was economic—more pay and an 8-hour work day. Other unions, in particular the International Workers of the World (IWW), were more militant. They believed in class conflict and resorted to violent means including general strikes and sabotage to achieve their goals.

The labor movement declined in importance during the 1920s. The AFL lost over a million members during the decade, and efforts to unionize new industries proved unsuccessful. There were several factors responsible for the decline in unionism in the 1920s. The "Red scare" after the end of World War I was one factor. Some unions, particularly the IWW, had been sympathetic to the Bolshevik Revolution in Russia. There was public concern that somehow Communists were infiltrating the United States and all unions were lumped in with the IWW. The sensational murder trial and execution of Sacco and Vanzetti, both of whom were anarchists, convinced many employers that bomb throwers and Communists were lurking behind every lamppost.

Another factor responsible for the decline of unionism was an unsympathetic attitude of the government; government opposition helped to break up strikes in the coal and steel industries in 1919, and conservative court decisions hampered union activity during the 1920s. Laissez-faire was advocated as public policy; unions were blamed for rising prices. Finally, business firms organized an attack on unionism by popularizing the open shop and organizing company unions.

The halcyon days of organized labor occurred during the New Deal of Franklin D. Roosevelt. In 1935 the National Labor Relations Act was passed. This law required employers to bargain collectively with representatives of their employees and prohibited employers from carrying on unfair labor practices and from interfering in the organization of unions for collective bargaining. The act was intended to stimulate the growth of organized labor, and it did just that. Union membership more than tripled during the 1930s, and many plants and industries which had previously escaped unionization were organized.

A split within the ranks of labor itself occurred in 1935 when union leaders within the AFL left it to form the Congress of Industrial Organization (CIO). The CIO was interested in organizing workers in the mass production industries. It was highly successful in the automobile and steel industries, securing recognition of unions for employees in these industries. Labor achieved at least a parity with management by the end of the 1930s. Labor also gained in terms of social welfare. The Fair Labor Standards Act of 1938 enacted minimum wages and maximum hours for labor engaged in interstate commerce.

During the latter part of World War II and in the immediate postwar period, a series of labor strikes incurred the enmity of the general public and convinced Congress that new legislation in the field of labor relations was needed. The Labor-Management Relations Act (Taft-Hartley Act) was passed in 1947 to eliminate some specific abuses on the part of labor unions and to equalize bargaining conditions between labor and management. The closed shop was outlawed and the union shop was permitted only under strict regulation. A notice was required 60 days before a strike or a lockout could be called, and the government could obtain an injunction against a union, postponing for 80 days any strike that would affect the national interest. Unions could be sued for breach of contract if they participated in jurisdictional strikes and boycotts. The pendulum, which had swung in favor of labor unions, swung back to a more centrist position.

The Decline of Unions

As reflected in Table 5-3, unions began to peak in importance as measured by the number of workers in the labor force in the 1950s. The reason was a shift from a goods-producing to a service society. The United States had entered a postindustrial age which represented a change in the type of work people do—from physically intensive to knowledge-intensive labor. In 1945, 43.4 percent of all workers were employed in manufacturing; by 1980 the percentage of workers employed in manufacturing had decreased to 28.4 percent of the labor force. Conversely, the number of persons in the service-producing jobs increased from 56.6 percent of the labor force in 1945 to 71.6 percent in 1980. In 1945, 38.5 percent of all workers employed in manufacturing belonged to unions; by

TABLE 5-3
UNION MEMBERSHIP AS A PERCENTAGE OF THE
U.S. LABOR FORCE, 1945–1980

Year	Union Membership
1945	21.9%
1950	22.3
1955	24.7
1960	23.6
1965	22.4
1970	22.6
1975	21.7
1980	21.2

Source: U.S. Department of Labor, Bureau of Labor Statistics, *Handbook of Labor Statistics 1980* (Washington: U.S. Government Printing Office, 1981), p. 507.

1980, the number of union workers employed in manufacturing decreased to 22.4 percent of the total manufacturing labor force. Unionism has never been strong in the service areas. White-collar workers tend to identify more with management. There is also a certain snob appeal about white-collar jobs, which is coupled with a tendency to look down on blue-collar manufacturing workers. By 1990 even more people will be employed in miscellaneous service-type jobs such as data processing, hotels, and restaurants.[12]

GOVERNMENT

For many years, the idea persisted that government in a capitalistic system, however it might be organized, should follow a laissez-faire policy with respect to economic activity. That is, its activities should be limited to the performance of a few general functions for the good of all of its citizens, and it should not attempt to control or interfere with the economic activities of private individuals. Laissez-faire assumed that each individual is a more or less rational being and a better judge of his or her own interests than any government could be. But all of this has changed, and the advanced capitalist countries of today, including the United States, represent a radical departure from laissez-faire. In the operation of capitalist economies, problems arose that seemed impossible for private individuals to solve and whose impact upon their lives brought a demand for government intervention. As a result, government regulation is a fairly common feature of economic life under capitalism.

Government intervention and participation in the U.S. economy can be divided into four areas. First, there is public finance, where government is a purchaser of goods and services as well as a tax collector. Government economic stabilization policies may also be considered a part of this area. Second, government regulation and control prescribe specific conditions under which private economic activity can or cannot take place. Government may interpose itself as a part of management in certain industries, such as public utilities, and regulate rates and the provision of services. It may also affect the character of private business operations both directly and indirectly through antitrust and other laws. Third, government (at all levels) is the single largest employer in the American economy, and as such it competes directly with private industry for labor. The government also affects the level of wages and salaries. Fourth, government owns and operates certain types of business enterprises and is a major provider of credit. In fact, a shift in emphasis from market to political decisions has taken place in the American economy in

---

[12]U.S. Department of Labor, Bureau of Labor Statistics, *Occupational Outlook Handbook, 1980–81* (Washington: U.S. Government Printing Office, 1981).

recent years, in great measure in response to increased demands from a wide variety of special interest groups.

Public Finance

Public finance is the clearest and probably most important example of the extent of government participation in the "mixed" economy of the United States. Taxes provide the government with control over the nation's resources and also affect the distribution of income and wealth. Government expenditures for goods and services divert resources from the private to the public sector of the economy. Government transfer payments redistribute income from one economic group to another. Through its own expenditures, the government has literally created whole industries. It has conducted much of the basic research in certain industries, and it has given impetus and direction to technological change. The direct subsidies and indirect benefits offered by government to special interest groups, e.g., farmers and shipbuilders, are too numerous to mention. In addition, preferential tax treatment is accorded to some firms and industries to achieve desired economic goals. Examples of special tax treatment include the investment credit, depletion allowances for mineral extraction companies, and accelerated depreciation.

The economic influence of the public sector has intensified steadily throughout this century, and has become particularly pervasive during the last 20 years. To some extent, this increase in influence can be attributed to a growing acceptance, at least until recently, of the government's taking charge of public welfare. Increased industrialization has resulted in changes in the size and complexity of business enterprises, and the regulatory operations of the government have been stepped up. Government expenditures for national defense are also an important component of budget expenditures, and account for around 30 percent of total government purchases of goods and services.

Economic growth has spurred a trend toward urban living. As a larger proportion of the nation's population has become concentrated in urban areas, the inevitable result has been an increase in demand for a vast variety of services that must be provided through the public sector. But regardless of the causes, the growth in both absolute and relative importance of the public sector to the U.S. economy is clear, as Table 5-4 indicates. Governemnt expenditures on goods and services accounted for around 21 percent of the gross national product. When transfer payments are added to government expenditures on goods and services, total government expenditures amount to one-third of gross national product.

The composition of taxes is also of importance in analyzing the role of government in the U.S. economy. Government expenditures are, at least in part, covered by taxes, including taxes on business firms and

TABLE 5-4
U.S. GOVERNMENT EXPENDITURES COMPARED TO
GROSS NATIONAL PRODUCT FOR SELECTED YEARS
(billions of dollars)

| | | Government Expenditures on Goods and Services | | |
| | | | | |
Year	Gross National Product	Total	Federal	State and Local
1929	103.4	8.8	1.4	7.4
1933	55.6	8.0	2.0	6.0
1939	90.8	13.5	5.2	8.3
1945	211.9	82.3	74.2	8.1
1950	284.8	37.9	18.4	19.5
1960	506.0	100.3	53.7	46.6
1970	982.4	218.9	95.6	125.2
1975	1,528.8	338.4	123.1	215.4
1977	1,899.5	396.2	144.4	251.8
1978	2,127.6	435.6	152.6	283.0
1979	2,388.5	476.1	166.3	309.8
1980	2,627.4	534.8	198.9	335.9

Source: *Economic Report of the President, 1981* (Washington: U.S. Government Printing Office, 1981), p. 233.

individuals. In view of this, where taxes are levied determines who ultimately pays for government expenditures. Taxes also have an income redistribution effect. Whenever any government extracts taxes, it lowers someone's income, but whenever that money is spent, it also raises someone's income.

There also has developed a belief among those who make public policy that variations in the rate of economic growth can be attributed to different tax systems. Many people feel that the reason why the Japanese growth rate is far superior to that of the United States is that Japanese tax policy favors saving and investment. The economic policies of the Reagan administration center heavily on tax-cutting measures designed to promote capital formation by increasing the rate of saving. Special types of incentives have been given to certain types of persons, corporations, or activities to influence shifts in behavior.

Economic Stabilization Policies. The acceptance of economic stabilization policies designed to promote stability and the use of the tax transfer payment mechanism to promote the redistribution of income tend to characterize the economic role of Western governments, including the

U.S. government, in much of the 20th century. Economic stabilization policies include the use of fiscal and monetary devices. Fiscal policy in the United States is effected through the federal budget, which can be used as a flywheel to change the level of economic activity in the economy. Taxes represent a withdrawal of income from the income stream, while government expenditures represent an injection of income into it. When the government's income, as represented by taxes and other revenues, exceeds expenditures, the net effect is to dampen down the level of economic activity in the economy. On the other hand, when government expenditures exceed revenues, the net effect is to stimulate the economy. Budgetary surpluses or deficits, then, can be used to effect changes in the level of economic activity.

Monetary policy is also an economic stabilization tool used by the United States and other Western countries. It involves operations by the central banking authorities affecting the stock of money, its rate of turnover, and the volume of close money substitutes. The Federal Reserve is technically a privately owned corporation, but is actually an independent government agency subject to loose control by Congress and the president. It may be regarded as the central bank of the United States, comparable, for example, to the Bank of England in the United Kingdom and the Deutsche Bundesbank in West Germany. The Federal Reserve may take action to counteract either inflation or deflation.

It effects monetary policy in the United States through openmarket operations, control over discount rates,[13] and legal requirements concerning the reserves that commercial banks have to maintain against demand deposits. Raising discount rates and legal reserve requirements are used as antiinflation measures; lowering them achieves the opposite result. The Federal Reserve also may either buy or sell U.S. government bonds. If it buys bonds from commercial banks, demand deposits are increased and banks have more money to lend. Conversely, if it sells bonds to commercial banks, the reverse is true.

Entitlements. There has developed in the United States what Daniel Bell refers to as a "revolution of rising entitlements."[14] This revolution is manifested in many forms. It includes the belief that, for example, on an individual basis, anyone who wants to work should be entitled to a job, if necessary under government auspices. Also, anyone who is sick is entitled to medical care, and anyone who wants an education should have it. What this means is an enormous expansion in services in the society. The federal government, through a variety of welfare programs, made a

---

[13]The discount rate is the interest rate charged when commercial banks borrow from the Federal Reserve. In turn, the discount rate affects what commercial banks can charge their customers.

[14]Daniel Bell, *The Cultural Contradictions of Capitalism* (New York: Basic Books, 1978), pp. 232–236.

commitment during the 1960s and 1970s to alleviate social inequalities. The composition of the federal budget has been altered considerably since 1960. Transfer payments have increased more rapidly than any single component in the budget, as Table 5-5 indicates. Total outlays for transfer payments and for other social welfare programs amounted to around 50 percent of the federal budget in 1980. When state and local government expenditures on social welfare programs are also taken into consideration, total government expenditures on social welfare programs amounted to $400 billion in 1980. In the state of California, on any given day, about 40 percent of the population received some form of state transfer payment.

TABLE 5-5
MAJOR CATEGORIES OF FEDERAL GOVERNMENT EXPENDITURES
(billions of dollars)

Fiscal Year	Transfer Payments to Individuals	Total Expenditures
1958	17.8	82.8
1960	20.6	91.3
1965	28.4	118.5
1970	55.0	195.5
1975	131.4	328.8
1978	178.7	450.5
1980	234.7	578.2
1981	276.8	671.0

Source: Executive Office of the President, Office of Manpower and Budget, *Budget of the United States Government, Fiscal Year 1982* (Washington: U.S. Government Printing Office, 1981), p. 41.

There are a wide variety of entitlement programs ranging from food stamps to Medicare to welfare payments. The funds are provided from general taxes or government borrowing. For example, unemployment compensation provides aid to unemployed workers and is financed by a payroll tax upon employers.

There are the regular social security programs which were created under the Social Security Act of 1937, the most important of which is the old age, survivors, and disability insurance programs which is financed by a payroll tax upon both employer and employee.[15] The tax receipts are placed in a reserve fund, and payments are made to workers who have retired or who are disabled and to the spouses and young children of

---

[15]The combined rate in 1982 is 13.4 percent on incomes up to $32,100.

workers who have been killed. An expansion of the program occurred in the mid-1960s when free hospital care began to be provided for older persons, and voluntary governmental insurance become available to them. Entitlement programs have risen at a rate three times as fast as the U.S. gross national product, placing strains on government financing.

Regulation

Government regulation, particularly of business, is a second area in which government has become firmly entrenched in the U.S. economy. This sphere of public sector influence has developed by fits and starts. In the 1880s the trust movement threatened to envelope much of American industry. This brought about a public demand for some sort of control over the monopolies, with the result that the Sherman Anti-Trust Act was passed in 1890.

The Depression, which began with the stock market crash of 1929 and continued until the wartime mobilization of the early 1940s, was a crisis. In response to that crisis, many new government agencies were created, most of which impinged in some way on business firms. By the end of the Depression, the federal government had come to exercise extensive regulation and control over business. After that time, there was little increase in government intervention until the late 1960s and early 1970s when environmental protection, employment of minorities, and consumer protection became dominant issues.

Antitrust Regulation. One important area of government regulation is antitrust activity to prevent anticompetitive business practices. This activity generally has sprung from the concept that concentration interferes with the efficient operation of a competitive market economy and that the most effective method of regulation is to prevent it from occurring. Antitrust laws are designed to promote and maintain competitive conditions in industry. There is a fundamental social interest in the efficacy of the market system. Society wants the system to work so as to get the maximum output of the goods and services at the lowest possible prices, using the most efficient production techniques.

Anticompetitive practices can be divided into several categories. First, there can be an industry in which a few firms are dominant and price competition is therefore minimal. Second, mergers between business firms can create an anticompetitive market situation. Third, anticompetitive business practices may involve certain types of market abuses such as price fixing and market sharing.

Public Utility Regulation. Certain types of industries vitally affect the public interest by providing a particular type of service that is considered too important to society to be left to the vagaries of the market or to private enterprise to provide as it sees fit. An example is the provision of electric power to homes and industries, an absolute necessity if society is going to function effectively. In other countries with systems similar to our own, industries directly affecting the public interest are owned and operated by their governments. In the United States, when one or both of two conditions exist in an industry, a *natural monopoly* is usually created instead by a state or the federal government. First, economies of scale will occur if output is concentrated in one firm, with the result that one firm can supply the market more efficiently than two or more firms; and second, unrestrained competition between firms in the industry is deemed by society to be undesirable. Included under the category of natural monopolies are electricity, gas, telephone service, and broadcasting.

Social Regulation. During the 1970s the federal government in particular extended its participation in the market system. More and more effort was directed toward cushioning individual risks and regulating personal and institutional conduct. Social regulation is broad-based in terms of objectives. It encompasses such areas as occupational health and safety, equal employment opportunity, consumer product safety, and environmental protection. These areas have specific social goals—a cleaner environment, safer consumer products, employment of minorities, and so forth. A number of important regulatory commissions; most of which were created during the 1970s, function to enforce the laws designed to achieve these social goals.

The important ones, in 1981, are the Consumer Product Safety Commission, the Occupational Safety and Health Administration, the Equal Employment Opportunity Commission, and the Environmental Protection Agency. For each of these relative newcomers to the federal government hierarchy of administrative agencies and commissions, jurisdiction extends to most of the private sector and at times to productive activities in the government sector itself. However, each of these newer agencies has a rather narrow range of responsibility. For example, the Equal Employment Opportunity Commission is responsible only for employment policies in a given firm, whereas the Federal Aviation Administration (FAA) is responsible for all the activities of any who fly.

Justification for social regulation is based in part on the belief that imperfections in the market system are responsible for various social problems. In a market economy, the price mechanism gives individuals no opportunity to bid against the production and sale of certain commodities and services they regard as undesirable. There may be a great number of people whose total amount of satisfaction would be much increased if they could prevent the production and sale of, say, alcoholic beverages or the emission of noxious fumes from a chemical plant, and who would be glad to pay the price to obtain satisfaction of their negative preference if given the opportunity to do so. But there seems to be no way in which the market price mechanism can take these negative preferences into account. The only way in which these preferences can be exercised, if at all, is through government action that places controls on the output of both public and private goods that are deemed deleterious to the public interest.

Government as an Employer

One measure of the magnitude of the public sector is the number of persons employed directly by one or another governmental unit. When the armed forces are included, some 16 percent of the total labor force is employed directly by the public sector. It is likely that this percentage will increase in the future, particularly at the state and local levels of government, since the demand for social services is expected to increase. In addition, numerous other jobs are related indirectly to government employment. An army base, defense plant, or state university often supports the economy of a whole area. The public sector sets wage standards in many areas and competes against the private sector for labor resources. However, the productivity of the public sector is low in comparison to productivity in the private sector, and as the public sector expands relative to the private sector, productivity in general declines. Unfortunately, many public sector jobs involve make-work and provide little opportunity for creativity.[16]

In the private sector, the profit-and-loss system produces an incentive to stimulate efficiency. Competition between business firms also encourages maximum efficiency in the use of capital and other resources, including labor. Both factors are lacking in government, for it is not in the business of making a profit or loss, nor is there a need to be competitive, because there is no competition between government units. There is no rationale to be productive because the stimulus is not there. No government agency has ever gone broke. In fact, some observers have argued that agency managers have strong disincentives to improve production if such gains lead to budget cuts. The prestige of an agency manager is often measured by the number of employees the agency has; thus the fewer the employees, the lower the prestige. The disincentive possibility means that Congress or its state equivalent must in effect fill the role played by the profit-and-loss system.

In a study on productivity in the federal government, the Joint Economic Committee of the U.S. Congress reached several conclusions.[17] First, if overall federal productivity were increased by 10 percent, person-

---

[16]U.S. Congress, Joint Economic Committee, *Productivity in the Federal Government* (Washington: U.S. Government Printing Office, May 31, 1979), pp. 1–12.
[17]*Ibid.*

nel costs could be reduced by more than $8 billion without a cutback in services. Resources would then be free for use in the private sector. Second, potential savings are even greater from increasing the productivity of state and local employees. Third, there is no relation between growth in compensation and growth in productivity of federal government employees. The Postal Service, for example, has had the highest average annual increase in yearly compensation, but one of the worst productivity records. Finally, although comparisons with the private sector are difficult, available evidence suggests that productivity in the federal government sector has risen less rapidly than in the private sector.

Government Ownership of Business

Government ownership of business is quite limited in the United States in comparison to other major Western industrial countries. In France, for example, the railroads, coal mines, and most of the banking system, airlines, electric power facilities, and insurance companies are state-owned. The government also has a large interest in the petroleum and natural gas industries and is involved in the production of motor vehicles and airplanes. In the United Kingdom, the coal mines, steel industry, railways, trucking, and the electric and gas industries are state-owned. In Germany, government ownership is limited to the railroads, airlines, public utilities, and coal mines. However, in all three countries, private enterprise is still dominant in that it employs by far the greater percentage of workers and contributes the greater part of the gross national product.

In the United States, all levels of government own and operate productive facilities of many kinds. Airports, but not railway terminals, are usually government-owned. Governmental units own and operate the plants that provide water, gas, and electricity to thousands of cities and towns, as well as owning local transportation systems, heating plants, warehouses, printing companies, and a wide variety of other facilities. Government also produces, either directly or indirectly, all our artificial rubber, atomic power, and many other goods. It carries on projects connected with reforestation, soil erosion, slum clearance, rural electrification, and housing. All of this does not mean that government, ownership and operation is necessarily preferred to private. In many cases, the resources required were too large, and risks too too great, or the likelihood of profit too small to attract private enterprise, and government was compelled to perform the tasks instead.

One illustration of this point is the Tennessee Valley Authority (TVA), a major public enterprise for the production and distribution of electrical power in the southeastern United States. At one time, the area adjacent to the Tennessee River was among the most impoverished in the United States. Flooding and soil erosion were common occurrences, and most homes in the area were without electricity. The area was also generally unattractive to industry. The TVA was created to erect dams and hydroelectric plants to provide electric power, to improve navigation on the Tennessee River, to promote flood control, to prevent soil erosion, to engage in reforestation, and to contribute to the nation's defense through the manufacture of artificial nitrates. It was opposed by private companies, in particular the utility companies, because it was empowered to sell electricity in direct competition with them. However, the utility companies in the Tennessee Valley area had never considered it profitable to provide anything more than minimal service. The TVA was also supposed to serve as a yardstick of efficiency, but government ownership and operation of power facilities does not always mean lower rates or greater efficiency. Opinion on TVA's efficiency is mixed. The TVA is efficient compared to other government agencies, but compared to private business it doesn't look as good.

Government credit programs constitute a gray area in that they do not involve outright state ownership of industry. However, federal credit programs have an impact on private industry that should be mentioned. Direct, insured, and federally sponsored agency loans passed the $500 billion mark in 1980 and have continued to increase. These programs have three main functions: the elimination of gaps in the credit market, the provision of subsidies for the purpose of stimulating socially desirable activity, and stimulation of the economy. The first two of these functions are microeconomic in effect in that they are supposed to affect the types of activity for which credit is made available, the geographical location of those activities, and the types of borrowers who have access to credit. For example, Federal Housing Administration (FHA) and Veterans' Administration (VA) mortgage insurance programs have resulted in an increased demand for housing. The third function is macroeconomic in nature in that federal lending affects the level of economic activity on a large scale—in particular, the gross national product and employment.

SUMMARY

Three important types of economic organizations have developed in the United States—big business, big labor, and big government. The three have developed partly in response to the needs and deficiences of the market mechanism. Big business, as represented by large corporations, developed first, and pervades all areas of economic activity ranging from manufacturing to banking and from communications to retailing. Whether this is good or bad is a matter of opinion. Large-scale production and distribution can effect economies of scale and the end result can be lower prices for consumers. However, largeness can result in a lessening of innovation and price competition. In all advanced industrial countries, regardless of their political and economic ideologies, large industrial entities are a fact of life.

Labor unions in part offset the power of corporations and also reduce the power of market forces in labor markets by creating a monopoly for certain types of workers. Unions gained in popularity and strength during the Depression of the 1930s. However, union membership began to peak during the 1950s and has been declining as a percentage of the total labor force. There has been a decline in employment in the manufacturing sector of the economy, where union membership has been the highest, and an increase in employment in the service sector, where union membership has never been strong. The increased education and mobility of American workers is also a factor that has tended to work against an increase in union membership.

Undoubtedly, the most important modification of the U.S. market system has been achieved through an increase in the role of the public or government sector. Public education has been provided, business monopolies have been curbed, and taxes and transfer payments have been used to redistribute incomes. Fiscal and monetary policies have been used, albeit with limited success, to attain full employment and price stability. A variety of government regulations have been adopted to achieve various social goals such as a cleaner environment and the employment of minorities. The social security program has been expanded over time to reduce economic insecurity. Government purchases of goods and services amount to around 21 percent of the gross national product. It is clear that government intervention in the economy has become large enough to justify the classification of the United States as a mixed rather than a strictly market system. How successful this mixture has been is the subject of the next chapter.

REVIEW QUESTIONS

1. In what ways can the development of large corporations be regarded as a departure from a market system?
2. What is a multinational corporation?
3. In what ways can the development of labor unions be regarded as a departure from a market system?
4. How can the distribution of income be altered by government tax and transfer policies?
5. What is meant by the term *entitlements*?
6. What, in general, is monetary policy? Who has control over monetary policy?
7. What is fiscal policy? How is fiscal policy implemented in the United States.?
8. What are some of the factors responsible for the increase in the role of government in U.S. society?
9. Discuss the purpose of antitrust regulation.
10. What are some of the factors responsible for the decline of unionism in the United States?

RECOMMENDED READINGS

Ash, Roy L. *The Political World, Government Regulation, and Spending.* Los Angeles: International Institute for Economic Research, 1979.

Barnett, Richard J., and Ronald E. Muller. *Global Reach.* New York: Simon and Shuster, 1974.

Bell, Daniel. *The Coming of Post-Industrial Society.* New York: Basic Books, 1976.

Committee for Economic Development. *Redefining Government's Role in the Market System.* New York: 1981.

Dunlop, John T. *Business and Public Policy.* Cambridge: Harvard University Press, 1980.

Kristol, Irving. *Two Cheers for Capitalism.* New York: Basic Books, 1978.

Scherer, Frederic M. *Industrial Market Structure and Economic Performance,* 2nd ed. Chicago: Rand McNally, 1980.

Schnitzer, Martin. *Contemporary Government and Business Relations.* 2nd ed. Boston: Houghton Mifflin, 1982.

Weidenbaum, Murray. *Business, Governemnt, and the Public.* 2nd ed. Englewood Cliffs, N.J.: Prentice-Hall, 1980.

6

An Appraisal of the United States Economy

INTRODUCTION

"Optimism," said a character in one of Voltaire's plays, "is a mania for maintaining that all is well when things are going badly."[1] There does not appear to be much room for optimism, at least as far as the immediate future of the U.S. economy is concerned, with inflation becoming a hallmark of life and U.S. industry taking a beating in international competition. By the end of 1980 the Japanese became the world's largest producer of automobiles, the first time in 56 years that any country has replaced the United States at the top. The financial problems of Chrysler and Ford became acute, leading the Reagan administration to impose voluntary import quotas on Japanese cars in April 1981. The opening words of an International Workers of the World (IWW) song of the early 1900s, "Times are getting hard, boys, money is getting scarce," may be as relevant to the United States in the early 1980s as they were then. By most standards, the United States has entered the 1980s with a rather serious set of problems, the worst of which are unemployment and inflation.

However, these problems are an extension of the 1970s, a decade which few persons will remember with any feeling of nostalgia. The

---

[1]Voltaire, *Candide* (New York: Bantam Books, 1976), p. 32.

economy's most disruptive decade since the Depression of the 1930s witnessed the contradiction of no growth and inflation, a condition called *stagflation* by economists. Stagflation was accompanied by an energy shortage in the land of supposedly limitless resources, the depreciation of the dollar, and a decline in real incomes and productivity. Keynesian economic policy prescriptions, which had once worked when demand was slack, did not seem to work any more.

A new international division of labor developed, which may be the most important structural shift in recent years. Newly industrialized countries such as Brazil, Mexico, South Korea, and Taiwan began to take over the traditional, routinized manufacturing activities—shipbuilding, steel, textiles, and so forth. Conversely, Japan deliberately adopted a strategy of encouraging a movement to high-value-added production of sophisticated technology, and began to obtain an ever-increasing share of the world's markets in such areas as automobiles and electronic equipment. There is the feeling that U.S. economic influence in the world has crested.[2]

Economic performance is not a straightforward concept. Any number of standards can be used to define and measure it. There are several standard measures that are acceptable—real economic growth, inflation, and unemployment. All are interrelated. What is clear is that the performance of the U.S. economy, particularly during the 1970s, has not been good. The U.S. economy has to undergo a fundamental change if it is to retain a measure of economic viability let alone leadership in the remainder of this century. United States industry will need large amounts of new capital to increase primary processing capacity, and the problem of a capital shortage—because of a low rate of household savings and because of declining profit margins of many U.S. firms—is a real one. The rest of the world is catching up with the United States.

ECONOMIC GROWTH

A high standard of living in the present is made possible by the economic growth of the past. A rising standard of living is made possible by continued economic growth and a rising level of employment. In the United States, the rate of unemployment has been high for several years. This problem has been compounded by the fact that the size of the labor force is constantly expanding. Thus, it is necessary to absorb new entrants into the labor force by providing more employment opportunities. If the economy does not grow, there is no way in which unemployment can be reduced and new jobseekers absorbed into the labor force. Further,

[2]Daniel Bell, *The Cultural Contradictions of Capitalism* (New York: Basic Books, 1976), p. 215; also Charles P. Kindleberger, "An American Climacteric?" *Challenge* (January–February 1974), pp. 18–27.

the nation will not be able to obtain the resources to solve its social problems and to provide schools, medical care, hospitals, and other social needs.

Table 6-1 presents U.S. real gross national product in 1972 dollars. A measure of economic growth is the rate of change of real GNP, either total or per capita, over time. The total real GNP of the United States measured in 1972 dollars rose from $1.1 trillion in 1970 to $1.5 trillion in 1980. The rate of change from year to year during the 1970s was the lowest for any decade since the Great Depression of the 1930s. The end result was a slippage in living standards relative to other countries. By 1978 the United States ranked fifth among the nations of the world in per capita GNP.[3] West Germany, a major world competitor, had a higher per capita GNP, and Japan's per capita GNP was only 7 percent below that of the United States.

TABLE 6-1
REAL GROSS NATIONAL PRODUCT, UNITED STATES, 1970 TO 1980

Total Real GNP

Year	Billions of Dollars of 1972 Purchasing Power	Percentage Change from Previous Year
1970	1,086	−0.2
1971	1,122	3.4
1972	1,186	5.7
1973	1,255	5.8
1974	1,248	−0.6
1975	1,234	−1.1
1976	1,300	5.4
1977	1,372	5.5
1978	1,437	4.8
1979	1,483	3.2
1980	1,481	−0.2

Source: *Economic Report of the President* (February 1981), pp. 234–235.

Productivity

Productivity growth has long been recognized as one of the most important determinants of national economic growth and stability. A nation's ability to consume ultimately depends upon its ability to pro-

---

[3]International Monetary Fund, *International Financial Statistics*, Vol. 32, No. 4 (April 1979), pp. 122, 156, 214, 352. Middle East countries, such as Kuwait, are not included even though they, too, have a higher per capita GNP than the United States.

duce. If money incomes increase but productivity does not increase, real purchasing power will fall. Increased productivity will also help reduce inflation by tempering the growth of unit labor costs.

Unfortunately, the productivity of the United States has fallen to the point where it may be eventually in the position of being replaced by Japan as the world's number one economic power. During the period 1972 to 1978, for example, industrial productivity rose 1 percent per year in the United States and over 5 percent per year in Japan.[4] The productivity of the United States has shown a steady decline over the last three decades. As measured by the growth in output per worker—the most widely used measure of productivity—the average annual rate of increase declined from 3.0 percent during the period 1950–1965 to 2.4 percent during 1965–1973, to only 0.6 percent during 1973–1980 with actual declines in 1978, 1979, and 1980. In the absence of productivity gains, there can be no general improvement in real U.S. living standards.

Table 6-2 presents the productivity performance of the United States during the period 1970–1980, with 1977 used as the base year. Average real output per hour is used as the measure of productivity. The productivity slowdown during the 1970s contributed to a deterioration in the ability of American industry to compete in the world economy. All of the

TABLE 6-2
ANNUAL INDICES OF PRODUCTIVITY IN THE
UNITED STATES, 1970–1980
(1977 = 100)

Year	Real Output per Worker
1970	86.1
1971	89.3
1972	91.4
1973	94.8
1974	92.7
1975	94.8
1976	97.9
1977	100.0
1978	99.8
1979	99.4
1980	99.0

Source: Joint Economic Committee, Congress of the United States, *The 1981 Midyear Report: Productivity* (Washington: U.S. Government Printing Office, 1981), p. 3.

---

[4]Joint Economic Committee, Congress of the United States, *The 1981 Midyear Report: Productivity.* (Washington: U.S. Government Printing Office, 1981), pp. 2–3.

industrialized Western countries experienced a marked decline in productivity, particularly after 1973. But the reduction experienced by the U.S. economy exceeded the decline in every other country except the United Kingdom and Sweden. Thus, a primary goal of U.S. economic policy during the 1980s must be to restore healthy productivity growth. To do this, it is necessary to pursue macroeconomic policies designed to reduce inflation and achieve high economic growth, as well as microeconomic policies designed to enhance productivity directly.

International Comparisons of Economic Growth and Productivity

The performance of the United States must be placed in a global perspective. No longer is it possible for the United States to exist in splendid isolation and ignore the rest of the world. In an increasingly interdedent world, no economy operates in a vacuum. Japan has already surpassed the United States as the leading producer of automobiles and steel products in the world. In many industries, the United States lags behind other countries in the introduction of new technology.

All the world's industrial countries have fallen victim to a hydra-headed economic monster of slower growth, higher inflation, and higher unemployment. However, there has been wide variation among industrial countries in economic performance levels. Real economic growth and productivity is one basic measure of economic performance. Another measure is the rate of employment and unemployment, and a third is the keeping of purchasing power of earnings as stable as possible.

Table 6-3 presents an economic performance index for eight major

---

TABLE 6-3
ECONOMIC PERFORMANCE INDEX
FOR EIGHT MAJOR INDUSTRIAL COUNTRIES

1960–1973		1974–1980	
Japan	145.9	Japan	37.8
West Germany	123.9	West Germany	29.0
France	85.5	France	18.0
Italy	67.7	Canada	16.5
Canada	64.2	Sweden	15.3
Sweden	55.6	United States	15.2
United States	50.4	Italy	13.4
United Kingdom	43.1	United Kingdom	2.2

Source: New York Stock Exchange, Office of Economic Research, *U.S. Economic Performance in a Global Perspective* (February 1981), p. 11.

industrial countries, including the United States, for two time periods, 1960–1973 and 1974–1980. The economic performance index involved a division of the real economic growth rate for each country by its unemployment and inflation rates. All else being equal, the higher the rate of economic growth, the higher the index; the higher the rate of inflation or unemployment, the lower the index. The higher the index, the better economic performance. The table indicates that for both periods, Japan's economy performed best, with West Germany second. However, there was a marked deterioration in the performance of all countries during the 1974–1980 period. Though Japan ranked first in both periods, its economic performance index for the 1974–1980 period (37.8) was but one-quarter the 145.9 registered for the 1960–1973 period. The performance of the United States was poor for both time periods.

Table 6-4 compares the average annual compound rates of real economic growth for the same countries during the time periods 1960–1973 and 1973–1979. Gross domestic product is used as the measurement of economic growth.[5] The table indicates that the performance of the United States relative to the other countries is somewhat mixed. For the period 1960 to 1973 the performance of the U.S. growth rate ranked it fifth among the eight countries. The growth rate was less than half of that for Japan. However, the U.S. growth rate for the 1973–1979 period, although low compared to the previous time period, actually was relatively better than the other countries in that there was less of a decline—4.1 percent in 1960–1973 to 2.7 percent in 1973–1979 compared to a drop in the Japanese growth rate from 10.5 percent to 4.0 percent. Only three

TABLE 6-4
REAL ECONOMIC GROWTH RATES
FOR EIGHT MAJOR INDUSTRIAL COUNTRIES

1960–1973		1973–1979	
Japan	10.5	Japan	4.0
France	5.6	Canada	3.2
Canada	5.6	France	2.9
Italy	5.3	United States	2.7
West Germany	4.5	Italy	2.4
United States	4.1	West Germany	2.4
Sweden	3.9	Sweden	1.7
United Kingdom	3.2	United Kingdom	0.8

Source: New York Stock Exchange, Office of Economic Research, *U.S. Economic Performance in a Global Perspective* (February 1981), p. 17.

---

[5]Gross domestic product is the value of all output produced within the geographic confines of a country.

countries—Japan, Canada, and France—had growth rates during the second period that were higher than the United States. The growth rates of all countries deteriorated during the 1973–1979 period. Moreover, the deterioration continued into 1980 and 1981, with the United States showing a negative rate of economic growth for 1980, and the United Kingdom for both years.[6]

Table 6-5 compares productivity in the United States and other countries for two periods, 1960–1973 and 1973–1979. Productivity is measured in average annual compound rate of change of real output per man-hour. Again the performance of the United States has been poor, particularly during the second period. This has contributed to a deterioration in the ability of U.S. industry to compete in a world economy. All major industrial countries showed a decline in productivity growth after 1973, but the decline experienced by the U.S. economy exceeded the decline in every other country except the United Kingdom and Sweden. Overall, when the 1973–1979 period is compared with the 1960–1973 period, productivity growth declined twice as sharply in the United States as it did elsewhere, while the rate of increase in unit labor costs accelerated four times as rapidly here as abroad.

TABLE 6-5
ANNUAL PERCENT CHANGE IN MANUFACTURING PRODUCTIVITY
FOR EIGHT MAJOR INDUSTRIAL COUNTRIES
1960–1973 AND 1973–1979

	1960–1973	1973–1979	Percent Decline
Japan	10.3	6.9	33.0
Italy	7.2	3.7	48.6
Sweden	6.7	2.4	64.2
France	5.8	4.8	17.2
West Germany	5.5	5.3	3.6
Canada	4.6	2.2	52.2
United Kingdom	4.0	0.5	87.5
United States	3.1	1.4	54.8

Source: Joint Economic Committee, Congress of the United States, *The 1981 Midyear Report; Productivity* (Washington: U.S. Government Printing Office, 1981), p. 4.

The famous baseball pitcher Satchel Paige once made the statement, "Never look back for you don't know who is gaining on you." Perhaps this advice is good for the United States because the rest of the world is indeed gaining on us, as Table 6-6 indicates. The United States still re-

---

[6]*Washington Post*, September 20, 1981, Section F5.

TABLE 6-6
REAL GROSS DOMESTIC PRODUCT PER WORKER
FOR EIGHT MAJOR INDUSTRIAL COUNTRIES, 1950–1979
(United States = 100)

	1950	1960	1970	1979
Belgium	55.6	59.7	73.7	90.7
Canada	84.5	89.5	92.6	94.8
France	42.4	53.7	71.0	88.8
West Germany	37.3	56.0	71.3	87.9
Italy	25.5	34.9	53.4	59.5
Japan	15.5	23.8	48.7	66.4
United Kingdom	53.4	53.7	57.6	59.5
United States	100.00	100.00	100.00	100.00

Source: Joint Economic Committee, Congress of the United States, *The 1981 Midyear Report: Productivity* (Washington: U.S. Government Printing Office, 1981), p. 5.

mains first in the world in terms of productivity as measured by real output per worker. However, if current trends continue, it will not be very long before other industrial countries match or exceed U.S. productivity levels. The productivity slowdown hits particularly hard at U.S. industrial firms that compete head-on in the world market with highly productive foreign firms. The U.S. auto industry is a case in point, with Japan's automated factories outproducing older U.S. auto plants. Consistently the U.S. automobile industry has found that there is as much as a 50 percent differential in labor productivity in favor of the Japanese auto industry.[7] In 1955 there were 150 television set manufacturers in the United States. In 1980 the only television sets that were produced in the United States were produced by Japanese firms.

INFLATION

The 1970s witnessed the worst combination of unemployment and inflation in modern U.S. experience. The average rate of unemployment ranged from a high of 8.5 percent in 1975 to a low of 5.3 percent in 1973.[8] However, the unemployment rate for the decade was in excess of 6 percent—the highest rate for any decade since the 1930s. During the same

[7]Congress of the United States, Office of Technology Assessment, *U.S. Industrial Competitiveness: A Comparison of Steel Electronics and Automobiles.* (Washington: U.S. Government Printing Office, 1981), p. 47.

[8]*Economic Report of the President* (Washington: U.S. Government Printing Office, February 1981), p. 244.

decade, the inflation rate was the worst for any decade in this century. In fact, the rate of inflation was 12 percent in 1974, the highest peacetime rate since after the Civil War. The rate of inflation decreased to less than 6 percent by 1976, but was back to double-digit levels by 1978. By 1980 the misery index, a term used by President Carter during his successful 1976 presidential campaign, was in excess of 20 percent—an unemployment rate of 7.8 percent plus a rate of inflation of 12.4 percent. Both unemployment and inflation have a deleterious effect on the American economy—unemployment in terms of a loss of income that can never be regained and inflation in terms of the impact it has on consumer purchasing power, saving, and business investment. In 1979 median family income rose by 11.6 percent over 1978, but the price level increased by 11.3 percent.[9] The purchasing power of the median family rose at an annual average rate of only 0.7 percent in the 1970s.[10]

Explanations for Inflation

It is convenient to find scapegoats for problems, and the Organization of Petroleum Exporting Countries (OPEC), by quadrupling oil prices in 1974, provided and continues to provide the scapegoat for some American politicians and the general public. There is no question that OPEC pricing policies have contributed to inflation, but it might be added that inflation in the United States and other industrial countries caused OPEC to raise its prices originally. So a vicious cycle developed—inflation, oil price increases, more inflation, more price increases. However, OPEC is only a partial explanation of the problem. West Germany, which is far more dependent on OPEC oil than the United States, had a much lower rate of inflation, a higher rate of economic growth, and a lower rate of unemployment than the United States during the 1970s. Evidently there must be other causes of inflation.

One of the prime causes has been the rather inept record of the U.S. federal government in controlling spending. As Table 6-7 indicates, a deficit has existed in the federal budget for every year during the 1970s and has continued in 1980 and 1981. Large deficits were incurred for the 1975–1979 period, as both the Ford and Carter administrations stimulated the economy after the 1975 recession to reduce the rate of unemployment.

Table 6-7 does not reflect the impact these deficits have on the American economy. The federal government, by borrowing mainly from banks and other financial institutions to finance the deficit, has increased the money supply.

---

[9]*Ibid.*, p. 198.
[10]*Ibid.*, p. 202.

TABLE 6-7
FEDERAL BUDGET RECEIPTS AND OUTLAYS
FISCAL YEARS 1970–1980
(billions of dollars)

Fiscal Year	Receipts	Outlays	Deficit
1970	193.7	196.6	− 2.8
1971	188.4	211.4	−23.0
1972	208.6	232.0	−23.4
1973	232.2	247.1	−14.8
1974	264.9	269.6	− 4.7
1975	281.0	326.2	−45.2
1976	300.0	366.4	−66.4
1977	357.8	402.7	−45.0
1978	402.0	450.8	−48.8
1979	466.0	493.6	−27.7
1980	520.0	579.6	−59.6

Source: U.S. Office of Management and Budget, Annual Report for 1981, p. 4.

Government competes with private industry for the supply of loanable funds. There is a constant rollover of the federal debt as it becomes due; thus the government is always in the money market, bidding for loanable funds. This results in a diversion of credit from the private to the public sector. It is easier to borrow than to raise taxes, but borrowing creates the inflationary bias in the economy. But as the rate of inflation increases, the normal response of the Federal Reserve is to reduce the money supply. Interest rates rise as a result of competition for loanable funds. Higher interest rates tend to hurt such crucial sectors as construction and home building. Continuation of deficits in the federal budget simply fuel inflation and do nothing to dampen the expectation of society that prices will continue to rise in the future.

The cartoon character Pogo once said, "We have met the enemy and he is us."[11] Government is supposedly us, giving us what we want or what it thinks we want. Often there is ambivalence in terms of what the public wants—lower taxes and better social services. The idea that solutions can be bought for any problem has encouraged overpromising by government and has inflated the expectations of the governed. A "revolution of rising entitlement" developed in the United States in the last decade which was reflected in an enormous increase in spending on social welfare programs. Experience showed that while some of these programs were worthwhile, others were expensive exercises in futility. Spawned in

---

[11]The syndicated comic strip *Pogo* was drawn by Walt Kelly.

the process were vast new constituencies of government bureaucrats and public beneficiaries whose political clout will make it very difficult to kill programs off even if they are abject failures.

Another contributing factor to inflation is the development of a service economy. An imbalance has developed between the industrial and scientific sector and the human and government services sector in relation to productivity, wage increases, unit costs, and inflation. Wage increases in the industrial and scientific sectors are easier for the economy to absorb because there may be at least some gain in productivity. If wages rise in the automobile industry by 10 percent, unit costs will rise. But labor costs are only a part of the total costs of producing an automobile and may be offset by increases in productivity. The service industry, which has replaced manufacturing as the main employer in the United States, offers no such hope. Labor costs are the major costs in the service industry, amounting to around 70 percent of total costs, and it is difficult to increase productivity significantly without the use of capital inputs.[12] As a result, wage increases which cannot be matched by increased productivity result in an inflationary gap.

International Comparisons of Inflation

Given the recent U.S. experience with inflation, it may be somewhat surprising to learn that our inflation experience compared to other major countries has not been bad. As Table 6-8 indicates, the U.S. average

TABLE 6-8
COMPARATIVE INFLATION RATES
FOR EIGHT MAJOR INDUSTRIAL COUNTRIES

	1960–1973	1973–1980
West Germany	3.3	4.7
United States	3.2	9.1
Canada	3.3	9.3
Japan	6.1	9.6
Sweden	4.7	10.3
France	4.6	10.9
United Kingdom	5.0	16.0
Italy	4.7	16.8

Source: New York Stock Exchange, Office of Economic Research, *U.S. Economic Performance in a Global Perspective* (February 1981), p. 31.

---

[12]U.S. Congress, Joint Economic Committee, *Productivity: The Foundation of Growth*, Staff Study (Washington: U.S. Government Printing Office, November, 1980).

annual rate of inflation (expressed as a percentage increase in consumer price indexes) was the lowest of the eight countries for the period 1960–1973, averaging 3.1 percent. During the 1973–1980 period, the average annual rate of increase in inflation for the United States was 9.1 percent, a rate which was exceeded by all other countries with the exception of West Germany. When both periods are taken into consideration, West Germany ranked first and the United States second. The table does not reflect the individual yearly rate, but only the average inflation rate for each period. The rate of inflation accelerated in 1980. Italy's rate reached 21.2 percent, the United Kingdom's 18.4 percent, Sweden's 13.7 percent; the Unted States' 12.5 percent, France's 12.3 percent, and Canada's 10.0 percent.

EMPLOYMENT AND UNEMPLOYMENT

A low rate of unemployment is another desirable goal of any economy. In fact, government economic policy in most of the advanced industrial countries of the Western world has been to prevent mass unemployment of the type that occurred during the 1930s. Keynesian economic policies that stressed the stimulation of aggregate demand were accepted as an integral part of government policy. To a considerable extent, liberal social policy was associated with the rise of Keynesian economics. Economic growth became tied to various social objectives, the chief of which has become full employment and a steady increase in consumption.

This has meant that the United States and other Western governments have increased spending and run larger budget deficits when unemployment rises; equally, governments have been called upon to increase social expenditures. Some inflation becomes an inevitable concomitant of government full-employment policies. Where workers once feared losing a job, which was a common experience during the Depression, they now expect a job and an ever-rising standard of living, and this puts pressure on the government to deliver.

An inflation-unemployment dilemma began in the United States around the latter part of the 1960s. As inflation increased, so did unemployment. A goal of full employment with price stability was becoming more difficult to achieve. This fact was reflected in the attitudes of various administrations as revealed in the *Economic Report of the President.*[13] In the Kennedy administration, 4 percent unemployment was set as the goal consistent with full employment. There was recognition of

---

[13]Lester C. Thurow, *The Zero-Sum Society* (New York: Basic Books, 1980), p. 73.

the fact that a certain amount of unemployment would always occur for one reason or another.[14] By the time of the Johnson administration, an unemployment rate of 4.5 percent was accepted as a norm for full employment and price stability. By the end of the Ford administration, the *Economic Report of the President* was listing a goal of 5 percent unemployment as being consistent with full employment. During the Carter administration, 6 percent became the implied target for full employment. These changing goals indicate the fact that it has become more difficult to achieve a low level of unemployment and price stability. The trade-off has become higher and higher as the years have passed.

Unemployment Rates for the United States

Table 6-9 presents the average percentage annual rate of unemployment in the United States for the period 1970–1980. These rates, which are by no means comparable to the very high unemployment rates that existed during the Depression, are higher than those rates which pre-

TABLE 6-9
UNEMPLOYMENT RATES IN THE UNITED STATES
BY DEMOGRAPHIC CHARACTERISTICS, 1970–1980

		White		Black	
Year	All Workers	Male	Female	Male	Female
1970	4.9	4.5	5.4	7.3	9.3
1971	5.9	5.4	6.3	9.1	10.8
1972	5.6	5.0	5.9	8.9	11.3
1973	4.9	4.3	5.3	7.6	10.5
1974	5.6	5.0	6.1	9.1	10.7
1975	8.5	7.8	8.6	13.7	14.0
1976	7.7	7.0	7.9	12.7	13.6
1977	7.0	6.2	7.3	12.4	14.0
1978	6.0	5.2	6.2	10.9	13.1
1979	5.8	5.1	5.9	10.3	12.3
1980	7.1	6.3	6.5	13.3	13.1

Source: Economic Report of the President (February 1981), p. 269.

---

[14]There is frictional unemployment which occurs when workers are between jobs, and structural unemployment which occurs when industries decline or become automated. Coal mining is an example of the latter.

vailed during the 1950s and 1960s. Moreover, there is a difference in the rate of unemployment based on such descriptive characteristics as race and sex. Unemployment rates are higher for blacks than for whites. The rate of unemployment is highest for teenagers 16 to 19, with black teenagers more than twice as likely to be unemployed as white teenagers. There is less difference based on sex, with the unemployment rates for males and females, white or black, somewhat similar.

International Comparisons of Unemployment Rates

Table 6-10 compares unemployment rates in eight major industrial countries for two time periods, 1960–1970 and 1970–1980. The rates are adjusted to U.S. concepts and definitions. As the table indicates, the rate of unemployment in the United States was the highest for the countries in both periods, with the exception of Canada. However, the low rate of unemployment in Sweden and West Germany results to a considerable degree from the fact that both countries have a very low rate of population growth. The number of entrants into the Swedish and West German labor forces are almost counterbalanced by the number of workers who retire. The table also does not reflect the increase in unemployment that occurred in all of the countries in 1980 and 1981. In the fall of 1981 the British unemployment rate was 12.2 percent—the highest rate since the Depression. The unemployment rate in France reached 8 percent in the same period. On the other hand, the Japanese unemployment rate was less than 3 percent in 1981, reflecting in part its policy of lifetime employment for many of its workers. The West German rate was around 3

TABLE 6-10

UNEMPLOYMENT RATES FOR EIGHT MAJOR INDUSTRIAL COUNTRIES

	1960–1970	1970–1980
Japan	1.3	1.7
Sweden	1.6	2.0
West Germany	0.7	2.4
Italy	3.2	3.7
France	1.9	4.0
United Kingdom	2.7	4.6
United States	4.8	6.3
Canada	5.1	6.9
Weighted Average	2.7	4.0

Source: New York Stock Exchange, Office of Economic Research, *U.S. Economic Performance in a Global Perspective* (February 1981), p. 45.

percent, but the country can export its foreign workers (*Gastarbeiten*) when times are slack.

THE U.S. ECONOMY IN THE 1980s

The U.S. economy at the beginning of this decade appears to be in a state of paralysis that may or may not be permanent. In fact, the title of the opening chapter in Lester Thurow's book *The Zero-Sum Society* probably sums up the condition of the U.S. economy quite well: "An Economy That No Longer Performs."[15] The economy is stagnant, productivity is low, and inflation is high. There are a number of explanations advanced to explain the condition of the U.S. economy. One explanation places the blame for the poor performance of the economy on a decline in the Protestant work ethic.

Japan outperforms the United States because Japanese workers supposedly work harder and with greater enthusiasm. A more viable explanation is that the Japanese workers do well because they have more modern machinery and plants. The rate of saving in Japan is much higher than it is in the United States. These savings provide the Japanese with the resources needed for capital formation. There is also the belief that U.S. business managers have lost their capacity to manage effectively. They are too preoccupied with short-term goals and avoid risk taking. Finally, special interest groups have come to dominate the decision-making process of the U.S. government. The ability to make decisions collapses into lengthy adversary procedures.

Saving and Investment

Saving is a precondition for investment to take place. There is a direct relationship between saving, investment, productivity, and economic growth. By any measure, the United States lags behind the rest of the industrial world in its ability to make resources available for investment through saving. Gross saving by both the private and public sectors of the U.S. economy is a smaller percentage of gross domestic product than it is for any other major industrial country. The Japanese gross saving rate is more than twice that of the United States, while personal household saving rate by Japanese households is usually three to four times as high. But as Table 6-11 indicates, Japan is not alone in saving more than the United States. The table presents the household saving ratios expressed as a percentage of disposable income for the United States and other

---

[15]Thurow, *op. cit.*, p. 3.

TABLE 6-11
SELECTED SAVINGS RATIOS, UNITED STATES AND OTHER
COUNTRIES, 1965–1969 AND 1970–1976

	Household Saving Ratio		Gross Private Saving Ratio		Gross Saving Ratio	
	1965–69	1970–76	1965–69	1970–76	1965–69	1970–76
Japan	18.6	22.0	29.6	31.7	36.6	37.0
West Germany	12.1	15.8	21.6	21.2	26.4	25.4
France	NA	13.6	NA	20.5	25.2	23.5
Italy	15.7	21.0	22.1	24.3	23.5	22.5
United States	7.4	7.8	16.9	15.8	19.7	17.8
United Kingdom	5.9	8.1	14.5	14.6	19.6	18.5

Source: Board of Governors of the Federal Reserve System, *Public Policy and Capital Formation* (April 1980), p. 67.

major industrial countries for two periods, 1965–1969 and 1970–1976. The table also presents the ratio of total private saving (corporate and household) to gross domestic product, and the ratio of total saving (private and public) to gross domestic product, for the same periods.

There are a number of explanations for the low rate of saving in the United States relative to other countries. Cultural differences may partially explain variations in saving rates among the countries. The United States is a consumer-oriented society in which instant gratification is the norm. The Japanese have traditionally been thrifty. Government policies after World War II and extending up to the present have been designed to encourage saving. The same also holds true for West Germany.

United States tax laws favor consumption at the expense of saving. For example, the United States does not use the value-added tax, which is a major source of government revenue in France, Italy, the United Kingdom, and West Germany. The value-added tax, like any sales tax, tends to inhibit consumption. The taxpayer burden on investment income is higher in the United States than it is in any of the other countries in Table 6-10. In 1980 the average tax on investment income in the United States was 33.5¢ per dollar compared to an average tax on investment income of 14.4¢ per dollar in Japan and 11.8¢ per dollar in West Germany.[16]

---

[16]New York Stock Exchange, Office of Economic Research, *U.S. Economic Performance in a Global Perspective* (February 1981), p. 27. Investment income consists of capital gains, dividends, and interest.

Deficiencies in U.S. Business Management

The premise of an article which appeared in the *Harvard Business Review* in 1980 is that the U.S. business managers are at least in part responsible for the poor performance of the U.S. economy.[17] Too many managers are more interested in short-run profit than in long-term growth. Partly to please stockholders, managers feel it necessary to show continually growing profits, quarter to quarter, at the expense of research and development programs that may not pay off for 8 to 10 years. Also, many executive compensation plans tie bonuses to year-to-year returns.

United States managers are also accused of not being innovative. For example, U.S. auto firms have not had a major innovation since the development of automatic transmission during the 1930s. They wouldn't significantly reduce the size of their cars until after the 1973 oil embargo, which brought small, fuel-efficient cars from Japan to the U.S. domestic market. Business bureaucracy has also been criticized. The bigger the firm, the bigger the bureaucracy: excessive paperwork; committees reviewing committees; institutional caution and delay; and the Parkinson's law effect of superiors creating more subordinates. Some corporate mergers, particularly those of the conglomerate type, may also inhibit innovation.

Interest Group Pluralism

The foundation of any liberal society, as Daniel Bell points out, is a willingness on the part of all groups to compromise private ends for the public interest.[18] There has to be a set of reciprocal obligations between individuals in a group situation to hold the institutions of a society together. In the United States there has been a loss of cohesiveness, resulting from the fragmentation of society into a congeries of special interest groups ranging from environmentalists to the National Rifle Association. There has been a shift from market to political decisions. Everybody organizes and goes out to fight. The result is an increase in conflict and in the politics of confrontation. There is the loss of *civitas,* a spontaneous willingness to obey the law and to respect the rights of others. Each group goes its own way and pursues its own goals, but the interests of society count for little.

Paralysis or lack of nerve can result on the part of the national leadership. When it becomes necessary to take an action that requires a sacrifice, each interest group expects someone else to make it. It is becoming

---

[17]Robert H. Hayes and William Abernathy, "Managing Our Way to Economic Decline," *Harvard Business Review* (July–August 1980), pp. 67–77.

[18]Daniel Bell, *The Cultural Contractions of Capitalism* (New York: Basic Books, 1978), p. 245.

more difficult to live by consensus. Presidents are now measured on the basis of immediate performance, reflecting the immediate-gratification syndrome which pervades U.S. society. One-term presidents have become the norm for the times.

Government Economic Policy: Supply-Side Economics

Supply-side economics has received considerable attention in the early 1980s. The term *supply-side economics* is really a reaction against the *demand-side economics* of John Maynard Keynes, which guided government stabilization policies in most countries since the end of World War II. The Keynesian prescriptions—tax tinkering and government spending to stimulate aggregate demand—became an article of faith in the Western world. Everything worked fine when demand was slack and unemployment was on the increase. But times have changed, and inflation, not unemployment, has become the *bête noire* of Western society. The economic pendulum has swung from underutilization of capacity to an overstraining of resources, and policies designed to stimulate demand simply fire up inflation. Economies have become more complex, and techniques have to be adapted to provide solutions to stagflation—low growth and inflation. One thing that is necessary is an increase in investment in the United States. Investment spending that results in expansion of capital and in increases in productivity will result in increases in the nation's productive capacity.

There is nothing new about supply-side economics. Supply was an important component of 19th-century classical economics, with emphasis placed on increasing total output by concentrating on the quantity and quality of such productive elements as labor, natural resources, physical plant and equipment, and financial capital. This emphasis has been updated, and today supply-side economics is advocated as a solution to the problem of stagflation. Attention is placed on the supply side of the economy, where certain impediments to economic growth have developed.

Foremost among these impediments is a low rate of saving and investment which has retarded capital formation and reduced the growth rate of productivity. The solution, according to the supply-side economists, is to reduce taxes, particularly those taxes that impinge upon saving and investment. Incentive and response logic is at work—cut taxes and saving and investment will increase. Given the right incentives, the free market is better equipped than the government to bring about lower prices and more supplies of what people want and need. Output and productivity will go up and inflation will go down.

The Reagan tax cuts reflect a belief on the administration of the efficacy of supply-side economics. The cuts are designed to favor those persons who make $50,000 or more, for they do the bulk of saving in U.S. society. Saving is supposed to increase and to be channeled into investment. The flow is tax cut → saving → investment → increased productivity, but if the flow is interrupted (if saving does not occur), then the logic of the tax cut is defeated. There is no question but that low productivity, saving, and capital formation are major reasons for the poor performance of the U.S. economy. Measures designed to increase productive capacity and productivity are necessary.

Increases in consumption spending, a mainstay of Keynesian economic policy, do not increase productivity unless the increased consumption spending is a catalyst to more investment spending. But supply-side economics is not limited to tax cuts. The Reagan administration is continuing a process begun by the Carter administration, namely, the dismantling of a plethora of government regulations that generated costs and lowered productivity. Too much attention has been placed on the benefits of regulation, but none was given to costs.

ECONOMIC INEQUALITY: INCOME DISTRIBUTION

The United States is experiencing a period of rapid economic and social change, exacerbated to a considerable degree by inflation. The traditional family unit, headed by one breadwinner who is male, is no longer typical of American society. The family of today is more likely to be headed by a single parent, male or female, or by two breadwinners, male and female. This has had an impact on the economy in terms of an increased demand for various goods and services.

Rising entitlement expectations resulted in an enormous expansion in the demand for services. Because of the pressure of rising entitlements, there has been a constant tendency for government expenditures to increase, requiring more borrowing to pay for services and stimulating more inflation because of an imbalance in productivity. The new "class struggles" of the United States, and for that matter Western society, are less a matter of conflict between management and labor in the enterprise than the push and pull of various organized segments to influence outlays from the national budget.[19] This conflict is all related to the distribution of income, which is an important issue in both market and nonmarket economies.

Trends in Income Distribution

Recent decades have witnessed no real movement toward greater equality in the distribution of income in the United States. There is an

---

[19]*Ibid.*, p. 24.

apparent conflict between the goals of an egalitarian society and the existence of marked income inequality. However, in a market economy there is bound to be inequality because income distribution is based on institutional arrangements, such as the pricing process, that are associated with this type of system. High prices are set on scarce agents of production and low prices on plentiful agents. This explains why engineering graduates make more than liberal arts graduates. In terms of rewards to labor, those persons whose skills are scarce relative to demand enjoy a high level of income, while those persons whose skills are not scarce do not. In a market economy people are supposedly rewarded on the basis of their contribution to marketable output, which, in turn, reflects consumer preferences and income. The implication is that persons whose productivity is low will earn little, regardless of whether the low productivity is attributable to lack of effort, lack of skill, or low demand for the skill.

Table 6-12 presents income distribution in the United States for a 30-year period. The frame of reference is personal income, which includes that part of national income actually received by persons or households and income transfers from government and business. Wages and salaries, rent, interest, and dividends are parts of personal income. The table indicates that there has been little change in the distribution of family income based on quintiles. The lowest fifth of family income recipients received around 5 percent of total income during the period while the highest fifth received around 42 percent.

TABLE 6-12
DISTRIBUTION OF FAMILY INCOME IN THE UNITED STATES
1947–1979
(percent)

	1947	1960	1971	1979
Lowest Quintile	5.0	4.9	5.5	5.3
2nd Quintile	11.9	12.0	11.9	11.7
3rd Quintile	17.0	17.5	17.3	17.2
4th Quintile	23.1	23.6	23.7	24.4
Highest Quintile	43.0	42.0	41.6	41.4

Source: U.S. Bureau of the Census, *Current Population Reports, Consumer Income, 1979*, Series P-68, No. 124 (March 1981), p. 47.

Whether or not this income inequality is desirable is a matter of opinion. Is income inequality necessary for economic growth? It is generally argued that growth is tied to performance. The theme is that the whole incentive structure is based on having income differences. Industrial growth and income distribution are correlated: in order to have the former, it is necessary to have increased financial resources, which are obtained only through higher profits. Moreover, any economy based primarily upon the ownership of private property is bound to create some inequality in the distribution of income.

On the other hand, it may be possible to have economic growth with a more even distribution of income. It is contended that Japan, which has had the most rapid rate of economic growth of all industrial countries, has the most equal distribution of pretax income.[20] On an a priori basis, however, one is tempted to attribute the high rate of Japanese economic growth to various characteristics of their culture rather than to a relatively equal distribution of income.[21] The Japanese growth rate is an integral extension of a century of development, the roots of which can be traced to the emergence of a mercantile class during the latter part of the Tokugawa Shogunate. Growth continued during the Meiji period up to the present, and the basic reasons for it have survived—a pervasive spirit of enterprise that combines the profit motive with economic nationalism.

Demographic Characteristics of U.S. Income Distribution

Political and economic tradition in the United States have focused attention on the rights of the individual—equality of opportunity, voting rights, and support for those individuals who in some sense have fallen below society's norm of acceptability. However, an age of group consciousness has developed, and the United States has become a society of groups, each demanding a larger share of the national economic pie, which has not grown much in recent years. Minorities argue that group parity is a fundamental component of economic justice and that incomes should be distributed on the basis of group parity, not individual parity. Therefore, it is necessary to present a more complete analysis of income distribution based on such social characteristics as sex, race, and age. There are disparities in income distribution that are related to these characteristics. Affirmative action policies represent a demand for government economic policies to focus on eliminating differences in income groups. Equality of result, based on group rights, involves the principle of redress for past wrongs.[22] Income, status, and power are to be distributed on the basis of group representation.

Sex. In 1979 the median income of households headed by a male was $20,140 while the median income of households headed by a female was $8,510. The median income of single men was $13,365; conversely, the

---

[20]Thurow, *op. cit.*, pp. 7–8.
[21]Japan has the lowest rate of welfare expenditures for any industrial country.
[22]John Rawls, *A Theory of Social Justice* (Cambridge, Mass.: Belknap Press, 1971), p. 45.

median income for single women was $10,000.[23] There are several reasons for these differences in income based on sex. A greater percentage of males were in the labor force in 1979. Also, a greater percentage of males worked full time in 1979. A third factor was a greater concentration of males in the higher-paying occupations. For example, well over one-half of all women in the labor force were concentrated in the relatively low-paying clerical and service occupations. On the other hand, men outnumber women by a ratio of 3 to 1 in the management, professional, and technical areas. Finally, long-term comparisons of median income of full-time workers based on the sex classification reveal that in 1947 the median income of women was 59 percent of the median income of men compared to 58 percent in 1979.

Race. In 1979 white household median income was $17,330, while black median household income was $10,220, or 59 percent of white median income. Hispanic median household income was $13,420, or 77 percent of that for white households. The much lower household income for blacks can be explained in part by the high concentration of black households headed by women. About 46 percent of black households were headed by women compared to 25 percent for white and Hispanic households. There is also a difference in income between workers who are single. Single black males had a mean income of $11,320 in 1979 compared to a mean of $15,897 for single white males; single black females had an average income of $8,158 compared to a mean income of $12,095 for single white females.[24]

The differences in income can be explained in part by a greater percentage of blacks in part-time employment. Full-time employment is higher for white males than for black males and higher for white females than for black females. However, the median incomes of both white and black male full-time workers are substantially larger than the median incomes of white and black female full-time workers.

Age. For both men and women, income increases from the early work years and peaks in the age bracket 45–54.[25] For example, the highest average annual income for males with a college education was reached at age 49. After this point was reached, average annual incomes declined for college-educated males. This pattern was also true for college-educated females and for both males and females with high school educations. The pattern holds true for all occupational categories, with the exception of unskilled workers. This in itself does not prove discrimination, for there

[23]U.S. Department of Commerce, Bureau of the Census, *Current Population Reports, Monthly Income of Households in the United States, 1979* (Washington: March 1980), pp. 1–4.

[24]*Ibid.*, p. 4.

[25]*Ibid.*, pp. 38–45.

are a number of factors at work. As family income needs decrease, many men wish to increase their leisure time and are less willing to work overtime. In the case of women over 40, a majority have not participated in the labor force for an extended period of time. Women often break the continuity of their employment to bear and rear children. When there is a return to the labor market it is at a later age, and the general lack of work experience results in a lower wage.

Discrimination

Differences in the distribution of personal income does not in itself prove discrimination. There has to be an allowance for differences in ability and motivation among people. Neither Congress nor the Supreme Court can repeal the human condition that some people can run faster and jump farther than others. Nevertheless, discrimination has to be accepted as one factor responsible for income differences.

In the case of blacks and members of other minority groups, there has been overt discrimination. Blacks have systematically been denied the same educational opportunities as whites over an extended period of time. This fact is reflected in the occupational mix of blacks. The majority are concentrated in the low-pay, low-skill jobs. There has been discrimination in hiring and promotion policies involving minority groups. Many of the differences in the employment status of blacks and other minorities have been due to their inability to obtain jobs commensurate with their training. This inability to some degree can be attributed to the restrictive practices of the trade unions, including union referral arrangements, complex seniority systems, and union shops.

Decisions concerning income distribution comprise one of the most fundamental starting points for any market economy. The question of what constitutes an equitable distribution of income is difficult to answer. It is hard to justify on purely ethical grounds the market economy position that those persons who contribute most to output should receive the most income. Problems arise because individuals and families differ with respect to age distribution, health problems, and many other ways, and therefore have different needs in an objective sense. Unfortunately, there are no accepted ethical standards for determining the degree to which contributions to output should be rewarded, nor are there any accepted economic standards for determining how much effort any individual is capable of making. The end result is that the Western market-oriented countries have accepted the idea that income distribution is much too important to be left solely to market-determined forces. In subsequent chapters, income distribution in other countries will be examined. Comparisons with the United States are made difficult by differences in statistical observation and classification as well as the social dimensions inherent in the concept of income distribution.

SUMMARY

The performance of the U.S. economy in the 1970s was poor in both absolute and relative terms. A number of problems developed: a low rate of economic growth, inflation, unemployment, irreconcilable group problems, and urban decay. A slippage occurred in the economic position of the United States relative to other countries. The rest of the world appeared to be catching up, and Japan was rapidly becoming the leader of the world in many areas of technology. Other countries were introducing new products and improving the process of making old products faster than we were. The political system seemed to lack the capacity to get things done because the politics of confrontation on the part of special interest groups ruled out the politics of compromise. In the international area, the Soviet Union became the military and geopolitical equal of the United States despite a much lower gross national product. Vietnam ended in a defeat, and the perceived weaknesses of the United States led to an embarrassing confrontation with the theocratic government of Iran. All in all, the 1970s will not be remembered in posterity as an American decade.

The 1980s may prove to be a key decade in U.S. history. The United States entered the decade with an economy that did not seem to work. Solutions seemed to be in short supply. One political party took the position that whatever worked for Franklin D. Roosevelt would still work 50 years later, and the other party, or at least its leader, seemed to think that whatever worked for Calvin Coolidge was good for today.

Energy, growth, and inflation are interrelated on many fronts. Major investment decisions have to be made to solve problems of energy and economic growth. The low rate of productivity in the United States has to be improved, and a higher rate of savings is necessary if the United States expects to remain competitive with other countries. The redistribution of income is certain to be a bone of contention during the decade, as groups press for increased entitlements. The degree of economic inequality remains rather high in the United States, but a certain amount of inequality is necessary for saving and capital formation. There is no consensus concerning what constitutes a just distribution of income.

REVIEW QUESTIONS

1. Discuss the relationship between savings and investment.
2. What is supply-side economics?
3. Present a good case against Keynesian economic policy.
4. Do Americans still live better economically than other people?
5. What are some of the factors contributing to inflation in the United States?
6. What are some of the factors contributing to the low rate of productivity in the United States?
7. Why is the level of savings higher in other countries than in the United States?

8. Increased productivity is the key to survival for the American economy during the 1980s. Do you agree?
9. What is the relationship between investment and productivity?
10. Is the United States in the process of decline as a world economic power?

RECOMMENDED READINGS

Bell, Daniel. *The Cultural Contradictions of Capitalism.* New York: Basic Books, 1978.
_____. *The Coming of Post-Industrial Society.* New York: Basic Books, 1976.
Business Week Team. *The Decline of U.S. Power.* Boston: Houghton Mifflin, 1980.
Congress of the United States, Office of Technology Assessment. *U.S. Industrial Competitiveness: A Comparison of Steel, Electronics, and Automobiles.* Washington, 1981.
Friedman, Milton, and Rose Friedman. *Free to Choose.* New York: Harcourt Brace Jovanovich, 1980.
Haberler, Gottfried. *Challenge to a Free Market Economy.* Washington: American Enterprise Institute, 1975.
Hayes, Robert H., and William Abernathy. "Managing Our Way to Economic Decline." *Harvard Business Review.* July–August 1980, pp. 67–77.
Joint Economic Committee, Congress of the United States. *The 1981 Midyear Report: Productivity.* Washington: U.S. Government Printing Office, 1981.
Kristol, Irving. *Two Cheers for Capitalism.* New York: Basic Books, 1978.
Stigler, George. *The Citizen and the State.* Chicago: University of Chicago Press, 1975.
Thurow, Lester C. *The Zero-Sum Society.* New York: Basic Books, 1980.
Servan-Schreiber, Jean-Jacques. *The World Challenge.* New York: Simon and Schuster, 1980.

PART 3
THE MIXED ECONOMIES

7

Mixed Economic Systems

INTRODUCTION

Many comparative economic systems texts tend to classify countries on the basis of *isms—capitalism, communism,* and *fascism.* A set of institutions is defined for each system and various countries are classified as belonging to one system or another. At one time there was certainly a clear-cut line of demarcation between the various systems, but developments in recent years have tended to obfuscate many differences that once existed. "Isms" may well be "wasms," for countries cannot be dumped into a box which is neatly labeled capitalism, socialism, or communism. Pure capitalism and pure socialism do not exist; institutional arrangements of each do.

There is less willingness on the part of Western society to leave all economic decisions to be resolved by the impersonal forces of the market. The idea, once prevalent in a capitalist society, that acting in one's self-interest benefits other members of society is no longer accepted as an article of faith. With large corporations, labor unions, and big government characterizing all advanced industrial countries of the Western world, the capitalist system of the earlier part of this century no longer exist.

Socialism as an economic system represents a distinct departure from the institutions of capitalism. But true socialism also does not exist. In countries that have utilized socialist policies, many vestiges of capitalism have been maintained. Probably the main alteration that has occurred when socialist political parties have come into power is in the distribution of income. One of the most distinctive features of Western society in the 20th century has been a demand for equality. The issue of equality became a question of income disparities between persons and of the role of government in reducing or containing them. This has meant an enormous expansion in income transfers and services on the part of government in all Western societies. Thus, what exists today in Western society is an amalgam of capitalism and socialism, with a set of characteristics that are listed below and also provide the framework for the remainder of the chapter.

Mixed Economic Systems

The term *mixed economic system* can be applied to the Western European countries, Japan, and also to the United States. A mixed economic system combines some of the basic features of capitalism and socialism. There is reliance on the market mechanism to allocate resources, but there is considerable government intervention in the form of economic and social policies. Four countries can be used as prototypes of mixed economic systems: France, Japan, the United Kingdom, and West Germany. But among these four countries, there is considerable variation in the extent and type of government intervention in the economy. In France there is reliance on economic planning, some industries are state-owned, and there is a well-developed welfare state. Conversely, Japan does not have a comprehensive welfare system, most industries are privately owned, and planning is a cooperative arrangement between business and government. Nevertheless, it is possible to identify certain characteristics that are applicable in some degree to the economy of each country.

1. The role of government in economic policy is pervasive. A commitment to full employment dominated economic policy in most Western countries for a period of at least 25 years after the end of World War II. Memories of the mass unemployment of the Depression remained fresh in the minds of Western government policymakers. Fiscal and monetary policies were subverted to the end objective of achieving full employment. Price stability, as an economic goal, was secondary in importance. During the 1970s, serious problems occurred to force at least a partial reevaluation of economic policy. Double-digit inflation and faltering growth rates, caused in part by OPEC oil price increases, focused attention on inflation and growth policies.

In the United Kingdom, the Thatcher government has combined tight money policies with an austerity program of less government spending to reduce inflation and increase productivity. British unemployment increased to 12.2 percent in late 1981, the highest rate since the Depression.[1] Conversely, in France, the Mitterand government adopted different solutions to somewhat similar problems—nationalization of private banks and an increase in social welfare expenditures. In each country, the government is the catalyst regarding economic policy; no longer is either economy left strictly to the forces of the marketplace for correction.

2. There has been the creation of elaborate social welfare programs, which has caused the name *welfare state* to be used in describing the economic and social systems of these countries, particularly the United Kingdom. These programs, which to some extent are a development of the immediate post-World War II period, provide a wide variety of social welfare transfer payments and constitute a sizable part of total government expenditures. With the collapse of the idea that market incomes are determined by impersonal forces beyond human control, Western governments have become heavily involved in altering the distribution of income through the use of transfer payments. Advanced industrial countries, with their delicate social and physical interactions, cannot tolerate extreme deprivation. It would be too easy for those with nothing to lose to disrupt the rest of society.[2]

3. There is a basic reliance on free enterprise and the market system in all four countries. Most industry is privately owned.[3] Facilities for production and distribution remain primarily in the hands of private enterprise. Nevertheless, the government plays an important role in these countries. Control over the budget and credit gives the government enormous leverage over the decisions of business firms. Tax policies are used to influence resource allocation. In all four countries, tax incentives are used to stimulate industrial development. In Japan there is a close working relationship between business and government. However, there is no effort made by the government to subsidize or bail out inefficient firms or industry.[4]

4. There is some reliance on economic planning of the indicative type, particularly in France. Planning, as it is utilized in France, is a system for centrally guiding the whole economy in the direction the planners would like it to go. Supporters of indicative economic planning of the French type contend that it is free from the elements of political

---

[1] *Fortune*, January 11, 1982, p. 72.

[2] A good example is the rioting and destruction of property which occurred in the United Kingdom in the summer of 1981. A major cause of the rioting was the high rate of unemployment that existed among teenagers and minorities.

[3] Even in France, which has gone through recent nationalization of banking and other industries, 82 percent of all industry is still privately owned.

[4] Yoshi Tsurumi, "How to Handle the Next Chrysler," *Fortune*, June 16, 1980, pp. 87–89.

authoritarianism and economic regimentation which are associated with Soviet-type command plans and from the defects of the unplanned, free market economies that existed in the United States and Western Europe prior to World War II.

5. There is some state ownership of industry. In France, the private part of the French banking system was nationalized by the Mitterand government in the fall of 1981. However, the major part of the banking system has been state-owned since 1945, when Charles de Gaulle nationalized it. Much nationalization that occurred in both France and the United Kingdom took place in the period immediately after World War II, for reasons that had little to do with political ideology. The French automotive firm Renault was nationalized by the de Gaulle government because its owners had collaborated with the Nazis.

In the United Kingdom, coal itself, as distinct from coal operations, was nationalized in 1938. The coal industry had a history of problems dating back to the beginning of the 20th century, the Liberal party recommended nationalization in 1919. In 1930 the government imposed by statute a cartel system, giving producers fixed quotas to produce and sell and the power to fix prices. Coal, then, had a history of unemployment, state interference, and cartelization before it was nationalized by the Labour government in 1948.

Before examining the economic systems of France, Japan, the United Kingdom, and West Germany, it is desirable to explore the above characteristics in some detail to provide a frame of reference to be followed. Perhaps the key point that should be remembered in connection with these countries is that although the free market is recognized as the normal mechanism of resource allocation, government plays a very important role in developing economic policy and redistributing incomes. Few subjects are as emotionally charged as how public policy should be used to influence the distribution of income. At issue is the question of how the total income of society is to be divided among its citizens.

ECONOMIC PLANNING

It can be said that the objectives of economic planning are certain general aims of economic policy expressed in qualitative terms: achieving a high rate of economic growth with full employment, achieving price stability and balance of payments equilibrium, improving the relative income difference between rich and poor, industrializing poorer regions, and so on. It is an attempt to harmonize the economic activities of different sectors of society in the interest of optimal economic growth and structural balance.

There are examples of economic plans in the United States history. In the late 18th century, both Alexander Hamilton and Albert Gallatin (secretary of the treasury under President Jefferson) prepared lengthy, detailed, and comprehensive plans for the development of the country. In fact, the rapid economic growth of the United States in the early 19th century may be ascribed largely to Hamilton's foresight and genius for planning. President Kennedy supplied another example of planning in the early 1960s when he established the goal of landing a man on the moon within 10 years. The government aided businesses in developing new technology, a plan was proposed, and the cost estimated in advance.

Economic planning can be classified as *imperative* or *indicative,* with gradations between these two extremes. The former would apply to a centralized macroeconomic plan in an economy dominated by its public sector. The government assumes control and regulation of output, prices, and wages. There is no reliance on the free market to allocate resources. Indicative planning would apply in an economy in which the government indicates a series of goals and either indirectly or directly stimulates certain desired economic activities through the budget, tax and transfer payment policies, and control over the supply of credit and interest rates to accomplish compliance by inducements. The free market, subject to some alterations, is recognized as the normal mechanism of resource allocation.

The Soviet Union and Imperative Planning

The Russian economic plan is an example of imperative economic planning. The planners, as would be true in any country, start with limited resources and must allocate the resources to each economic sector to maintain some kind of balance for the normal production of goods and services needed for the country. Russian economic planning consists of selected physical targets for output, employment, and consumption by sectors and regions. A plan is built around output goals and the expansion in capacity needed for leading industries and their supportive branches and for other sectors of secondary importance. A system of input-output balances is used to derive the various output and employment targets. Plans are drawn up on the basis of directives from the leadership of the Communist Party, which also controls the government. Consumer sovereignty is pretty much disregarded in the Soviet Union, and failure to fulfill the goals which have been defined by the planners redounds to the serious disadvantage of those who are responsible.[5] Needless to say, this leads to playing it safe by state enterprises, with avoidance of innovation.

---

[5]It has been said that a Russian plan is reducible to an input-output table, plus a firing squad, plus a monopoly on propaganda.

France and Indicative Planning

French economic planning is an example of indicative planning.[6] It is much less extreme or coercive than Russian planning, and it is essentially viewed as a set of directives or guidelines which help to guide the planning of private industry as well as the public sector of the economy. Nevertheless, there is a certain amount of government intervention in the implementation of planning, which has taken the form of indirect control over credit and taxation to encourage desirable objectives. There exists in France a whole range of measures which enable industries that conform to the plan to be rewarded. There is access to bank credit. There are tax concessions and, within the policy for regional development, subsidies for factories and equipment.

Defects in Economic Planning

Economic planning of the indicative type has been held up by its advocates as a cure-all for the problems of the Western world. However, planning has its defects as well as its virtues. Countries with some form of economic planning have not fared any better than the United States in the areas of employment and inflation, particularly in the latter part of the 1970s and the early 1980s.[7] Forecasting, which is supposed to be easier when economic planning is involved, has not been that successful. Even in Japan's carefully monitored economy, forecasting has had a poor record of success. It has proven to be quite difficult to predict variables in the Japanese private sector for a protracted time span, say, more than six months to a year. Random shocks in the world economy can throw off even the best of forecasts.

The merit of planning lies in the identification of problems that lie ahead, thus facilitating the taking of corrective measures. The U.S. energy problem provides an example. Even though the problem developed in 1973 with the Arab oil embargo, little has been done to formulate plans to develop new sources of energy.

FISCAL AND MONETARY POLICIES

Government fiscal and monetary policies play an important role in the operations of mixed economic systems. The primary purpose of each

---

[6]The term *indicative* may be a misnomer. Although French planning is not imperative or mandatory, it does attempt to guide the economy in a certain direction, and it does have the machinery to make its preferences effective. The nationalization of private French banks in 1981 will give the state even more control over credit.

[7]The French unemployment rate reached 8 percent in the fall of 1981 and the rate of inflation was around 10 percent. Both rates were comparable to the U.S. rates.

is economic stabilization which has dual goals of controlling tendencies toward inflation or large-scale unemployment. A third objective, which is interrelated, is a desirable rate of economic growth. The last refers to real per capita increases in goods and services over a time period. A high rate of economic growth is reflected in higher living standards. Full employment without economic growth is meaningless. In comparing the efficiency and effectiveness of various economic systems, economic growth is certainly a valid criterion. In the process of influencing price level stability and full employment, fiscal and monetary policies can also be used to influence the rate of economic growth.

Fiscal Policy

On the whole, fiscal policy means the government carries the major responsibility for providing the conditions requisite to economic growth in the Western European countries and Japan. To a considerable extent, this follows from the relatively substantial level of government participation in economic activity which is regarded in the United States as properly the sphere for private action. The term *public investment* would embrace a substantially wider range of economic activities in such countries as France and the United Kingdom than it would in the United States. Because of relatively large government ownership in public utilities, transportation and communication facilities, and many basic industries, expenditure policies in these countries are much more directly involved in the expansion of total productive capacity than is true in the United States. Public investment in the expansion of the capacities of these industries has been pursued vigorously to stimulate employment and economic growth.

Monetary Policy

Monetary policy refers to central bank actions to lessen fluctuations in investment and consumer spending through the regulation and use of the supply of money. The central banks of France, the United Kingdom, and West Germany are state-owned and thus have less autonomy than the Federal Reserve of the United States. The Bank of England enjoys autonomy in determining and guiding monetary policy, but its policies are closely coordinated with those of the government. In West Germany the law of 1957 which created the Deutsche Bundesbank provides that the central bank should keep in line with government economic policy, although the law adds that it should do this so far as it is consistent with its proper duty, which is to safeguard the currency.

As inflation has become the main economic problem in the Western

European countries and Japan, central bank monetary policies have become more important than government fiscal policies. The latter, which are easier to expedite during a period of unemployment, become a political liability during inflation, as both Ronald Reagan and Margaret Thatcher have found out. It is easier to cut taxes than to raise them; conversely, it is harder to cut government expenditures than to increase them.

STATE OWNERSHIP OF INDUSTRY

State ownership of industry is a distinct manifestation of socialism. The reasons for state ownership are perhaps obvious. It is alleged by the socialists that production for profit under a capitalist system leads to social waste and unemployment. Also, certain wants, such as public health and education, are difficult to express in the marketplace and, as a result, are not adequately fulfilled under capitalism. Since profit is the basic entrepreneurial motive in a free enterprise system, social costs—polluted streams, polluted air, and wasted natural resources—are not taken into consideration. There are also certain industries affecting the public interest that are considered by socialists as to be too important to be left in private hands. Banks and railroads are examples. Finally, state ownership of key industries gives the government greater control over the enforcement of fiscal and monetary policies.

For the most part, state ownership of industry in Western Europe has had no relationship to political ideology until the 1981 election of François Mitterand, the Socialist leader, as president of France. In most countries, certain industries have always been operated by government. In France, for example, a mixed system of public and private ownership and control existed before the Franco-Prussian War. The government of the United Kingdom, wishing to coordinate telegraph services with the post office, had the postmaster general take over all telegraph companies in 1869. In 1896 the post office bought all the long-distance telephone lines from private telephone companies, and in 1911 it bought all privately owned telephone properties. In Germany, government ownership of industry predated Bismarck. In Prussia state ownership of mines existed until 1865, when a mining law did away with state operations. Also in Prussia, ownership of the railroads was assumed by the state by 1876, and the other German states soon followed suit.[8] In Japan government con-

---

[8]State control and regulation of industry has always been important in Germany. Under the Nazis all the economic activities in Germany, with the exception of transportation and agriculture, were centralized under the control of an economics minister, and many restrictions were placed on German enterprise.

trol and operation of certain industries dates back to the Meiji Restoration of 1868.

State Ownership of Industry in France

A wave of nationalization took place in the United Kingdom and France in the period immediately following World War II. However, it is necessary to point out that socialism was only one of several factors which were responsible for this development. France emerged from the German occupation a stripped and debilitated economy, desperately short of raw materials, consumer goods, and food supplies. Transportation was paralyzed; industrial production had fallen to 40 percent of the 1938 level; a generalized black market had replaced the usual channels of trade; and an inflated currency threatened to bring the whole economy down in chaos. The view was adopted that, in order to achieve economic recovery, the French government had to play an important role. The immediate postwar years were consequently characterized by a policy of economic *dirigisme* as opposed to a quick return to a liberal or market economy, which was the way that West Germany chose. The policy brought with it some important nationalizations, affecting the gas and electric power industries, almost the whole of coal mining, the Renault motor works, the Bank of France, the four largest deposit banks, and the larger insurance companies.

Renault: A Case Study of State Ownership. Renault is one of the oldest manufacturers of automobiles. The first Renault car was produced in 1898. In 1914 taxis built by Renault carried French soldiers to the First Battle of the Marne. From 1918 to 1939 the company was the largest producer of automobiles in Western Europe. However, Louis Renault, the company's owner, was accused of collaborating with the Nazis during World War II, and as punishment the company was nationalized by the de Gaulle government in 1945. Since that time the company has been owned by the government and run by government appointees.[9] Renault has been run on strictly commercial lines and is expected to pay its own way. It pays taxes and uses the same accounting system as any private company in France. It is France's leading exporter, a factor that has led the government to avoid general interference with managerial decisions. In 1980 its total world sales amounted to $20 billion and its profits were $185 million.[10] It is one of the 25 largest multinational corporations in the world and owns 46 percent of the common stock of the U.S.

---

[9]Representatives of the ministries of industries, economy, defense, and transportation are on the supervisory board.

[10]*Forbes,* July 6, 1981, p. 98.

auto firm American Motors. It also has 20 percent of the stock of Mack Trucks.

State Ownership of Industry in the United Kingdom

When the Labour party came into office in the United Kingdom in 1946, a limited number of industries were brought under state ownership. Coal was one industry that was nationalized. For reasons that have already been pointed out, it is probable that the Conservative party, had it remained in office, would have nationalized the coal industry also. The Bank of England was already in effect a public institution. Its change to nationalized status was hardly more than a change of title. The railroads, nationalized by the Transportation Act, were pretty much subject to government control from the outset.

The nationalization of the British steel industry by the Labour party, however, was a much more specific socialist measure, and it aroused considerable controversy. The industry was nationalized because it was considered desirable for the government to assume control over an industry upon which the British economy was dependent. There was also the belief that there was too much concentration of economic power by a few companies in the industry. Through trade associations, these companies had adopted price fixing and other cartel practices.

British Steel Corporation: A Case Study of State Ownership. The British steel industry was nationalized by the Labour government in 1951, and denationalized by the Conservative government when it came into office in the same year. The industry was renationalized in 1967 by the Labour government, which was once more in office, and the 14 largest companies, accounting for 92 percent of total raw steel output, were merged into the state-owned British Steel Corporation. The government saw the nationalization as the only way to inject large amounts of capital into the industry and also to eliminate obsolete facilities. Unions regarded nationalization as a means to insure job security and high pay for their members.

The end result of nationalization has been a poor performance by the British Steel Corporation. It has lost money in each year from 1976 to 1981. In 1980 it lost $3.8 million, which was covered by the British Treasury. The company cannot compete successfully in the international steel market against Japanese and South Korean steel producers. The number of employees fell from 250,000 in 1971 to 110,000 in 1981, with most pared from the labor force because of low productivity and increasing company losses.[11] Management of British Steel is at the mercy of politics and the unions.

---

[11]*Fortune,* September 21, 1981, p. 92.

INCOME DISTRIBUTION AND SOCIAL WELFARE

Despite Marxist predictions of inevitable collapse, capitalism has shown a surprising ability not only to survive but also to expand and to adapt to the democratic conditions of modern industrialized society which, it must not be forgotten, it has strongly helped to create. One manifestation of this adaption has been the development of what can be called *welfare statism*. Actually, a precursor of the welfare state was the social welfare program developed in Germany in 1883, when Bismark's opposition to socialism and his jealousy of the trade union movement led him to sponsor health insurance and old age insurance. Bismark, a political pragmatist of the first order, realized that social legislation was necessary in order to remove the causes upon which socialism was developing. Another precursor of the modern welfare state was the social welfare program of the Liberal government in the United Kingdom. Developed in 1908, the program included social insurance for health and unemployment, old age pensions, and assistance to low-income workers through the statutory fixing of minimum wages.

The fundamental premise of the welfare state as it has developed in the capitalist countries is that governments must intervene to achieve certain economic and social objectives. In general, the development of the welfare state stems from a dissatisfaction with the distribution of income. Under a purely capitalistic market economy, it was held that market forces would compensate people on the basis of their contributions to total output. However, this idea has been modified because it was easy to recognize the fact that large incomes accrued to some persons, not on the basis of their contributions to total output, but through inherited wealth or through the exercise of other special privileges. Moreover, capricious economic and social changes often worked hardships on the most productive of individuals. The social Darwinist concept of "survival of the fittest" made little sense when a depression caused millions of efficient and productive people to be out of work.

Government Distribution Policies

The public sector of an economy is engaged in two major types of activities, both of which can be measured by the expenditures incurred in carrying them out. One activity involves a government in the provision to its citizens of a broad array of goods and services including expenditures on roads, education, and police protection. These expenditures represent a transfer of resources from the private sector of an economy to the public sector, and they also represent the contribution of the government sector to total gross national product. A measure that can be used to indicate the extent to which Western governments contribute to the national output of goods and services is the ratio of government expenditures on goods and services to gross national product.

The other activity involves the use of transfer payments as an instrument for the redistribution of income, generally with the dual objectives of greater income equality and the provision of some minimum standard of living for everyone. Transfer payments, as distinguished from government expenditures on goods and services, involve only the transfer of income from one group to another and provide no equivalent value in terms of goods and services. Transfer payments in most Western countries have come to include family allowances, old age pensions, accident benefits, and unemployment compensation. Some services, such as free medical care, are normally considered to be direct government expenditures for services which absorb resources the same way as do other expenditures for goods and services.

The economic influence of governments is of paramount importance in the analysis of mixed economic systems. This influence has intensified in all major industrial countries, including the United States, and will be measured in the following chapters by using several criteria:

1. The relationship of government expenditures to gross national product to indicate the extent to which resources have been diverted from private to public use.
2. The relationship of transfer payments to national income to indicate the extent to which the percentage of earned income has been redistributed by government action.
3. The relationship of taxes to gross national product to indicate the extent to which governments have control over economic resources.

Table 7-1 presents government expenditures as a percentage of gross domestic product for selected countries for two time periods, 1973 and 1980. Japan and the United States had the lowest percentage relationship

TABLE 7-1
GOVERNMENT EXPENDITURES AS A PERCENT OF
GROSS DOMESTIC PRODUCT

	1973	1980
Canada	36.0	40.1
France	38.5	46.3
Japan	35.4	31.6
Netherlands	48.1	60.4
Sweden	46.1	63.2
United Kingdom	41.1	44.3
United States	32.0	33.1
West Germany	40.5	46.1

Source: Bank for International Settlements, *Fifty-First Annual Report,* June 1981, p. 24.

of government outlays to gross domestic product, while Sweden and the Netherlands had the highest. Included as expenditures are government expenditures on goods and services and transfer payments.

Resource allocation to the public sector is accomplished by the process of taxation. This means that the cost of public activity is borne by the taxpayers of a nation. Taxation will have an income redistribution effect if various income groups have a different proportion of money income after payment of taxes than they do before. This will occur particularly if the tax system is progressive. However, there are limits to the extent to which progressive taxation can be used, and in France and West Germany the bulk of social welfare expenditures are financed by indirect taxation, in particular the value-added tax. It can be said with respect to countries with mixed economic systems that the growth of social welfare expenditures has brought with it an increase in the dependence of the government on indirect taxation.

Income Distribution and Equality

Condercet and Tocqueville argued that what was distinctive about modern society was a demand for equality. That thrust has continued today, long after it first emerged as a powerful political force. Income redistribution in favor of the lower-income groups has long been a cardinal objective of socialism. While very few socialists would favor complete income equality, recognizing that there are differences in ability and talent, most would favor the elimination of wide income disparities between rich and poor. The socialists object to the concentration of wealth in the hands of a few persons, which leads to considerable income inequality. The rentier class, or "coupon clippers," are looked upon with disdain. The socialists would attempt to correct this unequal distribution of income through the use of progressive income taxes, gift and inheritance taxes, and a wide variety of transfer payments which are designed to raise the incomes of the poor. In Western society, much of this has already occurred, but not to the extent that many socialists would like. The state has become inevitably the arena for the fulfillment of both private and group wants, but there comes a point where demands cannot be easily matched by state revenues.[12]

---

[12]Joseph Schumpeter once wrote as follows: "The fiscal capacity of the state has its limits not only in the sense in which this is self-evident and which would be valid also for a socialist community, but in a much narrower and, for the tax state, more painful sense. If the will of the people demands higher and higher public expenditures, if more and more means are used for purposes for which private individuals have not produced them, if more and more power stands behind this will, and if finally all parts of the people are gripped by entirely new ideas about public property—then the tax state will have run its course and

It is difficult to reach an agreement on what can be considered an optimum distribution of income. Individuals and groups view an economic system from their own positions in society. Unanimity of opinion is therefore impossible, and it is highly doubtful if an agreed-upon concept of optimum income distribution can be achieved.[13] If such is the case, the actual effect of taxes and government expenditures on the distribution of income will not be determined on the basis of a particular theory of optimum distribution, but rather as a result of a struggle between the dominant political forces in a society at a particular moment in time. The results will be strongly modified, of course, by political decisions made in the past. This does not mean that theories will play no role whatever, for each social group must have a rationale for its position.

Some industrial countries display more income inequality than others. Comparisons are made difficult because of all the different aspects inherent in the concept of income distribution. Probably the main bone of contention between capitalism and communism concerns how each system distributes its income. But even among countries which are considered capitalistic and countries considered communistic, there are wide variations in patterns of income distribution. It is also apparent that no one country has a lock on what can be considered a "just" society. Discrimination of one form or another is just as likely to exist, regardless of the country.[14]

Comparisons between countries are also difficult because of differences in statistical observation and classification. Typically, the data used would have to involve the distribution of income before taxes and transfers because government taxes, expenditures on goods and services, and transfer payments alter the distribution of income.

SUMMARY

The four countries that have been discussed in this chapter—France, Japan, the United Kingdom, and West Germany—have mixed economic systems, meaning that

---

society will have to depend on other motive forces for its economy than self-interest." ["The Crisis of the Tax State," *International Economic Papers*, No. 4 (New York: Macmillan, 1954), pp. 5–38.]

[13]Even when arbitrary differences such as class or sexual privileges are eliminated there will be differences in income, status, and authority between persons, differences arising out of talent, motivation, effort, and achievements. And individuals will want to exercise the reward and powers of those achievements. The question of justice arises, as Daniel Bell wrote in *The Coming of Post-Industrial Society* (pp. 9–12), when those on top can convert their authority positions into large discrepant material and social advantages over others.

[14]During the 1970s it was fashionable for various groups in the United States to accuse the country of various forms of discrimination—racism, sexism, and so forth. It was inferred that somehow these and other forms of discrimination did not exist elsewhere. The Soviet Union is probably more guilty of sexism than the United States.

they have elements of both capitalism and socialism. The governments of these countries pursue economic and social policies of participation and intervention to a higher degree than exists in the United States. Although private enterprise is dominant and a market system prevails in all four countries, government participation in economic activity cannot be minimized as an influence and covers several specific areas, which can be summarized as follows:

1. Economic planning, which involves a certain amount of state intervention, is used in varying degrees, ranging from the formal French indicative plan, which is usually set for a four-year period of time, to more informal forecasting and general direction plans.
2. Fiscal and monetary policy measures are an important part of economic policy. These measures have been generally used to maintain a high level of aggregate demand during most of the postwar period; in the 1970s, however, inflation had become the dominant economic problem.
3. State ownership of key industries which can influence the volume of public expenditures is a fact of life. These industries are indeed very large businesses and are often the largest employers in the country.
4. Transfer payments, through the medium of social welfare expenditures, have served to create what can be considered as the "welfare" state. These payments, which are broad and comprehensive in terms of their coverage, have an important impact on income redistribution between and within income groups.

It is assumed that a mixed economic system, through government direction and participation, can ameliorate or eliminate some of the major flaws of a purely capitalistic system, namely, unemployment and economic insecurity, as well as accomplish a high rate of economic growth. Whether this is actually the case is highly problematical. The performance of the British economy over the last three decades has generally been poor, particularly in terms of economic growth. Inflation has become a problem in the Western European countries, and few have given evidence that they can control it. Economic policy measures that worked when unemployment was the only problem are no longer relevant for the times.

REVIEW QUESTIONS

1. How are supplies of productive agents allocated or distributed among industries in mixed economic systems?
2. Discuss the effects of great income inequality on the distribution of goods and services in a capitalistic system.
3. Discuss some of the reasons for the nationalization of industry in the United Kingdom and France.
4. All important economic decisions would be made without reference to price relationships under socialism. Do you agree?
5. The term *mixed economy* is probably more applicable to the economic systems of the Western European countries than the terms *capitalism* and *socialism*. Do you agree?

6. Discuss the role of government with reference to monetary and fiscal policies in a mixed economy.
7. Discuss the importance of economic planning in a mixed economic system.
8. The major flaws of a capitalistic system—unemployment, income inequality, and social waste—have been eliminated in such countries as France and the United Kingdom. Do you agree?
9. Discuss the importance of social welfare expenditures in a mixed economic system.

RECOMMENDED READINGS

Beveridge, William. *Full Employment in a Free Society*. 2nd ed. Atlantic Highlands, N.J.: Humanities Press, 1960.

Dobb, Maurice H. *On Economic Theory and Socialism*. London: Routledge and Kegan Paul, 1965.

Ebenstein, William. *Today's Isms*. 7th ed. Englewood Cliffs, N.J.: Prentice-Hall, 1973.

Friedman, Milton. *Capitalism and Freedom*. Chicago: University of Chicago Press, 1962.

Myrdal, Gunnar. *Beyond the Welfare State*. New Haven: Yale University Press, 1960.

Sweezy, Paul W. *Socialism*. New York: McGraw-Hill, 1949.

Tinbergen, Jan. *Economic Planning*. New Haven: Yale University Press, 1966.

Wright, David M. *Capitalism*. Chicago: Regnery, 1962.

8

France

INTRODUCTION

In May 1981, François Mitterand, a socialist, was elected president of France, and the Socialist Party gained control of the French National Assembly, thus creating a mandate for more government control of the French economy. A shift has been made toward increasing the public share of the public-private resource mix in an economy which has been managed through economic planning by the French government since the end of World War II. The election of President Mitterand was a combination of a number of factors—inflation, unemployment, and general resentment against the rich. Perhaps the most important factor was the general ennui on the part of the French voters when it came to Mitterand's predecessor, Valéry Giscard d'Estaing, and to conservative governments that had ruled France since Charles de Gaulle created the Fifth Republic in 1958.

But regardless of the reasons for the change in governments from conservative to socialist, the fact remains that there will be changes in the economic structure of France away from private enterprise and capitalism. There will be less reliance on the market system and more reliance on state ownership and direction. The government's control over the French economy will be very strong.

The state has nationalized most of the privately owned banks. It will have a monopoly or dominant position in a number of industrial sectors, including practically the whole steel industry, all aluminum production, half of glass production, the whole electronics sector, half of the computer industry, and an important part of the pharmaceutical and metallurgical sectors. Furthermore, the nationalized sector will be the principal customer and supplier of many other industrial sectors.

THE ECONOMIC SYSTEM

The French government participates directly or indirectly in business and industry to a far greater degree than is the case in the United States or West Germany. It controls all the railroads and coal mines and virtually all the electrical power production, and has controlling interest in the airlines. The Bank of France and the four largest deposit banks were controlled by the government before the Mitterand government came to power. A segment of the insurance industry is nationalized. The government has a large interest in the petroleum and natural gas industries, and is involved in the production of motor vehicles and planes. Direct regulation and selective intervention in other industries is also common. Investment plans of major companies are often discussed with government agencies able to help provide financing; and the government controls mergers and other changes in the organization of private firms.

However, state intervention in the French economy is not new. It dates back to the time of Jean Baptiste Colbert (1619–1683), who was finance minister under King Louis XIV. It was Colbert's belief that France could and should be the greatest industrial country of Europe. He developed a policy of supporting national commercial and industrial interests by governmental means. To promote foreign trade, industries were created out of state funds. He also fostered mercantilism, the theory of national economy which held that commerce should be regulated so as to secure a favorable balance of trade, thus building up the store of precious metals within a country. A canal was dug from the Bay of Biscay to the Mediterranean to improve the flow of trade between the different areas of France, while the highway system was made into the best in Europe. The greater part of the country became a customs-free area within which trade could flow freely.

The Industrial Revolution, for the most part, largely bypassed France. Through the end of the last century, France was primarily an agricultural country, with the *petit bourgeoisie* or small business owners concentrated in the cities. There was an industrial base in northern France, concentrated in the steel, textile, and coal-mining industries, but by no means was France the industrial equal of England or Germany. Although France was a capitalist country, capitalism was on a more limited scale in comparison to the United States, England, and Germany. The state continued to play an important role in the French economy. In industry, the

French railway system was developed by the government, and the telephone system was made a government monopoly in 1889.

World War II and Nationalization of Industry

An increase in government ownership of industry resulted from a series of nationalizations that occurred immediately after World War II, The Bank of France, the four largest deposit banks, 34 insurance companies, the electric and gas industries, the coal mines, Air France, and one automobile company were nationalized.[1] There were several reasons for nationalization.

One reason for nationalization was a desire to continue the Popular Front program of 1936, which was an assault on economic institutions that had for decades preserved a hopelessly outmoded capitalism.[2] Manufacturing and agriculture were both protected by high tariffs and import quotas and, in many cases, by subsidies and by producers' agreements allocating production and markets. This had led to a static economy with restrictive competition and little incentive to improve production methods or to experiment with new products. The Depression had created mass unemployment and social unrest in France. The Popular Front sponsored social programs similar to those developed by Franklin D. Roosevelt during the New Deal.

A second reason for nationalization was the need to develop a blueprint for France's future after the war, which called for formal and systematic economic planning that would rehabilitate the war-torn economy and stimulate economic growth. Discussions in France concerning the way in which economic recovery could most quickly be accomplished led to the view that an active role would have to be played by the French government. A policy of economic *dirigisme* was selected as opposed to a quick return to a liberal or market economy, which was the way that West Germany chose. This policy, coupled with the Monnet Plan, which give the government control over investment in industries damaged by the war, could be carried out best by the nationalization of a number of basic industries such as coal.

Nationalization under Mitterand

Socialism, as mentioned previously, represents a departure from the institutions of capitalism. The socialists contend that there are several major flaws in a capitalist system—unemployment, income inequality,

---

[1]The automobile and aircraft companies were nationalized for cooperating with the Germans.

[2]The Popular Front was an amalgam of a number of political groups and was headed by socialist Leon Blum, who became the first socialist president of France.

and social waste. They would amend these flaws by altering some of the capitalist institutions that presumably are responsible for them. There would be more public ownership of industries considered vital to the national interest. Income distribution would become more of a public function, and income disparities between haves and have-nots would be reduced through progressive income taxation and through transfer payments designed to raise the incomes of the poor.

Great emphasis would be placed on social welfare measures—medical care, family allowances, and retirement benefits. Decisions concerning the kinds and quantities of goods to produce, the allocation of available productive factors to various industries and enterprises, and the distribution of resources between consumption and capital formation would be made by the government through some form of planning and through greater control over the allocation of credit. There also would be at least a major modification of private profit making.

Industry. With this as a blueprint, it is easier to follow the objectives of the new socialist government of President Mitterand. On October 26, 1981, the French General Assembly approved measures designed to restructure industry and banking. Five industrial groups will come under full state control. They are the Companie Générale d'Electricité, Saint Gobain (glass and chemicals), Pechiney-Ugine-Kuhlmann (aluminum and chemicals), Rhone-Poulenc (pharmaceuticals), and Thomson-Brandt (electronics and arms). Two other companies are being nationalized, but not entirely: the Dassault aviation firm is to have 51 percent state ownership, as is the arms division of Matra. The USINOR and SACILOR steel firms will be nationalized by a simple conversion of large state credits into shares. The French government also plans to take over the holdings of two U.S.-based companies, ITT and Honeywell.

Table 8-1 presents the financial size of major French companies that will be nationalized by the French government. Also included are firms

---

TABLE 8-1

MAJOR COMPANIES OWNED BY THE FRENCH GOVERNMENT

(millions of dollars in 1980)

Company	Revenues	Assets	Industry
Renault	$18,955	$12,385	Automotive
Elf Aquitaine	18,150	19,935	Energy
Générale d'Electricité	10,400	6,909	Electrical equipment
Saint Gobain	10,291	9,399	Glass, chemicals
Pechiney-Ugine-Kuhlmann	9,018	7,586	Metals
Le Groupe Thomson	8,646	8,174	Electrical equipment
Rhone-Poulenc	7,146	6,573	Chemicals

Source: Forbes, July 6, 1981, pp. 96–97.

that were nationalized in the past—the French auto firm Renault and the petroleum firm Elf-Aquitaine. It is interesting to note that one-half the auto industry, as represented by Peugeot, is not nationalized. Nationalization also raises problems for French holdings in the United States. At issue is whether French investments in the United States will be maintained or managed differently after their French parent companies have been nationalized. There is also the large issue of French government ownership or control of U.S. businesses in a variety of sensitive industry sectors, including energy, natural resources, and defense contracting.

Banking. The banking system before the election of Mitterand was a mixture of public and private ownership. France's four largest banking firms, which control around 60 percent of all deposits in the country, have been state-owned since 1945. The Mitterand government has planned to nationalize most of the privately owned banks, leaving only 7 percent of the nation's bank deposits in the hands of privately owned institutions.[3] The action makes France the only non-Communist country in the world to have credit almost totally under government control. The rationale for state control of credit is the desire on the part of the Mitterand government to restimulate an economy beset by low growth, double-digit inflation, and unemployment. The government, then, is in the position of deciding how credit is to be allocated, a decision which is made in a pure market system by the forces of supply and demand.

Public Finance

French public finance is highly centralized. The national government accounts for about 86 percent of total tax receipts and local governments for the remaining 14 percent. Both national and local governments rely extensively on indirect taxes as revenue sources. In 1980 approximately 72 percent of all national and local government tax receipts came from indirect taxes, and the remaining 28 percent from direct taxes. The most important national tax, the value-added tax, and the most important local tax, the retail sales tax, are indirect taxes. The most important direct taxes, the personal income tax and the corporate income tax, are both national taxes and have no counterpart at the local level. The property tax, which is the major source of tax revenue to local governments in the United States, is not an important source of revenue at the local level in France.

---

[3]*Time*, September 28, 1981, p. 74.

The French Tax System. The tax system in France has several characteristics which tend to be somewhat different from the tax systems of
other industrial countries. Greater emphasis is placed on sales taxation in
France than in other advanced industrial countries. The value-added tax
is the keystone of the French tax system and accounts for one-third of the
revenues of the national government.

Tax incentives are used for a variety of purposes—to stimulate scientific research and development, to encourage the modernization of plants
and equipment, to facilitate regional development and the decentralization of the Paris region, to encourage housing construction, and to develop export markets. These tax incentives are available under both the
value-added tax and the income tax.

Another major characteristic of the French tax system is the role of
tax innovation. In the value-added tax, France developed a tax which has
been adopted by many other countries and which has been proposed from
time to time in the United States. Value added is the difference between
the selling price of a product and the costs of the various inputs used by
the enterprise in the course of the manufacturing and distribution
process.

In France, the tax is calculated by applying the tax rate to gross sales
and then crediting all taxes on purchases against the tax due; thus each
enterprise pays a tax only on the difference—the value added. The value-
added tax is normally applied to transactions at every stage in the production and wholesale cycle, with each taxpayer enjoying a tax credit to
ensure that each enterprise is taxed only on the value each adds to the
taxable product. The rates of the value-added tax vary considerably, with
low rates applied to goods regarded as necessities and higher rates applied
to goods regarded as luxuries.

French taxes also include the personal income tax, which is progressive and is levied on income from wages and salaries, dividends and
interest, capital gains, and profits from industrial-commercial activities.
However, the progressivity of the tax is lessened by the *family quotient
system* which allows income to be divided into a certain number of
shares based on the number of dependents in a family. Each adult is
entitled to one share, and each dependent child is entitled to half a share.
The income tax is then levied equally on each share.

Government Expenditures. Total French government expenditures
amounted to 46 percent of gross national product. France has two budgets—the national budget and the social budget. The national budget is
general in nature in that it contains the receipts from basic revenue
sources, such as the value-added tax and the personal income tax, and it
contains the national expenditure, including expenditures on goods and
services, gross capital formation, interest on the public debt, and capital
transfers.

The social budget covers both social security expenditures—old age and disability insurance, medical care, family allowances, and worker's compensation—and outlays for veterans' pensions and miscellaneous welfare payments. The social budget is used because the bulk of French social welfare expenditures is financed, not out of general national revenues, but by special taxes on employers and, to a lesser extent, on employees. These taxes are not paid to the national treasury, but to special social security funds from which the benefits are paid.

There are two separate social welfare systems—a family allowance system and a general social security system. Both systems are comprehensive in terms of coverage. The family allowance system, which is financed by a tax on employers, provides tax-free monthly payments for the second, third, and subsequent children in a family; a special allowance for families with only one wage earner; prenatal and maternity allowances; and, in certain circumstances, a housing allowance. The general social security system provides health insurance, maternity benefits, pension benefits, and old age and survivors benefits. Sickness benefits compensate for the loss of earnings, as well as the medical costs of being sick. In addition, special systems exist for farmworkers, coal miners, railroad workers, public utility employees, seamen, and public employees. There is some intermingling of the general and special systems, with workers receiving benefits from both systems. Total transfer payments from the social welfare system—family allowances and social security—accounted for 22.5 percent of French national income in 1980.[4]

Until the election of François Mitterand, there was little taking from the "classes" and giving to the "masses" taxation in France. The value-added tax, rather than the personal income tax, has been the single most important revenue source. The progressivity of the income tax was reduced through the family quotient system and income splitting; and tax evasion among the French of all social classes was a fact of life. A result was that France had the most unequal distribution of income of all the major Western industrial countries.[5] Conspicuous consumption was the "in" thing at such watering places of the rich as St. Tropez and Cannes. The Mitterand government has raised income, wealth, and inheritance taxes, and has doubled levies on yachts, speedboats, and luxury cars.[6] It remains to be seen whether or not the "soak the rich" tax policies of the Mitterand government will have a deleterious effect on the French economy in terms of investment.

---

[4]"France," *Economic Surveys* (Paris: Organization for Economic Cooperation and Development, May 1981), p. 47.

[5]Malcolm Sawyer and Frank Wasserman, "Income Distribution in OECD Countries," *OECD Economic Outlook*, July 1976, p. 14.

[6]"Bad Times for the Good Life," *Newsweek*, November 30, 1981, pp. 46–47.

The Banking System

France has a comprehensive banking system which is headed by the Bank of France. The system includes three types of banks—commercial banks, investment banks, and medium- and long-term credit banks. Unlike the banking systems of West Germany and the United Kingdom, the French banking system is, with some exceptions, publicly owned. This provides the government with control over the allocation of credit to all sectors of the French economy. Ownership provides the government with direct leverage for the implementation of credit policies which are consonant with the French economic plan.

The Central Bank. The Bank of France was organized by Napoleon Bonaparte in 1800 as a privately owned company. In 1803 it was given a monopoly for note issuance in the Paris area, and in 1848 that monopoly was extended to all of France. With the victory of the Popular Front government of Leon Blum in 1936, legislation was passed which gave the French government the dominant position in the management of the bank. In 1946 the Bank of France was nationalized, the shareholders receiving negotiable government securities in exchange for their stock.

With the nationalization of the Bank of France, the French government was able to assume ultimate control over monetary policy. A National Credit Council was created and given power to regulate the operations of all classes of banks in France, this power being exercised through the Bank of France. Members of the council represent government departments concerned with economic problems and various economic and financial special interest groups. Within the policy framework set by the council, the Bank of France has the responsibility for implementing monetary policy. It utilizes all sorts of credit control measures—changes in the discount rate, the imposition of rediscount ceilings, the control of minimum reserves to be held by the banks in the form of Treasury paper, open market operations, and certain measures of qualitative control. However, the power of the Bank of France to implement monetary policy is circumscribed, to a certain extent, by the existence of specialized credit institutions, which have considerable influence on both the volume of money market demand and the character of the investment program for which financing is sought.

The Commercial Banks. The three largest commercial banks—Banque Nationale de Paris, Crédit Lyonnais, and Société Générale—were nationalized in 1945. The three banks are among the 10 largest commercial banks in the world.[7] These commercial banks operate branch banks

---

[7]*Fortune,* August 11, 1980, p. 202.

throughout France and the world, and they actively compete against each other for the demand and time deposits of the French public. The size of these banks makes it easier to implement the state economic plans and to carry out monetary policy. Nationalization of private banks such as the Crédit Commercial de France by the Mitterand government has increased the extent of state control over commercial banking.[8]

Specialized Credit Institutions. There are in France a number of public and semipublic credit institutions. It is through these institutions that the French government exercises its considerable financial powers to determine the allocation of savings into particular investment channels. They are diverse in that some are banks while others are not. But as a common feature they tend to specialize in one or a few lines of activity. Their funds are made available by grants from savings deposits, bond issues, and the French Treasury. The French Treasury plays a central and dominant role in the French capital market, and it accounts for around 50 percent of savings in France. The Treasury controls the capital market to the extent that no important borrower can have access to funds without its consent. Moreover, control over the financial circuits of the country means that the Treasury has a priority claim on resources. The Treasury is also in the business of lending money through its various credit intermediaries.

The Caisse National de Crédit Agricole. The Crédit Agricole, with assets of over $100 billion, is exceeded in size only by two U.S. banks—Bank America and Citicorp.[9] It is the umbrella organization for 94 regional agricultural banks, in which capacity it receives all of their long-term deposits and assumes the risks on their long-term loans. It is a public institution which is controlled by the Ministry of Agriculture. It receives funds from the Treasury and private depositors and through the issue of bonds in the capital market.

The Crédit National. The main function of this government-owned institution is the provision to private industry of a part of the funds from the national budget for investment purposes. The Treasury retains the right to restrain its borrowing and lending activity directly. It makes several types of loans, all of which are made at subsidized rates of interest. These loans go to specially favored economic sectors, particularly exports and energy, at an interest subsidy of 2 to 3 percent.[10] Loans are also made to small business firms.

---

[8]French banks in which foreign investors have a joint interest apparently have escaped nationalization.

[9]*Fortune*, April 15, 1981, p. 55.

[10]Jacques Melitz, "The French Financial System: Mechanisms and Propositions of Reform," paper presented to the Conference on the Political Economy of France, American Enterprise Institute, Washington, May 29–31, 1980.

The Caisse de Dépots. This state-owned institution manages the funds of the social security and postal savings systems. It is a type of intermediary virtually unique to the French banking system, under which the nationwide network of savings banks do no lending of their own. Instead, the Caisse de Dépots receives most of the savings banks' deposits and is responsible for their distribution. It lends a part to local governments and to the Treasury itself to finance the federal deficit. It controls the levers on a wide range of credit policy instruments. With the Bank of France, it controls the marginal cost of money to the banking sector and thus influences interest rates.

Credit Policy. The French financial system is characterized by a small number of very large financial institutions ranging from commercial banks to the French Treasury. Since virtually all credit is channeled through these institutions, monetary and credit policies are easier to expedite. The government can and does influence most aspects of this centralized system. It sets lending priorities for banks, limits their total credit extension, and controls their cost of funds. This control is the key enabling influence for the implementation of French industrial policy. The existence of a small number of lending institutions makes it easier to allocate credit to those industries claiming the highest priority in the French economic plan.[11] Even closer state control is envisioned by the Mitterand government.

Labor-Management Relations

The French trade union movement is dominated by several large labor confederations which, although ideologically different, are united in a general unwillingness to accept the basic institutions of capitalism. The largest trade union confederation is the Confederation Générale du Travail (CGT), which is Communist-led and has a membership of 1.5 million workers. It is militant in philosophy and activity and supports the French Communist party. The CGT is divided into departmental unions and industrial federations. To be affiliated with the CGT, each union must first join a departmental union which brings together all unions of a region, regardless of their trade. Other important unions are the Confederation Française Democratique du Travail (CFDT) and the Force Ouvriere (CGT-FO), both of which support the Socialist party.

Employers are also organized into associations. The most important employers federation is the Conseil National du Patronat Française (National Council of French Employers). It consists of some 170 trade asso-

---

[11]U.S. Congress, Joint Economic Committee, *Monetary Policy, Selective Credit Policy, and Industrial Policy in France, Britain, West Germany, and Sweden,* 97th Congress, 1st Session (Washington: U.S. Government Printing Office, 1981), p. 35.

ciations and three major federations. The trade associations represent their members in the negotiation of collective agreements. Another employer's association is the Center des Jeunes Patrons. This association supports government economic planning, maintenance of full-employment policies, and participative labor-management relations.

Given the rather diverse political views of labor and management, relations between the two groups have not exactly been harmonious. Labor-management agreements have tended to transcend the normal areas of wage demands and working conditions. Profit-sharing and works councils have also entered into the bargaining process. It is in the works council where plant managers and the elected officials of all the employees sit together and express their views. Several unions may represent the workers in a particular plant. This means that management must face different unions, acting through different channels. The situation is much more complex and ambiguous than in other countries, where management usually faces only one union and handles problems with this union through collective bargaining.

Since most unions supported the election of François Mitterand, it can be expected that unions will gain in terms of political influence. The Mitterand government has proposed a 35-hour work week, an increase in the minimum wage, increases in social welfare benefits, and changes in profit-sharing plans of employers. One potential source of conflict is between the objectives of Mitterand and his Socialist party and the Communist-led trade unions. Mitterand, who is outspoken in his opposition to Russian-style communism, will have to balance deep differences between the various factions who supported him for election.[12] Among the most intransigent of these factions are the Communist trade unions.

Government and Business

State intervention in the economy is not just a recent occurrence in France. It dates back many centuries and has come to be accepted as a permanent feature of the French economy. Public policies in France have included both protection and promotion of key industrial sectors through a wide variety of mechanisms, including financial subsidies of many types, price controls, encouragement of mergers to increase the size and market power of French-owned corporations, export promotion, and facilitation of inward flows of technology in industries such as computers, semiconductors, and aerospace.[13] In addition, there is considerable gov-

---

[12]Mitterand, more than any Western European leader, has been consistent in supporting the positions of President Reagan against the Soviet Union.

[13]Joseph Zysman, *Political Strategies for Industrial Order: State, Market, and Industry in France* (Berkeley: University of California Press, 1977), pp. 59–67.

ernment ownership in the French economy, and this has been increased by the Mitterand government. In fact, the sharp distinction between public and private sectors of countries such as the United States and Japan has never existed in France. The French government is highly centralized with an elite bureaucracy that has considerable autonomy in shaping industrial policy that affects both nationalized and private industries. Although a variety of government agencies influence policy making, much of the power resides in the state-owned financial institutions. Thus, government is very much a part of business.

Some specific government control devices are discussed below. They include public investment both in the nationalized sector of the economy and into officially approved private channels, compulsory profit sharing, taxes and subsidies, and price controls.

The Nationalized Industries. Nationalization of important sectors of the economy has given the government control over the prices and products of key industries. It has also given the government considerable control over the allocation of credit through the public lending institutions which channel savings into favored sectors of the economy. A shortage of capital after World War II gave the government considerable leverage in the manipulation of credit to influence business decisions.

The nationalized industries function for the most part under the nominal control of public boards on which representatives of labor, management, and the customers of the enterprise in question are represented. In practice, however, the government has retained a strong hand through its authority to appoint the general managers, whose powers have increased at the expense of the public boards. More and more basic policy is determined by the ministries under whose jurisdiction the nationalized industries fall, and in some cases by interministerial committees. Basic decisions with respect to prices, costs, and investment have become the responsibility of various government agencies.

The nationalized industries have been operated within the framework of a number of objectives, the principal of which have been the raising of production to meet certain economic goals, the implementing of a large-scale modernization program to expand capacity and raise productivity, the lowering of industrial costs, the subsidizing of various economic and social groups, the improving of working conditions and labor relations, and the achieving of financial balance in the accounts of the nationalized enterprises.

Compulsory Profit Sharing. Aside from the nationalized industries, the interference of the French government in business is considerable. For example, in January 1968, the government established an obligatory profit-sharing plan affecting the employees of all private enterprises in France employing more than 100 persons. The workers' share of profits is calculated on the percentage contributed by labor to the total value added by the enterprise. Prior to calculating the amount of profits which are to be distributed to the workers, however, enterprises are permitted to deduct from taxable profits the corporate income tax as well as a 5 percent return on invested capital, including legal reserves. Employers and employees are supposed to form company works committees to select the method by which profits are distributed.

Monetary and Fiscal Devices. The French government has been very active in the use of monetary and fiscal devices which are designed to foster investment and influence regional development. Regional development is a fundamental goal of French economic policy, and many tax incentives are provided to industry to encourage industrial decentralization. Special grants are provided to firms that locate in regions that have below average incomes. Exemptions from local business taxes and special depreciation provisions are also provided. The government has also used tax incentives to encourage corporate mergers.

Price Controls. Direct price controls have been used extensively since the end of the war. Three separate systems of controls were established in 1945 and form the basis of current controls: *liberté totale,* in which industries are subject to no price controls or in which the price of a product is free of control through several stages of production; *liberté surveillée,* in which industries are subject to direct price controls fixed by the government; and *liberté controlée,* in which producers or distributors may set or change prices but are required to explain to the government the reasons for their decisions. The price control authorities may accept or reject their reasons, and in either case firms must delay price changes for a 15-day examination period.

Recourse to price controls has varied considerably in the postwar period. The trend, however, has been toward the relaxation of controls. Price controls were dropped in 1976. But both price controls and wage guidelines were imposed again in late 1981 by the Mitterand government in an attempt to slow inflation.

Economic Planning

There was a time when French economic planning received considerable attention in Western countries. It was regarded as a middle-ground approach between an unplanned, free market capitalist system and an imperative, or directive, planned economic system.[14] The worst evils of each system were presumably eliminated by French planning, which provided a series of blueprints for the economy to follow over a specific

---

[14]Stephen Cohen, *Modern Capitalist Planning: The French Model* (Berkeley: University of California Press, 1977), pp. 7–27.

period of time. There was no element of overt coercion, but the government could influence the allocation of resources into areas that were in conformance with the objectives of the plan. Priorities were set in the plan, thus providing business firms with a frame of reference in terms of investment decisions. There also developed the belief that economic planning was responsible for the above average postwar rate of economic growth in France.

However, in succeeding decades following the end of World War II, French economic planning began to become less important. By the 1970s indicative planning as originally conceived had been largely abandoned—in part a victim of the increasing complexity of the expanding French economy and in part because of its openness to international market interferences. Planning has survived, however, and may well regain influence as the focal point of the decision-making process of the Socialist government. For one thing, the institutions that were set up to facilitate economic planning have equipped the government with the tools for regulating the economy and promoting economic growth. The gamut of French industry, ranging from aerospace to steel, have all benefited from state support and a state-created environment of steadily increasing demand. The French planners also have established over time a series of specialized credit institutions to ensure the access of priority industries to credit and to direct subsidies from the French Treasury. The Socialists, who believe in a strong government role in the French economy, have inherited the planning mechanism with its institutions that have already expedited state control of the economy.

The instruments through which planning has been expedited since its inception are simple and direct. The state spends money, the state lends money, and the state owns and operates major enterprises in both the infrastructure and the final goods manufacturing sectors. Thus, it is desirable to examine the development of French ecomomic planning from its inception after World War II, keeping in mind that planning was a part of a policy of economic *dirigisme* which began with the Monnet Plan and started to decline in importance under the governments of Georges Pompidou and Valéry Giscard d'Estaing.

Development of French Planning. The formation of the Popular Front government under Socialist Premier Leon Blum marked the first phase of the development of economic planning in France in that it extended the responsibility of the government more deeply than ever before into the economy. The Popular Front nationalized the armament industry, introduced a graduated income tax, and institutionalized a government protected system of collective bargaining.

In 1944 the National Council of the Resistance produced a plan for France's future which called for the nationalization of primary resources and energy, state control of banks and insurance, and the participation of labor in industrial management. Most of the nationalization measures were formalized following World War II.

Formal economic planning occurred with the creation of the Commissariat Général au Plan in 1946. The Monnet Plan, or "First French Plan," was developed with the objective of reconstructuring six basic areas of the French economy—coal, electricity, steel, cement, transportation, and agricultural equipment. Its primary objectives were set out in terms of the growth in capacity and output needed in these sectors. The corresponding investments were, in large part, financed out of funds provided by the Treasury. Controls were placed over new capital issues and over the distribution of medium- and long-term credit. Priority allocations of raw materials, building permits, and permits to install new equipment were also used in order to channel production and investment in the desired direction.

Altogether, seven plans have been completed, with an eighth in progress. The First Plan was designed to develop basic sectors of the economy which would exert a motive force on all economic sectors. The state, through the First Plan, achieved a dominant influence over the direction of investment. The First Plan covered the period from 1947 to 1953.

Less authoritarian, or directive, methods were used by the French government in succeeding plans. The First Plan was of necessity an imposed reconstruction of the French economy. By the early 1950s, however, the worst scarcities had been eliminated and direct controls—allocations of goods and wage and price controls—moderated considerably.

The Second French Plan (1954–1957) differed from the First Plan in that it applied to the entire economy rather than to a few basic sectors. The objectives of the Second Plan were improving productivity in the agricultural sector of the economy, modernizing processing industries, constructing housing, upgrading the less developed areas of the country to the level of more prosperous areas, and developing export markets.

The Third Plan (1958–1961) had as a general goal a high rate of economic expansion—a 20 percent growth rate in four years—with monetary stability and balanced foreign payments. Its objectives were also similar to those for the Second Plan. In 1958 the franc was devalued in an attempt to achieve a more favorable balance of foreign payments—a move which proved successful.

The Fourth Plan (1962–1965) included social as well as economic objectives. Social action was taken in support of the less favored sections of the population—farmers, the aged, low-income workers, and students. This was accomplished by increasing subsidies and allowances to students, implementing a guaranteed minimum wage to aid low-income workers, improving welfare benefits to the aged, and increasing loans and price supports to farmers.

Other objectives included attaining a 24 percent increase in gross domestic output, full employment of the labor force, increasing exports and a favorable balance of payments, and increasing the level of fixed gross investment to 22 percent of disposable income.

The Fifth Plan (1966–1970) ran for five years instead of four as in the three preceding plans. There were two innovations in the Fifth Plan. For the first time in the development of French planning, an incomes policy was adopted. The objective of the incomes policy was to develop goals for distribution of increases in national income among income groups. Under the incomes policy, average annual increases in incomes, in real terms, were planned over the five-year period of the plan. The second innovation was the adoption of a warning system to identify inflationary or deflationary trends in time to take remedial action. The plan also contained social and economic goals which were to be attained during the planning period.

The Sixth Plan (1971–1975) placed emphasis on attaining a computer industry which would achieve technological parity with the U.S. computer industry.[15] A variety of policy instruments, including fiscal incentives, manpower training, and market forces were coordinated in order to support the industry. The plan also gave priority to the aerospace industry. Another strategy of the plan was to rely upon a rapid expansion of industrial products—a consequence and a condition of diversification and fast development of the industrial sector. The plan aimed at an annual increase of 2.5 percent in the general price level, but fell far short of this goal because of the Arab oil embargo. For social investment, the main one was that which concerned job training. An objective was to double postschool job training between 1970 and 1975.

The Seventh Plan (1976–1980) included a detailed outline for strengthening French science and technology. It was necessary to mitigate the impact of petroleum price increases by conservation and substitution; therefore, a massive acceleration of investment in the available alternative, nuclear power, was required. The development of competitive export sectors was given priority. The plan recommended an increase in employment in the sciences and included proposals for the organization of research. Desirable fields of research and development included the information industries, electronics components, and scientific instrumentation.[16]

The Eighth Plan (1981–1985), as altered by the Mitterand government, has become more target-oriented. One objective of the Mitterand government is a reduction in the work week to 35 hours. Social welfare benefits of all types are to be increased. Credit is to be channeled into

---

[15]Congress of the United States, Office of Technology Assessment, *U.S. Industrial Competitiveness: A Comparison of Steel, Electronics, and Automobiles* (Washington: U.S. Government Printing Office, 1981), p. 195.

[16]Programme 25, *Le VII Plan de development economique et social, 1976–1980* (Paris, 1976), pp. 294–301.

regions removed from the Paris area to promote industrial decentralization. The French aerospace industry, one of the strongest in the world, will be given increased access to credit.[17]

The Mechanics of French Planning. French planning is essentially a forecast of the direction the economy should take over a period of time. The government, in concert with representatives of agriculture, business, and labor, draws up a plan for the future development of the economy. Reliance is placed on input-output tables and national income sector accounts in the development of the plan.

The Commissariat au Plan (Planning Commission) is the administrative agency responsible for the development of the plan. The commission has no power of its own, but prepares the plan, submits it for approval to government authorities, and sees to its implementation once it is approved. It is then responsible to the premier for its actions. It is headed by a commissaire général (director) and has a staff of about 40 planning specialists and 50 executive personnel. A large contribution toward the work of preparing the plan comes from other public or semipublic offices.

At the regional level, there are Regional Economic Development Committees, which are consultative bodies set up in 1965. These committees represent local regions and organizations and are responsible for an analysis of the economic and social impact of the plan in the region they represent.

Three interministerial agencies were created in 1966—the Administrative, the Public Enterprise, and the Private Enterprise committees. These committees were created to supervise the implementation of the plan and to offer solutions for any problem that arose in the administrative, public, or private sector of the economy.

Instruments of French Planning. French economic planning relies on priority allocation of investment funds and on tax incentives to accomplish its implementation, rather than on authoritarian directives or exhortations. Physical restraints are few and are primarily limited to the granting of permits which are required for opening new petroleum refineries or expanding old ones. Special installation permits are required for new plants and plant extensions of more than a certain size in the Paris area.

Credit Allocation. Allocation of credit is an important instrument of French planning. The Treasury, operating out of several types of budgetary funds, is a major source of funds which finance investment in the public and private sectors of the economy. The major part of these funds is channeled through a special Treasury account called the Fund for Eco-

---

[17]*Quarterly Economic Review of France,* Third Quarter, 1981 (London: Economist Intelligence Unit, 1981), pp. 9–10.

nomic and Social Development. The fund makes three types of loans, which are as follows:

1. Loans to the nationalized enterprises, which are made directly through the Treasury;
2. Loans to basic industries in the private sector, which are made by the fund but with the Crédit National acting as intermediary; and
3. Loans to other industries, which are made by the Crédit National out of funds provided by the Treasury.

Since interest rates are below what the borrower has to pay in the market the fund can see that there is conformity with the objectives of the Plan, both in the nature of investments and the priority of investments.

There are other ways in which investment can be influenced to favor the objectives of the Plan. One is selective control by the Ministry of Finance over all capital issues; another is control by the Planning Commissariat over long-term borrowing from the major semipublic credit institutions—Crédit National, Crédit Foncier, and Crédit Agricole.[18] These public institutions can make long-term loans out of advances from the Fund for Economic and Social Development, from their own resources, and from funds raised in the capital market.

Selectivity in the granting of short-term credit was utilized for the first time in 1963. Although the basic reason for the use of selectivity was in connection with a stabilization plan to reduce the inflationary pressures prevalent in the economy, favoritism was shown by the commercial banks to borrowers who intended to follow the objectives of the Fourth Plan, particularly with respect to investment in labor surplus areas. This favoritism represented an attempt by the government to influence investment decisions through the short- and medium-term lending policies of the commercial banks.[19] Favorable consideration was also to be shown to borrowers who intended to finance investments that would reduce costs and prices.

Tax Incentives. A second instrument of French economic planning is the use of tax incentives. These incentives are selective as between one activity which conforms to the aim of the Plan and another which does not.[20] There are several examples of selective tax measures:

---

[18]The Crédit National deals mostly with industrial credit, the Crédit Foncier with real estate credit, and the Crédit Agricole with farm credit.

[19]The commercial banks were asked, not ordered, by the government to pursue a selective lending policy.

[20]The use of tax incentives is not a new phenomenon in France. Its use dates back to the time of Colbert and French mercantilism. It reflects a view that taxation should not be neutral but should be used to achieve certain economic objectives. However, the neutrality aspects of the French tax system considerably outweigh the incentive aspects. Tax incentives are basically confined to regional development, housing construction, exports, and

1. As mentioned previously, incentives are provided under the value-added tax. Special credits under the value-added tax are also provided for the construction of housing.[21]
2. Although dividends are not generally deductible from taxable income in computing the corporate income tax, corporations can make this deduction provided that the proceeds paid for the stock have been used in connection with regional development or plant and equipment modernization plans. Application for deduction must be filed with the Planning Commissariat, and approval or disapproval is given by the Ministry of Finance.
3. A reduction is also given on the transfer tax on land and buildings when the transfer is connected with the program for regional development and industrial decentralization.
4. There is partial relief or total exemption from the business license tax for firms that help promote the Plan's regional development program.

The use of tax incentive devices to hasten the modernization and decentralization of French industry is an essential feature of the French tax system. Tax incentives are used by many European countries to accomplish the same objectives, plan or no plan. It happens to be that modernization and decentralization of industry are objectives of the French Plans. Since this is the case, tax incentives can be considered a legitimate instrument of French planning.

Public Investment. Public investment is also an important instrument of French economic planning. A large part of French gross fixed investment is financed out of public funds. In 1981 total gross fixed investment financed by the French government amounted to about $88 billion. Under the Mitterand government, public investment is expected to increase 23 percent in 1982. Much of this increase in investment will be to industry to finance research and development. There will also be an increase in spending on public job creation projects to reduce unemployment. Part of this investment will be financed by an increase in the deficit in the French budget.

AN APPRAISAL OF THE FRENCH ECONOMY

The performance of the French economy relative to the economies of other major industrial countries has been quite good, particularly during the period 1950 to 1970. It is hard to attribute this performance to the

---

scientific research, and to a considerable degree are automatic in that no government approval is needed.

[21]A shortage of housing is an acute problem in France. Tax incentives are considerable. Since tax credits are available under the value-added tax, this extension meant a reduction in the tax burden on housing construction.

economic plans because numerous factors in addition to economic planning had an impact on the post–World War II development of France. The
French economy had to be rebuilt after the war, and institutional arrangements were altered by the war and by the postwar nationalization of
certain industries. The new institutional arrangements provided the state
with the tools for a comprehensive strategy of promoting growth. French
economic policy as embodied in the economic plans was designed to
facilitate this growth. France had the second highest average growth rate
over the postwar period, and the second highest standard of living among
major European countries by 1970. French growth of real gross national
product averaged 5.6 percent from 1954 to 1970, compared to 5.7 percent
for West Germany and 2.8 percent for the United Kingdom.[22]

During the more immediate period 1974–1980, the performance of
the French economy, as measured by average annual increases in real
gross domestic product, was the best in Western Europe, and was exceeded only by Japan among the world's major industrial countries. However,
when other measures of economic performance—inflation and unemployment—are taken into consideration, the French economy ranked
third behind Japan and West Germany among major industrial countries,
but well ahead of the United States.[23] The prime contributing factor to
the third-place position of the French was the rate of inflation, which
averaged 11 percent annually for the period. The Arab oil embargo of 1973
had a particularly deleterious impact on the French economy. Not only
did the price of oil rise, but to mitigate this increase the French undertook
a massive investment program in alternative energy sources, particularly
nuclear power. Recourse was made to deficit financing to finance state
expenditures in nuclear power. Wages which were indexed to the cost of
living also rose.

There are those persons who feel that France has failed to live up to
its potential as a world power.[24] The French political system is a composite of squabbling factions that are often unable to unite toward a
common goal. The victory of François Mitterand can be attributed in part
to the unwillingness of various political groups of the center and right to
unite around the candidacy of Valéry Giscard D'Estaing. In other elections, political groups of the left were also fragmented when it came to
supporting a candidate. This factionalism carries over into the presidency, with Mitterand being criticized by groups that think he has not gone
far enough in nationalizing industry and creating a greater welfare state,
and by other groups that think he has gone too far. There is an abiding

---

[22]*Annual Supplement 1981* (London: Economist Intelligence Unit, December 1981),
pp. 1–3.

[23]*Ibid.*, p. 4.

[24]Alain Peyrefitte, *The Trouble with France* (New York: Knopf, 1981).

cynicism about government that makes stable political leadership almost impossible.

The election of François Mitterand as a Socialist president has brought about a series of changes in France. Certain industries have been nationalized, taxes on the rich have been increased, and welfare expenditures have also been increased. In 1982 the rate of inflation was 10 percent and the unemployment rate was in excess of 8 percent. There is the question of whether Mitterand can deal successfully with the disparate elements among his supporters, who range from Communist trade unions to moderate Socialists. Centralism and bureaucracy, which created problems for previous French governments, remain to be dealt with by the Mitterand government. The competitiveness of the French economy in world markets can deteriorate, particularly if taxes and transfer payments have a deleterious impact upon production.

SUMMARY

More state control of the French economy occurred after the election of a Socialist government in 1981. However, state control is not new in France, dating back to the time of Louis XIV and his finance minister Jean Baptiste Colbert. In late 1981 the Mitterand government implemented plans to nationalize most private banks and a number of large French business firms. Taxes were levied on the rich, and transfer payments were increased for the lower-income groups. The mix of public-private ownership of business was tilted more toward public ownership, but France remains basically a mixed economic system. The French economy depends upon both public and private enterprise, and there is reliance on economic planning. The French Plans indicate directions that the general development of the economy should take but do not indicate special targets that each industry or firm should achieve. Special incentives, including special credit policies, tax incentives, and favorable treatment of exports, are used to stimulate industrial growth according to the plan.

REVIEW QUESTIONS

1. French economic planning can be called indicative rather than imperative. Explain.
2. Discuss the reasons for the postwar nationalization of certain of the French industries.
3. The French government plays an important role in the banking system. Do you agree?
4. The French government can influence the decisions of business firms to invest in several ways. What are these ways?
5. Discuss the policy instruments which are used to implement the French Plans.
6. What is the function of the Bank of France?
7. What are some of the changes the Mitterand Socialist government has made in the French economy?

8. Presidents Reagan and Mitterand have taken diametrically opposite approaches to solve the problems of inflation and economic stagnation. Compare the approaches.

RECOMMENDED READINGS

American Enterprise Institute. *Proceedings of Conference on the Political Economy of France,* Washington, D.C., 1980.

Carré, Jean Jacques. *French Economic Growth,* Palo Alto, Cal.: Stanford University Press, 1975.

Cohen, Stephen S. *Modern Capitalist Planning: The French Experience.* Berkeley, Cal.: University of California Press, 1977.

Economic Assessment Unit. *The Major European Economies, 1980–1985.* London: Economist Intelligence Unit, 1980.

Gray, Phillip & Martin Shaw. *French Politics & Public Policy.* London: F. Pinter, 1980.

Marceau, Jane. *Class & Status in France.* Oxford: Clarendon Press, 1977.

Peyrefitte, Alain. *The Trouble With France.* New York: Alfred A. Knopf, 1981.

Price, Roger. *The Economic Modernization of France.* London: Croom-Helm, 1975.

Zysman, John. *Political Strategies for Industrial Order: State, Market, & Industry in France.* Berkeley, Cal.: University of California Press, 1977.

9

Japan

INTRODUCTION

International economic experts feel that Japan is in the process of replacing the United States as the world's leading industrial power.[1] This feeling was substantiated by motor vehicle production statistics for 1980. The United States was the leading producer of motor vehicles from 1908 to 1979, but in 1980 Japan assumed world leadership. In 1979 the United States produced 11,475,107 vehicles; in 1980 production dropped to 8,011,740 vehicles, a decline of 30 percent in one year.[2] In 1979 Japan produced 9,635,546 vehicles; in 1980 the Japanese produced 11,042,884 vehicles. American television was the world leader in the 1960s, but this field is now dominated by the Japanese. Japanese steel plants have a capacity roughly the same as the United States or almost as much as the entire European Economic Community, but their capacity is the most modern and sophisticated in the world.[3] In shipbuilding, Japan produces shipping tonnage equivalent to that of all Europe and the United States combined.[4] In pianos, hardly a traditional Japanese musical instrument, Japan is competitive in the U.S. market. The Japanese have taken over

---

[1]Ezra F. Vogel, "The Challenge from Japan" (unpublished paper presented at the Conference on U.S. Competitiveness, Harvard University, April 25, 1980).

[2]*Wall Street Journal*, January 26, 1981, p. 1.

[3]Congress of the United States, Office of Technology Assessment, *U.S. Industrial Competitiveness*, July 1981, p. 93.

[4]*Washington Post*, January 11, 1981, p. 2.

world leadership from the Swiss in the production of watches and from the Germans in the production of cameras. In the manufacturing of industrial robots, which facilitate mass production, Japan is the world's leader.[5]

The phenomenal performance of the Japanese economy is even more remarkable when one considers the economic base from which the country has to operate. The land area of Japan is small, the natural resources are limited, and the population is large. Japan is vulnerable to world upheavals because it imports such a high percentage of resources required to meet its energy needs. Dependence on exports and imports is a way of life for the Japanese economy. There has been considerable pressure on foreign reserves to cover a balance-of-payments deficit incurred to pay for the imports necessary to sustain industrial development. Thus, it is imperative for the Japanese to be successful in world competition so that they can earn the foreign reserves necessary to cover their import needs. Government policies encourage industries that can be competitive in international markets.

However, Japan is merely the cutting edge of the spread of industrial technology to other East Asian countries. South Korea, Hong Kong, Taiwan, and Singapore are already acquiring industrial capacity in many areas. In the future, developing countries with low labor costs such as South Korea are likely to be among the stronger international competitors. South Korea, although still a minor producer on the world scale, has quadrupled its output of steel in the period 1976–1980.[6] In fact, South Korea has already taken over some of the Japanese export markets in such areas as steel and television production.

It is difficult to argue with success, and the Japanese economy is the most successful in the world. It is important to examine the factors responsible for the success of Japan. How could a country come back from a zero point in August 1945, when the war ended and the economy was in ruins? Forty percent of the aggregate area of the cities had been destroyed, and urban population had dropped by over half. Industry was at a standstill, and agriculture, short of equipment and personnel, had declined. The per capita annual income was $20, and unemployment was 50 percent of the working population. The economy, with American aid, could go no place but up, but it went up at a rate unprecedented in the Western world. Success can be attributed to a combination of factors which the Japanese have melded together. Japan stands as a model to the world, especially the Third World, for its success transcends its culture and history.

---

[5]"Technology Duel: Japan's Robots March to a Lead over America's," *Wall Street Journal,* November 24, 1981, pp. 1, 24.

[6]Jean-Jacques Servan-Schreiber, *The World Challenge* (New York: Simon and Schuster, 1981), p. 170.

THE ECONOMIC SYSTEM

Japan has an economic philosophy which embraces the basic concepts of a modern capitalistic society. Economic phenomena are permitted free play to the extent that their actions are not inimical to national objectives. Implicit in this philosophy, however, is an element of control by the government over economic activity at whatever point it is considered necessary. Historically, however, there has been a close relationship between government and business in Japan.

An Overview

The Meiji Restoration of 1868 marks the beginning of the development of Japan as a modern industrial nation.[7] In the first years after the Restoration, the most important development in Japan was the development of an atmosphere conducive to economic growth. Fear of conquest by the leading maritime powers of Europe, as well as the United States, caused a deep sense of national emergency among the new leaders of the nation. In order to survive the encroachments of the Western powers, it was felt that Japan, by national policy, had to master the secret of industry. To gain the knowledge necessary to develop industry, Japanese students were sent to study the technology of Western nations, and engineers and technicians from Western nations were temporarily employed in Japan. The Japanese developed an ability to adapt the technology of the West for their own industrial purposes.

The government became a major operation of key industries. The modernization of Japan during the latter part of the last century included the nationalization of key sectors of the economy—the postal service, telephone and telegraph communications, and railways. The government also built and operated iron foundries, shipyards, machine shops, and factories. Tobacco, salt, and camphor became government monopolies. The government also provided technical and financial assistance to private interests in other industries. A financial and monetary base for the economy was provided in 1882 when the Bank of Japan was formed. Although the government was involved in providing the conditions requisite to economic growth and industrial development, private enterprises also flourished and developed during the Restoration.

Role of Private Enterprise. Japanese capitalism was characterized by the development of concentrated economic power in the form of business combines called *zaibatsus*. Each combine consisted of 20 to 30 major

---

[7]The Meiji Restoration of 1868 was called a "restoration" because the powers of government which the Tokugawa Shogunate had usurped were restored to the emperor of Japan, who came to be known posthumously as the Emperor Meiji.

firms, all concentrated around a large bank. These major firms represented each of the important industrial sectors in the economy, so that a group would typically include a shipping company, a steel company, an insurance company, and so forth. Zaibatsu combines were larger than any American corporation and were under the control and management of a few family dynasties. The Mitsui combine, for example, employed 1,800,000 workers prior to World War II, and Mitsubishi employed 1,000,000 workers. There was a working relationship between the zaibatsus and the Japanese government in that the latter, through military force or otherwise, provided penetration of new markets.

With the defeat and subsequent occupation of Japan in 1945 came the problems of reform and reorganization of the economy. A new constitution, which incorporated Western principles of democratic parliamentary government, was promulgated in November 1946. The dissolution of the zaibatsu into a number of independent business enterprises was one part of American occupation policy. This policy, in effect, retarded postwar industrial recovery, for it diluted the base upon which the prewar economy had been built. However, the zaibatsu combines have regrouped and form much of the economic base of Japan today. Japanese corporations are among the world's largest, and many are engaged in a wide variety of business activities.

However, Japan is also characterized as having a *dual economy.* Around each major business firm is a number of satellite companies. These satellite companies, which are often small, family-owned operations employing up to 100 workers, are important to the Japanese economy for the reason that there is a widespread practice of subcontracting on the part of large business firms.[8] They typically manufacture a subassembly or provide a service sold only to their major customer. The relationship between satellite companies and their major customer constitutes a bilateral monopoly, in which the satellite has only one customer for its product and the major firm has only one supplier for each of its inputs. The satellites are not considered a part of the main zaibatsu group and do not enjoy the same financial protection afforded to major business firms.[9]

Role of the Japanese Government. The Japanese government plays a very important role in the economy. There is extensive reliance upon fiscal and monetary policies to promote economic growth. Special tax incentives are used to promote a high rate of saving, investment, and exports. Tax policy is used to achieve specific policy objectives. For example, there are special tax incentives to promote the introduction of new products and technology. Probably most important of all is a close working relationship between government and business in Japan. This relation-

---

[8]William Ouchi, *Theory Z* (Reading, Mass.: Addison-Wesley, 1981), p. 18.
[9]*Ibid.,* p. 25.

ship extends back to the Meiji Restoration and is based to some extent on the realization that since Japan has few natural resources, there is a need to reach some consensus over resource allocation. Government and business leaders attempt to decide on policy objectives that will promote the national interests as opposed to the parochial interests of special interest groups.[10] An effort is made by business and government leaders to informally gather information, develop a common perspective, and thus lay the groundwork for policy before final decisions are made.

Although economic planning exists in Japan, it is indicative rather than imperative. The economic plans, as developed by the government, serve as guidance for public and private decisions. The Ministry of International Trade and Industry (MITI), which is directly responsible for industrial policy in Japan, uses different policies for different industries, and at various stages of development. These sector-specific measures are supplemented by macroeconomic policy and planning carried out by a number of other government agencies, including the Ministry of Finance, the Bank of Japan, the Economic Planning Agency, and the Science and Technology Agency. Fiscal and monetary incentives are used by the government to encourage compliance with the objectives of the economic plan.

Public Finance

One of the factors complicating the whole subject of public finance in Japan is the role that the industrial enterprise plays in the life of the average Japanese worker. It can be said that the enterprise has usurped many of the functions of the welfare state. One important characteristic of many Japanese companies is lifetime employment, which is the rubric under which various facets of Japanese life are integrated.[11] Once hired, a new employee is retained until mandatory retirement at age 55.[12] A number of functions that are normally provided, at least in part, by the public sector are provided by the Japanese enterprise. Such things as free medical care, low-cost housing, and subsidized meals are provided, all of which would count in the income redistribution process. Upon retirement, a company pays each retiree a lump sum separation amounting typically to five or six years' worth of salary. This means that social welfare expenditures in Japan are low in comparison with other countries.

Government expenditures and transfers are handled in the national

---

[10]Peter F. Drucker, "Behind Japan's Success," *Harvard Business Review*, January-February, 1981, pp. 83–90.

[11]Not all Japanese workers are guaranteed lifetime employment. Around 35 percent of the work force has lifetime employment.

[12]Ouchi, *op. cit.*, pp. 17–18.

budget, which consists of general accounts, special accounts, and government agency accounts. General accounts are incorporated into a general accounts budget and include expenditures for education, science and technology, social security, land conservation and development, allocations to local governments, and national defense. Main revenue sources are taxes, monopoly profits, and bond revenues. Special accounts are used for purposes where the government either undertakes specific projects or finances a specific expenditure with a specific revenue. The government agency accounts are for those public corporations which are financed by the government and whose budgets are subject to the approval of the Diet.[13] These agencies are the three public corporations—the Japan Telephone and Telegraph Company, the Japan National Railways, and the Japan Monopoly Corporation; two banks—the Japan Development Bank and the Japan Export-Import Bank; and several other credit institutions, including the Small Business Finance Corporation and the Housing Loan Corporation.

Taxation in Japan. The two most important taxes in the Japanese tax system are the personal and corporate income taxes. In 1980 these taxes accounted for 62 percent of national government revenue obtained from tax sources.[14] The tax rates are altered frequently, for the national government has the authority to alter the rates and base annually and usually does. Annual changes in the tax laws constitute an important part of the government's budgetary policy and are called the "tax cut" policy. Because of a high rate of economic growth, the national government has reduced both the rates of the personal and corporate income taxes almost every year since 1950. Since the income elasticity of both taxes is greater than 1, if tax rates had not been cut, tax revenues would have increased at a much faster rate than national income.

An important characteristic of the Japanese tax system is an enormous number of special tax provisions under which taxes are reduced selectively to accomplish specific national policy objectives. Examples of these objectives and provisions are considered below.

Savings. To stimulate savings, provisions of the personal income tax provide for tax exemption of interest income from small deposits. For example, the annual interest on the first 3 million yen ($13,700) deposited in a Postal Savings account is tax-exempt.[15] In addition, an individual can set up several Postal Savings accounts in the names of family

---

[13]The Diet is Japan's legislative body to which representatives of the political parties are elected.

[14]Ministry of Finance, *An Outline of Japanese Taxes, 1980* (Tokyo, 1980), p. 195.

[15]The yen as of November 1981 exchanged at 210 to $1. The interest on Postal Savings accounts was 6.5 percent. Multiplying 6.5 percent by $13,700 gives tax-free income of $900 a year per account.

members, so that each can get the maximum tax-free interest.[16] Income from dividends and capital gains is subject to a flat rate tax which is less than half the rate of the income tax on ordinary income. These inducements contribute to a savings rate that is the highest in the world.

Investments. Considerable use has been made of accelerated depreciation provisions to stimulate investment. These provisions are selective in their application and apply only to industries designated as contributing to exports or to the modernization of the economy. For example, industrial robots are more widely used in Japan than in any other country in the world. To facilitate use of the robots, the Japanese government permits companies to write off 53 percent of the cost of a robot during the first year of its use.[17] The government also sponsors a number of programs to provide low-cost loans to small and medium-sized companies that want to install robots.

New Products and Technology. There are provisions to promote the introduction of new products and technology. These include exemptions from personal or corporate income taxes from the sale of new products approved by the Ministry of Finance, duty-free importation of certain types of machinery and equipment, and favorable tax treatment of certain royalties and patents.

Exports. There are provisions to stimulate exports. A certain part of income from exports is exempt from the personal and corporate income taxes. Accelerated depreciation privileges are also granted to export industries, provided that income from exports in one year shows a gain over the preceding year.

Government Expenditures. In 1980 total government expenditures of all types amounted to 19 percent of Japanese gross national product, a lower percentage than any other major industrial nation.[18] These expenditures are broken down into two categories—general government consumption expenditures and expenditures on capital formation. General consumption expenditures are evenly divided between the national government and local governments. Japan has had a long tradition of local autonomy, and the importance of local finance in relation to national finance is greater in Japan than it is in the United Kingdom, France, or West Germany.

Expenditures on capital formation are made by the national government and amount to around 10 percent of gross national product. These

---

[16]"Japan's Strategy for the '80s," *Business Week*, December 14, 1981, p. 50.

[17]"Technology Duel," *Wall Street Journal*, November 24, 1981, pp. 1, 24; also *An Outline of Japanese Taxes*, p. 188.

[18]"Survey of Economic Conditions in Japan" (Tokyo: Mitsubishi Economic Research Institute, July 1981), p. 12.

expenditures are made in the *Financial Loan and Investment Program*, which is a separate budget entity. It contains expenditures for capital investments which are to be used over an extended period of time. Items included in the Financial Loan and Investment Program are expenditures for the following: housing, water, and sewage facilities; agriculture and small industries; roads, transportation, and regional development; and key industries and export promotion.

Government expenditures and tax policies have placed more emphasis on the attainment of a high rate of economic growth than on income redistribution. Priority within the budget is given to expenditures that increase capital formation and thus the capacity of the nation to increase its output of goods. A lower priority has been assigned to social welfare expenditures, in part because of the policy of lifetime employment provided by large industrial enterprises. The industrial enterprise is regarded as a family where employees, rather than being hired, are adopted as members of the family, and their participation in it is based on grounds larger than actual contribution in terms of skill. The wage system is not simply compensation for work but is rather a kind of "life income" determined by the employees' ages and family changes. The basic wage often comprises only 50 percent of annual income; the remainder is paid in the form of various allowances and benefits.[19]

Fiscal Policy. Fiscal policy has played an important role in the development of the Japanese economy. Changes in the level of taxation, in expenditures in the government general accounts budget, and in the government financial loan and investment program are the three devices which have been used to affect the level of aggregate demand. Maintenance of a high rate of economic growth, as opposed to income redistribution and the provision of socially desirable goods and services, has been the dominant objective of fiscal policy. However, this emphasis on economic growth can also be recognized as an acceptance of responsibility on the part of government to provide a sustained rate of economic growth, which redounds to the advantage of the Japanese people in the form of a continued increase in the per capita output of goods and services. Government fiscal policy, which has supported a continuous increase in private and public investment, has been conducive to a high rate of economic growth in Japan.

The Banking System

The financial system of Japan can be divided into a number of institutions, with the Bank of Japan forming the nexus of the system. Japanese

---

[19]Ouchi, *op. cit.*, p. 25.

banks may be classified under the headings of ordinary banks, long-term credit banks, and foreign exchange banks. There are also financial institutions which specialize in financing small and medium-sized enterprises and agriculture, forestry, and fisheries. In addition, there are government-owned financial institutions which operate to supplement the functions of the private financial institutions. Included among the government financial institutions are the Japan Development Bank, Postal Savings, the Export-Import Bank of Japan, the Housing Loan Corporation, and the Small Business Finance Corporation. Most of these financial institutions were created after the end of World War II and currently play an important role in the financial operations of the nation.

The largest borrowers of funds in Japan are the corporate business concerns, which dominate investment activities in the country. The biggest source of saving is private individuals who invest their money in Postal Saving accounts. This money, along with government trust and pension funds, is funneled into government lending institutions mentioned above. Large and medium-sized Japanese corporations borrow from private Japanese banks or issue stocks and bonds to raise money; small companies that are usually the subcontractors to the larger ones get most of their loans from the government through the Small Business Finance Corporation.

The Central Bank. The Bank of Japan was established in 1882. Since its establishment, the Bank has always served as the fiscal agent for the government. It provides the government with lending facilities and has also assumed over the years a wide range of activities, including the handling of public receipts and payments, Treasury accounts, government debt, and the buying and selling of foreign exchange.

The Bank of Japan also carries out a wide variety of activities with commercial banks and other institutions. These include receiving deposits, making loans, discounting bills and notes, and buying and selling Treasury bills. A lack of financial capital has caused commercial banks to turn to the Bank of Japan as a source of funds. Since the commercial banks are dependent upon the central bank for credit, discount policy has played an important and effective role in maintaining general economic stability. A restriction of central bank credit has an immediate and significant impact on commercial bank policy.

Commercial Banks. The commercial banks are privately owned and are divided into two types—city banks and local banks. City banks are located in large cities and operate on a nationwide scale with a network of branch offices widely distributed throughout the country. Since the Meiji period, these banks have played a principal role in supplying the funds necessary for the rapid expansion of the economy. City bank loans, for the most part, are granted to large-scale enterprises; however, in recent years they have become more oriented toward the consumer mass market and have gone into the area of consumer credit. The city banks account for one-third of the total fund resources of all financial institutions, public and private, in Japan and account for 58 percent of the deposits of all banks.[20] There are 15 city banks in Japan.

Local banks are commercial banks conducting business principally in local economic areas. There are 63 local banks, and each is based in a prefecture and extends its operations to neighboring prefectures.[21] Loans to small and medium-sized enterprises make up the greatest part of local bank loans, and time deposits of individuals make up the greatest part of total deposits. Local banks also lend to local public entities and are an important supplier of call loan funds.

In addition to the commercial banks, there are also long-term credit banks and trust banks. To raise funds for loans, they are allowed to issue debentures up to 20 times their combined total of capital and reserves. Trust banks provide long-term funds for investment in equipment. Both the long-term credit banks and the trust banks are privately owned.

Government Financial Institutions. The government itself is engaged in substantial financial activities through the ownership of a number of specialized credit institutions. Funds to support these institutions are obtained from the special counterpart fund in the budget and from individual savings in the form of postal savings, postal annuities, and postal life insurance. These savings and the surplus funds from special budgetary accounts are deposited in a Trust Fund Bureau, which can use these funds for loans to public enterprises and the financial institutions. Loans are also made to the private sector of the economy, particularly to industries that are export-related. However, as a rule, this type of financing is undertaken in cooperation with private lending institutions.

The Export-Import Bank. Through its specialized credit institutions, the government provides capital for long-term industrial development, export financing, and agriculture as a part of its policy for stimulating economic growth in an economy where capital is scarce. The Japan Export-Import Bank provides long-term loans at subsidized interest rates to exporters of Japanese products. For example, loans have been provided for the construction of tankers, textile machinery, and rolling stock. Loans have also been provided for the financing of projects, such as the development of iron ore mines in India and the construction of textile mills in South America. The Bank also provides import financing and debt guarantees to attract foreign capital into Japan. To stimulate economic development in Southeast Asia, the government set up a special account with the Bank and called it the Southeast Asia Development Cooperation

---

[20]Bank of Tokyo, *The Financial System of Japan* (1980), p. 33.
[21]A *prefecture* is an administrative unit which corresponds to a metropolitan area or a province.

Fund. Funds were provided out of the national budget. The fund was eventually transformed into an independent corporation and currently finances long-term investment in Southeast Asia.[22]

Japan Development Bank. Another important government-owned financial institution is the Japan Development Bank. This bank was created in 1951 for the purpose of aiding in the reconstruction of the economy. Most of its loans were originally concentrated in the electric power, shipbuilding, and coal industries. However, in recent years its loans have been channeled into the petrochemical and rubber industries and also into the promotion of regional development, city transportation, and international tourism. The bank provides long-term loans at low interest rates to basic domestic industries. Through its control over investment resources that are in the hands of official financial agencies like the Japan Development Bank, the government is able to exercise some control over national investment and thereby exert some influence with respect to its economic plans.

Other financial institutions directly owned and operated by the government include the Small Business Finance Corporation, which exists for the purpose of supplying long-term loans to small businesses when financing by ordinary financial institutions proves difficult, and the Agriculture, Forestry, and Fisheries Finance Corporation, which provides long-term, low-interest loans for agricultural equipment investment on the part of agricultural cooperatives and individual farming enterprises. Funds for both corporations are obtained from the general accounts (national) budget and from investments in securities and the provision of call loans.[23]

Monetary Policy. The Bank of Japan has three instruments which are used to control the volume of credit and money—bank rate policy, open market operations, and reserve deposit requirements. Bank rate policy involves the lowering or raising of discount rates and interest rates. The alteration of these rates is the most important monetary policy instrument in Japan because city banks rely heavily on loans from the Bank of Japan, and industries, in turn, rely heavily on bank loans. Costs in general and the availability of bank funds are highly responsive to changes in the discount and interest rates on commercial and export trade bills, overdrafts, and general secured loans. In addition, the Bank also can place a lending ceiling for each bank, above which it can impose a penalty rate or refuse to make loans. Open market operations are inhibited by the lack of a well-developed capital market and are not important as an instrument of monetary policy. Legal reserve requirements are far below the standard

---

[22]Bank of Tokyo, *Banking in Modern Japan* (Tokyo, 1980), p. 35.
[23]*Ibid.*, pp. 37–38.

of reserve requirements in other major countries, and manipulation of these requirements by the Bank of Japan is a supplementary instrument of monetary control.

In Japan the function of monetary policy is more circumscribed than that of fiscal policy. In general, monetary policy has been expansionary in order to facilitate a high rate of economic growth. Successive cuts in the official discount rate had brought it down to the all-time low level of 4.25 percent in June 1972. However, in 1974 and 1975 the discount rate was raised to 9 percent because of inflation caused by the oil embargo. After 1975, the discount rate was lowered as the rate of inflation subsided. In 1981, the average Japanese discount rate was 7.5 percent, a relatively high rate compared to previous time periods. The Japanese have relied more on monetary policy in recent years as an antiinflationary device.

Labor-Management Relations

An outstanding feature of Japanese trade unions is that they are usually company unions, organized enterprise by enterprise. The typical Japanese labor union is made up of the employees of a single company or of a single operational unit within a company, regardless of their occupation. The end result is that there are many trade unions in Japan—more then 70,000 in 1980.[24] Approximately one-fourth of the Japanese labor force belongs to trade unions, with each union loosely tied to one of four central labor organizations. The central organizations enjoy little authority over the company unions, which carry on the bargaining with employers. Negotiations between labor and management are mostly conducted within each enterprise; however, there are several points of difference between Japanese labor practices and those practiced in other countries.

Many Japanese firms, in particular the larger ones, provide lifetime employment for their employees. This makes for a very different balance of power between union and management in Japanese firms. The employees know that their future depends on their company's future and that labor work stoppages could hurt their company's competitive position.[25] Since it is difficult to obtain employment by leaving one company for another, the union will rarely press its demands so far as to seriously damage the company. Forcing a company into bankruptcy, for example, would put workers at the mercy of the labor market.

Wages and positions within a company are determined largely on the basis of age and length of service. Japanese companies also provide a

[24]Bureau of Statistics, *Japan Statistical Yearbook*, 1980 (Tokyo: Office of the Prime Minister, 1980), p. 127.

[25]"Japan's Unions Try a New Approach," *Wall Street Journal*, February 18, 1982, p. 28.

number of fringe benefits for their employees. Thus, negotiations between labor and management in Japan are limited primarily to wages. During February through April each year, unions begin what is called the *shunto* or "spring wage struggle" with their respective companies. If there is not mutual agreement, the union may go out on strike. But since there is one union for each company, concerted strike efforts are rare. Unions may also resort to public demonstrations to make the public aware of their demands.[26]

However, this is not to say that labor-management relations are ideal. There is industrial conflict in Japan as evidenced by the frequent wildcat strikes on the government-owned national railways. Worker-days lost by strikes, although much lower than in the United States, are higher than in Sweden or West Germany, and work stoppages are also high in comparison to West Germany and France.[27] With emphasis currently being placed on automation, the potential for labor conflict may well increase in Japan during the 1980s. The failure of successive conservative governments to develop labor-oriented welfare programs in the allocation of national resources also presents a potential for labor unrest.

Japanese employers are also organized into several major confederations, the largest of which is the Federation of Economic Organizations (*Keidanran*). It is made up of financial, industrial, and trading associations and almost all of Japan's largest business firms. Membership in the federation is institutional, and its work is carried out in standing committees. It is interested in national economic planning and the development of the economy. Keidanran wields considerable influence in government economic affairs because many business and political leaders are bound together by a common educational background and family and matrimonial ties. This provides the Japanese with a mechanism for reconciling industrial policy objectives with political and social goals.[28] Also, both business and the nation depend upon export-import exchange to survive.

Government and Business Relations

A combination of free enterprise and government control in Japan dates back to the Meiji Restoration in 1868.[29] The government was active

---

[26]Solomon B. Levine and Koji Taira, "Labor Markets, Trade Unions, and Social Justice: Japanese Failures?" *Japanese Economic Studies* (Spring 1977), pp. 66–95.

[27]Douglas A. Hibbs, "Industrial Conflict in Advanced Industrial Societies," *American Political Science Review*, Vol. 70 (December 1976), pp. 1033–1058.

[28]Ezra Vogel, *Japan as Number One* (Cambridge: Harvard University Press, 1979), pp. 16–33.

[29]However, the Tokugawa Shogunate encouraged the development of Western-style factories to produce iron, coal, armaments, and other products considered militarily essential.

during the Meiji era in introducing Western industrial methods into Japan and also took the lead in promoting the development of industries of strategic importance. Throughout the period from the Russo-Japanese War of 1904 to World War II, responsibility for development and innovation was shared between the government and the large zaibatsu combines. Fundamental shifts took place in government policy during the economic and political crisis of the 1930s. To counteract the effects of the worldwide Great Depression, the government militarists gained the ascendancy in Japan and war appeared inevitable. Government intervention in the economy increased. The electric power industry was nationalized in 1938, and strategic industries were brought under direct government control.

When World War II was over, the American occupation authorities attempted to democratize the Japanese economy by destroying the concentration of economic power which was held by the zaibatsu combines during the period before World War II. Antimonopoly and antitrust decrees which prohibited interlocking directorates, mergers, and undue restrictions of production, prices, and technology were utilized.[30] The whole approach to the dissolution of the zaibatsu combines ran counter to the need for extensive economic planning to rehabilitate the economy, and the antitrust decrees were dropped by 1950. Japanese government policies, particularly with respect to the promotion of exports, favored mergers which resulted in large-scale business operations and the revival of the zaibatsu arrangement. Selective or discriminatory treatment became an integral part of postwar Japanese economic policy. Special financial privileges, subsidies, and low interest rates were used to favor certain industries, certain types of economic activity, or certain groups of firms.

The Ministry of International Trade and Industry. The Ministry of International Trade and Industry (MITI) is probably the most important and powerful government agency in Japan, at least as far as Japanese business is concerned.[31] It is literally responsible for the regulation and guidance of all Japanese business firms. Its crucial role is to decide in broad terms the direction in which each industry should proceed. Although the powers of MITI were reduced somewhat in the late 1970s, at one time it had the power to grant licenses to companies to deal in foreign exchange. Without licenses, companies could neither import raw materials nor export finished goods, so MITI could decide which industries were the most important.

Building a steel industry was one of Japan's most important postwar priorities. MITI encouraged Japanese banks to supply the capital that

---

[30]Jerome B. Cohen, *Japan's Economy in War and Reconstruction* (Minneapolis: University of Minnesota Press, 1949), pp. 429–435.
[31]Drucker, *op. cit.*, p. 83.

purchased equipment and technology from the West, mostly from the United States. Tax incentives, low interest rates, and other forms of financial privileges were also given to the steel industry. When the Japanese steel industry became strong, MITI began to confine its support to a consultative capacity.

In March 1980, MITI published a document which set Japanese priorities for the 1980s.[32] The agency recognized the fact that the Japanese economy was being adversely affected by forces over which it had little control. High energy costs were affecting those industries—steel, aluminum, and coal—that depend upon the importation of oil and coal. Japanese success in exporting automobiles to the United States and Europe had increased the resentment of U.S. and European auto makers and their unions. By 1980 the Japanese had succeeded in capturing almost one-fourth of the U.S. automarket and from 10 to 20 percent of the European auto market, depending on the country. The end result was that restrictions were imposed on U.S. and European imports of Japanese automobiles. Thus, the Japanese plan to base their economic future on the high-technology industries which require far less energy, with the main thrust in semiconductors, communications, and information processing.[33]

Government Savings and Investment. To facilitate the development of high-technology industries, MITI and other government agencies will provide financial aid. As mentioned previously, funds from the national budget are channeled through various lending institutions to help provide industries with the financies necessary for expansion and development. The government and its agencies account for as much as one-fourth of all investment spending in Japan—a high percentage for an economy largely based on private enterprise. In 1981 MITI lent the high-technology industries $500 million in no-interest loans through the Agency of Industrial Science and Technology.[34] The Development Bank of Japan lent the computer and electronics industry an additional $210 million for projects related to some aspect of government policy.[35] Preferred interest rates were given to the high-technology industries.

Figure 9-1 presents the financial relationship between government and industry in Japan. Funds flow from the national budget into many lending accounts. The Japan Development Bank derives most of its financial support from the government-owned Postal Savings system and lends only to company projects that are a part of government policy. It has

---

[32]Ministry of International Trade and Industry, *Vision of Industry in the Eighties* (Tokyo, March 1980).

[33]"Japan's Ominous Chip Victory," *Fortune*, December 14, 1981, pp. 52–57.

[34]"Japan's Strategy for the '80s" *Business Week*, p. 40.

[35]*Ibid.*, p. 41.

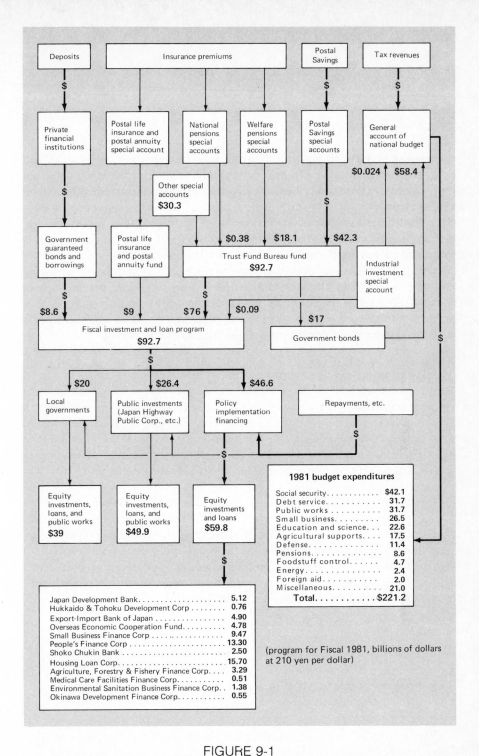

FIGURE 9-1
HOW GOVERNMENT CHANNELS ASSETS INTO JAPANESE INDUSTRY
Reprinted from the December 14, 1981 issue of *Business Week* by special permission, ©
1981 by McGraw-Hill, Inc., New York, NY 10020. All rights reserved.

financed such projects as the commercialization of Sony's Trinitron tube for color television.

Economic Planning

Japanese economic planning is indicative rather than imperative and similar to French planning in that it develops goals for industrial development, social welfare, labor relations, and related major economic and social sectors. Plans, as announced, represent the consensus of not only government, but also of private groups, including business, labor, and the academic community. Each group is expected to fit its self-interest into a framework of national needs, national goals, and national aspirations.[36] This forces Japanese leadership groups to take responsibility for thinking through policies that the national interest requires. The private sector has full knowledge through its government input of any government planning.[37] In the Japanese connotation, planning or plans represent goals which the Japanese government would like to see achieved.

Development of Japanese Planning. Since the end of World War II, there have been several sets of economic plans. The first set of plans was aimed at the reconstruction of the postwar economy. When this was accomplished, a second set of plans was adopted for the purpose of developing a viable economy in the absence of economic assistance from the United States. A third set, including the National Income Doubling Plan and the Economic and Social Development Plan, placed emphasis on economic growth. These sets of plans coincided with the actual stages of postwar economic development.

Japan's Economic Planning Agency designed a Seven-Year Plan (1979–1985) to restructure the economy. The plan concentrates on correcting an imbalance among various sectors of the economy, restructuring older industries, and improving the quality of life. There will be a shift from an economy based primarily on heavy industry to one based on high-technology, knowledge, service, and information industries. Specific goals established in the plan are as follows:[38]

1. Achieve an annual average rate of real economic growth of 5.7 percent through 1985 and to reduce the rate of unemployment to less than 1.7 percent.
2. Stabilize the consumer price index at a level of 5 percent increase annually.

---

[36]Drucker, *op. cit.*, pp. 86–87.

[37]Phillip Caldwell, "The Automobile Crisis and Public Policy," *Harvard Business Review* (January–February 1981), p. 82.

[38]*Economic Planning Agency, Economic and Social Development Plan, 1979–1985* (Tokyo: Japan Times, 1980).

3. Increase expenditures on social overhead capital by at least 100 percent of the amount for the 1979 budget. The ratio of transfer payments to national income is to be increased to 16 percent by 1985.
4. Energy independence, at least as far as oil is concerned, is to be achieved by 1985. Development of alternative sources of energy is a high-priority concern.
5. Government assistance to private research and development is to increase 100 percent during the 1979–1982 period and at a minimum of 10 percent a year for the remainder of the plan period.
6. Movement is to be to energy-efficient industries based on combining scientific computers and data processing. Emphasis will be placed on the development of computers, semiconductors, microprocessors, industrial robots, optic fibers, and bioengineering.[39]

The Mechanics of Japanese Planning. Economic planning is optional on the part of the government and the initiative for it rests with the prime minister. Unlike the French economic plans, which have been usually for four-year periods, Japanese plans do not adhere to a particular time schedule. The plans usually set a goal of long-range economic growth per annum over a base period and provide guiding principles for the accomplishment of various economic and social objectives.

The National Resources Development Law, which was passed in 1950, provided the current framework for economic planning. The formulation of a plan involves the creation of a set of objectives and the collection and analysis of data which lead to the preparation of a formal framework within which the plan is to operate. The Economic Council, which consists of not more than 30 members appointed by the prime minister, is responsible for the development of a plan, and the Economic Planning Agency, which is attached directly to the office of the prime minister, is responsible for the technical work associated with economic planning.

The Economic Council is comprised of key members of the financial community, industry, and government, who are appointed to a two-year term by the prime minister. In addition, a number of experts on technical matters are utilized in the formulation of the plan. There is a General Policy Committee and a number of specialized committees, each of which is concerned with certain areas of the economy, such as agriculture and forestry. Their reports are appended to the draft of the plan, which is sent by the council to the prime minister.

The Economic Planning Agency is responsible for the technical work associated with economic planning. It also has the responsibility for coordinating the principal policies and plans of other executive agencies of the Japanese government, analyzing and measuring national economic

---

[39]Servan-Schreiber, *op. cit.*, pp. 141–145.

resources, and preparing policies and plans concerning the development of electricity resources. It has as its advisory agent the Economic Council.

To carry out its functions, which are not limited exclusively to long-term economic planning, the Economic Planning Agency must work through various executive departments and such agencies as the Bank of Japan, whose support is crucial because it is the center of Japanese financial policy formulation. It is also necessary to work with the Ministry of Finance, because of its control over expenditures and the budget, which affect the successful operation of any plan. Planning policies involving foreign trade, agriculture, transportation, and labor are effectuated through cooperation with the various ministries that are responsible for these activities. However, the Economic Planning Agency does not possess the power of a ministry and can exercise little independent initiative or coordination.

As in the past, government and business have been closely associated in working out national economic policy. From this association, the plans which concern the future of the Japanese economy develop. These plans are more than just estimates of the future, for the government is able through various fiscal devices and through control over various financial institutions such as the Japan Development Bank, to encourage or compel growth along the desired lines.

AN APPRAISAL OF THE JAPANESE ECONOMY

The growth rate of the Japanese economy has been the highest for any major industrial country, even during the 1970s when growth rates began to decline for all countries. During the period 1960–1973 the average annual rate of economic growth in terms of real gross domestic product was 10.5 percent for Japan, compared to 4.5 percent for West Germany and 4.1 percent for the United States.[40] During the period 1973–1979 the Japanese growth rate declined to an average annual rate of 4.0 percent, compared to 2.7 percent for the United States and 2.4 percent for West Germany.

Contributing to a higher Japanese growth rate was a high rate of increase in labor productivity. The rate of labor productivity growth in Japan was at an average of 9.9 percent annually for the period 1960–1973, compared to 5.8 percent for West Germany and 3.1 percent for the United States; for the period 1973–1979 the average annual rate of increase in labor productivity was 3.6 percent for Japan, 1.4 percent for the United States, and 4.2 percent for West Germany.[41] Japan also had an economic

---

[40]New York Stock Exchange, Office of Economic Research, *U.S. Economic Performance in a Global Perspective* (February 1981), p. 17.
[41]*Ibid.*, p. 19.

performance index higher than that of either the United States or West Germany, as Table 9-1 indicates.

TABLE 9-1
ECONOMIC PERFORMANCE INDEX FOR JAPAN
AND OTHER MAJOR INDUSTRIAL COUNTRIES
1974–1980
(U.S. = 100 percent)

	Percent
Japan	248.7
West Germany	190.8
France	118.4
Canada	108.6
Sweden	100.7
United States	100.0
Italy	88.2
United Kingdom	14.5

Source: New York Stock Exchange, Office of Economic Research, *U.S. Economic Performance in a Global Perspective* (New York, February 1981), p. 12.

The performance of the Japanese economy during the decade of the 1970s was somewhat erratic, as Table 9-2 indicates. In 1974 there was

TABLE 9-2
GROWTH IN REAL GROSS NATIONAL PRODUCT
IN JAPAN, 1970–1980
(annual increase in percent)

Year	Percentage Increase
1970	9.9
1971	4.7
1972	9.0
1973	8.8
1974	−1.2
1975	2.4
1976	5.3
1977	5.3
1978	5.1
1979	5.6
1980	4.2

Source: Mitsubishi Economic Research Institute, "Survey of Economic Conditions in Japan" (July 1981), Table 1, p. 12.

actually a decrease in real gross national product, reflecting Japanese vulnerability to the oil shortages of 1973. Japan derived 80 percent of its oil supply from the Middle East. This vulnerability to oil cutoffs led Japan to reappraise its whole industrial strategy based on the knowledge that oil is no longer cheap and inexhaustible and that new industries must be created that rely less on imported energy sources. Plans for the 1980s include the development of sophisticated computer technology.

Actually, the Japanese growth rate is an integral extension of a century of development, the roots of which can be traced to the emergence of a mercantile class during the latter part of the Tokugawa Shogunate. A continuity of growth continued during the Meiji Restoration up to the present, and the basic reasons for it have survived: a pervasive spirit of enterprise which combines the profit motive with economic nationalism; a regulatory but sponsoring relationship of government to business; the mangerial competence of the business and financial class; and the frugality and industry of the masses of workers. A new element has contributed to the continued evolution of the growth process, namely, the absence of major military expenditures in the national budget. With the United States assuming the major responsibility for Japan's defense, the Japanese are able to divert their resources into more productive channels. Defense-related expenditures accounted for only 5 percent of national budget expenditures for 1981 and less than 1 percent of Japanese gross national product.[42]

Strengths of the Japanese Economy

With the United States and Western Europe caught in the economic malaise of the late 1970s and early 1980s, Japan has emerged as the world's most viable economy. Its rate of unemployment is lower than all major Western industrial countries, averaging only 1.7 percent of the work force during the period 1970–1080, compared to 4.0 percent for France, 6.3 percent for Canada, and 6.9 percent for the United States.[43] In the fall of 1981 unemployment rates in France and the United States were in excess of 8 percent, while unemployment rates in the United Kingdom were close to 13 percent.[44] Japanese unemployment rates were around 2 percent, reflecting in part the lifetime employment policy of many Japanese firms which denies the possibility of job layoffs. For those workers not guaranteed lifetime employment, unemployment compensation is less than it is in other industrial countries, and the differentials between

---

[42]"Survey of Economic Conditions in Japan," p. 13.
[43]*U.S. Economic Performance in a Global Perspective*, pp. 17–25.
[44]*Washington Post*, December 13, 1981, p. 2.

low-level wages and unemployment benefits is sufficiently great that low-paid workers are anxious to retain their jobs. The main factor contributing to a low unemployment rate is a high growth rate resulting from a constantly expanding economy.

Japan has a more equal distribution of income than other industrial countries. This may appear surprising, for the level of transfer payments is low in comparison to other countries. There are several factors that explain the more even distribution of income in Japan: less inherited wealth than in other countries, a lower rate of stock and bond ownership, and lower incomes for top executives in comparison to workers. There is also less ostentatious living on the part of business executives in comparison to the life styles of the workers.[45] Moreover, when workers take cuts in pay, managers also take similar cuts. The result of all of this is that there is less class conflict in Japan than there is in France, the United Kingdom, or even the United States. F. Scott Fitzgerald is reputed to have made the statement, "The rich, they are different from you and me." There are rich people in Japan, but they are not all that noticeable.

The existence of a coherent industrial policy gives Japan a sense of national purpose. One end result is the sudden emergence of Japan as the world leader in the semiconductor industry—an industry which had previously been dominated by the United States. Japan has set a national goal to win by 1990 a worldwide market share of 30 percent and a U.S. market share of 18 percent of the computer market.[46] Japan is the world leader in the production of industrial robots and plans to provide business with $140 million over a seven-year period to develop robots that are capable of assembling an entire automobile.[47] There is a certain samurai spirit about the Japanese—a desire to be the best in the world in any line of activity.[48]

Government leaders are committed to business success, and their ability to work with business leaders provides a more stable environment for investment. This relationship is in almost diametric contrast to the business-government interface in the United States, which can be described as being basically adversary in nature.[49] Although different historic and cultural patterns explain at least part of the differences in relationship between government and business in the United States and Japan, the contrast is in favor of the Japanese. There is a more realistic assessment of the Japanese role in the world economy, and cooperation between business and government is based on a desire to win.

---

[45]Ouchi, *op. cit.*, p. 27.
[46]"Japan's Strategy for the '80s," *Business Week*, p. 68.
[47]*Fortune*, December 7, 1981, p. 38.
[48]Drucker, *op. cit.*, p. 90.
[49]John T. Dunlop, ed., *Business and Public Policy* (Cambridge: Harvard University Press, 1980).

There are several other factors contributing to the strength of the Japanese economy. Japan has a disciplined and well-educated work force. The Japanese are thrifty by nature, and the rate of savings is among the highest in the world. The country is homogeneous with respect to race, history, language, religion, and culture. Living in close proximity in a small country, and confronted with both natural and human-made disasters, the Japanese have survived through their capacity to work together in harmony. Finally, the entrepreneurial and managerial talents of the Japanese are among the best in the world.

Weaknesses of the Japanese Economy

Japan is vulnerable to changes in the world economy. It imports a high proportion of resources required to meet its energy needs. High energy costs have made it more difficult for certain Japanese industries, in particular aluminum, chemicals, and steel, to compete in world markets. Japanese success in the United States and Western Europe has created pressure to curb the flow of Japanese imports into these areas. The economic malaise which has affected both the United States and Western Europe in 1981 also has an adverse impact on Japanese imports. Japanese dependence on its export trade makes a healthy and viable world economy a necessity.

Japanese economic growth has not been an unmixed blessing. The Japanese have come to the realization that they have paid heavily for their obsession with economic growth. Tokyo, Osaka, and other metropolitan areas have become megalopolitan nightmares, hopelessly congested and permeated with fumes. The Japanese are having to undertake a vast restructuring of the nation and its economy. To check pollution and urban congestion, factories have had to be dispersed to the countryside and dozens of new towns have been created and linked together by networks of highways and express railways.

Various changes in the work force can create social problems. The impact of industrial robots could be considerable, particularly if they replace workers. This could cause social unrest. The intrusion of women into a male-dominated society and work force may also create problems. Women in Japan are concentrated in part-time jobs and in the service occupations. With professional workers in short supply, Japanese employers are hiring more women. Japanese workers of both sexes are following a phenomenon in the United States and Western Europe, namely, a disdain for the dirty factory jobs and a desire for white-collar jobs. The Japanese work force is also aging. With pay raises and promotion based on seniority, younger workers feel that there is less opportunity for advancement and are more likely to change jobs. This tends to work against one of the most fundamental institutions of Japan—lifetime employment by large Japanese firms.

In Japan a complicated set of reciprocal obligations between individuals in a group situation has held the institutions of the society together. These ties, before World War II, were centered in the nation as represented by the army, religion, and in the emperor. Those ties were transferred, after the shattering military defeat in World War II, into the mundane tasks of economic reconstruction and growth. The success of Japan up to now has been awesome, but a double problem can emerge. First, if economic growth falters, the consensus built up between groups could falter. The foundation of Japanese society is a willingness to compromise private ends for the public interest. Second, if economic growth continues to increase affluence, discretionary social behavior may eventually work against economic growth. For example, there may be a substitution of leisure for work. Resources also could be transferred to the creation of more social goods and services. This could result in inflation and a decrease in productivity.[50]

SUMMARY

The Japanese economic system is essentially capitalistic. With the exception of certain public services and monopolies which are operated by the Japanese government, private enterprise is dominant in the economy. The government leaves the initiative for production and distribution in private hands, and it has for many decades devoted itself to creating an environment which is favorable to investment by private enterprise. Business firms have flourished under the protection of the government, and leaders in both fields are often connected by common educational and marital ties.

Nevertheless, the government intervenes constantly to turn industry into directions thought to be desirable for the economy as a whole. By controlling the flow of funds from the Bank of Japan to commercial banks and from thence to industry, the government has exerted pressure on industry. Through tax benefits, special depreciation allowances, and favorable interest rates, the government has stimulated savings and investment. Pervasive pressures are exercised one way or another on the investment decisions of business firms. The government also has controlled a considerable proportion of the nation's investment during the boom of the last decade. A policy of tax reductions has served to stimulate aggregate demand, which in turn has caused yearly surpluses in the budget. From this source came 25 percent of the nation's savings over the last decade.

The rate of economic growth has been the most rapid of all major industrial

---

[50]Because of the pressure of rising entitlements, there is a constant tendency for state expenditures in the Western world to increase, requiring more taxes to pay for services and stimulating more inflation because of an imbalance in productivity.

countries. Although the increase can be predicted in part on the fact that the economy had nowhere to go but up after the devastation brought about by World War II, other factors are much more important in explaining the growth rate. A stimulus to growth has come both from rising consumption demands at home and market opportunities abroad. Other stimuli include a reverse gap between productivity and wages, an abundant labor supply, a high rate of personal savings, and an undervalued currency.

Economic planning is indicative rather than imperative. A series of plans have been used since the end of World War II to accomplish set economic objectives. Japanese planning points out a series of desirable goals which the economy should try to achieve. Industry has a frame of reference within which to operate. No direct coercion, which would be used in imperative planning, is used to make industry operate within the framework of the plan. The government, however, has indirect and more subtle ways to assure compliance with the objectives of planning. Control over the supply of credit gives the government leverage in enforcing compliance. Selective fiscal measures which are designed to favor exports or certain types of industries, investment, or personal savings can also be used to encourage conformance with the plan. The national budget can also be used to allocate expenditures into desirable areas. Even where no fiscal and monetary controls exist, it is customary for the government to provide personal guidance to industry or, conversely, for industry to consult the government before making major business decisions.

The Japanese economy is not free from socioeconomic problems as it enters the 1980s. There is still a dependence on foreign sources of energy and raw materials. The work force is aging and there are shortages of workers in the technical areas. The much-heralded consensus between government, business, and other sectors of the economy could break down if prosperity is not maintained. There is also the possibility that more Japanese workers will opt for leisure time at the expense of working, and social welfare expenditures could divert government expenditures away from capital formation into consumption.

REVIEW QUESTIONS

1. Comment on the Japanese system of lifetime employment with one firm. Would this system work in the United States?
2. The Japanese economic system involves management by consensus. Discuss. Would this system work in the United States?
3. Discuss the relationship between government and business in Japan.
4. What factors are responsible for the high rate of economic growth in Japan?
5. Discuss the objectives of Japanese economic planning.
6. Explain some of the factors which have been responsible for a high rate of personal savings in Japan.
7. Discuss the ways in which the Japanese government provides financial support to business.
8. What is the role of the Japan Development Bank in the Japanese banking system?
9. What are some of the problems confronting the Japanese economy?

10. Discuss the role of the Ministry of International Trade and Industry (MITI) in the Japanese economy.

RECOMMENDED READINGS

Allen, G. C. *Japan: Government Intervention in the Developed Economy.* London: Croom Helm, 1979.

Drucker, Peter F. "Behind Japan's Success." *Harvard Business Review,* January–February, 1981, pp. 83–90.

"Japan's Ominous Chip Victory." *Fortune,* December 14, 1981, pp. 52–57.

"Japan's Strategy for the '80s." *Business Week,* December 14, 1981, pp. 39–119.

Kahn, Herman, and Thomas Pepper. *The Japanese Challenge.* New York: Morrow, 1980.

Magaziner, Ira C., and Thomas M. Hout. *Japanese Industrial Policy.* London: Policy Studies Institute, 1980.

Martin, Benjamin, and Everett M. Kassalow. *Labor Relations in Advanced Industrial Societies.* Washington: Carnegie Endowment for International Peace, 1980, Chapter 2.

Ministry of Industry and Trade (MITI). *Vision of Industry in the Eighties.* Tokyo, March 1980.

Ouchi, William. *Theory Z.* Reading, Mass.: Addison-Wesley, 1981.

Servan-Schrieber, Jean-Jacques. *The World Challenge.* New York: Simon and Schuster, 1980.

Suzuki, Yoshio. *Money and Banking in Contemporary Japan.* New Haven: Yale University Press, 1980.

Vogel, Ezra F. *Japan as Number One.* Cambridge: Harvard University Press, 1979.

10

West Germany

INTRODUCTION

The Federal Republic of Germany, or West Germany, was created out of the western portion of the German *Reich*, which portion had been divided in 1945 into a British, an American, and a French zone of occupation. In 1949 free elections for a Parliament (*Bundestag*) were held, and the Federal Republic of Germany, with its capital at Bonn, was formally established as a federal republic made up of 11 states (*Länder*) and West Berlin. A policy of decontrol of the economy was pursued under the direction of Ludwig Erhard, an economics professor who was to become minister of economics and then chancellor of West Germany. He believed that the incentives of a free market economy would serve to liberate long-dormant productive capacities. His policies were enormously successful, and the West German "economic miracle" was created.

The reconstruction of the West German economy since the end of World War II has enabled the country to gain the position of one of the great industrial powers of the world and certainly the outstanding industrial country of the Western European mainland. The task, however, was not easy, for when the Third Reich was defeated by the Allied powers, Germany was divided into two parts. Eastern Germany, which consisted of the provinces of Prussia, Silesia, Pomerania, Brandenburg, and Upper Saxony, fell under the Russian sphere of influence, and from these provinces the Republic of East Germany was formed. Western Germany, which consisted of the provinces of Westphalia, Bavaria, Lower Saxony,

Württemburg, and the Rhineland-Palatinate, fell under British-French-American influence and eventually became the Federal Republic of Germany.

For practical purposes the history of current Germany begins with the end of World War II. Germany had lost the war, damage to industrial capacity was considerable, and the country was split in half. Yet, like the legendary phoenix, West Germany rose from the ashes to become one of the world's leading industrial powers. There were several factors that can explain this renaissance, which are as follows:[1]

1. The amount and extent of war damage was overrated. The amount of industrial capacity that was destroyed by Allied bombing was counter-balanced by that which was constructed during the war. At the end of the war, Germany found herself with better than prewar industrial capacity. War damages and dismantling policies pursued by the Allies led to re-placement of old plants with newer, more modern ones.
2. Although split in two by the partition, the western part of Germany retained most of the prewar industrial base. This base was concentrated in the capital goods industries. These goods were needed, not only for German reconstruction, but for world markets in general. While other countries concentrated on the production of consumer goods for export, West Germany concentrated on the production of capital goods.
3. A low level of imports and a favorable trade balance caused by the Korean War also contributed to the recovery of the West German economy.

Marshall Plan aid also played an important role in the revival of West Germany. Some $4.5 billion were spent in helping Germany recover from its war losses. This aid supported the modernization of plants and equipment by supplying foreign exchange and investment funds.

Postwar Reliance on Market Forces

The German economy relied on market forces and incentives instead of controls to accomplish recovery from the devastation brought about by the war. Anti-inflationary and sound currency policies were pursued. To channel profits into investment and saving, income tax rates were modified in favor of savers and investors. A policy of free markets was adopted, but was by no means uniformly applied to all sectors of the German economy. This policy was carried out under the direction of the future Federal German minister of economics, Ludwig Erhard, who, with the support of the non-Socialist parties, gambled that the incentives of a free market economy would stimulate long-dormant productive capacities. He felt that the function of the government was to provide the economy

---

[1]Henry C. Wallich, *Mainsprings of the German Revival* (New Haven: Yale University Press, 1955), pp. 7–9.

with principles and broad guidelines of economic policy. Government was to see that neither social privileges nor artificial monopolies impeded the natural process by which economic forces reached and maintained a state of equilibrium and that the operation of supply and demand was allowed full play.[2]

Erhard felt that the contradistinction was not between free and planned economic systems, nor between capitalist and socialist economic systems, but between a market economy with free price level adjustments and an authoritarian economy with state control extended over production and distribution.[3] In this market economy, any mistake in judgment in the management of production or distribution produced concomitant repercussions through price changes in the marketplace. In a state-directed economy, the same mistakes would not be reflected in changes in the pricing mechanism, but would be covered up, eventually causing serious misallocation of resources. Market reaction to mistakes would be eliminated and the consumer deprived of all freedom of choice.

Postwar German economic policy revolved around the combination of personal freedom and social welfare within the framework of a competitive economy. Social welfare programs became among the most comprehensive and extensive in Europe. The German government, in addition to its expenditures on social welfare measures, also relied heavily on tax incentives to stimulate savings and investment. In 1948 special depreciation allowances for various types of investment were introduced. High income tax rates, introduced after the war to finance reparations and to combat inflation, were reduced to stimulate saving. Corporate tax exemptions permitted tax-free reinvestment of 10 or 15 percent of total profits.

Tax incentives were designed primarily to stimulate investment on the part of German enterprises. It was felt that the paramount postwar need was to rebuild productive capacity so as to increase production in all fields. In general, consumption was penalized through taxation, and private capital formation was promoted. This led to criticism that German fiscal policy favored the upper-income groups and discriminated against the working class. However, under conditions that were prevalent, this was probably the most direct way of stimulating economic growth in a free market system.

Postwar Monetary and Fiscal Policies

Postwar German monetary and fiscal policies were oriented toward production. Incentive elements favored the strong and discriminated

---

[2]Edward Hartrich, *The Fourth and Richest Reich* (New York: Macmillan, 1980), pp. 1–105.
    [3]*Ibid.*

against the weak. Considerable income inequality was permitted. Although the position of the economically weak and less viable segments of the economy was buttressed through the provision of a comprehensive social welfare program which consumed and distributed a sizable part of the national income, there is no question that the bulk of the economic gains went to business firms and individual entrepreneurs. Monetary and fiscal policies were tight and served to intensify competition among business firms to create markets for their products.[4] General policies aimed at stimulating aggregate demand and thereby insuring a sellers' market were avoided. To the contrary, aggregate demand was held relatively constant and aggregate supply was stimulated through various factors, such as tax incentives.

To a major degree, the free market policy adopted after World War II remains the policy of Germany today. Nevertheless, there are marked differences between the West German and United States economies. For one thing, a considerable segment of German industry is nationalized. Moreover, there is stronger government penetration and control over financial affairs in West Germany through state ownership of the central banking system and through the high proportion of transfer payments generated through the state budget.

THE ECONOMIC SYSTEM

A postwar reliance on a free market system represented somewhat of a break with traditional German reliance on state intervention in economic affairs, which predated Hitler by a considerable time period. The West German economic system, then, is a mixed economic system in which there is both public and private ownership of the agents of production. The bulk of German industry is in private hands, and pricing decisions are determined in the marketplace. It has been the government's stated policy to denationalize some of its holdings as it did in the case of the Volkswagen company in 1961. Distribution is also primarily a function of private enterprise, with the government responsible for seeing that it is shared equitably by all income groups. To this extent, allocation of resources, as determined in a purely competitive market economy, is circumvented.

The West German economy can be divided into two sectors, private and public, each of which contributes to the total output of goods and services. The private sector is the more important in terms of consumption, production, and employment. The public or government sector is also important not only from the standpoint that it contributes to consumption and investment but also because it has come to play the para-

---

[4]Wallich, *op. cit.*, pp. 121–131.

mount role in the maintenance of full employment and the redistribution of income. For a variety of reasons the government sector has entered into certain business activities that it shares to a greater or lesser extent with private enterprise. During the Bismarck era the railroad system was nationalized, and foundations were laid upon which the war economy of a later period could be built. Bismarck was also the chief architect of most of the social legislation which exists in Germany today.[5]

Public Finance

Almost any government activity influences the private as well as the public sector of an economic system, whether or not an effect is intended. Taxes divert resources from the private to the public sector of an economy, and the level of taxation relative to gross national product indicates the extent to which the influence of the state exists. In Germany the combined federal, state, and local budgets control about 40 percent of the gross national product. A considerable part of gross domestic investment in financed out of tax revenues, and income redistribution is facilitated by one of the most comprehensive social welfare programs in the world. However, the tax structure is heavily weighted against consumer expenditures, and the main thrust of fiscal policy has been toward capital accumulation, at first for reconstruction and subsequently for expansion of production capacity. Government savings as one source of capital formation have been high, averaging as much as 40 percent of total national savings. The government has also relied extensively upon preferential tax treatment to stimulate the rate of savings in the private sector of the economy, and the impact of tax policy on capital formation in the postwar period has been considerable.

In West Germany the budgets of the state and local governments constitute an important expenditure source in the economy. In comparison with the French public finance system, which is highly centralized, the German system allows the states (*Länder*) to have large separate budgets, which, when combined with local budgets, provide a greater volume of expenditures than the central government. The social security system is similar to that of the French in that the tax-transfer arrangement is largely independent of the federal budget.

The German Tax System. The present tax structure of West Germany is primarily the inheritance of history and political processes. There is a similarity between the German and United States tax systems in that

---

[5]Bismarck was Chancellor of Germany from 1871 to 1890. He was a political pragmatist of the first order who realized that concessions to the working classes had to be made in order to check the rise of socialism. He sponsored social legislation in order to remove the causes upon which socialism was developing and to maintain military efficiency, which was dependent upon the health and happiness of the German people.

there is a *tripartite structure,* meaning that legislative authority over tax matters is divided between federal, state, and local governments, and certain taxes are regarded as the prerogative of each.

The Value-Added Tax. The value-added tax was introduced in January 1968. It was devised in accordance with a Common Market tax harmonization directive which called for a value-added tax in all Common Market countries by January 1, 1970. The tax is levied at a general rate of 13 percent of value added in each stage of the production process. There are numerous items, however, to which a lower rate applies. For example, many food and agricultural products are taxed at a rate of 6.5 percent, and exports and certain items and services are exempt from the tax. In the case of imports, the importer pays an import equalization tax equal to the value-added tax applicable to the same good produced domestically.

Excise Taxes. Federal excise taxes and customs duties are also an important source of revenue to the national government. Excise taxes are levied on a variety of commodities, including tobacco, mineral oil, salt, tea, sugar, matches, and alcohol. A tax on beer is administered separately by the states and is an important source of revenue. In 1981, the beer tax accounted for about 11 percent of state revenues. The manufacturer, producer, or importer of products subject to excise taxation is expected to shift the tax to the buyer by including it in the purchase price of the product. Revenue from the two major excise taxes on tobacco and gasoline account for approximately 15 percent of federal tax revenue, and the impact of the excise tax structure places a heavy burden on the individual taxpayer.

Income Taxes. Income taxes are levied by the states partly as a matter of historical right and partly under powers delegated by the federal government, and the proceeds are divided between the government and the states. Corporations are taxed on distributed profits at flat rates and on undistributed profits at graduated rates. Individuals pay a personal income tax at rates ranging from 22 to 56 percent. Income splitting is permitted for personal income tax purposes in that incomes of married persons are reckoned together, divided into equal parts, and each part subjected to the tax.

The federal portion of the proceeds from the personal and corporate income taxes amounts to 40 percent and the state portion 60 percent. The state portion is allocated on the basis of the share of total income taxes collected by each state. Although this would tend to weigh the portions heavily in favor of the more densely populated and heavily industrialized states, there is a federal statute which provides for an equitable distribution of revenue among the various states. This is accomplished through equalization payments which are made by the affluent states to the needy states. All states are required to grant a part of their share of income taxes to the municipalities located within their territories.

Municipal Trade Tax. The municipal trade tax is the most important source of revenue for local governments. It is a tax on business profits, on business capital, and, in some communities, on the payrolls of commercial enterprises. The basic purpose of the tax is to compensate local governments for the cost of maintaining schools, roads, police protection, and public welfare. Collection of the municipal trade tax is the responsibility of a community, and only business enterprises located within its boundaries are liable for the tax.

Tax Distribution. The tripartite structure of the German tax system is unique among European countries. The division of total tax resources results in a distribution of tax revenues among federal, state, and local governments in a ratio of roughly 5:4:1. In 1980, for example, total tax collections at the federal level of government amounted to $85 billion, total tax collections at the state level amounted to $70 billion, and at the local level $20 billion.[6] This has meant a division of taxes, with the value-added tax the most important revenue source for the federal government and the personal income tax the most important source of revenue to state governments.

Combined federal, state, and local taxes, including the very heavy social security levies, absorb approximately 40 percent of the German gross national product. Social security levies alone absorb 10 percent of the gross national product, and the total burden indicates the measure of the tax burden resting on the German economy. This burden, however, is mitigated by the high proportion of transfer payments and the existence of tax incentives to stimulate investment.

Government Expenditures. Expenditure policy has emphasized a comprehensive social security system with constantly expanding individual benefits, public investment in the form of low-cost housing, transportation facilities and other civil construction, and economic assistance to private enterprise. In fact, a substantial part of public investment has been effected through the financing of private enterprise.

Social Welfare Expenditures. Nineteenth-century Germany was the first nation in the world to adopt comprehensive social security legislation. Current social security programs are extensive and costly. Social security levies amount to approximately 10 percent of the gross national product, and expenditures on social insurance and other welfare programs amount to approximately 13 percent of gross national product. Social insurance and company-provided fringe benefits supplement the wages of the average German worker by about 70 percent.[7]

German social welfare benefits include old age and survivors benefits

---

[6]Deutsche Bundesbank, *Annual Report for 1980* (Frankfurt am Main, April 1981), p. 17.
[7]*Ibid.*, p. 12.

which are financed from general revenues of the federal budget and from taxes levied on the employer and employee.[8] Cash payments include an old age pension, a disability pension, a widow's pension, children's supplements, and funeral grants. There are also sickness and maternity benefits financed by a tax on workers, unemployment compensation financed jointly by a tax on employer and employee, and work injury compensation financed solely by a tax on the employer which varies according to risk.

Family allowances are financed out of general revenues of the federal government and payable to families with one or more children. In addition, government-mandated paid vacations of four weeks also add to social welfare benefits. Manual and office workers usually receive Christmas or other kinds of annual bonuses totaling, on the average, one month's pay.

Public Investment Expenditures. Public investment from all government sources has accounted for approximately one-fourth of total investment since the late 1960s. The bulk of support has come from savings on the part of the federal government which have been derived from budgetary surpluses, funds secured from accumulations in the social security system, moderate amounts of government borrowing, both through bond issues and through direct credits from financial institutions, and surpluses in the budgets of the various German states.[9]

Housing is a major area of government support. An acute need after World War II was the repair and construction of residential housing. There was also the need to provide for the refugees from East Germany. To encourage the construction of housing, tax incentives and direct subsidies were offered by all levels of government. For example, newly built homes were exempted from the local real estate tax. Generous depreciation allowances were provided for the construction of houses and apartments, and rents for many dwellings were subsidized. Loans at subsidized interest rates as low as 1 percent per annum were also made to encourage housing construction.

All levels of government continue to be active in financing and subsidizing houses. Housing construction continues to be supported out of subsidies financed by general taxes, interest subsidies, and accelerated depreciation allowances. Tax revenues have been channeled into housing

---

[8]A characteristic of many European social security systems is their fragmentation into a number of funds or special systems. In Germany, for example, there are special systems for miners, public employees, self-employed artisans, self-employed farmers, and building and clock workers. Contributions and benefits vary according to the system. The contributions and benefits above pertain to the general social security system.

[9]It is necessary to remember that Germany is a federal republic. The fiscal systems of state and local governments are much more important than in most other European countries.

investment, reflecting the postwar priorities of German fiscal policy. This means that the average German is subsidizing, to a certain extent, the cost of housing through the taxes paid to the various levels of government. Government-subsidized housing has contributed to a higher level of demand than would otherwise exist in the housing industry.

A high proportion of savings, then, emanate from the government sector of the economy and are channeled into areas which are government-approved. Agriculture has been another one of these areas. For example, agricultural enterprises are entitled to special depreciation provisions which are over and above the normal rate. Structural subsidies are paid to stimulate an increase in the size of the farming unit, and interest subsidies are paid to stimulate capital investment. Under the annual *Green Plan*, which is designed to improve the technical and economic organization of farms and to raise farm incomes, the federal government spent $3.8 billion in 1980, an amount which is considerably less than the total amount of subsidies to farmers.

It should be clear that combined federal, state, and local budgets absorb a very large percentage of the German gross national product, and many economic functions are influenced by government tax and expenditure policies. This means that a high degree of control over the economy can be exercised by governmental units through manipulation of taxes and expenditures. A wide variety of tax incentives have been used to stimulate economic growth, and many economic sectors have been favored by government use of tax revenues. Tax policy has sought to create incentives to work, save, and invest in business enterprises, but, in turn, heavy reliance has been placed on indirect taxation, such as the turnover tax and the value-added tax, which discriminates against consumption. Expenditure policy has sought to buttress the position of the average German by providing comprehensive social security measures.

Income Redistribution. The important thing to note concerning government outlays for transfer payments and goods and services is that they require the diversion of resources from the private to the public sector of an economy. To the extent that the government provides services, real resources are diverted to the public sector as a result of the purchase of goods and factor services by governmental units. The recipients of these services benefit through obtaining them at a price below their real cost as measured by the government expenditures necessary to provide the services. Transfer payments do not necessitate a direct diversion of real resources from private to public use, but they do require a diversion of financial resources, generally in the form of taxes on the consumer's current money income.

Fiscal Policy. West German budgetary policy has sought to avoid deficits; therefore, much heavier reliance is placed on monetary than fiscal policy for control of the business cycle. Fiscal policy began to be used in the early 1970s and is innovative in the use of selective tax devices to accomplish various objectives. For example, when inflation threatened as a result of the oil embargo in the middle 1970s, income taxes were increased and a 10 percent selective tax was levied on domestic business investment. In 1980, the West German economy was hit by a downturn. Personal income taxes were cut and transfer payments, in the form of children's allowances, were increased.[10] Both federal and state budgets were allowed to run deficits.

The Banking System

The German banking system has a mixed public-private relationship. The central bank, the *Deutsche Bundesbank*, is publicly owned, but the commercial banks are privately owned. Two government financial institutions, the *Kreditanstalt für Wiederaufbau* (Reconstruction Finance Corporation) and the *Industrie Kreditbank*, provide funds to business firms. There is direct government intervention in the flow of credit from the financial institutions to the various sectors of the economy through the provision of saving out of budgetary surpluses, which is made available for capital formation. Government lending to households and enterprises includes loans financed by its own funds, as well as loans made by public institutions which it controls. In addition, government authorities mobilize loan funds outside of the budget by subsidizing interest payments.

Central Banking. The historical and deep-rooted conflict between federalism and centralism is reflected in the development of central banking in Germany. The *Reichsbank*, Germany's first central bank, was formed in 1876; but to placate the supporters of federalism, banks in the various German states were given the right to issue bank notes. In 1924 the Reichsbank was reorganized under the auspices of the victorious allies' Dawes Commission to make it more independent of the German government. In 1935 it was given the sole right to issue bank notes, but lost its autonomy during the Nazi period (1933–1945), when it became a monetary instrument which was subservient to the economic objectives of the government.

Following World War II, the Reichsbank was reorganized as the Bank Deutscher Länder, an interim central bank which existed pending the creation of a federal republic. However, it lost the function of note issuance to the central banks of the German states. In 1957 it was reorganized into the Deutsche Bundesbank and given the exclusive right to issue bank notes. The capital stock of the Bundesbank was given to the federal

---

[10]Deutsches Bundesbank, *op. cit.*, pp. 16–18.

government and increased authority was also given to the government through the use of appointive powers which were granted to it. The Directorate of the Bundesbank is composed of the president, vice-president, and no more than eight additional members—all of whom are appointed by the president of the Federal Republic.

The current central banking system consists of the Deutsche Bundesbank and 10 *Landeszentralbanken* (central banks of the states). The Bundesbank, unlike many central banks in other countries, operates with a considerable degree of autonomy with respect to open market operations and credit policy. It is, however, obliged to advise the government on all matters of importance in the area of monetary policy and to support general economic policies of the government, particularly in the area of currency stability.

Commercial Banks. German commercial banks are privately owned and are of three types: nationwide banks; state, regional, and local banks; and private banks. Commercial banks account for over 50 percent of total short-term deposits and short-term credits, but less than 10 percent of total long-term lending. German banks, remembering the banking crisis of 1931 when withdrawals of foreign short-term deposits brought down the superstructure of long-term credits, have pursued a highly liquid position with respect to loans.

There are three nationwide banks—the Deutsche Bank, the Dresdner Bank, and the Commerzbank. These banks have a nationwide network of branch banks. They have about one-fourth of the short-term deposits and short-term credits of the entire banking system and conduct the bulk of Germany's international banking business.

There are 105 state, regional, and local banks which specialize in short- and medium-term lending. Some of these banks engage in general banking business; others are highly specialized. Underwriting is the main capital market function of these banks, and a large part of their holdings of bonds is related to the underwriting business. They also hold substantial amounts of fixed interest securities for their own accounts.

There are also private bankers who make short-term loans. Their strength stems from a close personal association maintained with their clients.

Savings Banks. Savings banks are municipally owned and are oriented toward local needs—housing, small business loans, and municipal projects. They provide the largest source of capital for the bond market and derive their funds from personal savings. Savings banks, as a rule, engage in both savings and short-term deposit transactions. Credits extended by the savings banks are mostly loans to medium-sized and small firms and to the handicraft industries.

There are also 12 central *giro institutions* (Girozentralen), which act as reserve depositories and clearinghouses and which carry out various banking functions, such as foreign exchange transactions and the issue of securities. Most of them are also provincial banks making long-term loans to communities and associations after raising funds by issuing bonds on the capital market.

Specific-Purpose Banks. Government savings from budgetary surpluses and accumulations by the social security system have been most important in the development of the German economy. Some of these savings are loaned to private enterprises, partly through such specialized credit institutions as the Reconstruction Loan Corporation, the Equalization of Burdens Bank, and certain agricultural banks.

The Reconstruction Loan Corporation had as its original purpose the provision of loans for the reconstruction of German industry. It has now become the main instrument for the extension of long-term credits to developing countries in the framework of the German foreign aid program.

The Industry Credit Corporation provides short- and medium-term loans, primarily to the machinery construction industry and the chemical industry.

Monetary Policy. The Deutsches Bundesbank has recourse to the standard instruments of monetary policy—control over the rediscount rate, control over minimum reserve requirements, and open market operations—to accomplish stabilization objectives.

Instruments of Monetary Control. The Bundesbank exercises control over monetary policy through various instruments which it can use to regulate the availability of credit and liquidity of the banking system:

1. It has control over the rediscount rate and the rate it charges for advances on commercial paper. Moreover, the quantity of open market paper which the Bundesbank stands ready to discount is subject to limits which are believed to be three times the liable capital plus the reserves of any given institution.
2. It has control over minimum legal reserve requirements for commercial banks and other credit institutions up to a maximum of 30 percent for sight deposits, 20 percent for time deposits, and 10 percent for savings accounts. Any credit institution that fails to meet reserve requirements is subject to a penalty surcharge, which is usually 3 percent above the rate charged by the Bundesbank on advances.
3. It can engage in open market operations by buying and selling Treasury bills and bonds, bills of exchange, and bonds that have been admitted to the official stock exchange.
4. It can encourage or discourage the placement of banking funds abroad by making it less or more expensive for commercial banks to make covered investments in the foreign exchange market, thereby increasing or decreasing the supply of funds available in the domestic money market.

The influence of the Bundesbank on credit, however, has been obviated considerably during the postwar period through the existence of several factors which have been present in the German economy. For one thing, the interest elasticity of investment has been low, reflecting a strong investment demand, and interest rate changes via changes in the rediscount rate have had little effect. Furthermore, German banks have also possessed considerable excess liquidity during the postwar period and have not had to resort to rediscounting commercial paper to any significant degree. The existence of an export surplus has provided the foreign exchange to enhance the liquidity of the banking system. High interest rates have attracted foreign accounts which in turn have increased bank liquidity, thereby circumventing attempts at effective rediscount policy.

Use of Monetary Policy. Monetary policy is invested with the primary responsibility for price level stability and for confining short-run fluctuations in levels of economic activity to moderate proportions. Credit restraint and easing has taken the form, primarily, of sharp increases and decreases in the rediscount rate. Excess reserves of commercial banks have been affected through changes in minimum reserve requirements. Open market policy has been generally limited to Treasury bills.

Government control over the supply of credit is more indirect than direct. As mentioned previously, a substantial part of savings during the postwar period has emanated from combined federal, state, and local governments' budgetary surpluses. Indirect influence on the capital market has been exerted through the allocation of government savings to government approved projects, such as housing construction.

Government incentives in the form of privileges and bonus payments have been used to increase the level of personal savings. Savers have received premium payments amounting to 20 to 30 percent for savings accounts and 25 to 35 percent for amounts held with building and loan associations provided that balances are immobilized for a specified period of time. Moreover, individuals in certain income brackets may receive greater premiums by deducting such deposits and premiums for taxable income.

Labor-Management Relations

The trade union movement in West Germany is dominated by one labor confederation, the *Deutsche Gewerkschaftsbund* (DGB), which was established in 1949 as a federation of 16 basic industrial unions comprising every segment of the German economy. For example, office and production employees in the textile industry are organized into a textile union. The DGB represents about one-fourth of the workers in the West German labor force and is the successor to the separate, politically oriented trade union federations which existed before the Hitler era. It has approximately 8.5 million members. The three principal unions within the DGB are the metalworkers, with approximately 2.1 million members, the public service and transport workers with 1.2 million members, and the chemical, paper, and ceramics workers with 600 thousand members. The multi-industrial form of organization is dominant in German trade unionism.

There are approximately 1.5 million workers who belong to other unions. White-collar workers and higher-ranking civil servants, reflecting class division and higher occupational distinction, have their own unions. The white-collar workers belong to the *Deutsche Angestellten Gewerkschaft* (DAG), which has 600 thousand members. Civil servants belong to the *Deutscher Beamtenbund* (DB), which has 750 thousand members. These two unions, unlike the typical German union, are not multi-industrial in terms of organization.

On the employers' side, the principal organization is the German Confederation of Employers Association, comprising 39 national organizations that cover the major branches of industry and 15 industrial employers' confederations, which in turn are made up of local and regional associations. The basic employers' association, however, usually covers geographically a state and industrially a single product. These associations are responsible for collective bargaining with the union. Employers in Germany are better organized than workers and possess more of a united front in collective bargaining than their union counterparts.

Codetermination. A unique feature of labor-management relations in German industries is codetermination of business policies on the part of labor and management. Under the Works Constitution Act of 1952 and succeeding laws, in particular the Works Constitution Act of 1976, labor participation in management decisionmaking was established and broadened. Originally, codetermination was applied only to workers and management in the iron, steel, and coal-mining industries. In 1976 it was broadened to cover all companies with 2,000 or more employees. For public corporations, there must be an equal representation between labor and management on a supervisory board with a chairman to act as tiebreaker. For private companies, supervisory boards must have equal representation from labor and stockholders, plus one representative who is supposed to be neutral. This neutral representative, who is elected by both groups, is supposed to function as a tiebreaker.

The purpose of codetermination is to give workers a voice in determining public policy. *Supervisory boards* make investment and other long-run decisions for companies. There are also *works councils*, which cover all aspects of job conditions. The council discusses with management working space and working conditions. All individual worker dismissals must be brought to the works council before notice can be given, and it may intervene by filing suit in a labor court against the dismissal. The burden of proof is placed on the employer. The works council cannot block major investment decisions by management or interfere with large-scale capital transfers; it is basically restricted to making the best out of the general environment provided by a firm's supervisory board. As such, it acts to smooth the transmission of most decisions between labor and management.

Demands of Labor. German unions have generally exercised restraint in their demands for wage increases. Germany has lost less time to work stoppages since World War II than any other industrialized Western country. During the period 1967–1976 West Germany averaged 56 days lost in major industry strikes per year compared to 1,349 days lost for the United States.[11] In pay, which includes fringe benefits, the German worker ranks among the top in the industrialized world. In pay, security, fringe benefits, and safety, the federal labor laws and the firm-level labor contracts largely fulfill the "social market" principle of sharing the benefits of a successful economy. Conversely, German firms face high labor costs which have affected their competitive position in world trade. Thus, the Germans are having their own problems when it comes to competing against the Japanese. Any product that is produced by labor-intensive techniques will leave Germany far ahead of most countries in terms of costs. West Germany is, therefore, beginning to suffer a sustained loss in world market share.

Government and Business

Government ownership of industry is partially concentrated in areas where state ownership is traditional. For example, telephone, postal communications, and railway transportation are supplied by public enterprises. In addition, various public utilities and, to some extent, bank services are owned and supplied by the public sector. Government ownership also extends to areas that are the domain of private enterprise in the United States. The federal government owns more than 3,000 firms, accounting for 10 percent of national income.[12] The federal and state governments together own 40 percent of the stock of Volkswagen. The federal government controls two-thirds of aluminum production and one-half of coal production. Publicly owned firms function much like privately owned firms. There is little direct government involvement in management, nor much special assistance.

Participation on the part of the federal government in business is channeled primarily through several holding companies. One of them,

---

[11]Douglas Hibbs, Jr., "Industrial Conflict in Advanced Industrial Societies," *American Political Science Review*, Vol. LXX, No. 4 (1976), pp. 382–387.

[12]Congressional Research Service, *Major Structural Differences of the Economies of the U.S., Germany, and Japan* (Washington: Library of Congress, 1979), p. 47.

Vereinigte Elektrizitaets und Bergwerke, A.G., controls subsidiaries which produce coal, lignite, and coke. Another holding company, Vereinigte Industrienunternehmen, A.G., holds interests in firms producing steel, aluminum, and chemicals. The third holding company, A.G. für Berg und Hüettenbetriebe, has control over coal mining, transportation, and engineering firms. The federal government also controls titles to real estate properties through another holding company, Industrie Verwaltungs Gesellschaft.

Business Activity in the Third Reich. Under the Third Reich, every economic activity in Germany, with the exception of agriculture and transportation, was centralized under a group—Industry, Commerce, Banking, Insurance, Power, or Handicrafts—and each functional group was subdivided into divisions. For example, the Metal Division was one subgroup in the Industry group. The Metal Division was further divided into subgroups—Mining, Iron Making, Nonferrous Metal, and Foundries. These subgroups were also organized along regional and geographic lines.

Mergers and cartels became a standard form of business development under the Third Reich. There was a strong government-sponsored concentration movement in industry and business. Thousands of small industrialists and business people were eliminated, and many new combinations and cartels were formed. Large firms were assigned the responsibility for founding and operating the new firms and industries made necessary by the national self-sufficiency programs. It was felt by the Nazis that cartels would result in greater industrial proficiency, and power over the cartel arrangement was transferred to the minister of economic affairs, who could decide whether the arrangement was desirable. The minister was given the power to make outside firms join cartels, and he could prohibit the establishment of new firms.

Postwar Business Development. Postwar Allied occupation policy was aimed at breaking the strength of monopolies and cartels. Deconcentration procedures were taken in the coal and steel industry, the chemical industry, and banking.[13] This action was designed to reduce the degree of monopoly which existed under the Nazis. Decartelization policies were also followed. More extreme forms of cartels, such as sales syndicates and market quotas, were eliminated. However, firms, like Krupp, that had been ordered to divest themselves of parts of their industrial empires were able to avoid the implementation of these orders. In banking, the Allies broke up the three major banks which had dominated the prewar German banking system, but by 1957, the same three banks had been reestablished.[14]

---

[13]This policy is similar to postwar occupation policy in Japan which sought to break up the zaibatsu combines.

[14]The three banks are the Deutsche Bank, the Dresdner Bank, and the Commerzbank.

Postwar German business development has been marked by a return to earlier patterns under which control over large sectors of the economy rests in the hands of a small number of business firms and bankers. Even though official government policy has sought to prevent continued mergers and business concentration, progress has been limited to some extent because of the opposition of the government's political backers in industry. The government's opposition to cartels was manifested in the Law of Cartels, which became effective in 1958 and was amended in 1965. Such business practices as pricefixing and marketsharing have also been curtailed to a degree. The concentration of German business has, to a certain extent, been inimical to the free market policy pursued by the postwar governments.

The federal government, then, exercises a degree of control over business in several ways, such as through functions which in other countries are carried out by private enterprise, but which are publicly owned and operated in Germany; through the national budget, which absorbs and disburses a large part of the national income; through tax incentives which have been designed to stimulate savings and investment; and through a high degree of administrative authority which is wielded by government agencies. However, intervention in economic affairs is a tradition which predates the current government by a considerable time period. Bismarck used state intervention to make Germany a world power. During the Hitler period, intervention was carried to its ultimate extreme in order to prepare the economy for war. Actually, the postwar trend toward a more liberal free market economy represents a break with past traditions and a reaction to extreme state controls.[15]

AN APPRAISAL OF THE GERMAN ECONOMY

Principal responsibility in West German public policies for stimulating economic growth has rested on fiscal devices. Close to one-fifth of federal government expenditures are devoted to physical investments in roads, schools, transportation, and particularly in housing. Savings derived from budget surpluses and the social insurance system have been diverted into investment in government-approved areas, such as housing construction. The federal tax structure is heavily weighted against consumer outlays in that the turnover tax, now replaced by the value-added tax, and other taxes on consumption account for approximately three-fifths of federal budget revenues. Numerous tax preferences are given for approved forms of savings and for various classes of business income, and

---

[15]It may be noted that articles 85 and 86 of the Treaty Establishing the European Economic Community are directed against arrangements which permit, restrict, or distort competition within the Common Market.

the burden of the personal income tax weighs heaviest on the lower- and middle-income ranges.

Until recently the West German growth rate has been second only to Japan's in terms of annual increase. For the period 1950 to 1964, its gross national product increased at a rate of 6.7 percent a year compared to 3.1 percent for the United States and 9.6 percent for Japan. In terms of gross domestic fixed investment for the same period, the rate of growth was 10 percent for West Germany, 2.3 percent for the United States, and 16 percent for Japan.[16]

During the periods 1960–1973 and 1974–1980, the overall performance of the West Germany economy was solid when measured by the economic performance index (see Table 10-1), which is a composite of real economic growth, consumer price index, and the rate of unemployment. In overall economic performance, West Germany ranked second only to Japan and well ahead of the United States for both time periods. The prime contributing factor to the successful performance of the West German economy was the ability of the monetary authorities to keep inflation under control. The West German consumer price index increased at an average annual rate of 3.2 percent from 1960 to 1973 and 4.7 percent from 1973 to 1980.[17] In 1980 the consumer price index increased at a rate of 5.5 percent, well below the 13.5 percent for France and 16.1 percent for the United Kingdom.[18] In large measure the ability of the Germans to moderate inflation stems from their memory of the cata-

---

TABLE 10-1
ECONOMIC PERFORMANCE INDEX
FOR EIGHT MAJOR INDUSTRIAL COUNTRIES

1960–1973		1974–1980	
Japan	145.9	Japan	37.8
West Germany	123.9	West Germany	29.0
France	85.5	France	18.0
Italy	67.7	Canada	16.5
Canada	64.2	Sweden	15.3
Sweden	55.6	United States	15.2
United States	50.4	Italy	13.4
United Kingdom	43.1	United Kingdom	2.2

Source: New York Stock Exchange, Office of Economic Research, *U.S. Economic Performance in a Global Perspective* (February 1981), p. 11.

---

[16]Angus Maddison, *Economic Growth in the West* (London: Allen and Unwin, 1964), p. 37.

[17]New York Stock Exchange, Office of Economic Research, *U.S. Economic Performance in a Global Perspective* (New York, February 1981), p. 11.

[18]Deutsches Bundesbank, *op. cit.*, p. 62.

strophic inflation which wrecked Germany during the period after World War I.

The real rate of economic growth for West Germany lagged behind Japan and France for both time periods. During the period 1960–1973 the real rate of economic growth averaged 4.8 percent a year for West Germany, compared to 10.6 percent for Japan and 5.7 percent for France. For 1973–1980 the annual average rate was 4.4 percent for Japan, 2.9 percent for France, and 2.3 percent for West Germany. Unemployment rates, however, have remained low in West Germany. These rates are helped by a labor force which is not growing in size and by the presence of millions of *Gastarbeiten* (foreign workers) who have most of the menial jobs and who are the first to be fired when there is an increase in unemployment.

Table 10-2 summarizes the performance of the West German economy from 1974 to 1980. The real rate of change in gross national product is used as a measure of economic growth. The rate of unemployment is expressed as a percentage of the German work force including *Gastarbeiten*. Annual increase in the consumer price index, with the base year of 1970 set as 100 percent, is the third measure of performance.

TABLE 10-2
ECONOMIC PERFORMANCE OF THE WEST GERMAN ECONOMY
1974–1980

	Increase in Real GNP	Unemployment	Consumer Price Index
1974	+0.5%	2.2%	7.0%
1975	−1.5	4.0	6.0
1976	+5.2	4.0	4.3
1977	+3.0	3.9	3.7
1978	+3.2	3.8	2.7
1979	+4.6	3.3	4.1
1980	+1.9	3.3	5.5

Source: Deutsches Bundesbank, *Annual Report for 1980,* April 1981, p. 2.

West Germany still has one of the world's healthiest economies. The deutschemark is one of the world's most stable currencies. There are some clouds on the horizon, however. Dependency on oil has made the economy vulnerable to flare-ups in the Middle East. In 1980 West Germany had to pay an average of 79 percent more than in 1979 to buy one barrel of imported petroleum. The oil price rise had immediate repercussions on the domestic price level, particularly on the cost of energy. Germany, like the United States, will face increased pressure from the Japanese in world competition. The general economic malaise of the Western European countries also will have an impact on West German exports. Unemployment rates in such countries as Belgium and the United Kingdom reached their highest levels since the Depression.

SUMMARY

The West German economy can be considered as a mix between private and public enterprise. The government has sought to establish a free market economy exempt from most controls. Policies have been pursued which can be considered as favorable to a free enterprise system. Certainly, from the standpoint of production and distribution, market forces determine each, just as in the United States. The pricing mechanism is the basic determinant, not some central authoritarian planner. Consumer sovereignty prevails in that the German people are free to purchase whatever products they desire.

Nevertheless, the government plays a much more important role in the economy than does its counterpart in the United States. A considerable segment of the economy is nationalized, and the government, through this segment, can influence the level of investment. Some nationalized industries are in direct competition with private industries for resources, but there is no striking economic consequence because public enterprise has coexisted with private enterprise since the days of Bismarck. There is also little danger that further encroachment on the private sector will occur on the part of the public sector. Since the end of the war, there has been no trend in this direction.

The government has made a wide use of fiscal incentives to accomplish various socioeconomic objectives. For example, fiscal encouragement has been directed toward housing construction. Private contractors have been accorded a variety of investment and tax allowances; they have been especially favored if they produce new homes to let at low rents. Tax credits and depreciation allowances have also been used to stimulate investment in ship construction to help rebuild the German merchant marine. On the other hand, special real estate taxes are levied to punish landowners who do not construct houses on their property. Savings are stimulated through the use of special premium allowances or tax exemptions.

An impressive portion of the West German national product is devoted to social welfare programs. These programs are extensive and are constantly expanding. Roughly half of government expenditures come under the purview of transfers, which is indicative of the welfare state character of Germany. Some of the income redistribution effect of transfer payments has been counterbalanced by a shift from progressive income and corporation taxes to indirect taxes, such as the value-added tax, which are burdensome on the consumer.

REVIEW QUESTIONS

1. Discuss the factors that were responsible for the rapid postwar recovery of the German economy.
2. Compare the West German and United States economic systems. Are there any major differences between the two systems?
3. Describe the West German tax system. Is there a similarity between it and the United States system?
4. Government tax and expenditure policies play a significant role in the operation of the West German economy. Do you agree?
5. Discuss the relationship of the Deutsche Bundesbank to the rest of the West German banking system.

6. Discuss the relationship between government and business in West Germany.
7. Compare the overall performance of the West Germany economy to other major industrial countries.
8. What is codetermination?

RECOMMENDED READINGS

Congressional Research Service. *Major Structural Differences of the Economies of the United States, Germany, and Japan.* Washington: Library of Congress, 1979.

Knott, Jack. *Managing the German Economy: Budgetary Politics in a Federal State.* Lexington, Mass.: Lexington Books, 1981.

Hartrich, Edward. *The Fourth and Richest Reich.* New York: Macmillan, 1980.

Kohl, W. L., and G. Bavesi, eds. *West Germany: A European and Global Power.* Lexington, Mass.: Heath, 1980.

Leminsky, Gerhard. "Worker Participation: The German Experience." In *Labor Relations in Advanced Industrial Societies,* edited by Benjamin Martin and Everett M. Kassalow. Washington: Carnegie Foundation for International Peace, 1980, pp. 139–160.

Schnitzer, Martin. *East and West Germany: A Comparative Economic Analysis.* New York: Praeger, 1972.

Wallich, Henry C. *Mainsprings of the German Revival.* New Haven: Yale University Press, 1955.

Zweig, Konrad. *Germany through Inflation and Recession.* London: Center for Policy Studies, 1976.

11

The United Kingdom

INTRODUCTION

One hundred years ago England was at the apogee of its power. The British dominated the world, bringing their culture and religion to such assorted "poor benighted heathen" as the Zulus of Natal, the "Fuzzy-Wuzzies" of the Sudan, and the Afghans and Pathans of northern India. The British Empire extended from England to Africa, and from India to New Zealand, and British business interests owned and operated everything from diamond mines in South Africa to tea plantations in Ceylon and paper mills in Canada. Brittania ruled the waves, and British citizens throughout the world were able to apply the Roman words, *civis Romanus sum*,[1] to themselves and know that they would enjoy the protection of the British government.

However, the days of Kipling and the British Empire are long since gone, and the society that once produced Charles Dickens and Alfred Tennyson now produces author Barbara Cartland and comedian Benny Hill. The British economy has fallen on hard times. Slow growth, low productivity, inflation, unemployment, and balance-of-payments crises have plagued the British economy over the last two decades. Successive governments have had little success with these problems in anything but the short run. Prime Minister Margaret Thatcher's electoral victory and

---

[1] "I am a Roman citizen." Because one British citizen of Greek extraction was killed in a riot in Greece, the British declared war on Greece.

the policies she has adopted can be explained partly by the inability of previous governments to manage the economy successfully and, in particular, to restrain inflation. It remains to be seen whether her policies are successful. The "British disease" may be too far advanced for Mrs. Thatcher or, for that matter, anyone else to cure.

It may well be that the United Kingdom represents a watershed in Western society. Oswald Spengler, a German philosopher, wrote a book called *Decline of the West* which forecasted the decline of Western civilization.[2] Spengler claimed to be able to discern the outline of a life cycle through which, he believed, all civilizations must pass. Western civilization was compared with Greco-Roman civilization in terms of form, duration, and meaning. His view of Western civilization was a gloomy one. The West, according to Spengler, had already passed through the creative stage of culture into a period of material comfort. The end of a creative impulse begins the process of decline. There is no prospect for reversing the decline, for civilizations blossom and decay like natural organisms and true rejuvenation is impossible. He uses a biological metaphor to describe the fateful trajectory of a civilization: "For everything organic the notions of birth, youth, age, lifetime, and death are fundamental."

The Industrial Revolution first took place in the United Kingdom, and that may be part of its problem. An agressive country (Germany and Japan are examples), entering later into the industrialization cycle, is able to take advantage of newer technologies and older countries' experiences in plant layout and design, while countries that industrialized earlier have older and more inefficient plants. The United Kingdom began to lose ground in the areas of advanced technology, first to the Germans and then to the United States. British economic dominance of the world had crested by 1910, and eventually the economy began to live off of the foreign earnings that its corporations earned during the halcyon years of the British Empire. Many British industries today are in an advanced stage of atrophy and need large amounts of capital to increase primary processing capacity. In many crucial areas British industry has lost its product advantage to the younger and more viable industries of Germany, France, and the United States. But these industries, too, face a challenge from the Japanese and South Koreans.

The remainder of the chapter will be devoted to a discussion of the British economy as it enters the 1980s. To most Americans, the problems of the British economy are a familiar litany of woe: high inflation, low investment, low productivity, declining industrial competitiveness, and, in recent years, increasing unemployment and declining living standards. The causes of the British problem are controversial as are the cures. Prime Minister Thatcher has focused on a different approach to the prob-

---

[2]Oswald Spengler, *Decline of the West* (New York: Knopf, 1939), pp. 1–7.

lem from her predecessors. This approach will be presented in some detail, but first it is necessary to examine the institutional arrangements of the British economy.

THE ECONOMIC SYSTEM

The British economy is mixed. Although private enterprise is dominant, the government plays an important role in economic activity in three ways: through the nationalized sector of the economy, through social welfare measures aimed at achieving income redistribution and economic and social well-being, and through fiscal and monetary policy measures which are used to pursue such macroeconomic goals as full employment.

The process of nationalization took place in the period immediately following World War II. Affected by the nationalization program of the Labour government were the Bank of England, the railways, the coal mines, the steel industry, trucking, and the public utilities—especially the electrical and gas industries. The owners were compensated at approximately the market price of their holdings. In the case of some of the industries, nationalization was neither as revolutionary nor as controversial as might be supposed. The Bank of England was already, in effect, a public institution; its changed status was hardly more than a change in title. The railroads and coal mines had been losing money for years, and the owners were perfectly willing to accept nationalization.

Apart from the nationalized industries, economic activity is organized pretty much in the capitalistic fashion. Business firms are free to organize in any of the traditional forms and may make their decisions on the usual capitalistic bases of price and cost. Through the use of monetary and fiscal policies, however, the government can exert indirect control on the activities of private enterprises. For example, the government has wide powers to encourage the development of industries in areas which are depressed because of the dependence on a single industry, usually coal mining or shipbuilding. The government can also influence and control industrial, residential, and public construction.

Public Finance

The British budget is a powerful weapon for influencing the general level of activity in the economy. Its purpose is not only to raise revenue to meet government expenditures, but also to regulate the national economy. It is part of the budget's job to help bring about a balance between the total goods and services that are likely to be available to the nation and the total claims that will be made upon them.

The budget does not include all public sector expenditures. It includes all national government expenditures other than payments out of the National Insurance Funds. However, it does not include either local governmental expenditures or nationalized industry investment, although it does cover grants to local authorities and loans and deficit grants to the nationalized industries, as well as the British government's contributions to the National Insurance Funds. The expenditure figures in the budget are one measure of the national government's contribution to the demand for good and services.

The nationalized industries, local authorities, and other public bodies need to borrow from year to year mainly to finance expenditures on capital projects. Most of this borrowing is done from the National Loans Fund, which is responsible for the bulk of domestic lending by the government. The National Loans Fund and the Consolidated Fund, which balances current revenue against current expenditures, are the two basic components of the budget.

The British Tax System. Taxation in the United Kingdom is fairly evenly balanced between direct and indirect taxes. The most important direct tax is the personal income tax. No other European country, except Sweden, imposes personal income taxes to a greater degree than does the United Kingdom, nor do personal taxes account for nearly so high a percentage of gross national product in France, Germany, or the United States as they do in the United Kingdom and Sweden. There is also a heavy reliance on indirect taxes on tobacco, alcohol, and gasoline. The tax yield on these three commodities amounts to nearly 7 percent of the British gross national product, over half as much again as Sweden, twice as much as Germany and France, and three times the American proportion.

Personal Income Taxes. For many years the British income tax structure included an income tax and a surtax. However, in 1973 this system was replaced by a single graduated income tax. The minimum and maximum rates of the British income tax were among the highest in the world, exceeded only by the tax rates of the Scandinavian countries. A distinction was made between earned and unearned income, with rates increasing to 98 percent on the latter. In 1980 minimum and maximum rates were lowered on both earned and unearned incomes. The minimum rate on earned income was reduced to 30 percent on income up to £11,250 (approximately $25,300), and the maximum rate was reduced to 60 percent on income in excess of £27,750 (approximately $63,710). The top rate on unearned income was reduced from 98 percent to 75 percent. There are allowances for children which vary with ages and flat allowances for single and married taxpayers. In 1980 the personal income tax accounted for 11 percent of gross domestic product.[3]

---

[3]Lloyds Bank, "The British Economy in Figures" (London, 1981), p. 1.

Other Taxes. In addition to the personal income tax, there is also a corporate income tax. In 1980 the 42 percent rate was applied to corporate incomes up to £60,000 (approximately $135,000) and the 52 percent rate was applied on incomes of £100,000 ($230,000) and above. Capital gains are taxed at a flat 30 percent rate. However, there are generous allowances for capital investment. Britain has experimented with a wide variety of subsidies to promote investment or regional development or both. It has used, at one time or another, accelerated depreciation, high initial depreciation allowances, investment allowances, and investment grants.

There is also a value-added tax which is calculated at a single flat tax rate of 15 percent of the value of a given good or service. There are certain exemptions to the value-added tax, including necessities such as drugs and medicines. Excise taxes are also levied on consumer goods, especially tobacco, alcohol, and gasoline. One feature of the excise taxes is the large proportion they represent of the total sales price. For example, the tax on cigarettes is 90 percent of the purchase price.

Finally, in the United Kingdom as in other countries, the social security system is financed largely from payroll taxes. At one time, contributions from both employees and employers were paid at a flat amount per employee per week. Since 1975 the social security tax has been levied as a percentage of the employee's earnings. In 1980 the rate was 6.7 percent for fully covered employees. Employers paid a rate of 10 percent on the first £120 of earnings a week.

Government Expenditures. Total central government expenditures for the fiscal year 1980–1981 amounted to $83 billion. These expenditures can be divided into two categories—current and capital. Current expenditures can be divided into four categories: expenditures for goods and services, subsidies, current grants to the personal and public sectors, and interest on the public debt.[4] Capital expenditures include gross domestic fixed capital formation, capital grants, and loans.

When local government and central government spending are added together, total public expenditures of all types are around 44 percent of the gross national product. One reason for this is that the public sector contribution to investment is much higher in Great Britain than in the United States because of the importance of public enterprises. These enterprises own about 38 percent of the nation's capital assets and are responsible for nearly 42 percent of the annual fixed investment of the nation.

The Welfare State. The United Kingdom has a comprehensive social welfare system. It can be divided into two categories: the medical care and social security program which includes family allowances, and the national health insurance program which provides unemployment and

---

[4]Bank of England, "Monthly Quarterly Bulletin," December 1981.

sickness benefits, old age pensions, maternity benefits, and death grants. Both programs were developed partly as a result of deprivations sustained during World War II and partly as a remembrance of prewar British capitalism, which was characterized by high rates of unemployment as well as excessive and widespread inequalities in the distribution of wealth and income. In 1924, for example, two-thirds of the total wealth in the United Kingdom was held by 1.6 percent of all wealth owners (property owners— real estate, stocks, bonds).[5]

Medical Care and Family Allowances. The best-known social welfare program is medical care, which is provided in the United Kingdom under the National Health Service as a free public service and is not a part of the regular social insurance program. All residents are eligible for health services. General practitioner care, specialist services, hospitalization, maternity care, and treatment in the event of industrial injuries are provided by the National Health Service. There are charges for some medical prescriptions and cost sharing by the patient for such things as false teeth and hearing aids. Most of the cost of the National Health Service program is financed by the British government out of general revenues from the budget. The employer and employee pay flat-rate weekly contributions that meet about one-fifth of the total cost of medical care.

In addition to medical care, there are family allowances which are cash payments for the benefit of the family as a whole. They are of recent origin in the United Kingdom, dating back to 1946, and are financed out of general revenues rather than from taxes on employers and employees. They are paid to families with two or more children under certain age limits.

National Insurance. Separate and apart from the National Health Service, there exists a comprehensive program of social security which comes under the category of national insurance. This program provides fixed-rate sickness benefits for up to one year to working men and women and widows. Dissatisfaction with this program has led to a rapid increase in the number of individuals who purchase private medical insurance. Old age pensions and unemployment benefits are similar in makeup to sickness benefits. As a corollary to regular old age pensions, there is a graduated pension scheme which provides higher rates to higher-paid contributors. A maternity allowance is paid to women who give up paid employment to have a baby, and there is also a lump-sum maternity grant which is paid to most mothers. There is a death grant which is payable on the death of an insured person or the wife, husband, or child of an insured person. Finally, there are widow's and widowed mother's allowances, the latter allowance based on the number of dependent children.

---

[5]James Wedgwood, *The Economics of Inheritance* (London: Routledge, 1929), p. 42.

Income Redistribution. The British government is an instrument for effecting changes in the distribution of income. Taxes and transfer payments are the major means for accomplishing this objective, with taxes reducing the incomes of some persons and transfer payments adding to the incomes of others. Income redistribution is accomplished through the progressivity of the personal income tax. The top bracket rate and rates at higher income levels make the progressivity of the personal income tax one of the highest in the world.[6] Even for the average workers, the marginal tax rate is high in comparison to rates in such countries as France, Germany, Japan, and the United States. The basic, or lowest, income tax rate of 30 percent is much higher than the basic tax rate of 14 percent for the United States. Moreover, personal exemptions are low in comparison to other countries even though numerous special provisions have been adopted. The tax on investment income, which once reached a maximum rate of 98 percent but which is now 75 percent, is also high by world standards.

Other taxes, in particular excise taxes on alcohol and tobacco, tend to add an element of regressivity into the British tax system, thus counterbalancing to some extent the progressivity of the income tax. In comparison to the United States, the total tax burden in Great Britain is higher at all levels of income.[7] With marginal rates in excess of 40 percent for the average production worker and higher for professional workers, the incentive to substitute leisure for paid employment is considerable.[8] Tax policy may have had a significant impact on the poor performance of the British economy, particularly in the area of saving.

Income redistribution is also accomplished through the provision of government assistance to individuals and families. For the family with children, family allowances and general social welfare measures are provided, and for the aged, an old age pension is provided. There are also supplementary benefits to individuals and families whose incomes are below a defined scale. For the infirm, there are sickness benefits; and for all persons, there are general health and medical benefits. Inequality in the distribution of factor income among British social classes is mitigated to some extent by the mechanism of transfer payments, the bulk of which are directed to households in the lower-income segments of the population. Low-income families gain, as well as persons in the nonworking population.

---

[6]Joseph A. Pechman, "Taxation," in Richard E. Caves and Lawrence B. Krause, eds., *Britain's Economic Performance* (Washington: Brookings Institution, 1980), pp. 207–208.
[7]*Ibid.*, p. 211.
[8]From 1959 to 1975 the average income tax burden of the middle-income groups tripled. See Royal Commission on the Distribution of Income and Wealth, *Third Report on the Standing Reference*, Report 5, Command Paper 6999 (London: Her Majesty's Stationery Office, 1977), pp. 13–66.

Greater Income Equality. A great deal has been written in recent years concerning the strong influence of egalitarian considerations upon economic policies pursued by the British government. A prime goal of the British welfare state when it was created in 1945 was a more equal distribution of income. This was to be accomplished through a progressive income tax levied on both earned (wages and salaries) and unearned (interest and dividends) income and an inheritance tax. However, the structure of the income and inheritance taxes has changed frequently since 1945 because the tax philosophies of the two major political parties, Conservative and Labour, differ markedly. Each party makes changes in the tax structure when it comes in to power. The Conservative government of Prime Minister Margaret Thatcher places emphasis on a reduction in government spending, enforced by stringent cash limits on expenditures, and a shift from direct to indirect taxation.

Table 11-1 shows the distribution of before- and after-tax income for the upper 1 percent and 5 percent of income earners for selected years. In 1949, for example, the upper 1 percent of all income units received 11.2 percent of before-tax income and 6.4 percent of after-tax income, while the top 5 percent received 23.8 percent of before-tax income, while the top 5 percent received 23.8 percent of before-tax income and 17.7 percent of after-tax income. As can be seen from the table, there was little change in income distribution from 1957 to 1967, but a rather sharp change from 1967 to 1977. The fact that there are relatively few people with high incomes makes the redistribution of income difficult because the extra revenue that can be squeezed out of them is small.

TABLE 11-1
DISTRIBUTION OF INCOME FOR THE UPPER 1 PERCENT AND 5 PERCENT OF BRITISH INCOME UNITS FOR SELECTED YEARS

	Before Taxes		After Taxes	
	Top 1 Percent	Top 5 Percent	Top 1 Percent	Top 5 Percent
1949	11.2%	23.8%	6.4%	17.7%
1953	9.8	21.9	5.8	15.9
1957	8.2	19.1	5.0	14.9
1960	8.5	19.9	5.1	15.6
1961	8.1	19.2	5.5	16.0
1967	7.9	19.2	5.0	15.5
1975	6.2	16.8	4.0	13.7
1977	5.5	16.3	3.8	13.8

Source: Central Statistical Office, *National Income Blue Book* (London: Her Majesty's Stationery Office, 1980), Table 6, p. 19.

Inequality of Wealth. Inequality in the distribution of wealth is perhaps more closely identified with the United Kingdom than with any other major industrial country because, after all, the Industrial Revolution really developed in this country. A concomitant of the Industrial Revolution was the concentration of property in the hands of a few persons. Vast fortunes were made, particularly during the development of the British Empire with its markets and resources. These fortunes, for the most part, were not touched by taxation, but were allowed to accumulate and be passed down from generation to generation.

Studies of the distribution of wealth are not often made. One of the first studies of the distribution of wealth in the United Kingdom covered the years 1912 and 1924.[9] In 1912, 43 percent of all wealth was owned by 0.2 percent of all wealth owners, while well over half of the wealth of the country was owned by only 0.8 percent of wealth owners.[10] During the intervening 12-year period World War I occurred, causing some dislocations in the British economy. The tax structure was also revised considerably in 1914 and in subsequent war years by the imposition of a surtax on incomes exceeding a particular level—$7,200 in 1914 and $4,800 in 1918. Minor shifts occurred occurred in the distribution of wealth. In 1924 two-thirds of the wealth was owned by 1.6 percent of all wealth owners, compared to 0.9 percent in 1912.[11] Some 93 to 94 percent of all of the wealth was owned by 13.3 percent of the owners in 1912 and by 23.0 percent of the owners in 1924.

Considerable shifting in the distribution of wealth has occurred since 1924, as is indicated in Table 11-2. The share of the highest 1 percent fell

TABLE 11-2
PERCENTAGE DISTRIBUTION OF PERSONAL
WEALTH HELD BY WEALTH OWNERS IN THE
UNITED KINGDOM, 1924 AND 1976

	1924	1976
Top 1 percent	61%	25%
Next 2 to 5 percent	21	21
6 to 10 percent	7	14
11 to 20 percent	5	17
21 to 100 percent	6	23

Source: Royal Commission on the Distribution of Income and Wealth (Diamond Commission), Report No. 7, Command Paper 7595 (London: Her Majesty's Stationery Office, July 1979).

---

[9]Wedgewood, *op. cit.*, p. 47.
[10]*Ibid.*
[11]*Ibid.*, p. 48.

from 61 percent in 1924 to 25 percent in 1976. The main influences at work on the distribution of wealth have been an increase in real income, which has allowed many persons to buy their own homes and to accumulate other assets, and the impact of the estate tax, which reduced wealth inequality directly and also encouraged wealthy persons to distribute their incomes before death. However, the role of inheritance in the creation of the largest wealth holdings remains large. Notice that the top 20 percent of the wealth holders still own 77 percent of the total personal wealth in Britain.

The Banking System

The British banking system consists of the Bank of England, which is the central bank of the nation, and a few large commercial banks which have assumed an oligopolistic structure as a result of mergers and integration. Besides the commercial banks, whose primary function is the financing of the economy in general, there are other institutions whose activities are more specialized but whose aggregate importance is very great. These are the merchant bankers and the acceptance houses, whose primary concern is with the financing of foreign trade. The insurance companies and building societies are the most important suppliers of investment capital in the United Kingdom.

The Bank of England. The Bank of England was chartered by an act of Parliament in 1694. In 1844 it was given the sole right of note issue. By the second half of the 19th century, the public service aspects of the Bank's activities began to eclipse its private banking business. It became the lender of last resort to the money market and the regulator of the great international gold and capital markets in London.

In 1946 the Bank was nationalized by an act of Parliament. The government acquired the entire capital stock of the Bank and was empowered to appoint the governor, deputy director, and directors of the Bank for fixed terms. The Treasury has the power to give directions to the Bank, after consultation with the governor.

The Bank has the overall responsibility for the management and control of the monetary and financial system. It exercises monetary control through a combination of open market operations and discount policy. This is done on the basis of institutional arrangements peculiar to the British monetary system. Unlike the Federal Reserve System of the United States, the Bank does not lend to commercial banks, but only to discount houses, whose main business is to underwrite the weekly Treasury bill issue with call loans secured mostly from London clearinghouses.

Credit is restricted by selling Treasury bills or government bonds through discount houses and securities dealers, thus absorbing cash from the banking system. The discount market chiefly consists of 12 major houses which are members of the London Discount Market Association, the organization which is responsible for bidding on Treasury bills each week. To restore their cash and liquidity positions, banks can withdraw their call loans from the discount houses; the discount houses, in turn, may be forced to borrow money from the Bank of England at a penalty rate, which is set higher than the average yield from the discount houses' earning assets.

The Commercial Banks. The commerical banking system operates under private ownership and management. There are five major commerical banks—Barclays, Lloyds, Midland, National Provincial, and Westminster. Two other large banks are the District Bank and Martins. These banks undertake all normal types of banking business, such as deposits, advances, bill discounting, and foreign exchange. They do not participate directly in industry; their financing of industry is limited to short-term advances and overdrafts which are formally repayable on demand. British banks have a traditional preference for financing working rather than fixed capital expenditures.

Discount Houses. *Discount houses* play a very important role in the British financial system. Their most important function concerns the financing of Treasury bills. The discount houses purchase the Treasury bills on a weekly basis with loans which they obtain from the commercial banks or with their own funds. This purchase provides the government with day-to-day finance. The discount houses are also the intermediary through which the Bank of England acts as a lender of last resort to the banking system. As mentioned above, the discount houses obtain a substantial amount of their funds to purchase Treasury bills from the commercial banks on a *call loan* basis. If loan repayment is demanded by the banks, the discount houses can borrow from the Bank of England through rediscounting bills or by advances against collateral. The minimum rate at which the Bank of England will make funds available to the discount houses is called the *bank rate,* and it is the key rate in the whole structure of interest rates in Great Britain.

Other Financial Institutions. Capital funds are also provided through other sources, such as insurance companies, building societies, investment trusts, and pension funds. The insurance companies, pension funds, and builing societies are the dominant sources of long-term finance. Insurance companies are privately owned and provide a supply of capital to the long-term market.

Building societies, also privately owned, are second only to the insurance companies as a source of long-term loanable funds. The building societies rely on the savings of the public, and they provide financing for about two-thirds of private home building. The societies offer both shares and deposits to the public. Shares are nonmarketable and pay a higher rate of interest.

Investment trusts are also an important source of long-term capital funds. In the past, trusts played an important part in the development of the Commonwealth countries. During the period from 1870 to 1914, they also contributed much to the economic development of the United States.

In investment banking, there is no doubt about the power of the government to exercise control. Under the Banking Control and Guarantee Act of 1947, the government has the power to regulate new access to the capital market and establish priorities which are deemed essential to the national interest. The act also empowered the Treasury to guarantee long-term loans made to facilitate industrial development.

Monetary Policy. Monetary policy in the United Kingdom is used as a stabilization device and consists of several arrangements.

Hire purchase controls are used to regulate the volume of consumer expenditures. This type of control is a selective control in that it involves the amount of down payment required to consummate the purchase of consumer goods and also involves the maximum period of repayment. It has proven to be an important monetary policy instrument and has an advantage over other monetary and fiscal policy instruments in that it can be imposed immediately.

The use of the *bank rate* is also an important monetary policy device. The bank rate is the price which the Bank of England will pay when rediscounting bills. It is a penalty rate which is usually set above the market rate of discount and has its impact on the discount houses. As mentioned previously, the discount houses occupy a special position in the market for Treasury bills, and from the standpoint of monetary policy the Treasury bill is a major instrument in the money market. The discount houses link the commercial banks to the Bank of England. They purchase Treasury bills with money borrowed at call from the commercial banks; if they have to borrow from the Bank of England, the bank rate, or "penalty rate," can be employed. Changes in the bank rate force changes in other interest rates.

Open market operations constitute another monetary policy instrument. It refers to the buying and selling of Treasury bills and other short-term obligations in the money market by the Bank of England. These transactions affect the liquidity of the commercial banks by expanding or contracting their balances with the Bank of England.

A direct control, which takes the form of special deposits, can be imposed on commerical banks by the Bank of England. The purpose of this device is to alter the liquidity ratio of commercial banks. The *liquidity ratio*, which is the ratio of liquid bank assets to total assets, is set at

30 percent of total bank assets. Special deposits have the effect of reducing the liquidity ratio.

Monetary, as well as fiscal, policy has been an integral part of the policy of "stop-go," which British anticyclical policy has been called. Aggressive use of monetary policy as a stabilization device has been made by both Conservative and Labour governments during the postwar period in an attempt to maintain full employment as well as to preserve a semblance of price stability.

Labor-Management Relations

Unions occupy a powerful position in the United Kingdom. During the postwar period full employment contributed to the development of union power, and wages increased faster than productivity. In general, labor-management relations have been rather acrimonious, with some of the worst labor disputes occurring in the public sector. Many British labor unions are afflicted with a class struggle mentality, and there is no question that union intransigence on issues involving productivity has been a factor contributing to the general decline of the British economy during the postwar period. British unions are politically active and constitute the main base of support for the Labour party.

Unlike the United States, where union membership expressed as a percentage of the work force has decreased, union membership in the United Kingdom has increased, particularly during the period 1968–1980. In 1980 union membership amounted to about 48 percent of the British labor force of 26 million workers.[12] To some extent this increase in union membership was caused by an increase in the rate of inflation which led workers to seek the protective security of unions. Also, as the importance of the public sector increased, there was a greater incentive to join a union that would represent worker interests in the complex negotiations for benefits conferred by the state.[13]

There are some 500 trade unions in the United Kingdom, and most belong to the British Trades Union Congress (TUC). The TUC is a permanent association which is constituted by the affiliation of trade unions. The executive body of the TUC is the General Council. The members of the General Council are elected at the annual meeting of the TUC. Affiliated unions are entitled to send to the annual meeting one delegate for every 5,000 members. These unions vary in size and character and in the

---

[12]Central Statistical Office, *Monthly Digest of Statistics* (London: Her Majesty's Stationery Office, August 1981), Table 7.

[13]Robert Price and George S. Bain, "Union Growth Revisited: 1948–1974 in Perspective," *British Journal of Industrial Relations*, Vol. 14 (November 1976), pp. 339–355.

views they hold regarding organization. There are craft unions, industrial unions, general workers' unions, and nonmanual and professional organizations. Although the unions operate individually, they come together, industry by industry, through federations which are set up for the purpose of collective bargaining. A single union may have members in several industries and may therefore be affiliated with several federations.

Current industrial relations in the United Kingdom are governed by two acts, the Trade Union and Labor Relations Act of 1974 and the Employment Protection Act of 1975. The Employment Protection Act is the more important in that it sets employees' rights. Under the provisions of the act, maternity pay and guaranteed weekly payments became a legal requirement, along with such things as time off with pay for union duties. Written terms for dismissal and redundancy (British term for being laid off) have to be provided. Government intervention in all aspects of collective bargaining came to be an increasingly important policy priority. The Advisory, Conciliation, and Arbitration Service (ACAS) was created to adjudicate collective bargaining disputes. Decisions of the ACAS can be appealed to the Employment Appeal Tribunal.

Government and Business

As Table 11-3 indicates, the government has control over a number of industries, such as coal, inland transportation, telecommunications, civil aviation, and steel. The nationalized industries are major users of national resources; employ, on the average, about one-twelfth of the labor force; produce about one-tenth of gross domestic product; and account for about one-fifth of domestic investment. Two industries were nationalized during the 1970s—shipbuilding and aerospace—and the British National Oil Company (BNOC) was formed chiefly on the basis of the North Sea oil assets previously owned by the National Coal Board. The steel industry was nationalized after World War II, denationalized by the Conservative party when it come to power in 1951, and nationalized again by the Labour government in 1966.

There were several reasons for the government takeover of these industries:

1. They were of key importance to the economy, not only as to production, but as to volume of aggregate employment as well.
2. They had not been efficient in the past and needed reorganization along radically different lines.
3. They needed large capital expenditures, which were forthcoming only from the government or through loan guarantees.
4. The nationalized energy sector could be coordinated more easily into a national energy policy.

TABLE 11-3
THE BRITISH NATIONALIZED INDUSTRIES

Industry	Government Agency
British Aerospace	Industry
British Airways	Trade
British Gas Corporation	Energy
British Railways Board	Transport
British Shipbuilders	Industry
British Steel Corporation	Industry
British Airports Authority	Trade
British National Oil Corporation	Energy
British Transport Docks Board	Transport
National Coal Board	Energy
National Bus Company	Energy
Post Office–Telecomunications	Industry
Electricity Industry in England and Wales	Energy

Source: T. G. Weyman-Jones, "The Nationalized Industries: Changing Attitudes and Changing Roles," in Peter Maunder, ed., *The British Economy in the 1970's* (London: Heinemann, 1980), p. 196.

The Coal Industry. The coal industry illustrates all of the reasons mentioned above. It has had a long history of problems. The first step toward state ownership occurred with the passage of the Coal Act of 1938 when the Conservative government made provision for the nationalization of royalties. Production quotas and minimum prices were set by the government. Actual nationalization of the coal industry occurred under the provisions of the Coal Industry Nationalization Act of 1946. The National Coal Board was created and given responsibility for running the coal mines. It was not set up as a department of the government. The Nationalization Act, which created the board, laid down the rule that the coal industry should break even, after paying interest charges on the capital advanced by the government to finance the industry. Within this particular statutory obligation, the industry is left free to conduct the day-to-day management as it sees fit. The National Coal Board has the authority to phase out the operation of unprofitable mines and to transfer unemployed coal miners to more profitable areas.

Nationalization and Pricing Policies. In 1967 explicit price and investment rules were established for the nationalized industries.[14] On pricing,

---

[14]*Nationalized Industries: A Review of Economic and Financial Objectives*, Command Paper 3437 (London: Her Majesty's Stationery Office, November 1967).

marginal cost pricing was laid down, though accounting costs were to be covered by revenue. Unit prices proportional to marginal cost were recommended for the apportionment of fixed costs among consumers where necessary to cover total costs. Social cost-benefit analysis was proposed for investment appraisal, and it was stated that the returns on investment should be presented in terms of discounted net present value. A test discount rate of 8 percent was laid down for project appraisal. The government explicitly recognized the noncommercial operations undertaken by nationalized industries and stressed the need to distinguish social obligations from commercial operations. When social obligations were involved, subsidies from the government could be provided to cover costs.

In 1978 the government recognized that in many cases prices are market-determined, and even where this is not so the difficulties of practical application in marginal cost pricing can be severe. The main focus of current policy was shifted from those matters affecting individual services and projects to the opportunity cost of capital in the industry as a whole.[15] A real rate of return on assets was defined and was to be achieved by the nationalized industries on new investment as a whole. The real rate of return is principally related to the real rate of return in the private sector, taking into consideration questions of the cost of finance. It was set initially at 5 percent and is to be reviewed every three to five years. Thus the main ways over which the government has sought to exercise control since 1978 are the real rate of return and the financial target together with the general level of prices.[16] Individual prices and investment priorities are left largely up to the industries themselves.

Government Influence on Private Enterprise. The government influences the development of British industry through the use of monetary and fiscal policies and through laws governing mergers, restrictive trade practices, and resale price maintenance. It also has control over credit and investment policies and can establish priorities that it deems to be in the national interest. A case in point is the National Enterprise Board, which was created by the Industry Act of 1975. It purpose is to provide financial aid to business firms in exchange for a share in their equities. Priority was to be given to the manufacturing industry. Shares of British Leyland and Rolls-Royce, two companies with financial problems, were transferred to the National Enterprise Board when it was set up. To some extent the board was set up to bail out ailing business firms, but in the process state control over these enterprises was increased through equity ownership. The Thatcher government has cut back some of the board's activities in

---

[15]*The Nationalized Industries*, Command Paper 7131 (London: Her Majesty's Stationery Office, March 1978).

[16]Andrew Likierman, "The Financial and Economic Framework for Nationalized Industries," *Lloyds Bank Review*, No. 144 (October 1979), pp. 16–32.

private investment. The board is to direct investment toward private companies involved in the development of advanced technology or located in areas of the country where unemployment is high.

In Great Britain, as in the United States, legislation seeking to improve the performance of the private business sector has proceeded both to regulate the structure of markets and to govern the conduct of firms in the marketplace. The aim of British legislation with respect to mergers and monopolies has been expressed in a number of acts, the most important of which is the Monopolies Act of 1973. Monopolies in Great Britain are not presumed illegal per se as they are in the United States, but there is provision for review of monopoly situations by the Monopolies Commission. Dominant firm situations may be referred if a firm holds at least one-fourth of total sales in a relevant market, whether it be national or local. Restrictive trade practices are dealt with in the 1976 Restrictive Trade Practices and Resale Prices Acts. Defined as restrictive practices are price-fixing agreements, control over input supply, and other anticompetitive practices by firms.

AN APPRAISAL OF THE BRITISH ECONOMY

By any standard the performance of the British economy has been abysmal, particularly during the 1970s. A good example of the performance of the economy can be provided by comparing per capita gross domestic product for the United Kingdom and for other major industrial countries. In 1967, for example, the per capita domestic product for the United Kingdom was $1,980, compared to $2,190 for France, $2,030 for West Germany, and $1,150 for Japan. By 1979 per capita gross domestic product for the United Kingdom was far below those for the other countries: $7,170 for the United Kingdom, $10,680 for France, $12,450 for West Germany, and $8,720 for Japan.[17]

The United Kingdom ranks last on the economic performance index of major Western industrial countries. Table 11-4, which has been used in other chapters, compares performance for two time periods, 1960–1973 and 1974–1980. The United Kingdom ranks last for both time periods. In the 1974–1980 period the United Kingdom was a bad last, with an index one-sixth that of Italy's.

Contributing to the poor performance of the British economy was a very low rate of economic growth, averaging less than 1 percent per year for the period 1974–1980; a rate of inflation which averaged 16 percent per year for the same period; and a combined rate of growth of capital efficiency and labor efficiency which averaged a negative 0.3 percent per

---

[17]*National Accounts of OECD Countries, 1967–1979* (Paris: OECD, 1980), p. 225.

TABLE 11-4
ECONOMIC PERFORMANCE INDEX
FOR EIGHT INDUSTRIALIZED NATIONS

1960–1973		1974–1980	
Japan	145.9	Japan	37.8
West Germany	123.9	West Germany	29.0
France	85.5	France	18.0
Italy	67.7	Canada	16.5
Canada	64.2	Sweden	15.3
Sweden	55.6	United States	15.2
United States	50.4	Italy	13.4
United Kingdom	43.1	United Kingdom	2.2

Source: New York Stock Exchange, Office of Economic Research, *U.S. Economic Performance in a Global Perspective* (New York, February 1981), p. 11.

year.[18] The unemployment rate during the period, which reached 10 percent by the end of 1981, was the highest since the Depression. The performance of the British economy has been poor over the last 20 years, defying solutions on the part of successive Conservative and Labour governments. Labor troubles, low productivity, large imbalances in trade and payments, and double-digit inflation may bring the United Kingdom to the edge of national bankruptcy and polarized social conflict. Class divisions run deep in the United Kingdom. In the face of this dismal scenario—which is not a prediction, but only a possibility—it is important to compare the economic policies of Prime Minister Margaret Thatcher to those of her predecessors.

Demand Management Policies

Policies to deal with British economic problems have changed from government to government. Until Margaret Thatcher, however, they generally consisted of aggregate demand management policies aimed at short-run stabilization of output, employment, and the balance of payments, frequently combined with an incomes policy to control inflation. The main instrument of demand management policy was fiscal policy. The instruments of fiscal policy are the standard tax and transfer payments devices that are used by the United States and other countries. In particu-

---

[18]*U.S. Economic Performance in a Global Perspective.* February 1981, p. 19.

lar, however, the British have tended to place reliance upon changes in the tax system to manage the economy. For example, to stimulate investment demand and hence the rate of economic growth, income taxes have been cut. To counteract inflation and excess demand, income taxes have been raised.

Stop-Go Stabilization. The term *stop-go* has been applied to British stabilization policy. It refers to deliberate government action to alternately restrain and stimulate economic activity. It has been followed rather continuously through the use of fiscal and monetary measures. Alternating policies of contraction and expansion of aggregate demand can be illustrated as follows:

1. In 1965 rising prices and a deteriorating balance-of-payments position brought about tax increases and budget cuts. Fiscal policy was switched to stop.
2. In 1971 fiscal policy was switched to go as a result of increased unemployment in 1970. To encourage consumer demand, reductions were made in indirect taxes and the budget was expansionary. Monetary policy was relaxed and banks lending increased. The end result was a rapid increase in demand, particularly of private consumption.
3. In 1976 economic policy switched to stop. Balance-of-payments problems and lack of foreign confidence in the British pound sterling became the immediate priorities of the government. Fears arose that the falling exchange rate would interact with money wage increases and domestic inflation to create a cycle of depreciating exchange rates and accelerating depreciation. Restrictive fiscal and monetary policies were adopted.
4. In late 1977 economic policy switched to go. Inflation had slowed, but the rate of unemployment was high. Fiscal policies were relaxed in that there was a decrease in personal taxes and an increase in public expenditures.

Incomes Policy. Both Conservative and Labour governments have used incomes policy as an antiinflationary measure. This type of policy subjects income increases to state control or to voluntary implementation at government request. Conservative governments in Britain have preferred statutory policy, Labour governments voluntary policy. In the 1960s the purpose of incomes policy was to limit average wage increases to average productivity increases, thus securing constant unit labor costs for any given level of output. In the 1970s, with inflation much higher, the aim of incomes policy was to reduce the increase in unit labor costs to manageable proportions. As the inflationary problem in the United Kingdom worsened, experiments with incomes policy became a prominent and persistent feature of national policy. In 1976 an incomes policy that provided for a norm increase of 5 percent was created. In 1977 a pay norm to be a maximum of 10 percent (except in the case of productivity agreement) was established. In both cases the norms were voluntary guidelines established by the Labour government.

Supply-Side Economics and the Thatcher Government

Margaret Thatcher came to office in the wake of the Labour government's unsuccessful attempts to use demand management and an incomes policy to deal with the problems of the British economy. She espoused an economic program based on monetarist theories and a belief in a freely operating market economy. She came to office committed to a policy of increasing aggregate supply through a decrease in the role of the state in the economy and an improvement in incentives for individuals in the private sector. To increase incentives and reward initiative, personal income tax rates were cut. Short-term stabilization policies, as reflected in stop-go, were rejected in favor of policies considered necessary for reducing inflation and creating the conditions for an increase in total real output and employment in the long run.

The following policies were adopted by the Thatcher government:

1. Greater reliance was placed on monetary policy as opposed to fiscal policy. The role of monetary policy became the linchpin of economic policy. Emphasis changed from the structure of interest rates to control over the money supply through progressive deceleration, over the medium term, of the growth rate of one of the money aggregates. This aggregate, called M3, consists of notes and coins in circulation plus all sterling bank deposits held by the private and public sectors.

2. An attempt has been made to increase total output by decreasing the interference of the government in the economy and by promoting the free operation of markets. Income taxes were reduced, with the stated purpose of increasing incentives to work. As mentioned previously, the basic income tax was reduced, top rates on both earned and unearned incomes were reduced, and personal tax allowances were increased. The base of the corporate income tax was changed, and subsidies to industries in depressed areas were reduced. Foreign exchange controls were lifted and quantitative credit controls were removed.

3. The government also intended to limit its role in the price and income determination process. There was more of a commitment to collective bargaining because it was felt that an incomes policy has only a temporary effect on wages. It was believed that monetary policy would affect wages by influencing expectations in that a restrictive monetary policy would moderate wage demands. However, the government decided that public sector pay had to be restrained because high public sector settlements were contributing to excessive government expenditures.

An Evaluation of Supply-Side Policies

The results, at least by early 1982, of Prime Minister Thatcher's economic policies have not been good. The unemployment rate is the highest since the Depression, and the rate of inflation has not fallen significantly. Any success on wage and price inflation that the government experienced resulted more from increases in the rate of unemployment and the appreciation of the pound sterling than from a decrease in the money supply. In fact, the growth rate of the money supply and public sector borrowing requirements exceeded the goals set by the Thatcher government.[19] Wage settlements, although moderating, still remain well in excess of any increase in productivity. The Thatcher government probably made too many commitments at one time. It was committed to cutting inflation, reducing government spending and borrowing, decreasing personal taxation, and increasing defense expenditures.

Toward the end of the 1970s, inflation increasingly became the focus of economic policy, not only in Great Britain but also in the United States and other Western countries. However, it was not until Prime Minister Thatcher came to office that inflation became the sole priority of economic policy, and monetary policy totally replaced traditional Keynesian methods of demand management. Since the exponents of monetary policy believe that there is a clear relationship between the growth rate of money supply and the rate of inflation in the medium term, a reduction in the money supply is supposed to reduce the rate of inflation.[20] But the problem was monetary policy is that its curative effects may kill the patient in the process. By the time inflation is ultimately wrung out of the economy, unemployment, high interest rates, and the decline of industries sensitive to high interest rates can cause considerable social unrest.

It is also important to remember that Mrs. Thatcher was elected because the demand management policies of her predecessor, Michael Callaghan, were unsuccessful in dealing with the problems of the British economy. This leads to the question of whether or not the British economy can be saved. Its industries, for the most part, are not competitive with those of other countries. The British in their history have demonstrated a unique capacity to "muddle through" any crisis, but the economy as it enters the 1980s presents a litany of woe: high inflation, low investment, low growth of productivity, declining industrial competitiveness, and, in recent years, increasing unemployment and a lower

---

[19]Bank of England, *Quarterly Bulletin*, September 1980, p. 264.

[20]Memorandum by H. M. Treasury, Memoranda on Monetary Policy, Treasury and Civil Service Committee, House of Commons, Session 1979–80, H. C. 720, pp. 11–12.

standard of living. The causes of British troubles are controversial, as are the possible cures, if indeed there are any.

SUMMARY

The economic record of the United Kingdom since the end of World War II shows a fairly high level of employment, a low rate of economic growth, and inflation. There has been a persistently sensitive balance-of-payments problem caused by several factors: the need to import roughly 50 percent of the nation's food supply and virtually all of its industrial raw materials; the burden of debt payments resulting from the war; overseas payments required in consequence of postwar policy commitments; and the loss of many of its markets, which was brought about by the dissolution of the British Empire.

The United Kingdom, like its European neighbors, has a nationalized sector of industry as well as an important public investment sector. Decisions in both areas have been conditioned by overall economic policy considerations. Economic policy directed to the private sectors of the economy has relied on general monetary and fiscal measures coupled with such specific fiscal measures as a purchase tax, which has been used to curb inflation, and investment allowances, which have been used to stimulate regional economic development.

Another important area of government intervention in the economy is the comprehensive social welfare system. Budgetary expenditures here have been a significant component of total consumption. An important key to the high level of employment which has characterized the British economy since the end of the war lies in the fact that total demand has been well sustained from the public sector.

The economic health of the United Kingdom is poor and there is serious doubt that the problems which confront the country can be remedied. The Thatcher government made a radical departure from the demand management policies of its predecessors by espousing an economic program based on monetarist theories. Short-term stabilization policies were rejected in favor of long-term policies aimed at reducing the rate of inflation and a greater reliance on a free market economy. It is difficult to reach any conclusions on the effectiveness of this economic program except to say that although inflation has come down, unemployment has increased. It may be that the problems of the British economy are insoluble.

REVIEW QUESTIONS

1. What are some of the problems confronting the British economy?
2. Discuss the economic policies of the Thatcher government.
3. What is meant by *stop-go* economic policy?
4. Discuss the relationship of the Bank of England to the British banking system.
5. Discuss the role of fiscal and monetary policy as economic stabilization devices in the United Kingdom.
6. What trends have developed over time in the distribution of income and wealth in the United Kingdom?

7. The rate of economic growth in the United Kingdom has lagged behind growth rates of other major countries. What are some of the reasons for this lag?
8. What is the function of the National Enterprise Board?
9. Discuss some of the reasons for the nationalization of such industries as coal and steel.
10. Discuss pricing policies in the nationalized industries.

RECOMMENDED READINGS

Caves, Richard E., and Lawrence B. Krause, eds. *Britain's Economic Performance.* Washington: Brookings Institution, 1980.

Chaloner, W. H. *The Coming Confrontation: Will the Open Society Survive to 1989?* London: Institute of Economic Affairs, 1978.

Gaskin, Maxwell, ed. *The Political Economy of Tolerable Survival.* London: Groom Helm, 1980.

Harris, Ralph. *The End of Government?* London: Institute of Economic Affairs, 1980.

Kramnick, Isaac, ed. *Is Britain Dying?: Perspectives on the Current Crisis.* Ithaca, N.Y.: Cornell University Press, 1979.

Maunder, Peter, ed. *The British Economy in the 1970's.* London: Heinemann, 1980.

Morris, Derek, ed. *The Economic System in the U.K.* 2nd ed. Oxford: Oxford University Press, 1979.

Posner, Michael. *Demand Management.* London: Heinemann, 1979.

Prest, A. R., and D. J. Coppock, eds. *The United Kingdom Economy: A Manual of Applied Economics.* 8th ed. London: Weidenfield and Nicholson, 1980.

Pryke, Richard. *The Nationalized Industries: Policies and Performance since 1968.* London: Maxwell, 1981.

PART 4
THE ECONOMIES OF MODIFIED CENTRAL COMMAND

12

Modern Command Economies

INTRODUCTION

Modern society offers two institutions through which resource allocation decisions are made. These are the market and government means of resource allocation. In reality, of course, no economic society allocates all of its resources through a single institution. Instead, each economy in the world is mixed, to one degree or another, between market-determined and government-determined resource allocation. A continuum can be used to show some of the major alternative techniques which can be used to affect resource allocation. These techniques range from those which are applied directly and completely by the government to those where the public sector's influence is very indirect. At one end of the continuum, government allocation influence is direct and complete, and at the other end market forces are dominant.

The communist economies of today show considerable variation in terms of their positions on the continuum. There are alternative allocative techniques which are used in different countries. Hungary is a case in point. Its New Economic Mechanism, with its emphasis on the forces of the marketplace and the incentives of the profit motive, has meant the partial dismantling of centralized state planning. In East Germany, as another example, agriculture with very minor exceptions has been collectivized, while in Poland most of agriculture remains in private hands. There is private ownership of industry in Yugoslavia and Hungary, but in the Soviet Union private ownership of industry is nil. No two countries

245

can be fit into the same mold. However, there are various institutional arrangements which are common to the communist countries. These arrangements are the subject of this chapter.

ECONOMIC PLANNING

The method of deciding key economic questions in communist industry, e.g., what to produce, how much of each item, for whom, and the allocation of resources necessary to achieve the desired production and distribution, is through state economic planning. Although communist economies make use of a system of money and prices, the prices of goods and services and those of agents of production are not determined by the competition of buyers and sellers in the market and hence are not reliable guides for the making of economic decisions. A communist economic system has the ability to make economic plans and to see to it that these plans are carried out. This is because the productive wealth of the system, consisting of land and capital, is owned by society as a whole; and society, as reflected through the state, is the only business entrepreneur of any importance and controls most lines of economic activity.

So both production and distribution are implemented through the use of economic plans. Formally approved state plans, buttressed by rules of behavior and various types of incentives, govern production and distribution decisions. The plans represent an attempt to balance the supply of and demand for resources in order to achieve an equilibrium. In a market economy consumer choice influences resource allocation, but this is not true for a planned economy. Planning is not only concerned with every branch of economic activity, but embraces many aspects of communist economic life. It is not content with merely making the system operate; it also has such objectives as increasing national wealth or the rapid industrialization of the economy. In other words, economic planning can have both short- and long-term goals. It relies on orders for its implementation; it is controlled by a central planning agency, by financial organizations, and, above all, by the political authorities.

Economic plans may be divided into several categories. First of all, there are general plans which may be laid down for a period of 15 to 20 years. These plans are primarily concerned with long-term problems of structural changes on the national scale, technology, the training of labor, and the like. Secondly, there are medium-term plans, usually covering a period of five years and concerned mostly with changes in the capacity and rate of production of different industries and enterprises. This type of plan is subject to perpetual revision as it is carried out, and, as a matter of fact, there seems to be no real reason why the planning process should be broken down into five-year intervals. Thirdly, there are annual plans within each five-year plan. These plans provide a detailed description of production plans for the year and serve as a control mechanism to ensure compliance by the enterprises. Finally, there are quarterly plans within each annual plan, and even monthly plans for plants or groups of plants within specific branches of industries.

It is also necessary to distinguish between physical input-output planning and financial planning. Actually, economic planning consists of both types. The basic planning in the communist countries is in real terms and involves physical output targets of the most important industrial and agricultural commodities and the allocation of labor at the national level, the balancing and transfers of important types of raw materials and equipment, and total national capital investment. The financial plan is important as a control mechanism. It is used to control the execution of the national physical, or real, input-output plan. Although subordinate to the physical plan in the overall planning system, it is used to maintain a discipline in the physical planning process—a discipline which is imposed by the banking system. The financial plan is also used to maintain a balance between consumer disposable income and the volume of consumer goods and services available. It consists of three parts—the state budget, the credit plan, and the cash plan of the central bank. The credit and cash plans control the outlay of short-term credit and the currency and coin issued by the central bank. The latter plays an important role in financial planning because it exercises several control functions, such as seeing that credit loans to enterprises are used in conformance with physical planning objectives.

There is in economic planning the need to balance plan targets with available economic resources. There are two ways in which this problem is resolved: (1) through the use of material balances or (2) through the use of input-output analysis. Material balances present an intended relationship between supplies and their allocation for specific commodities. The balances, which are normally expressed in physical units, provide a basis for the financial counterpart of the plan. Input-output analysis involves interbranch balancing, which means that the economy is divided up into a number of branches, each of which has assigned inputs and outputs. Table 12-1 illustrates that these branches are presented on a statistical grid showing how much each economic sector buys and sells from every other major sector. For example, the grid shows how much of the output of the steel industry goes to the auto, construction, or farm machinery industries. At the same time, it shows how much the steel industry itself receives from these other industries.

Mechanics of Planning

Economic planning is a complicated process in which production and consumption are controlled by the central planning authorities on the basis of predetermined economic and political objectives. Typically, pri-

TABLE 12-1
THE USE OF COMMODITIES BY INDUSTRY, UNITED STATES, 1972
(percent distribution, based on producer's prices)

For the distribution of output of a commodity, read the row for that commodity.

Commodity number	Commodity	11 New construction	36 Stone and clay products	37 Primary iron and steel manufacturing	38 Primary nonferrous metals manufacturing	39 Metal containers	40 Heating, plumbing, and structural metal products	41 Screw machine products and stampings	42 Other fabricated metal products	43 Engines and turbines	44 Farm and garden machinery	45 Construction and mining machinery	58 Misc. electrical machinery and supplies	59 Motor vehicles and equipment	60 Aircraft and parts	61 Other transportation equipment	62 Scientific and controlling instruments	Total commodity output
1	Livestock and livestock products	0.5	(*)	(*)	(*)			(*)	(*)	(*)	(*)	(*)	(*)		(*)	(*)	(*)	100.0
2	Other agricultural products	(*)	0.1		0.2	0.1	0.2	0.1	0.1	(*)	(*)	(*)	(*)	0.1	(*)		(*)	100.0
3	Forestry and fishery products		.1	.1												(*)	(*)	100.0
4	Agricultural, forestry, and fishery services	2.4																100.0
5	Iron and ferroalloy ores mining		1.3	133.7	.7				.1				0.2					100.0
6	Nonferrous metal ores mining		1.3	1.2	84.9		.8						.1					100.0
7	Coal mining		1.7	14.0	.2		.2	.1					(*)	.5				100.0
8	Crude petroleum and natural gas																	100.0
9	Stone and clay mining and quarrying	35.4	32.2	3.5	.1	(*)	(*)	(*)	.1	(*)	(*)	(*)						100.0
10	Chemical and fertilizer mineral mining		5.4	6.4	(*)				(*)									100.0
26	Printing and publishing	.1	(*)	.2	.1	1.3	(*)	.2	(*)				.3	.1	.2	(*)	.1	100.0
27	Chemicals and selected chemical products	1.3	1.5	2.6	1.3	.1	.1	.1	.8				.4	.4	.4	.4	.1	100.0
28	Plastics and synthetic materials		.7		1.9	.1		.1	.2					.6			.5	100.0
29	Drugs, cleaning and toilet preparations		(*)	(*)	(*)	(*)	.1		.1					(*)		(*)	(*)	100.0
30	Paints and allied products	15.8	.8	.5	.9	2.6	3.9	.6	3.1	.1	.4	.4	(*)	5.4	.7	2.6	.2	100.0

#	Industry	(%)
31	Petroleum refining and related industries	100.0
32	Rubber and miscellaneous plastics products	100.0
33	Leather tanning and finishing	100.0
34	Footwear and other leather products	100.0
35	Glass and glass products	100.0
36	Stone and clay products	100.0
37	Primary iron and steel manufacturing	100.0
38	Primary nonferrous metals manufacturing	100.0
39	Metal containers	100.0
40	Heating, plumbing, and structural metal products	100.0
41	Screw machine products and stampings	100.0
42	Other fabricated metal products	100.0
43	Engines and turbines	100.0
44	Farm and garden machinery	100.0
61	Other transportation equipment	100.0
62	Scientific and controlling instruments	100.0
63	Optical, ophthalmic, and photographic equipment	100.0
64	Miscellaneous manufacturing	100.0
65	Transportation and warehousing	100.0
66	Communications, except radio and TV	100.0
67	Radio and TV broadcasting	100.0
68	Electric, gas, water, and sanitary services	100.0
69	Wholesale and retail trade	100.0
70	Finance and insurance	100.0
VA	**Value added**	**100.0**

(*) Less than 0.00005.
Source: *Survey of Current Business* (Washington: U.S. Government Printing Office, February, 1972), pp. 56–71.

ority has been given to the development of industries that will contribute the most to the attainment of national economic and political goals. Economic plans provide for a maximum rate of development of certain branches of an economy and lines of production through priorities in investment and materals and through human and financial resources. It is assumed that the accelerated expansion of certain key industries, such as the chemical, oil, gas, and power industries, makes it possible to increase the overall rate of growth of industrial and agricultural production.

The East German plan can be used to illustrate the intricacies of economic planning. The plan is initiated each April by the State Planning Commission (Staatliche Plankommission). However, the plan is based on the policy directives of the Council of Ministers (Ministerrat der DDR), which is the highest administrative organ in East Germany. The Council is also responsible for the approval of the final draft of the plan. Guidelines for the working out of the plan are developed by the State Planning Commission to be sent to districts and municipalities and to all enterprises. The connecting links between the Planning Commission and the various economic and political units are the industrial, agricultural, and trade ministries. Each ministry is responsible for the application of control figures to its given area of jurisdiction. These control figures are also sent down to ministry subdepartments at district, county, and local levels.

Figure 12-1 presents the framework of the plan. The lowest link on the plan is at the enterprise level (*kreisgeleitete Betriebe*). The purpose of this dissemination is to provide information which can be used as a basis for plan formulation by all production and distribution units. After the control figures have been made available to the various economic units and the lower levels of government, there is a plan counterdesign which starts with the formulation of plans by industrial and trade enterprises, state farms, and other local economic units. These plans cover all phases of their operations. The plans, which can be considered as target plans, then travel upward for their integration into the national plan. At each administrative level the plans cumulate into a national whole. Also at each level the plans must be defended.

The numbers correspond to the various state administrative units and enterprises that are involved in planning. For example, number 1 represents the initiation of the planning process when the basic targets of the plan are sent to the ministries for transmission to the various industries under their jurisdiction. The lines emerging from "1" represent the preparation and transfer of the plan. The ministries disaggregate the plan goals and transmit them to the respective executors. In East Germany the next step is number 4 when the plan directives go to the VVBs (Vereinigung Volkseigener Betriebe), which are associations of industrial and trade enterprises. Each VVB represents the most important link between

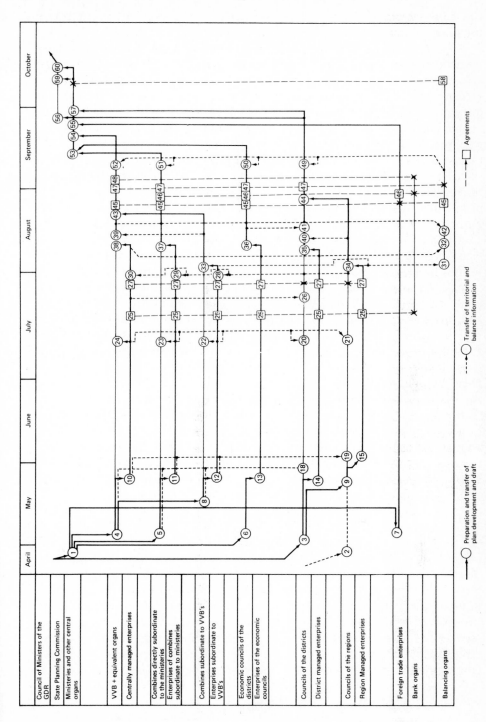

FIGURE 12-1. PREPARATION OF ECONOMIC AND STATE BUDGET PLAN

Council of Ministers of the GDR
State Planning Commission
Ministries and other central organs
VVB + equivalent organs
Centrally managed enterprises
Combines directly subordinate to the ministries
Enterprises of combines subordinate to ministries
Combines subordinate to VVB's
Enterprises subordinate to VVB's
Economic councils of the districts
Enterprises of the economic councils
Councils of the districts
District managed enterprises
Councils of the regions
Region Managed enterprises
Foreign trade enterprises
Bank organs
Balancing organs

April   May   June   July   August   September   October

○ Preparation and transfer of plan development and draft
○ Transfer of territorial and balance information
□ Agreements

the administration of the industrial system and the basic enterprise units.[1]

The comprehensiveness of the plan is apparent. As has already been mentioned, the state budget is an integral part of the plan. There must be a reconciliation of individual enterprise needs to the availability of bank credit. Consumer needs must be balanced against the supply of producer's goods. Foreign trade also must enter into planning decisions. All of this is done during the period from April to September. By October the final process of reconciliation is done by the State Planning Commission. Once the plans have cleared the national ministries, they are merged into the draft plan in which the directives and policy objectives of the Council of Ministers is adjusted to planning aggregates. When the national economic plan is prepared, it is sent to the Council of Ministers for approval. Once approved, the plan in essence becomes law, and it passes down the administrative ladder until it reaches the enterprises. It is to be emphasized that this annual plan is an operating plan which is to be followed within prescribed limits by all production and distribution units.

The basic method of East German economic planning involves the use of material balances which are usually carried on in physical terms and present an intended relationship between supplies and their allocation for specific commodities. Material balances are drawn up for all of the important types of industrial and agricultural products. Targets are reconciled with the limiting constraints of available resources. The balances, which are normally expressed in physical units, provide a basis for the financial part of the plan. According to the existing practice in East Germany, the overall balance of the national economy comprises several flows which have to be harmonized, including production, consumption, and accumulation, and primary, secondary, and final distribution of national income. The material balance method is cumbersome to handle, and moreover it obscures the repercussions of economic changes.

Defects of Planning

In the case of a system of central plan directives, a powerful bureaucracy develops which generally identifies the movements and regularities of economic life with the internal norms of the state apparatus. This bureaucracy generally tries—regardless of its stated intentions—to perpetuate and consolidate its position. Every system of guidance has its internal logic; in the case of the central system of planning directives, this means that deficiencies are often due to the fact that enterprises are circumscribed in terms of planning directives. It is impossible to guide a complex and interdependent economy on a directive basis without run-

---

[1]VVB's are in the process of being dissolved in favor of a two-level system.

ning the risk of serious economic trouble. The hierarchical nature of planning and administration makes a communist system unwieldy and not easily adaptable to the changes demanded by modern developments.

Under economic planning, not enough attention has been paid to problems arising at the microeconomic level. Communist economies have tended to neglect the problems of management and utilization of resources at the operational level. Seen from a purely economic point of view, planning provides practically no incentive to be efficient. A dual system of decision making, which cannot be avoided in the absence of frequent enterprise, contains a danger of incongruity and divergence. Experience shows that it is not easy in practice to reconcile targets set at the central level, even though they may be optimal, with the interest of the enterprises so that they do not act contrary to social interest.

PUBLIC FINANCE

A major difference between the fiscal systems of the communist countries and the leading noncommunist industrial countries of the West lies in the role and size of the budget. In the United States there are three basic levels of government—federal, state, and local—and each level operates its budget in substantial independence from the other. However, in the Soviet Union and the People's Republic of China, as well as in the satellite countries, the budget represents a financial control mechanism for carrying out the state economic plans. The budgets of both the Soviet Union and the People's Republic of China are centralized and represent a consolidation of all budgets—national, republic, and local. The end result is the consolidated state budget which assumes the key role in the distribution of the national income in each country.

Significance of the State Budgets

The state budgets of the communist countries are much larger in terms of the relationship of expenditures to national income than the budgets of the leading noncommunist countries. About half of the national income of the Soviet Union and China flows through their budgets. The reason for the size of the state budget is obvious. Under the communist system many things which would be financed in a capitalistic system by private enterprise or private individuals are financed by the government. So the budgets of the communist countries are much broader in coverage than their counterparts in other countries. For example, investment expenditures, which in the United States would be financed by private enterprise, are financed to a considerable degree by the state budget in a communist country. Many other expenditures, such as expenditures for health, education, and research, which would be financed at least in part by the private sector in a capitalistic economy, are financed out of the state budget.

In such communist countries as the Soviet Union and China, the national economic plan sets forth the level and distribution of economic resources necessary for the fulfillment of national objectives. The state budget of these countries is an integral part of the financial plan, which reflects financially the national economic plan. The financial plan involves the cash, credit, and investment financing which is necessary to implement the attainment of the physical output goals spelled out in the national economic plan. It is through the state budget that the turnover tax, deductions from profits of enterprises, and the other fiscal resources of the government are collected and redistributed. The state budget is a prime vehicle for the allocation of resources among various ends, whereas in a market economy, the market is a device for the organization of economic activity, and it functions by transmitting preferences to producers, who, in the process of adjusting output to correspond with these preferences, direct economic resources into alternative uses. The state budget is used as a control mechanism because it provides a considerable proportion of the investment funds for enterprises. These funds are provided for certain purposes within the framework of the financial plan. This control restricts the opportunity of enterprises to indulge in investments outside of those which are specified in the plan.

Taxation

An outstanding feature of the fiscal systems of China, the Soviet Union, and Yugoslavia is the predominance of indirect taxation over direct taxation. This is surprising in view of the fact that Marxist doctrine would hold that the use of such taxes discriminates against the working classes because they are regressive and inequitable. However, there are reasons for this reliance on indirect taxation. First of all, indirect taxes are easier to administer and harder to avoid than direct taxes. They are collected from thousands of enterprises rather than millions of individuals, and in the early stages of communist development, this was important because the administrative machinery of government was not well developed. Second, the role of the government as reflected by the size of the national budget is more important in the communist countries, so taxation by necessity must also be higher. Direct taxes would not provide the revenues which are necessary to support budgetary expenditures. The direct taxes would also have more of a negative impact on work incentives than indirect taxes.

Basic Types of Taxes. A very important tax in the Soviet Union is the turnover tax. It is applied primarily to consumer goods and is levied at early stages in the production process. It is a highly differentiated tax in that the rates vary from product to product and also from region to region. In addition to being a leading revenue source, the tax exercises an important control function in that it is used to regulate the level of aggregate demand. The tax is also often levied when, although goods are abundant, consumption is considered undesirable. For example, a high turnover tax is levied on such commodities as alcohol and tobacco and on such luxury items as furs and jewelry. The turnover tax is also used to regulate profits in that the rates can determine the amount of profits allowed to producers.

Deductions from profits represent another important source of revenue for the state budget, particularly in the Soviet Union. Profits, as defined in Soviet terms, can represent the difference between the total income received by an enterprise from the sale of its products and its production costs. They can also represent the difference between the government-determined price for a given commodity and the cost to an enterprise for producing it. When profits are made by an enterprise, they are utilized in two ways—one part is remitted to the budget and the other part is retained by the enterprise. The part which is returned to the budget can be viewed as a transfer of revenue rather than a direct tax. However, since it is a part of total profits over and above costs of production, it is incorporated in the final selling price. In this respect, deductions from profits can be considered to have the same effect as sales taxes since each can be shifted forward to consumers.

The personal income tax is not an important source of revenue in the communist countries. There are two reasons for a lack of reliance on the personal income tax. First of all, virtually all wage and salary earners are employed by state enterprises or enterprises which are closely controlled by the state. Therefore, a personal income tax would only be an administrative device for doing what could be done with less trouble by adjustment of the wages and salaries originally paid. Second, the communist countries rely on wage differentials to allocate labor. Material incentives play a very important role in stimulating worker productivity. It is felt that a direct tax, such as the personal income tax, would have a more negative impact on work incentives than indirect taxes. An indirect tax, such as a sales tax, is less visible than the income tax and would not have the effect of reducing the take-home pay of the worker. In the Soviet Union, the personal income tax on wage and salary earners was supposed to have been abolished after October 1, 1965. Although some staged reductions in the income tax have been carried out, the tax is still being used.

Fiscal Policy. There is little doubt that the three basic economic goals of full employment, price stability, and economic growth are highly desirable in both the noncommunist countries of the West and the communist countries. Both fiscal and monetary policy can be used to contribute to the attainment of these goals. Fiscal policy, as defined previously, deals with government receipts and expenditures. Receipts represent the flow of funds from the economy to the government to the economy. The significance of fiscal policy lies in the fact that it deals directly with matters which immediately influence consumption and investment expenditures, and hence the income, of the economy. Monetary policy, as also defined previously, is concerned with the provision of money, defined to include currency and demand deposits at commercial banks. It seeks to maintain a balance between real aggregate demand and supply through control of the aggregate monetary demand for goods and services.

In the Soviet Union the turnover tax is the basic fiscal policy instrument which is used to achieve a balance between supply and demand. Consumer goods are in short supply relative to the demand for them. Soviet economic policy has usually stressed the development of the industrial goods sector of the economy, and resources have been allocated for this purpose. Yet the Soviet workers receive income and have relatively few alternatives for spending it as far as consumer goods are concerned. The turnover tax is used to absorb the excess purchasing power of consumers. The production plans of the government provide that a given amount of goods be made available to consumers annually. On the other hand, in order to maintain incentives and partly because of errors in planning, consumers may receive more purchasing power than can be absorbed by the goods available to them. This excess purchasing power is siphoned off by the turnover tax which is applied at the various stages of production of the goods.

BANKING

Monetary systems vary considerably from country to country. This is particularly true when viewed from the standpoint of the relationship of central banks to governments. This relationship varies from the considerable constitutional independence which the Federal Reserve Banks possess in the United States to the integral role as an instrument of state economic policy which Gosbank plays in the Soviet Union. The United States is a country that always has been devoted to the doctrine of the separation of powers. Economic policy emerges from the interplay of various forces: the Federal Reserve Board certainly is free to hold, or openly advocate, rather different views in economic policy from those of the government. This is hardly the case in the Soviet Union or in China. On the contrary, Gosbank is an essential part of the Soviet economic control mechanism in that it contains the accounts of all state enterprises and can see that expenditures are made in conformance with basic economic objectives.

Central Banking

In some respects there is a similarity among all central banks—communist or otherwise. For example, Gosbank, the Bank of Japan, the Bank of France, and other central banks issue bank notes, serve as repositories for gold holdings, and make international payments. Gosbank serves as a fiscal agent for the Soviet government in that virtually all governmental receipts and expenditures flow through various deposit accounts. The same holds true of the People's Bank of China. In this respect, both are similar to the Bank of Japan, which has served since its inception in 1882 as the fiscal agent of the Japanese government. The Bank of Japan handles public receipts and payments, government debt, and Treasury accounts.

There is also a similarity from the standpoint of credit control between communist and noncommunist central banks. In France, for example, the central bank exercises tight control over the credit-creating banks. The central banks of the Soviet Union and China also control credit, but to a degree that is unheard of in the Western countries. In both communist countries, the central banks are essentially *monobanks* in that they combine the functions of both central and commercial banking. These monobanks, with the exception of a few specialized banks, represent the banking system of each country and purvey most of the total credit. This fact means that they are provided with a control mechanism in that they can supervise the amount of credit granted and the purposes for which it is used.

Monetary Policy

The function and instruments of monetary policy differ between the communist and noncommunist countries. Although the central bank is at the apex of the banking system in both types of economies, there are different institutional arrangements. In Japan and the Western countries, a well-defined commercial banking system and private capital ownership exists. Neither exists in the Soviet Union and China. In the noncommunist countries imbalances between aggregate demand and aggregate supply are adjusted through the use of both monetary and fiscal policies; in the communist countries reliance is placed on fiscal policy. The Soviet turnover tax, as mentioned previously, is an example of the use of fiscal policy to regulate consumer demand.

In the noncommunist countries, monetary policy is a flexible instrument used by the central banks in response to changes in the market economy. The basic tools of monetary policy include control over the minimum liquidity requirements of commercial banks, changes in the rate of rediscounting short-term commercial notes, and open market operations. The importance of each of these instruments varies from country to country. Monetary policy is implemented by the central banks through the commercial banks, with the ultimate objective of influencing changes in both the cost and the availability of credit. These changes are designed to affect the consumption and investment expenditures of both individuals and companies.

In the communist countries, monetary policy is not used as an economic stabilization measure to effect a balance between aggregate demand and supply, and the basic policy instruments are irrelevant because the investment decisions are made by the state in the economic plan rather than by private enterprise operating within the framework of a market economy. Instead, monetary policy is a part of the financial plan and is concerned with controlling the amount of money in circulation and providing credit for enterprises. Its role is passive in that it is not used to correct disequilibria between supply and demand through changes in the cost and availability of credit. In other words, in Japan and the Western countries, monetary policy is a flexible instrument which is used continuously to respond to market changes, while in the communist countries, monetary policy is inflexible and is used to expedite the implementation of the governments' financial plans.

Commercial Banks

A major difference between the banking systems of the communist and noncommunist countries is the virtual absence of commercial banks in most communist countries. In such countries as the United States and Sweden, commercial banks are a separate and integral part of the banking system. They are privately owned business firms operating for the purpose of making a profit. They provide facilities for time deposits on which depositors receive interest, extend credit to the great variety of borrowers by making loans and purchasing securities, and create and manage demand deposits. The essence of commercial banking in the noncommunist countries is the extension of credit through the creation of money. Their ability to create spendable purchasing power in the form of checking accounts is the attribute which gives commercial banks a unique quality among financial institutions. Commercial banks in most noncommunist countries are normally the largest single source of credit and the most diversified.

In the Soviet Union the functions of commercial banks have been assumed by Gosbank. In addition to serving as the central bank of the country, Gosbank has a monopoly over the provision of short-term credit. Each enterprise has an account in Gosbank, originally put there by the government, which is supposed to supply it with working capital, and when a sale is made between two industrial enterprises, the bank simply deducts the amount of the sale from the buyer's account and adds it to that of the seller. Under ordinary circumstances purchases and sales tend to offset each other, thus making no inordinate demand on an enterprise's working capital, but in the event that it is temporarily in need, it can obtain short-term credit from Gosbank. This credit is extended to enterprises for the purpose of procuring inventories and also for financing goods in transit.

Savings Banks

Savings banks exist for the purpose of making the accumulations of small savers available for use in financing the economic system, and savings are encouraged as a means of regulating consumer demand. Savings banks accept deposits from individuals and such personal organizations as trade unions or cooperatives, and pay interest on these deposits. They also perform other services, such as collecting rent and utility bills and selling government bonds. Most of their funds are invested in government bonds, and it is in this way that personal savings make their way back into the economy. Savings banks may exist as part of a nationwide system, as is the case in some of the satellite countries, or they may exist as a part of the central bank, as in both the Soviet Union and China.

Special-Purpose Banks

Special-purpose banks are included in the structure of the communist banking systems. For example, foreign trade banks operate to finance foreign trade transactions and to carry on a correspondent relationship with banks in other countries. Other banks exist as a channel for paying out to enterprises and institutions the funds provided by the state budget for investment. In the event that a particular enterprise is in need of funds for financing new construction, it may procure these funds from a special purpose bank in the form of a nonrepayable grant. If it is practical to finance the proposal out of future earnings, a short-term, interest-bearing loan can be arranged. An example of a special-purpose bank is the Construction Bank of China, which is responsible for giving out nonrepayable investment grants and issuing short-term loans to construction enterprises. Agricultural banks also exist for the purpose of financing rural credit cooperatives. However, separate agricultural banks no longer exist in most communist countries, and their functions have been assumed by the central banks.

ORGANIZATION OF PRODUCTION AND DISTRIBUTION

In the communist economic system, most productive and distributive enterprises are under the direct control of the state. There is some place for small private enterprises, particularly in Yugoslavia, but for the most part their operation is narrowly circumscribed. Some organizations are also left to local governments to operate on the grounds that their operation is largely of local importance. Such enterprises as public utilities, hospitals, theaters, and housing construction would fall into this category. Nevertheless, though the ownership and operation of these enterprises is entrusted to local governmental units, usually some agency of the central government has the ultimate responsibility for coordinating their operations within the general framework of the economic plans for the whole country.

The state exercises a monopolistic control over the basic economic structure and resources of the country. It owns and operates large-scale industries, mines, power plants, railways, shipping, and various means of communications. It engages in farming on its own account through the institution of state farms, and it largely controls peasant agriculture through the institution of collective farming. It has an exclusive monopoly of banking and foreign trade, and it controls the domestic channels of distribution in its role as manufacturer, farmer, merchant, shipper, and banker. In the field of labor relations, it is the sole employer of note, and as such, dominates bargaining between itself and the employees. Although trade unions are allowed to exist, their function is purely subsidiary to the interest of the state, and strikes are illegal.

The Enterprise

The *enterprise*, which is usually an individual firm, is the basic unit of industrial production. It has its own fixed and working capital, which is derived in part from the state budget and in part from bank loans and retained earnings. It is strictly subject to state planning and is managed by state appointees. Profits, if there are any, are turned over to the state treasury to be included as a part of revenue for the state budget, except for amounts which are assigned for retention by the enterprise earning them. Retained profits must, however, be used for specific purposes, such as bonus incentive funds. The enterprise is under an obligation to fulfill the production and financial plans set down by the state, which specifies targets or *success indicators* to be attained. These targets, for the most part, can be reduced to quantitative terms stated in physical or monetary units of measure. Quantity of output is often used as a success indicator, but often quantity may be achieved at the expense of quality or by providing a product mix that is not related to demand but which is easy to produce. Profit is also used as a success indicator.

When an enterprise is formed, it becomes an economic accounting unit with its own capital, both fixed and working, and its own account at the central bank. It then operates as a financial entity and is generally expected to conduct its affairs in such a way that income will cover expenses and leave some profits. However, the earning of profit is not a basic requisite for survival, as an enterprise can also operate with a planned loss. Prices of inputs and outputs are fixed, and the enterprise must operate within these constraints in fulfilling its plan, covering its costs, and making a profit.

The state prescribes the ultimate objectives to be sought by the enterprise in the annual national plan, and the enterprise prepares its own annual operating plan, which is an elaboration of the targets set forth in the annual national plan. This operating plan contains such targets as the volume of output and the introduction of new types of products. It also contains such information as the number of workers employed, cost of production, and the amount of wages payable to workers. The annual operating plan requires the approval of the central authorities before it can be implemented at the enterprise level. The operating plan is then formalized in terms of control figures and resource use.

In a country the size of the Soviet Union or China, one can well wonder how the operations of thousands of enterprises are coordinated. Although the managers of the enterprises have a certain degree of operational flexibility, major decisions regarding what to produce, how much to produce, and for whom to produce are made primarily by superior agencies. In both the Soviet Union and China there is a hierarchy of agencies that is responsible for developing and coordinating the economic plan.

In the Soviet Union there are several agencies or organizations that can exercise some sort of managerial control. The State Bank (Gosbank) can exercise monetary control since it holds the accounts of all enterprises. It can scrutinize an enterprise's receipts and payments to see if they conform to the objectives of the plan. The Ministry of Finance, in collecting tax receipts, can audit the accounts of an enterprise. Then, too, all industries in the Soviet Union are divided into functional groups under the control of industrial ministries which plan and control production and decide questions of technical policy, material supplies, financing, labor use, and wages. The Communist Party also exercises control over the enterprises. Each industrial enterprise has a Communist Party committee elected from the personnel who are party members. This committee is responsible for stimulating the workers to carry out the plan. The committee can also report any irregularities at the enterprise. However, as will be discussed in chapters which follow, there is also some decentralization of authority in the control of enterprises in some communist countries such as Yugoslavia and Hungary.

Agriculture

The organization of agriculture has always presented a problem to the Communists because the peasants have always been hostile to efforts to collectivize and regiment them. For ideological reasons the Communists regard it as imperative that agriculture be collectivized, but early Soviet experiments with collectivization invariably ended in disaster. Eventually after the most repressive measures were used on the peasants to enforce their compliance with Soviet collectivization policies, some sort of compromise was worked out whereby, in return for work on the collective farms, the peasants were given the privilege of farming their own private plots. This arrangement exists in other communist countries as well. The degree of collectivization, however, differs considerably among communist countries. In the Soviet Union there are a few individual peasants who own their land, but their numbers are exceedingly small relative to the total farm population. In Yugoslavia the opposite is true, for 80 percent of the agricultural land is privately owned and individuals are permitted to own up to 10 hectares (about 24.7 acres) of land.

In comparing the relationship of the government to agriculture in the communist and noncommunist countries, the fundamental distinction lies in the pervasiveness of government control and administration of the whole communist economic system, of which agriculture forms an integral part. The communist state exercises a monopolistic control over the agricultural resources. It engages in farming on its own account through the institution of state farms, and it largely controls peasant agriculture through the organization of collective farming. Through control of the state budget and the banking system, it can control the allocation of monetary resources to agriculture. This branch of economic activity is also subject to the system of state economic planning.

Agriculture in the communist countries is carried on by collective farms, state farms, and individual farmers. A *collective farm* is a production unit in which farm property is owned by the peasants and the produce is distributed according to their labor contribution. A certain amount of produce is also set aside for delivery to the state to be sold to consumers. A *state farm* is owned and operated by the government. Its annual budget and operating plans are prepared just like those of any state enterprise, and its equipment and machinery is owned by the state. It hires workers and pays them wages that are established by the state.

Marketing

In a communist economic system the state is typically the sole producer and distributor of goods. It performs the principal marketing functions of buying and selling, transporting, storing, standardizing, and grading goods. The role of middlemen in the exchange process was decried by the Communists as a capitalistic invention designed to gain profits and was eliminated during the early stages of communist development in the Soviet Union and other countries. This, however, failed to simplify the process of exchange, and in some respects there is a distinct similarity between distribution procedures in communist and noncommunist countries. In the Soviet Union, for example, the main channel of distribution for consumer goods is from producer to wholesaler to retailer to consumer, which also holds true for the United States. However, the Soviet government owns and controls each link in the production and distribution process.

Distribution at both the wholesale and retail level is usually the responsibility of two types of trading networks—the state trading network and the cooperative trading network. Although nominally collective, the cooperative network comes under close state control and is in fact little different from state trading. Both trading networks are governed by the annual economic plan. The plan determines the volume of goods to be distributed through the state and cooperative trading systems, and an effort is made to relate the volume of goods and services that will be made available to the income of consumers so that some sort of equilibrium is attained. Responsibility for the coordination of the distribution system is placed in the hands of a number of government agencies which perform such functions as drafting general plans for state and cooperative trade in accordance with the annual economic and financial plans and fixing wholesale and retail prices for state and cooperative outlets.

PRICING AND PROFIT IN A COMMUNIST ECONOMY

The problem of pricing in a communist economy is of a different order of magnitude from that under capitalism. For one thing, prices do not determine the allocation of resources to the same extent as in a market economy. Moreover, pricing is not merely a question of economics, but also of ideology and politics. In terms of ideology they have a rationality of their own, for the law of value is the communist rationality of prices. Value in the communist frame of reference is the amount of labor embodied in particular goods and services. Labor is the only factor of production credited with the capability of creating value. So the price or value of anything is determined by the amount of labor which is required to produce it. The relative prices of two products will be in the same proportion as the amount of labor required to produce them. If two hours of labor is required to make a pair of shoes and five hours are required to build a cart, the price of the shoes on the market will be two fifths of that of the cart.

A hang-up over the labor theory of value has caused the communists all kinds of pricing problems. For one thing, the theory virtually denies the role of demand in the determination of value. The idea of marginal utility is rejected because it is in conflict with the assumption that value is objectively determined by labor content, not by subjective valuation depending on the amount used. Moreover, the factor of scarcity has been ignored. The value of a thing in exchange for something else depends on the state of its supply and the state of demand for it. Behind supply and demand can be a great many interdependent determinants which cannot be ignored. When scarcity is considered, not only labor but capital and natural resources count as productive and value-creating.

However, pragmatism has transcended ideology in communist pricing policies, so that the actual formation and structure of prices incorporate little of the labor theory of value. In fact, actual prices are arrived at through the use of different plan variants which recognize the scarcity of resources and the significance of demand. But the fact remains that no fully workable pricing system has been devised. Prices do not reflect factor costs, as rent and interest are not necessarily fully accounted for in them, and furthermore, different criteria for price setting are used for different categories of products. As a result, prices still do not perform a rational allocative function.

Producer and Consumer Prices

A dual price system operates in communist planned economies—prices paid to producers and prices paid by consumers for retail goods. Producers' prices are those received by producing enterprises from other producing enterprises and from wholesale trading entities. The wholesale price is considered a producer price in the sense that it is a price charged by producers for the sale of a product when it leaves the factory. It consists of full production costs and the profit of the producers; it does not normally include distribution costs. Producer prices are normally based on an average cost for the entire branch of industry producing a given product. Included in average cost are not only wage payments and material costs, but capital charges and differential payments. In some cases, producer prices are actually set by the state at levels below average cost, so that enterprises operate with a planned loss, with the loss subsidized by state revenues.

Retail prices consist of all of the components which make up the prices charged by the producer to the retailer plus a retail price markup added as the last element of retail price formation. There is a virtual isolation between producer and retail prices in that what happens to the former has little impact on the latter. Retail prices are set to keep supply and demand in balance within the guidelines of the economic plan. However, the setting of prices is based on the macrosocial preferences of the planners rather than on the true interaction of supply and demand affected by consumer preferences. However, a certain amount of flexibility in retail prices is permitted. For example, "free prices," which are prices set by supply and demand, operate in the purchase and sale of certain agricultural products. Prices also may be allowed to fluctuate within ranges above and below the levels set by the state planning authorities.

The price structure of most products typically consists of production cost, profit of the producer, turnover tax, and wholesale and retail price markups. Profit, which is a matter for subsequent discussion, is designed to achieve a better use of resources at the enterprise level. The turnover tax occupies a distinct role in pricing in two ways. First, it is used to adjust demand to supply through the manipulation of rates on various goods. Typically goods in short supply or luxury goods carry a high rate. Secondly, the turnover tax is used to regulate profits. Since prices are fixed for the producer as well as the consumer, in effect the tax rates determine the amount of profits allowed to producers.

Price formation for a state enterprise may be described as follows: There is the enterprise price which consists of two components—enterprise costs and profits. Enterprise costs include material, wage, and social costs. The definition of these components differs from one country to another. One innovation in the field of enterprise pricing was the decision by East Germany and Hungary to permit enterprises to set their own prices to other producing enterprises, with the exception of the prices of most raw materials, which remain set by the state. This, however, has led to distortions as monopolistic sellers have increased prices at will. These prices were passed on, where possible, by the purchasing firm.

A profit markup is the second component of enterprise price. This markup is set within ranges permitted by the state and represents what can be considered as an average for a given industry. Profit for individual enterprises can be above this average by either increasing production of articles which meet buyers' preferences or by reducing unit costs. From profit there is a deduction which goes into the state budget.

The turnover tax is added to the enterprise price to give an industry price. As mentioned above, the size of the turnover tax is determined by the required level of the retail price. The rate is differentiated to reflect different elasticities of consumer demand for different products. Typically the tax is arrived at residually, i.e., the retail price is fixed first to balance supply with demand, and the tax is the difference between this price and the price paid to the producer.

The wholesale price is really a margin which is added to the industry price. This margin is the price at which wholesale organizations sell to the retail network. In the absence of wholesaling organizations, an enterprise wholesale price may also be charged. The turnover tax is included in the enterprise wholesale price, and therefore is paid by the producer.

The retail price consists of all the above components which go into the making up of the price of a product. It can be viewed as a retail markup added as the last element of retail price formation. The markup may be fixed by the state or it may be flexible within prescribed limits.

Free prices also are used along with ceiling prices in which the state prescribes a maximum retail markup.

A schematic presentation of price formation, which presents pricing policies followed by the East German clothing industry, is shown below.[2]

Enterprise price (including cost and profit markup)
+ sales taxes = industry sales price
+ wholesale margin = wholesale price
+ retail margin = retail trade sale price

Profit

Profit is an interesting phenomenon in a communist system. At first profit was decried as one of the most basic evils of a capitalist system. Although profit was used in communist economies, it was created merely as an accounting device to ensure that enterprises tried to cover their costs out of their own resources where possible and then handed the surplus over to the state. But certainly profit was not the rationale for the existence of an enterprise. However, profit has come to have a new and important role under communism. For one thing, it is used as a measure of enterprise efficiency. More important is the attempt to link profit with incentives. It is now common to tie the reward system to enterprise profit, for profit may be distributed in the form of bonuses to both labor and management. The proportion of profit distributed in this manner comes under the heading of the material incentives fund.

In setting profit directives, state planning authorities use as the criterion, or base, average production costs in an industry producing a given commodity. Profit is expressed as a percentage of average cost and is set in combination with turnover tax rates and distribution markups. However, the use of a single average profit rate in the price set for a particular product does not result in a uniform rate of profit for all enterprises, because production costs vary widely among enterprises. Through the tying of profit to bonus funds, enterprise managers do have an incentive to reduce production costs. As an end result, however, some enterprises may make large profits while other enterprises may end up with a loss. Profit consists of the difference between receipts from total output and costs of production. Since profit is supposed to accrue to society in the first instance, a certain part of it has to be handed over to the state budget and the remainder is retained for use by the enterprise.

The profitability of an enterprise can be measured by comparing the profit to costs of production to obtain a profit rate. There are, however,

---

[2]Staatsverlag der Deutschen Demokratischen Republik, "Gesetzblatt der Deutschen Demokratischen Republik," Teil 11, Nr. 24 (Berlin, May 10, 1972), p. 269.

weaknesses in this measure, and state planners are adopting other approaches. Profitability can now also be measured as the ratio of profit to the total annual average value of fixed assets and working capital. Fixed capital allocated to enterprises is no longer free, but is subject to capital charges now representing cost. The profit rate then becomes a composite of five factors:

1. The average prime cost of an enterprise, which includes wages, materials used, interest, and depreciation of fixed capital
2. The quantity of output actually sold by the enterprise
3. The price at which the output is sold
4. The average annual value of fixed assets
5. The average annual value of variable assets

Distribution of Profits

When an enterprise makes a profit, the first claimant is the state. A part of profit is allocated to the state budget, and the remainder is divided by the enterprise into a number of funds. Each fund is designed to accomplish a specific objective. There is a *production development fund*. Its purpose is to finance capital investment for the introduction of new technology, mechanization and automation, renovation of fixed assets, modernization of equipment, and other purposes that are designed to develop and improve production. There is also a *fund for social and cultural measures*, which has as its purpose the improvement of worker morale and productivity. It provides revenue for the construction and maintenance of child-care centers, expansion of recreational facilities, support of athletic programs, and housing construction. There is also a reserve fund, which is used for the purpose of paying off long-term loans.

A simplified scheme of profit use for the individual state enterprise can be presented as follows:

    Gross profits of the enterprise
    − Payments to the state budget
    − Interest on bank loans
    = Net profits of the enterprise

The net profits of the enterprise are divided into:

1. Production fund to finance fixed and working capital
2. Social and cultural funds to improve the social and intellectual life of the worker
3. Material incentive fund to stimulate worker productivity
4. Reserve or amortization fund
5. Profit residual that is not committed to any fund that goes to the state budget.

A specific example of profit distribution can be provided in the case of an East German state farm. The starting point in the distribution of profit is gross sales, which is obtained by multiplying the planned volume of sales per product by the set state price. From gross sales, production costs, including the cost of seed and fertilizer and depreciation, are deducted to get gross income. From gross income a deduction is made into the wage fund, and the remainder is called the socially clear income. This income may be considered as a residual that is divided between the state farm and the state. The example follows:

Total sales		$450,450.45
Less seed, fertilizer, and other costs, including depreciation		−225,225.22
Equals gross income		225,225.23
Less wage funds		− 90,090.09
Equals social clear income		$135,135.14
Less special costs	22,522.52	
Less production levy	18,018.02	−40,540.54
Equals gross profit		$ 94,594.60
Less land and production fund tax		− 18,018.02
Equals net profit		$ 76,576.58

INCOME DISTRIBUTION UNDER COMMUNISM

Income distribution is determined by the state within the framework of the economic plan. The total amount of wages to be paid and the production counterpart to support the wage funds depend on the division of the national income between accumulation and consumption and further of consumption between the social consumption fund and the wage fund. The total wage fund is partitioned into wage funds for all economic fields. In its economic planning, the government is able to determine the wages total for the economy by multiplying the planned number of workers by the rates of wages it has set. Wages are changed as seems necessary to effectuate government policy and achieve particular production ends. For example, in order to attract more workers to a given industry, wages paid by it may be raised while others remain static or are allowed to decline. Direct pressure on the part of workers would in general have little effect on wage determination.

The degree of state control over the wage fund at the microeconomic, or firm, level is smaller. Some latitude is allowed to enterprise managers in determining the size and the use of the fund. Typically the wage fund consists of several components, including basic wages. This component can be subdivided into two categories—time rates and piece rates. Both are based on work output indicators. In addition, bonuses may also be paid from the wage fund. The wage fund also provides for extra wages which are based on the difficulty of work; payments for night, holiday, and Sunday work; and wages for state holidays, vacations, and participation in public duties. As it stands, typical workers receive payments according to their work grade from the wage fund plus a bonus based on a performance standard.

Another source of income is provided from the material incentives fund. This fund is tied to enterprise profit. The significance and success of the profit criterion lie mainly in the fact that a direct link has been established between profit and incentive payment so that it is in the interest of enterprise personnel—and at the same time of society—to strive to maximize enterprise profit. The proportion of enterprise profits channeled into this fund varies in different communist countries. For example, in East Germany up to 20 percent of net profits can be placed in the fund. In East Germany, Poland, and Romania the size of the fund is based on complicated formulas in which a distinction is made between planned and above-plan profits, and further between profits made by exceeding production targets and those achieved by reductions in prime costs.

ECONOMIC REFORMS

With the exception of Yugoslavia, the communist countries of Eastern Europe were occupied by Soviet forces after the end of World War II. It was inevitable that sooner or later the Soviet Union would impose its type of economic system on these countries. Although this imposition did not occur at the same time for each country, by 1950 the basic rudiments of the Stalinist command type of economy had been established in Eastern Europe. This command economy was based on the ideological assumption that the only repository of human rationality is the Communist Party. Accordingly, the independent actions of individuals, groups, or institutions—which could only hinder the pursuit of rational goals—was replaced by the absolutist exercise of power by the party-state. This absolute rationality was embodied in the state plan, which prescribed practically all actions for each economic unit in the form of a state law to be carried out to the last detail. The same rigid relationship existed between the center and the unit, the state and the individual, in all walks of human life, particularly in politics, where it was seen as the only guarantee that the center could control the economy.

The advantage of a Stalinist command type of economy was that it ensured the structure of production and distribution according to the priorities postulated by the Communist Party. However, there was no scope for independence of decision making at the operational level. Producing units were bound by directive targets and a large number of other directive plan indicators. Economic accounting was done entirely in terms of physical units, and allocative decisions were not based on prices but on material balances. But the most important defect of the Stalinist command economy was its lack of flexibility and wastefulness. Resources were not allocated in the most efficient manner. There were shortages in the production of consumer goods, for top priority was assigned to the development of the capital goods industries. In each country under Soviet influence there was a command legacy of internal rigidity and resultant problems of economic performance. The attainment of Stalinist type objectives reinforced traditional autarky, nonspecialization, inappropriate specialization, and small-scale economics—problems that were to plague Eastern Europe's development as a viable economic region.

To improve economic efficiency, a series of reforms were instituted by the communist countries, particularly during the 1960s. Industrial and trading enterprises were given greater freedom to choose ways and means of plan fulfillment. Profit was accepted as the main indicator of enterprise performance, while the total number of success indicators were drastically reduced. Increased importance was attached to material as distinct from moral incentives. Planning was made less prescriptive and detailed; instead, efforts were made to lay down broad targets expressed in value terms. Prices were brought more in line with production costs to reduce the need for state subsidies and to enable average enterprises to be profitable. Similarly, procurement prices paid to the farms were raised in relation to industrial prices, to encourage agricultural production and to improve living standards in rural areas. There was some overhaul of the retail and wholesale trade network, designed to improve services to consumers and to enable effective transmission of customers' preferences to producing enterprises. A greater role was assigned to finance and credit, with a flexible use of interest rates.

With the exception of Hungary, there has been a general retreat from many economic reforms, the extent of the retreat varying from country to country. Changes in administrative organizations, planning methods, and performance indicators aroused the opposition of special interest groups. There was an ambivalent attitude on the part of Communist Party leaders, who feared a lessening of their authority and control. Caution and delay were often involved in the implementation of the reforms. The state was ready to take away what it had given at the first sign of real independence. Moreover, there were no political reforms to accompany decentralization of ecomic decision making at the enterprise level. Although there was an effort to achieve decentralization of decision making, there was no corresponding effort to provide more autonomy in terms of political rights. All economic decisions have had to be made within the constraints of a highly circumscribed political framework. Inevitably, the reforms have come into conflict with ideological and political issues.

HUNGARY: A CASE STUDY OF ECONOMIC REFORM

A series of economic reforms, the most important of which took place in 1968, has been a distinctive feature of the Hungarian economy.[3] These reforms have been designed to promote administrative and economic efficiency. They include measures designed to establish a consumer and producer price system that better reflects actual market scarcities. Broad guidelines are provided for enterprises to follow with respect to quality, style, and pricing. They also have been given the latitude to determine their own production mix on the basis of their preferences. A modified market economy is permitted in which enterprises can react to consumer preferences. In 1968 enterprises were made independent economic units with the right to determine the structure of their production and sales. They were also given the right to establish direct contacts with foreign firms, conclude contracts, and engage in independent foreign trade activities.[4]

Hungarian reforms, barring Russian displeasure, are expected to continue in the 1980s. The tax system is to be revised and simplified, while consumer subsidies are supposed to be cut and consumer prices are to increase, reflecting scarcity of various products.[5] There is also a goal of eliminating subsidies to inefficient enterprises.[6] Producer prices are to reflect true economic costs. The tax system is to be simplified by abolishing an assets tax, reducing wage taxes, and introducing a sales tax on final production. The government plans to link imported raw material and energy prices more closely to world market prices to encourage conservation. There is also a plan to increase the wages of workers in profitable state enterprises.[7] In the past, a lack of wage differentials between profitable and unprofitable state enterprises inhibited labor productivity and an efficient allocation of manpower. Inefficient workers and inefficient enterprises were subsidized by the state. Producer prices for three-fourths of

---

[3]The New Economic Mechanism of 1968 introduced the Hungarian reforms. It effected a substantial reduction in central government intervention in the economy at the enterprise level. However, the reforms were never designed to do away with a substantial government role in economic planning and decisions.

[4]A number of contracts have been signed between U.S. and Hungarian enterprises. Philip Morris has a licensing agreement with Hungary to produce and sell Marlboro cigarettes. Levi Strauss has an agreement with five Hungarian partners to produce and sell blue jeans in Hungary and the rest of Eastern Europe. Coca-Cola has an agreement with Hungarian bottling plants to produce and sell Coca-Cola. American and Hungarian enterprises are producing tractors for sale in both Western and Eastern Europe.

[5]Consumer prices in Hungary and other communist countries are both heavily subsidized and taxed. But low prices encourage excessive consumption at the expense of supply.

[6]This encouraged inefficiency because state enterprises never have to worry about going bankrupt.

[7]Good and bad workers in a particular profession tend to make the same income; and good and bad workers in different enterprises tend to make the same income. This hardly promotes overall efficiency.

Hungary's industrial output will be linked to export prices obtainable in the West at prevailing exchange rates. The purpose is to improve Hungary's hard currency balance of payments by reducing enterprise demand for raw material imports.[8]

A problem that the Hungarian government encountered in implementing reforms is resistance to any change in the status quo, both on the part of Communist Party hardliners and certain parts of the population. Job security and an income distribution system which does not distinguish between the competent and incompetent have inhibited labor productivity. The wages of workers in very profitable firms have only marginally exceeded those of the workers in unprofitable enterprises.

However, Hungary may well succeed in reforming its economy because the reform program has strong support from the Communist Party secretary, Janos Kadar, and much of the population. While the Soviet Union and the other Eastern European countries are implementing reforms in a piecemeal manner which usually does not mesh with their centrally planned economies,[9] Hungary has attempted to develop a totally reformed economic system. In essence, Hungary has developed a market-socialist economic system while maintaining its political allegiance to the Soviet Union.

SUMMARY

Probably the most important difference between the capitalist, socialist, and communist countries is the role that economic planning plays in communist resource allocation. Fundamental to the operation of planning is the public ownership of the agents of production, which joins industrial, agricultural, and trading companies into a single economic unit. Since there is no meaningful competition between rival firms, there is no price competition. In turn, the profit motive is rendered unimportant as an automatic regulator, which is its role in the market price system of a market economy. So in the absence of the market price system, economic planning is necessary to make the complex of state enterprises function. To organize the uninterrupted operations of these enterprises, full and exact account must be kept of the national requirements for their particular products and of the channels through which they must be distributed.

The state exercises a virtual monopolistic control over all economic resources. It owns and operates large-scale industries, mines, power plants, railways, shipping, and various means of communication. It engages in farming on its own account

---

[8]Joseph C. Kramer and John T. Danylyk, "Economic Reform in Eastern Europe: Hungary at the Forefront," in *East European Economic Assessment*, Part 1, Joint Economic Committee, Congress of the United States, 97th Congress, 1st Session, Washington: U.S. Government Printing Office, 1981, pp. 549–570.

[9]These reforms usually involve decentralization of decision making. For example, Bulgaria abolished its Ministry of Agriculture to promote the decentralization of the agricultural sector.

through the institution of state farms, and it largely controls agriculture through the institution of collective farming. It has an exclusive monopoly of banking and foreign trade, and it controls the domestic channels of distribution in its role as manufacturer, farmer, merchant, shipper, and banker. In the field of labor relations, it is the sole employer of note and as such dominates bargaining between itself and the employees. Although trade unions are allowed to exist, their function is purely subsidiary to the interest of the state, and strikes are illegal.

REVIEW QUESTIONS

1. Why is it difficult to fit the communist countries into a common economic pattern?
2. Discuss the role of input-output analysis with respect to economic planning.
3. Discuss the process of economic planning as illustrated in the East German plan.
4. Compare the role of the national budgets in the United States and the Soviet Union.
5. Discuss the role of profit in a communist economic system.
6. Compare the process of income determination in a market economy and a planned economy.
7. What were the objectives of the Hungarian economic reforms?

13

An Introduction to the Soviet Union

INTRODUCTION

The Soviet economy depends on economic planning rather than on a market system to make the basic economic decisions of what and how much is to be produced and to whom it is to be allocated. Interaction between buyers and sellers, which determines the prices of commodities, services, and the agents of production in a market economy such as the United States, is inoperative in the Soviet Union. Since land and capital are owned by the state in the name of society and since the state operates almost all lines of economic activity, it has the ability to make comprehensive economic plans and to see to it that they are carried out as thoroughly as possible.

The Soviet economy has entered into a period of increasing difficulty. There are problems of declining output growth, serious inflationary pressure, slow technological progress, and accumulated deficiencies in housing and other public needs. Attempts to alleviate these problems usually encounter resistance from party ideologues and bureaucrats. Moreover, the imbalance in the economic system is created by an orientation toward military spending. Even though the Soviet Union is one of the richest countries in the world in terms of metals and mineral resources, rising resource constraints, based in part on geographic impediments to transportation, place limits on the growth of the Soviet economy. The costs of obtaining and using natural resources have been rising in real terms as high-grade, well-located resources have been depleted and less accessible supplies have been drawn on. New deposits of oil are not being found and developed rapidly enough to offset declines in older fields.

From the standpoint of population, the Soviet Union is a little larger than the United States. Its population in 1980 was an estimated 262 million compared to 220 million for the United States. In land area, however, it is larger than the United States and Canada combined. Its length from east to west is 7,000 miles, and from north to south it is about 3,000 miles. In one respect the populations of both the United States and the Soviet Union are similar because each consists of a melange of different racial and ethnic groups. The people of the Soviet Union can be divided as Slavic or non-Slavic, or Russian or non-Russian. The Slavic group consists of Russians, Belorussians, and Ukrainians, and they are united by similar languages.[1] The non-Slavic group consists of Estonians, Lithuanians, Tatars, Armenians, Georgians, and others. The Russian population is limited primarily to the western, or European, part of the country.

The Soviet Union consists of 15 socialist republics. The largest is the Russian Soviet Federated Socialist Republic, which comprises 79 percent of the total area and around half of the population of the country. The second largest republic in terms of land area and population is the Ukrainian Soviet Socialist Republic. Within the republics, there are autonomous republics and regions which also reflect the ethnic diversity of the country.[2] For example, within the Russian Soviet Federated Republic there is the autonomous Soviet Socialist Republic of Yakutia, which has a land area of more than a million square miles, but is a very sparsely populated area far removed from Moscow. Its autonomy is largely a matter of administrative convenience. An example of an autonomous region is the Jewish Autonomous Region, which is in the Asiatic part of the Russian Soviet Federated Republic.

THE POLITICAL SYSTEM

Perhaps the most important point that can be made with respect to the political system of the Soviet Union is the interlocking relationship between the Communist Party and the administrative units of the government. Political and governmental power in the Soviet Union is com-

---

[1]There are three subdivisions of Slavs—eastern Slavs (Russians, Belorussians, and Ukrainians), western Slavs (Poles, Czechs, and Slovaks), and Southern Slavs (Serbo-Croatians, Slovenes, and Bulgarians).

[2]There are, in fact, over 170 different nationalities and more than 200 languages and dialects spoken in the Soviet Union.

pletely in the hands of the Communist Party. In other words, the Communist Party dominates the governmental administrative structure of the Soviet Union and has its members in practically all important offices and positions. Its policies are carried out by all governmental agencies and organizations.

Organization of the Government

The governmental administrative apparatus of the Soviet Union is divided into a multitiered arrangement with control extending from Moscow down to the rural soviets (elected government councils). The current arrangement is essentially as follows.

Territorial Administration. From a territorial administrative standpoint, the Soviet Union can be divided into several categories. First, there is the Soviet Union itself. As a federation of constituent republics, it has its own constitution. Then there are the 15 theoretically independent union republics which form the federation. Each republic has its own constitution, government, and party hierarchy. The republics are similar to American states, although they are generally larger in size. A distinctive feature of Soviet public administration is the fact that most of these republics were formed primarily on the basis of nationality. The federalist structure of the Soviet Union can be regarded as a concession to the non-Russian peoples' nationalistic sentiments. However, administrative safeguards modify the formal federalism of the constitutional structure of the Soviet Union. The Communist Party itself is a single, unified organization which exerts a countervailing centralism to ethnic federalism. Moreover, the highest administrative organs of the country are centralized in Moscow.

National Policy Administration. The state apparatus through which national policy is administered can be divided into two pyramidal hierarchies—one is the Council of Ministers of the USSR and the other is the Supreme Soviet of the USSR. The Council of Ministers is the executive branch of the Soviet government, the Supreme Soviet the legislative branch.

The Council of Ministers. The Council of Ministers is responsible for the development of economic policy and the enforcement of laws passed by the Supreme Soviet. It is also responsible for exercising general guidance in the sphere of relations with other countries and for directing the general organization of the country's armed forces. It is elected by and is responsible to the Supreme Soviet. To assist the Council of Ministers in coordinating economic activity, there are a number of committees whose responsibilities are to provide the information needed for decision making. One important committee is the State Planning Committee (Gosplan), which is responsible for the development of the national economic plans. There are five other committees—the All-Union Agricultural Committee, the State Committee for Science and Technology, the State Committee for Material and Technical Supply, the State Committee for Construction, and the CEMA Commission.[3] The Presidium of the Council of Ministers, which consists of a chairperson and six deputies, one of whom represents each of the six committees, is the policy-making body. There is also a Council of Ministers in each of the 15 constituent republics.

The Supreme Soviet. The Supreme Soviet of the USSR is the most important legislative branch in the Soviet Union. It is formally a bicameral legislature with coequal houses—the Soviet of the Union, whose deputies are elected on the basis of population, and the Soviet of Nationalities, whose deputies are elected on a territorial basis by nationality. The responsibilities of the Supreme Soviet are stronger in theory than in practice. In terms of real decision making it has little power and passes the bills that are submitted to it. A law is considered enacted if passed by both houses by a simple majority vote in each. There are standing committees for each house comprising the following areas: credentials, plans and budgets, industry, transportation and communication, building and the building materials industry, agriculture, public health and social security, public education, science and culture, trade and public services, legislative proposals, and foreign affairs.

The Communist Party

Control of the government machinery in the Soviet Union is in the hands of the Communist Party, which is the only political party permitted in the country.[4] Although membership in the Communist Party is limited to a small minority of the total population of the country (16 million in 1980), it maintains firm control over every aspect of Soviet life through well-organized and disciplined organization. Communists are assigned to key positions in all institutions and enterprises in Soviet society. In factories, offices, schools, and villages, primary units called *cells* operate. Cells consist of at least three party members and are responsible for the recruitment of members and for the selection of delegates to the local party conferences which in turn select delegates to conferences covering a somewhat wider area, and this process continues until finally,

---

[3]The Council for Mutual Economic Assistance (CEMA) is the consultative organ which coordinates the domestic and foreign economic policies of the USSR and the European satellite countries.

[4]The Communists argue that political parties are class organs and that, if several parties were permitted, there would be a return to class antagonisms.

in district and regional congresses, delegates are selected to the National Party Congress, which is supposed to be the highest body of party authority. Power actually rests in the Central Committee, the Politburo, the Secretariat, and the various staff departments of the central apparatus in Moscow.

The Central Committee. The Central Committee is elected at the meeting of the National Party Congress. It is composed of the Politburo, Secretariat, Party Control Committee, and a number of individual sections including those called Cadres Abroad, Economic Relations with Socialist Countries, International Affairs, and Relations with Bloc Parties. The Central Committee has no effective role as a decision maker; that function is performed by the Politburo. It does, however, provide a forum or sounding board for the elaboration of the major policies of the Communist Party and its top leaders. It is also responsible for the dissemination of the aims and objectives of the leaders to officials in various departments in the central apparatus and also downward to the various party committees in the republics and at lower levels.

The Politburo. The *Politburo* is, in effect, the supreme instrument of political power in the Soviet Union. When the Central Committee is not in session, it is responsible for all phases of national life—foreign policy, domestic economic policy, and military policy.[5] There are 15 full voting members who exercise the prerogatives and responsibilities of national policy making, and seven candidate members who participate in varying degrees in the policy-making process. Most members of the Politburo have collateral duties, meaning that they serve in other capacities in addition to their positions as party administrators.

The Secretariat. The Secretariat of the Central Committee ranks second only to the Politburo from the standpoint of decision making. Unlike the Politburo, which has no administrative responsibility, the Secretariat is responsible for the administration of the Communist Party. It consists of 11 members who are elected by the Central Committee in plenary session—a formality, since the slate is drawn up in advance by top party leaders. There is an overlap between the Secretariat and the Politburo in the sense that several members serve on each organization. The Secretariat is responsible for providing the leadership for the professional party organization, which consists of a hierarchy of subordinate secretariats at the republic, and lesser administrative levels. This hierarchy is responsible for insuring the implementation of state economic policy by the vari-

---

[5]The Politburo of the Central Committee is not to be confused with the Presidium of the Council of Ministers of the USSR and the Presidium of the Supreme Soviet. The last two are involved in the operations of the government as opposed to the Politburo, which is involved in the operation of the Communist Party.

ous governmental organs. It is also responsible for the allocation and mobilization of manpower and other resources of the Communist Party.

Party and Government Structure. Party and government structure parallel each other. For example, at the national or USSR level, the basic party administrative units are the Central Committee, Politburo, and Secretariat; the basic governmental administrative units are the Supreme Soviet and the Council of Ministers with their respective presidiums. The leaders of the party are members of both units. At the union republic level, the party administrative unit consists of the Central Committee and Secretariat, and the governmental administrative unit consists of the Republic Supreme Soviet and Council of Ministers. This interlocking relationship continues down to the rural soviet level. Although inefficiency may result at lower administrative levels because of communication problems, there is no question but the interconnection of party and government and party domination of the government confer on Soviet public administration exceptional unity of control and uniformity of ideological perspective.[6]

THE ECONOMIC SYSTEM

It can be said that the leaders of the Soviet Union are committed to the view that the future of the country depends upon the Soviet economy's productivity and efficiency. Emphasis is placed on the organization of material production. This organization is based on two fundamental characteristics of the Soviet economy: (1) The economy is run by the allocation of resources by administrative decisions rather than by a market mechanism; and (2) its operations are governed by a priority system which over the years has given preference to capital goods and military and scientific development over consumer goods. Because of these characteristics, consumer sovereignty, which means that the production of goods is determined by the combined prices made in the marketplace by millions of consumers, cannot develop in the Soviet Union. Through its control over economic resources, the state can manipulate the share of gross national product which is to be allocated to consumption, and through its investment policies the state can control the amount of inputs for those sectors of the economy that supply the consumer. Nevertheless, the Soviet leaders have heeded to some extent the expectations of the consumer for a higher living standard.

---

[6]This does not mean, however, that party and government organs function as two perfectly synchronized parts of a smoothly working administrative machine. To the contrary, there are cliques within the party and the governmental bureaucracies which often cause power rivalries or power disputes. These cliques have a vested interest in maintaining the status quo.

Economic Planning

The distinctive feature of the economic system of the Soviet Union is the fact that it operates on the basis of comprehensive economic planning. Fundamental to the operation of economic planning is the public ownership of the agents of production which has joined the multitude of industrial, agricultural, and trading enterprises together in a single economic unit. Since there is no competition among rival firms, there is no meaningful price competition. This, in turn, renders the profit motive impotent as an automatic economic regulator, which is its role in the market price system of a capitalistic economy. So in the absence of the market price system, economic planning is necessary to make the complex of Soviet enterprises function. To organize the uninterrupted operation of these enterprises, full and exact amount must be taken of the national requirements for their particular products and of the channels through which they must be distributed. Conversely, every enterprise must be constantly supplied with raw materials, fuel, equipment, and other means of production, the output of which must also be commensurate with national needs.

An important principle of economic planning in the Soviet Union is the priority given to the development of industries that will contribute the most to the attainment of national economic and political goals. Economic plans provide for a maximum possible rate of development of certain branches of the economy and lines of production through priorities in investments and materials and through manpower and financial resources. It is assumed that the accelerated expansion of certain key industries, such as the chemical, oil, gas, and power industries, makes it possible to increase the overall rate of growth of industrial and agricultural production. Economic planning also has political as well as economic overtones in that priorities in past and current plans have been given to industries which make the Soviet Union strong from a military standpoint.

It is necessary to stress the fact that there is a difference between formal and actual economic plans. In practice plans are changed often and some plans reflect aspirations. There constantly has to be a revision of targets to reflect changing economic conditions. As the communist countries have been entering higher stages of economic development, the number of alternative uses for resources and the complexity of economic processes have greatly increased. Consequently, the possibilities of errors have been multiplying, threatening the economies with greater waste and dislocation than before. So the longer the planning period, the less precision can be introduced in terms of plan targets. What happens then is that planning, particularly for periods of five years or longer, is continuous and the plans are constantly supplemented and extended in the process of their implementation.

The economic plans differ in their functional character. There are physical output plans, which involve production, distribution, and investment goals, and financial plans, which are derivatives of these plans. Then, too, plans differ in terms of time limits. There are long-range plans which extend for 15 to 20 years. These plans usually deal with a particular aspect of the economy, such as electrification. Medium-term plans, which cover a period of 5 to 7 years, develop targets or goals to be accomplished during this time. There are also annual plans which involve production plans to be followed by Soviet enterprises and other organizational units during the year. The annual plan can be considered an operational plan. Annual plans can be broken down further into quarterly or monthly periods. All of these plans are interconnected and interrelated, and it is important and necessary for planning agencies to ensure their unification in order to establish a proper relationship between production and consumption and between national requirements and resources. In terms of a frame of reference for the presentation of the methodology of Soviet planning, economic planning refers primarily to physical planning which involves product output and distribution, labor force utilization, and investment and which is developed on an annual basis.

The organization of economic planning can be divided into the following stages:

1. Drafting of the plan in conformity with the objectives of the Communist Party and the Soviet government
2. Endorsement of the plan by relevant government administrative units
3. Organization and control over the execution of the approved plan

Planning in the Soviet Union is directed by the Supreme Soviet and the Council of Ministers. The actual plans are drawn up by planning bodies which may be divided into three groups—state planning bodies, ministries and departments, and the planning bodies of enterprises and organizations. The state planning bodies are the State Planning Committee (Gosplan), which is a part of the Council of Ministers of the USSR, the state planning committees of the union and autonomous republics, regional planning committees, and district and city planning committees. These committees draw upon the economic and cultural plans for the country as a whole and for individual republics, regions, and districts. In the ministries and departments, plans are compiled by planning boards and sections, and at the enterprise level they are the responsibility of planning departments.

Gosplan. Gosplan is the agency responsible for translating broad policy decisions made by the Council of Ministers and the Central Committee of the Communist Party into concrete programs. It has the responsibility for working out national economic plans of all kinds and for their presentation for review by the Council of Ministers. It is also responsible for the supervision of the plans. Gosplan is organized into various economic planning sections for the branches of the national economy. One section is responsible for sector planning and is divided into the following sections: machine building, transportation and communications, consumer goods, agriculture, heavy industry, electrification and chemicalization of the national economy. Another section is responsible for the supply and distribution of materials, such as coal and metal products. This section provides a monitoring function over the supply of key materials. Gosplan is also responsible for setting wholesale prices for industrial and agricultural products and for setting retail prices. Through an institute which is attached to it, called the Scientific Research Institute of Economics, it also plays a leading role in theoretical economic research.[7] To check on Gosplan and its activities, there are various departments within the Secretariat of the Communist Party which serve as watchdogs.

Since the Soviet economic plan covers the entire economy, it is necessary to have planning units extending down to lower administrative units of government. Below the all-union Gosplan and subordinate to it in terms of planning are the republic Gosplans. These Gosplans are responsible for the preparation of plans for all of the industries under union republic supervision. They are also responsible for developing recommendations pertaining to the draft production plans of all enterprises located within the territories of their respective republics. There are also the Gosplans of the autonomous republics and regional planning commissions at the local level. They are responsible for drawing up plans for industry and transportation at the regional level, and for agriculture, social and cultural development, and housing and public construction. They also base their summary plans on plans developed at the rural soviet levels. The planning bodies at these levels draft the plans for enterprises under their direct control and check to see if they are implemented. There are also planning departments in industrial enterprises, state farms, and transport and trading enterprises. Their activities are guided by targets set forth in the national plan.

Gossnab. Gossnab is the State Committee on Material-Technical Supplies and is responsible for handling the distribution end of the plan. It is supposed to tie customers to suppliers at both the republic and local levels. Subject to general guidelines and within the limits set by central allocation, the local units of Gossnab make detailed arrangements for supply, sometimes from warehouses which they administer. Managers of enterprises are supposed to negotiate for supplies with the local Gossnab

---

[7]Alec Nove, *The Soviet Economic System*, 2nd ed. (London: George Allen & Unwin, 1980), pp. 37–40.

unit. Gossnab has 22 central distribution sections and each has the following responsibilities:

1. Identify special needs and assign priorities to such needs
2. Make the most economical assignment of each individual supplier to a group of users
3. Decide on long-term direct supplier-user contacts among plants or enterprises
4. Regulate the flow of products according to assigned priorities in the plan[8]

Drafting of the Plan. Control figures are drawn up by Gosplan before the five-year plan is drafted. These figures determine the principal trends and general scale of economic development during the duration of the plan. These control figures cover the volume and distribution of national income, the overall volume of capital investment and industrial production in the more important branches of industry, the volume of output and state purchases of farm produce, the volume of retail trade, expected increases in labor productivity, and the monetary income of the population. These control figures are based on the economy's achievements in preceding time periods and on estimates of future manpower availability and progress in technology and labor productivity.

Stages of the Planning Cycle. When the plan is designed, it is a draft plan which outlines the basic economic development tasks for the plan period. This drafting phase transforms government and party objectives into numerical targets which determine the amount of resources to be allocated for specific purposes.

When the draft plan has been completed, it is sent for approval to the Central Committee of the Communist Party and to the Council of Ministers of the USSR. After the plan is approved, it is broken down by sections and sent to the appropriate national ministry or department for consideration. It is also sent to the Gosplans of the republics, which are also supposed to prepare plans for the economic programs of their particular republics and ministries. The draft plan is then sent to planning commissions at the regional and local levels and to enterprises. The purpose of this dissemination is to provide information which can be used as a basis for plan formulation at the enterprise level and also at the various local, regional, and national administrative levels. An enterprise, for example, would receive information as to the kinds, quantities, and qualities of goals which it was expected to produce, quantities and kinds of labor, power, materials, capital goods, and other things which would be supplied to it, estimates of the productivity which the workers should achieve, and estimates of the workers' incomes and living standards.

---

[8]Sumer C. Aggerwal, "Managing Material Shortages: The Russian Way," *Columbia Journal of World Business,* (Fall 1980), pp. 26–37.

After the control figures have been made available to the various economic units and the lower echelons of government, there is a plan counterdesign which starts with the formulation of plans by industrial and trade enterprises, state farms, and other local economic units. These plans cover all phases of their operations in great detail. For example, plans of enterprises set forth what they are to make, in what quantities, and by what combinations of labor and capital. These are target plans which are supposed to serve as a framework for annual operating plans. The plans then travel in an upward route to their eventual integration in the national plan by Gosplan. At each administrative stage the plans cumulate into a larger whole. From the primary producing units—industrial, agricultural, and trading enterprises—the plans move through local soviets, rayons, krays, oblasts, autonomous republics, and the various ministries and planning agencies at the union republic and national level. Gosplan has the final responsibility for the preparation of the overall national plan. The problem is reconciling all draft plans into one national plan.

The process of reconciliation is the third stage of the planning cycle. Gosplan must adjust Politburo objectives from above with the aggregation of plans from below. It is also at this stage that various monetary plans are developed. These monetary plans, or financial plans as they can be called, represent a counterpart to the main economic plan which is expressed in physical terms. Two of the major financial plans are the state budget and the cash and credit plans of Gosbank. Each plan exercises important control functions which will be discussed later in the chapter.[9] The financial plans are approved and developed by the Ministry of Finance and Gosbank, and are reviewed by Gosplan in its preparation of the national economic plan. When the plan is prepared, it is sent to the Council of Ministers and the Central Committee of the Communist Party for ratification. Finally, the plan, with its tasks for each administrative and economic level, is passed down the line until it reaches the enterprise. The whole Soviet planning process is complex, for there has to be a flow of operational directives to the thousands of operating enterprises. Plans for various sectors must be coordinated with those of other sectors.

The Use of Material Balances. The basic method of Soviet economic planning has involved the use of material balances. These balances are usually carried on in physical terms and present an intended relationship between supplies and their allocation for special commodities. Material

---

[9]There is also the consolidated financial plan, which includes the state budget and the cash and credit plans of Gosbank. In addition, it includes the profits of all state enterprises and allowances for depreciation, increases in savings bank deposits, and other financial resources.

balances are drawn up for all of the important types of industrial and agricultural products. An example of the use of material balances can be presented roughly as follows:

Product

Resources	Distribution
Stocks at the start of the planning period	Production and operating needs
	Capital construction
Production	Replenishment of state stocks
Imports	Exports
Mobilization of internal resources	Other needs
	Stocks at the end of the planning period
Total	Total

However, given the complexities of the production and distribution processes, the material balance method has become more cumbersome to handle. So it has been replaced to some extent with input-output analysis which consists of working out a matrix of flows which looks like a chessboard. These flows represent an array of interrelationships between economic sectors. The economy is divided into many branches and each of them is supposed to achieve an annual output of a given quantity. Each branch also uses a certain portion of its annual output. The remaining portion of each branch's annual output is to be delivered to other branches. That part of production over and above that used up in the branch and other branches during the year constitutes net material production. This total is devoted to consumption and investment.

Economic planning has to reconcile a number of flows, including production, consumption, and saving; the utilization of labor resources; the distribution of national income; and personal money income and expenditure. The total amount of wages to be paid and the production counterpart to support wages depend on the division of national income between savings and consumption, and further, of consumption between social consumption and wages. This leads to the problem of relating the total flow of wages to the total value of consumer goods and services. The maintenance of balance between incomes from work and the resources allocated to personal consumption is a part of distribution policy and especially of wage planning. As prices of consumer goods and services may change, this also involves the problem of maintenance of the purchasing power of wages and the relationship between nominal and real wages.

Conditions for Planning. The essential conditions for planning are present in the Soviet Union. The state is in full control of the land, factories, transportation, and the raw materials necessary for the production of all commodities. It controls the quality and quantity of the labor force, which enables it to supply the economy with the necessary labor to fill planned targets. Through control of money and credit, it finances construction and the operations of enterprises in accordance with the financial plan. To exercise compliance with the plan, the state, through Gosplan, Gosbank, and other organizations, can maintain control over the plan's execution. Gosplan in particular has the responsibility for checking on the progress made in implementing the plan. This is done through the hierarchy of planning offices that exist down to the lower administrative levels of government. The Communist Party also performs a control function in that its members hold positions of authority in all enterprises and they can supervise the implementation of the plan at the enterprise level.

Limitations of Planning. Nevertheless, the whole process of planning has its limitations. The plan may estimate that a certain number of workers, given certain supplies of machinery, land, equipment, materials, and power, will turn out a specific number of units of product of definite quality in a given period, but the results of the workers' activities may be anything but those which are expected. There is also a certain lack of coordination and inefficiency in planning which can be attributed to the existence of a comprehensive bureaucratic structure. Enterprises are separated from the decision-making agencies at the top by a number of intermediary agencies. This means that they are separated from other enterprises by agencies that must check purchase and sales requests and disburse funds. Another defect in planning is that the setting of general production norms or indexes fails to take into consideration differences in the characteristics of various enterprises. Also, over the years since planning was developed, the Soviet Union has grown into a complex and modern industrial nation with increasingly sophisticated production techniques and greater demands for quality specifications of materals. This, in itself, has complicated the central planning process and has caused a need for more detailed microplanning.

Public Finance

The operation of any modern state requires the collection of large sums of money for the financing of various public services and for the general administrative expenses of government. This is as true of the Soviet Union as it is of any capitalistic country. However, there is a great deal of difference in the ways in which the two forms of economic organization acquire and dispose of their revenues. In the Soviet Union government expenditures are very large in relation to national income, since the government has to make expenditures for operating industries as well as carrying on normal governmental functions.[10] Since the government has provided the expenditures necessary for the operation of industrial and agricultural enterprises, it would stand to reason that it would receive part of the proceeds derived from the sale of goods and services by these enterprises. Both the Soviet and Western capitalistic governments will necessarily devote substantial sums of their national incomes to general administrative expenses, to war and defense measures, and to various forms of social services, but in the case of the Soviet state, additional sums must also be made available to finance industry operation.

The Soviet State Budget. In the Soviet Union the national budget is of paramount importance since it provides for the accumulation and distribution of much of the national income. The national budget, or Soviet State Budget, as it is called, is a consolidated budget which provides for the expenditures and revenues of the national, republic, and local units of government. It is also closely related in terms of revenues and expenditures to the national economic plan. It performs an important allocative function in that it is the major instrument for financing many types of investment and for controlling the utilization of investment in accordance with planning objectives. The budget is also instrumental in decisions to divide the national product between consumption and investment.

The Soviet State Budget is made up annually for the calendar year. It is prepared by the Ministry of Finance and includes the all-union or central budget, the budgets of the autonomous republics, and the budgets of regional, urban, and rural administrative entities. Republic and local authorities prepare their own budgets in conformance with the objectives of the national economic plan.[11] When the tentative budgets are prepared, they are transmitted upward—local government budgets to their respective republic's ministry of finance, and republic budgets to the Union Ministry of Finance—and coordinated at each step with the national economic plan. When the total budget—national, republic, and local—is integrated, it is sent by the Ministry of Finance to the Council of Ministers of the Soviet Union for approval. After the Council of Ministers has made changes and recommendations, the Soviet State Budget is then presented by the Ministry of Finance to the Supreme Soviet for final

---

[10]It is necessary to mention the fact that most state enterprises operate on the basis of what is called *khozraschet financing*. This means that they sell their products for money and use the resulting proceeds to finance normal operating expenses. However, the typical enterprise receives extensive support from the state budget. A major share of all capital investment of enterprises is financed from the budget.

[11]Only the principal headings or expenditures in the budgets require ultimate approval at the top of the budgetary hierarchy. Local and republic governments have some autonomy concerning expenditures for specific items such as fire protection and repairs of drains.

approval by its members before it becomes the law of the land and is published. The budget often provides an indication of Soviet economic policies for the coming year, for it is a part of the country's overall economic and financial plan for each year and reflects priorities in terms of resource allocation.

Government Revenues. Table 13-1 presents the principal sources of revenue for the state budget. Most of the revenue of the budget is derived from the operation of the national economy rather than from direct taxes on the incomes of individuals. The two most important sources of revenue are the turnover tax and deductions from the profits of state-owned enterprises. Both sources of revenue are obtained by setting the prices of goods at levels higher than the cost of production and appropriating the difference.

The Turnover Tax. The turnover tax is one of the most important sources of revenue in the state budget. It was established in 1930 when Soviet industry, unable to support itself, needed additional revenue for further expansion. It represents a flexible and varied portion of the price and is delivered directly to the state budget in accordance with sales of goods on which the tax is levied. The tax is collected by wholesale distributing organizations, individual enterprises, and procurement organizations dealing with consumer goods and foodstuffs. As a rule, the following procedure is followed: If enterprises making goods subject to the tax sell them directly to buyers or to trade organizations, then the turnover tax is paid by the enterprises themselves according to the place of production of such goods; if, however, goods are sold through wholesale organi-

---

TABLE 13-1
ACTUAL REVENUES
OF THE SOVIET STATE BUDGET FOR 1978

Revenue Sources	Billions of Dollars*	
Social Sector		$312.90
Turnover tax	$115.21	
Payments from profits	107.68	
Other receipts	90.01	
Private sector		48.08
State taxes on the population	30.28	
Receipts from social insurance	17.80	
Total revenues:		$364.08

*Because of rounding, components may not add to the totals shown. The exchange rate is 1 ruble equals $1.37 as of March 1978.

Source: Alex Nove, *The Soviet Economic System*, p. 235.

zations, then the turnover tax is paid by the latter at the place of sale of the goods. The burden of the turnover tax ultimately falls on the Russian consumer, so that it can be considered to represent a part of the flow of funds between the state and households.

The Russian turnover tax performs several important economic functions. In addition to being a principal source of revenue for the budget, it also serves to absorb the excess purchasing power of consumers. The production plans of the national government provide that a given amount of goods be made available to consumers annually. On the other hand, in order to maintain incentives, and partly because of errors in planning, consumers may receive more purchasing power than can be absorbed by the goods made available to them at controlled prices. This excess of purchasing power is siphoned off by the turnover tax, which has the impact of an excise or sales tax, as it is applied primarily to consumer goods. It is not a fixed-rate tax, with the yield an independent variable, but, to the contrary, a tax where the desired yield determines the rate, which also varies in response to particular supply and demand conditions. Since the turnover tax is tied to output and is collected either directly at factories or at wholesale distribution outlets, it guarantees a steady inflow of funds to the budget and is easy to collect and inexpensive to administer. Moreover, it is flexible device for establishing equilibrium prices on the bases of the level of output of consumer goods and disposable income.

Payments from Profits. Another important source of revenue in the state budget is payments from profits of state-owned enterprises and organizations. In fact, the turnover tax and payments from profits account for almost two-thirds of the total revenues of the state budget. In 1978, for example, the turnover tax accounted for $115.21 billion and payments from profits accounted for $107.68 billion out of total budget revenues of $364.08 billion. Payments from profits include capital charges, fixed rental charges, free remainder of profit, and deduction from profit. Thus, most of the Russian tax burden can be seen as equal to the total difference between cost of production and final sales prices of all goods and services.

Payments from profits are payable on the actual rather than the planned profits of enterprises, and such payments vary from industry to industry. The rate for a particular enterprise is fixed on the basis of its financial plan for the year. The final selling price of commodities produced by the enterprise is designed to cover the cost of production and planned profits. The latter may or may not occur depending upon the efficiency of the enterprise. Each enterprise has the right to retain part of its profits for such purposes as expanding its fixed and working capital, and the government, in setting the rate of the profit deduction, takes this into consideration. Nevertheless, the amount of profits returned to the state budget is high and can account for as much as 80 percent of total profits.

The distribution of enterprise profits falls into two categories—profits which are retained by enterprises and which are used to finance various incentive funds, and profits which are paid into the state budget. Retained profits can be used to finance an enterprise's material incentives fund, which is a part of the new economic reforms that have taken place in the Soviet Union, Its purpose is to provide an incentive system of bonuses to workers as a reward for increased productivity. Retained earnings are also used to finance an enterprise's social-cultural and production development funds. The former is used to support various services which are provided to workers by an enterprise, and the latter provides a source of revenue for the expansion of fixed and working capital. Depreciation deductions also provide revenue for the same purpose.

Social Insurance Taxes. The remainder of the revenues obtained from the operation of the national economy comes from social insurance taxes paid by enterprises as a fixed percentage of their wage bill, taxes levied on organizations such as collective farms, and income taxes levied on individuals. The social insurance taxes are levied as a percentage of wages and salaries, and these taxes vary from industry to industry. The revenue is paid into a state social insurance budget which is administrered by the trade unions. This budget is consolidated with the stage budget, and revenue is transferred to republic and local budgets.

Personal Income Tax. Direct taxes on the population are unimportant in the Soviet revenue system. The personal income tax accounted for only 8.2 percent of the total state budget revenues in 1978. It is progressive in nature, and in 1978 it ranged from a minimum of 0.59 percent to a maximum of 13 percent of monthly earnings withheld by the enterprises and paid to the Ministry of Finance. The income tax is differentiated between economic groups, with certain groups, such as workers and salaried employees paying a lower tax than other groups, such as doctors, lawyers, and artisans, with incomes from private practice. The personal income tax was supposed to have been abolished in the Soviet Union by 1965. This has not come about, although some liberalization in the amount of income which is exempted from the tax has occurred. Since 1971, the amount of income exempted from the tax has been 100 rubles ($137) a month.

There is also a rural counterpart to the income tax, a so-called agricultural tax which is levied on farmers who earn an income from agricultural activities on their private plots of land. It has as its purpose to discourage farmers from spending too much time on their own land at the expense of their work on collective farms.[12] The tax rate is progressive

---

[12]If farmers fail to work the stipulated minimum number of labor-days or workdays on the collective farms, the agricultural tax can be increased by as much as 50 percent.

and is based on the quantity of land in use rather than on the return on the land. As a source of revenue, the agricultural tax is of little importance, but it has a control function of regulating work.

Government Expenditures. Expenditures of the state budget are presented in Table 13-2. There are four main categories of expenditures—expenditures to finance the national economy, social-cultural measures, national defense, and administration. Expenditures for financing the national economy and social-cultural expenditures account for four-fifths of total outlays.

It can readily be seen that the main function of the state budget is the reallocation of funds within the economy. This reallocation process involves budget receipts of the turnover tax and deductions from profits, and budget expenditures on the national economy, social welfare programs, and national defense. The turnover tax and deductions from profits would represent an inflow of revenue into the state budget from the consumer and enterprise sectors of the economy. The turnover tax, for example, represents part of the net income of society fully returned to the state budget to cover social-cultural measures, outlays for development of the national economy, and other general state needs. These outlays represent an outflow of expenditures on enterprises, while other revenue in the form of salaries and transfer payments is directed from the budget

TABLE 13-2
ACTUAL EXPENDITURES
OF THE SOVIET STATE BUDGET FOR 1978

Expenditures		Billions of Dollars*
Financing the national economy		$193.6
Social-cultural measures		122.1
Education, science, and culture	$53.3	
Health and physical culture	18.1	
Social welfare measure	51.8	
Defense		23.6
Administration		3.1
Loan service		N.A.
Budgetary expenditure residual†		14.1
Total expenditures		$356.5

*Because of rounding, components may not add to the totals shown. The exchange rate is 1 ruble equals $1.37 as of March 1978.

†This includes such items as budget allocations for increasing credit resources of long-term investment banks.

Source: Alex Nove, *The Soviet Economic System*, p. 342.

to households. It can also be seen from looking at the state budget that the national government purchases large quantities of goods and services on its own account.

Financing the National Economy. Expenditures to finance the national economy accounted for approximately 54 percent of total budgetary expenditures in 1978. These expenditures include allocations to enterprises for capital investments and for working capital. Capital goods and construction industries are the major recipients of budget funds for investment purposes, for the government concentrates on growth-inducing investment in areas that constitute the base of economic power. Appropriations from the state budget are also used to finance the construction of transportation facilities, investment in state farms, and housing construction. State farms are government-owned and -operated and they are a major recipient of budgetary funds. Housing construction also enjoys a high priority in terms of allocation of budgetary funds because there is an acute housing shortage in the Soviet Union, particularly in the large cities. Funds allocated to housing construction are of two types: funds that are allocated to construction enterprises for building apartments and other dwellings, and funds which are made available .to individual home builders in the form of credits.

As mentioned previously, the state budget redistributes income within the economy. Payments from profits represent a withdrawal of income from the economy, but they reenter the economy through the budget as expenditures which are used to finance capital investment, increases in working capital, and housing. The turnover tax can also be considered as a device used to reallocate resources from consumption to investment.

Social and Cultural Measures. Expenditures for social and cultural measures, including education and training, public health, physical culture, and social insurance benefits, accounted for 34 percent of total expenditures in the 1978 state budget. A wide variety of social services are financed under the three subcategories of social and cultural measures— education, science, and culture; health and physical culture; and social welfare measures.

Expenditures on education, science, and culture include construction and maintenance costs of schools, payment of teacher's salaries, and provision of financial support for students. Expenditures for science include the support of scientific research. Certain defense expenditures are included under the science category. Expenditures on culture include support for museums, expositions, and the fine arts. Other expenditures that are financed under education, science, and culture include the costs of disseminating Soviet propaganda throughout the world.

The second subcategory of social and cultural expenditures includes spending on health and physical culture. Health expenditures cover outlays for medical and hospital facilities, training of medical personnel, and medical research. Physical culture expenditures support the athletic programs, which are carried on throughout the Soviet Union. Unlike the United States, where sports receive no subsidy from the federal government, the Soviet Union subsidizes its sports and provides special dispensations for its better athletes. In fact, success in sports, particularly in the Olympic Games, is of prime value to the Soviet Union from the standpoint of propaganda. Special sports schools are maintained throughout the Soviet Union and its Eastern European satellites, particularly the German Democratic Republic (East Germany).

The third subcategory, social welfare measures, represents expenditures for old-age and disability pensions, sickness and maternity benefits, and family allowances. Old-age pensions range from a minimum of 35 rubles a month ($50) to a maximum of 120 rubles a month ($175). The retirement age is 60 for male industrial workers with 25 years or more of work experience and 55 years for women workers with at least 10 years of work experience. Sickness and maternity benefits are also payable to all persons under the Soviet social insurance system. Paid vacations cover 15 working days as a minimum. Work injury pensions are also paid to Russian workers, including those on collective farms. Temporary disability benefits are paid from the first day of injury until recovery. Finally, family allowances are paid to families with two or more children, and there is an income supplement for those whose per capita income falls below 50 rubles a month.

National Defense. Outlays for national defense accounted for about 7 percent of total budget expenditures in 1978. However, the amount of $23.6 billion understates the amount that was actually spent for defense-related activities because a substantial proportion of military-space research is carried out under expenditures for science. These expenditures include outlays for research and development for complex military equipment such as aircraft and missiles and for nuclear energy and space activities. The general defense category includes monetary and material allowances for armed forces personnel, payment for supplies and repair of combat equipment, maintenance of military institutions and schools, and military construction. When general defense expenditures are added to outlays for scientific research allocated under the category social-cultural measures but relates directly or indirectly to national defense, total defense expenditures have ranged around 20 percent of the state budget and around 14 to 18 percent of Soviet gross national product.[13]

Soviet defense expenditures have placed a burden on the economy. For one thing, the best human and material resources are channeled into defense-related activities. Outside of these activities, the economy has

---

[13]Central Intelligence Agency, National Foreign Assessment Center, *Handbook of Economic Statistics* (Washington: U.S. Government Printing Office, 1981), Table 45.

generally been inefficient. With a labor force 45 percent larger and about equal real capital investment, the Soviet Union provides a larger population with less than half the goods and services available in the United States. Policies and priorities favoring defense have also worked to the detriment of agriculture because of the huge amounts of human and material resources claimed by the military and space establishment. In addition, there is a trade-off between defense and nondefense resource use. The resources foregone for defense could have resulted in a higher standard of living for the Soviet consumer. The most apparent trade-off has been between defense weapons and producer durable goods, with decreases in the latter leading to a decrease in capital stock, one of the primary ingredients in the growth process. So it can be argued that Soviet defense expenditures have had an adverse effect on the growth rate.[14]

Administration. Budget expenditures for administration is another category of expenditures. This includes financing for local and central government agencies such as planning and financial bodies, ministries, government departments, and the courts and judicial organs. In this connection, it is necessary to remember that the Soviet state budget covers a scope of activities which is much broader than equivalent activities financed in the budgets of capitalistic governments. The state budget covers the planned expenditures for all of the national, regional, and local Soviet governments.

Money and Banking

Money plays a subordinate role in the Soviet economy. To some extent this reflects the traditional Marxist view on money, which largely represented a reaction against capitalism where money reaches its peak of development and influence. Moreover, primary reliance on planning is in real terms; a channeling of investment funds occurs through the state budget rather than through financial markets. As long as plan balancing is done in physical terms, there is little need for prices in planning. Since prices have generally been fixed according to administration convenience, money values rarely indicate the value of goods in terms of real cost, and are, therefore, an uncertain guide to investment decisions. Money also does not provide automatic access to goods in the capital market. First, there must be authorization for the goods to be produced and, secondly, in addition to money, there must be plan authorization to acquire the goods.

This is not to say, however, that money is of no importance. Soviet

---

[14]Henry F. Becker, "Soviet Power and Intentions: Military-Economic Choices," *Soviet Economy in a Time of Change* (Washington: Joint Economic Committee, 1979), pp. 341–45.

money has many of the same functions as money in a capitalistic system. Within and outside the state sector, money serves as a unit of account; that is, all goods and services which are bought and sold are valued in monetary units. Money also functions as a medium of exchange in the Soviet Union in that wages and salaries are paid in terms of currency, and receivers of money can use it to purchase goods and services. However, the ownership of money does not give individuals command over the allocation of resources as it does under a capitalistic system, for resource allocation is determined by the national plan and not by the price system. It is also necessary to stress that money is an instrument through which the state maintains control over enterprises. The Gosbank, acting as the agent of the planning authorities, allocates credit to enterprises in conformance with the plan. Finally, economic reforms, even to the limited extent they have been implemented, imply a more important role for money, particularly in the area of pricing.

Similar to the control over other sectors of the Soviet economy, there is a plan to control the monetary aspects—the financial plan—which parallels and is coordinated with the production and distribution plans for each period of time. The three essential components of the financial plan are the following: the state budget, which is responsible for resource allocation between consumption and investment; the credit plan, which regulates the granting of credits by the banking system to enterprises during a stipulated period of time; and the cash plan, which controls the supply of money in circulation. By use of the components of the financial plan, the planners seek to coordinate the operations of the monetary and financial aspects of the economy with the production of physical goods and services. The financial plan is calculated prior to the production plan because it determines the income and expenditure patterns of all important sectors of the Soviet economy.

The Soviet banking system possesses the following characteristics:

1. Banking is centralized as a monopoly of the government. This means that through the direct operation of the banking system, the government can determine the volume of credit and hence the money supply.
2. The banking system is subordinate to the economic plan. It serves as an instrument of control through the verification of planned transactions.
3. Banks specialize according to functions. There are banks for savings and for investment. There is, however, a trend toward bank consolidation, and savings banks have become a part of the State Bank (Gosbank). For all practical purposes, Gosbank is the banking system of the Soviet Union because it provides for the cash and credit needs of the country.

The State Bank (Gosbank). The Gosbank is the keystone of the Soviet banking system. Within the framework of the centrally planned economy of the Soviet Union, it performs a number of functions:

1. It acts as the fiscal agent of the government in that it receives all tax revenues and pays out budgetary appropriations to enterprises and institutions.
2. It is responsible for granting short-term or commercial credit to all types of enterprises.
3. It carries the accounts of all business enterprises in the country. Each enterprise has an account in the Gosbank which is supposed to supply it with working capital, and when a sale is made between two industrial enterprises, the bank simply deducts the amount of the sale from the buyer's account and adds it to that of the seller. This, as will be explained later, gives the central government control over the progress of each enterprise within the economic system.
4. It is responsible for the preparation of the credit and cash plans which are a part of the financial plan prepared by the Ministry of Finance. In this capacity, the bank is exercising a planning function which involves currency needs and credit expansion.
5. It is also responsible for the emission of currency and for holding all precious metals and foreign currencies owned by the Soviet government. As the bank of issue, it can issue money and withdraw it from circulation, thereby helping to regulate the supply of money available to enterprises and individuals in accordance with the cash plan.

Organization of the Gosbank. At the apex of the Gosbank is the policy-making head office, which is in Moscow. The administrative apparatus of this office is divided into several departments, which have a variety of responsibilities. In addition to the main office in Moscow, there is a network of offices of the Gosbank throughout the Soviet Union. These offices are of three types—republic, regional, and local. Each republic has a principal office which is responsible for the coordination of policy between the main office and regional and local offices. Regional offices are responsible for the supervision of local offices and the transmission of credit plans to the main office. They are also responsible for the conformance of local offices to the credit plans of the Gosbank and for the dissemination of central bank policies into all areas of the Soviet Union. Local offices perform an important control function in that they possess the accounts of the various enterprises and collective farms and can enforce financial discipline in the sense that they can make sure that funds are used for only those purposes that are set forth in the financial plan. In addition to the republic, regional, and local offices, the Gosbank also operates savings banks which are responsible for the accumulation of individual savings and the sale of government bonds.

Financing the Gosbank. The funds that are used to support the operations of the Gosbank are obtained from several sources. One source is the state budget. Since the end of World War II, the state budget has annually shown an excess of revenues over expenditures. This excess is used to increase the credit resources of the Gosbank. There are also other transfers of funds from the budget to the Gosbank. For example, budgetary grants are made for capital purposes. Deposits of savings by the public in the savings banks operated by the Gosbank are also a source of funds. These savings banks do not make loans to the general public. Part of the income derived by the Gosbank is obtained from the difference between the interest paid on savings deposits and interest received from loans to enterprises. The reserves of the social insurance funds also provide a source of funds. Other sources are increases in note circulation and increases in the balances of enterprises and collective farms held on account with the Gosbank.

Planning Function. One of the most important functions of the Gosbank involves economic planning. The Gosbank has the responsibility for the preparation of the credit and cash plans. These plans are approved by the Council of Ministers. The extension of loans made by the bank is carried out in connection with the credit plan and is granted for needs arising in the course of the fulfillment of the plans of production and distribution. Through its drawing up of quarterly cash plans, the bank has a significant influence in determining the extent and composition of note issue. The purpose of the credit and cash plans is to adjust the supply of money to the real output goals of the national economic plan and to prevent expenditures outside of planning purposes. The credit and cash plans are used to implement the physical output plan and to preserve price stability. Both types of plans are used not only by the Soviet Union but by the other communist countries of eastern Europe and by China.[15]

The *credit plan* determines the amount of short- and long-term credit which is to be allocated to all enterprises and collective farms in the economy during the period of the national economic plan.[16] Both types of credit plans involve the preparation of a balance sheet statement which shows the sources and uses of funds.

The short-term credit plan is designed to provide loans to the various sectors of the economy for such purposes as financing the acquisition of inventories by enterprises. The sources of funds which are used to provide short-term credit are budgetary contributions, bank reserves and profits, balances of credit institutions such as savings banks, deposit balances of enterprises, and net changes in currency in circulation. The uses of funds include loans for the payment of wages, loans for temporary needs, loans against drafts in the process of collection, and loans for technological development. It can be seen that the purpose of the plan is

---

[15]The banking system of the Soviet Union is a model which is followed by other communist countries with the exception of Yugoslavia.

[16]The national economic plan is in real terms. The financial plan, of which the credit plan is a part, translates real output into monetary terms.

to collate the short-term needs of enterprises and collective farms with the supply of credit. This collation is carried down to the regional and local levels of the economy through the use of regional credit plans.

The long-term credit plan is prepared on an annual basis and is designed to provide loans for both productive and nonproductive investments which have completion dates of several years or longer. It, too, shows the sources and uses of funds during the year. The funds to finance fixed investment are obtained from three sources: loan repayments by collective farms, individuals, consumer cooperatives, and municipal enterprises; funds from the state budget, which include allocations for such purposes as construction, home building, and agriculture, and also temporary Treasury loans; and subsidies from the union republics, which are used to defray the cost of home building. The funds are used to provide loans to collective farms, individuals, consumer cooperatives, and municipal enterprises, and to repay temporary Treasury loans.

The *cash plan* controls the amount of currency in circulation. It is prepared quarterly and consists of a balance statement which shows the inflows and outflows of money. The inflow of money represents deposits in the Gosbank. These deposits represent currency receipts from a wide variety of sources—tax payments, deposits to the accounts of collective farms, rents and municipal services, receipts from retail sales, receipts from amusement and personal services enterprises, post office and savings banks receipts, and receipts from railroad, water, and air transportation. Monetary outflows under the cash plan go for wage payments, pension allowances and insurance payments, payments for agricultural products and raw materials, consumer loans, expenditures for individual housing construction, and cash disbursements by various economic organizations. The outflow side of the balance statement represents most of the money income payments of the Soviet Union. Withdrawals for wage payments constitute four-fifths of total monetary outflows of the cash plan. Inflows into the Gosbank represent the deposit of receipts of consumer expenditures which result from wage and other income payments on the outflow side. Thus, the cash plan is an instrument which is used to control the performance of the consumer sector of the Soviet economy in terms of the disbursement and use of money.

Control Function. The Gosbank also exercises an important control over the operations of Soviet enterprises. Since all financial transactions of enterprises are legally required to be accomplished through the Gosbank, this affords the bank an opportunity to view their economic performance with regard to real and financial plan fulfillment. Inasmuch as most transactions between enterprises are in terms of money through bank transfers, the flow of goods is necessarily accompanied by a counterflow of funds. By requiring that all purchases and sales of goods be matched against authorized payments and receipts, it is possible for the bank to exercise control over the budget of an enterprise as a regulator of production. The very status of an enterprise's account at the bank is an indicator of its efficiency. If it breaks even on its operation, its account should neither increase nor diminish. If it makes planned or unplanned profits, its balance at the bank will grow, but if it operates inefficiently and sustains losses, its balance will decrease.

It is clear that financial transactions that would normally take place directly between the parties to the transaction in capitalistic economies are obliged to be executed through accounts established in the Gosbank where the transactions and the performance of the units carrying out the transactions must come under the close scrutiny of bank officials. This procedure is not in reality basically different from capitalistic bank settlement procedures since most transactions in capitalistic countries are also carried out through bank accounts, although these transactions are not as closely examined by capitalistic commercial banks. In the Soviet Union, every purchase or sale of goods and raw materials must be reflected in changes in the accounts of the enterprises involved. It is by way of this settlement process that the Gosbank assumes its unique position to carry out many of its control functions.

Provision of Credit. Short-term credit accounts for an overwhelming percentage of the total credit granted by the Gosbank. The most important purpose of short-term credit is to finance accumulations of inventories by enterprises. Another important use of short-term credit is to finance accounts receivable. This provides working capital to the seller of goods while payments are in the process of collection. Short-term loans must be made for purposes which are consistent with the credit plan. They must be secured by real assets, such as goods in process or finished goods, and must carry a fixed maturity date. Interest rates, which are practically uniform as to borrower, are applied to all short-term loans, and penalty rates are charged on overdue loans. Interest proceeds are used as a source of revenue to cover the operating expenses of the Gosbank. As an allocator of resources, interest does not play an important role in the Soviet Union.

The Investment Bank. The Investment Bank (Stroibank) assumed the function that was formerly the responsibility of the Industrial Bank, namely the long-term crediting of capital and consumer goods enterprises. It also assumed responsibility for the following functions:

1. It has the responsibility for financing cooperative housing construction and the long-term crediting of individual housing construction and capital repair of houses in urban areas.
2. It finances the construction of schools, hospitals, and the like in urban areas.
3. It is responsible for investment financing in all state-owned sectors of

the economy, excepting agriculture, transportation, communication, and state-owned housing construction.

4. It is responsible for the short-term crediting of contract organizations working on construction projects for which it handles budget grants.
5. It controls the accounts and expenditures of funds for capital repair and maintenance by contract organizations in the construction field.

The Investment Bank derives its funds from budget grants, which constitute the bulk of its investment assets, and from depreciation allowances and profits of enterprises. It is a result of the creation of a highly centralized banking system in which the Gosbank plays the paramount role. The Investment Bank is an agent for the disbursement of budgetary funds in the form of grants to enterprises in accordance with their investment plans. Although most of its financing is long-term, it provides short-term working capital loans to the construction industry.

The Foreign Bank. Another Soviet financial institution is the Foreign Bank (Vneshtorgbank), which has been in operation since 1924. It is responsible for financing Soviet foreign trade and for carrying out a large part of Soviet international settlement operations. It is also designated as an agent for the Gosbank in many dealings with regard to gold and foreign exchange. It provides the state budget with any surplus of export proceeds over the amount which export producers would receive based on the domestic value of their products and pays subsidies to producers when export prices are below domestic costs. The Foreign Exchange Bank is organized as a shareholding bank with the Gosbank owning two-thirds of the shares. It has few offices of its own in the Soviet Union and, therefore, carries out its operations in the offices of the Gosbank; abroad, it carries out its business through local correspondence banks.

SUMMARY

In their structural arrangement, both the Soviet government and the Communist Party resemble a pyramid with its apex representing control by a central government and party hierarchy. There is an interlocking relationship between government and party, with party officials controlling the administrative structure of each organization. This merging of authority at the top continues with parallel lines of party and government organizations extending downward through the whole Soviet system. In addition to its control and supervision over the government administrative apparatus, the party is organized in every Soviet institution.

In the Soviet Union economic planning is responsible for resource allocation. It is based on the public ownership of the agents of production. However, the size and complexity of the Soviet Union make it difficult for planning to operate efficiently. Economic planning consists of a system of plans. There is a single national plan for the economic development of the country and a subset of plans for different sectors of the economy (sectoral planning) and for different areas (territorial planning).

Economic planning can be divided into long-term and annual planning. The basic form of long-term planning is the five-year plan in which important targets are established. Annual plans are subdivisions of the long-term plan. These operational plans are particularly important at the enterprise level. Long-term economic planning is essentially investment planning, and annual planning is basically production planning. The long-term plan is the principal form of state economic planning.

Public finance in the Soviet Union occupies a much more prominent role in the economy than it does in the economies of the United States and Western Europe. The state budget is very important, for through it flows a large part of national income. The budget is interrelated with the financial plan of the Soviet Union, which it used primarily as a check on the operation of the basic plan, which is expressed in physical value terms. The two main sources of state budget revenues are the turnover tax and payments from the profits of state-owned enterprises. The turnover tax is used to regulate profits and to maintain a balance between aggregate demand and the available supply of consumer goods. Budgetary expenditures include allocations to finance capital investments and to provide working capital to enterprises. Expenditures on social welfare measures constitute a major expenditure item in the state budget.

The banking system in the Soviet Union is a monopoly of the government. Gosbank is the principal instrument of the system and can be called a monobank because it performs the functions of both central and commercial banks. It serves as a collection agent for the payment of taxes and other revenues by state enterprises and other organizations. It also serves as a control mechanism to assure that the flow of funds between enterprises is in accordance with the objectives of the national plan. Gosbank plays an important role in economic planning in that it prepares the credit and cash plans, which are a part of the financial plan.

REVIEW QUESTIONS

1. Distinguish between the roles performed by the Council of Ministers and the Supreme Soviet of the USSR.
2. Discuss the interlocking relationship that is maintained between the Communist Party and the administrative units of the government. What does this relationship accomplish?
3. What is the difference between long-term and annual economic plans?
4. Discuss the procedures involved in the drafting and development of annual plans.
5. What is the role of the state budget in the Soviet economic system?
6. The turnover tax performs several important economic functions in the Soviet Union. What are these functions?
7. Why are direct taxes of little importance in the public finance of the Soviet Union?
8. In addition to performing central and commercial banking functions, Gosbank also performs control functions as well. What is the nature of these functions?
9. What is the role of the financial plan in the Soviet Union? What roles do the state budget and Gosbank perform in the formulation of the financial plan?
10. Gosbank is called a monobank. What is the meaning of this term?

RECOMMENDED READINGS

Aggerwal, Sumer C. "Managing Material Shortages: The Russian Way." *Columbia Journal of World Business* (Fall 1980), pp. 26–37.

Bailer, Seweryn. "The Harsh Decade: Soviet Policies in the 1980's." *Foreign Affairs* (Summer 1981), pp. 999–1020.

Bornstein, Morris, ed., *The Soviet Economy: Continuity and Change,* Boulder, Colo.: Westview Press, 1981.

"The Stalled Soviet Economy," *Business Week.* October 19, 1981, pp. 72–83.

Gregory, Paul R., and Robert C. Stuart. *Soviet Economic Structure and Performance,* 2nd ed. New York: Harper & Row, 1981.

Krylov, Konstantin A. *The Soviet Economy: How It Really Works.* Lexington, Mass.: Lexington Books, 1979.

Lee, Andrea. *Russian Journal.* New York: Random House, 1982.

Nove, Alec. *The Soviet Economic System,* 2nd ed. London: George Allen & Unwin, 1980.

Raymond, Ellsworth L. *The Soviet State.* New York: New York University Press, 1978.

U.S. Joint Economic Committee. *Allocation of Resources in the Soviet Union and China,* Part 6, Hearings before the Subcommittee on Priorities & Economy in Government, 96th Congress, 2nd Session, Washington: U.S. Government Printing Office, 1980.

_____.*Soviet Economy in a Time of Change,* vols. 1, 2, 96th Congress, 1st Session, Washington: U.S. Government Printing Office, 1979.

Wesson, Robert, ed. *The Soviet Union: Looking to the 1980's.* Stanford, Calif.: Hoover Institution Press, Stanford University, 1981.

14

The Economic System of
the Soviet Union

INTRODUCTION

The organization of production and distribution is a fundamental problem which confronts all economic systems. Production involves decisions pertaining to the types and quantities of goods which are to be produced. Related to production is the matter of allocating scarce resources among competing alternatives to attain maximum output. Once the production of goods has taken place, the problem of their distribution arises. Distribution, or *marketing*, refers to the process by which physical goods are brought from producers to consumers. It involves the organization of channels of distribution, transportation, storage, finance, and inventory planning. These functions have to be performed regardless of the type of economic system involved. In the Soviet Union, they are performed by the government, which owns, administers, and controls all of the wholesale and retail distribution facilities.

Distribution can also refer to the division of national income in terms of money, real goods, and services among the suppliers of the agents of production. Most of the Soviet national income is distributed in the form of wages. The Soviets use monetary incentives, such as wage differentials and bonuses, as key devices for motivating workers. Profits are also a part of national income. Government enterprises in all fields of economic activity can make both planned and unplanned profits, but the significance of these profits is quite different from profits in the United States and Sweden. They belong to the government and are used for capital development and other purposes. As mentioned in the preceding chapter, deductions from profits constitute a major source of income for the state budget. Profits are also used as an index of the effectiveness of production of Soviet enterprises, and the extent of their retention by enterprises depends upon the promotion of greater productivity through better organization of production and through economies in the use of raw materials and energy. Interest also figures in the national income to some extent, particularly in the form of payment on the savings deposits of individuals.[1]

In this chapter the organization of industry and agriculture in the Soviet Union will be discussed. In looking at this organization, it is necessary to examine the macroeconomic structures of industry and agriculture and their relationship to economic planning. To enforce planning in a country the size of the Soviet Union, there has to be a system of surveillance which is imposed by both government and party organizations. It is also necessary to examine the operation of individual industrial and agricultural enterprises, for they are the focal point of the primary, critical function of production. However, the production process in itself is incomplete until goods are distributed from producers to consumers. Also in this chapter, the role of unions in the Soviet Union and the process of income distribution among various types of workers will be discussed.

ORGANIZATION OF INDUSTRY

The organizational structure of Soviet industry is complex because an immense bureaucratic apparatus is necessary to plan and administer production and distribution policies in a country which is almost three times the size of the United States. There has, however, been a continual reorganization of the Soviet economic-administrative structure, the most recent occurring in 1965 when there was a change from the regional production council form of territorial organization to a ministerial form.

Administration of Industry

The administrative and policy-making framework of industrial organization resembles a pyramid, with the top being the Politburo of the Central

---

[1]Interest also takes the form of a rental charge for the use of capital. This charge is supposed to be levied only at the end of the period during which the capital has been utilized. Short-term credits provided by Gosbank to finance inventory accumulations of enterprises carry a rate of interest which is usually 2 percent.

Committee of the Communist Party and the bottom being the Soviet industrial enterprise. The Politburo is responsible for making major policy decisions, including those that affect industry. Then there is the Council of Ministers of the USSR, which is the most important governmental executive and administrative body in the Soviet Union, and Gosplan, which is directly subordinate to the Council of Ministers and which is responsible for the development of the long-term and annual economic plans. There is also Gossnab, the State Committee for Material and Technical Supply, which is also under the supervision of the Council of Ministers. This committee is responsible for implementing material and technical supply plans on a national basis and for ensuring that ministries, departments, and enterprises fulfill their delivery plans on time.

However, the direct links in the organization of industrial production are the all-union and union republic ministries, the ministries of the autonomous republics, regional and district departments and boards, and the enterprises.[2] The all-union and union republic ministries are responsible for the allocation of material and technical resources to different industries. These resources are distributed according to plan through various central and regional supply organizations. Each ministry is divided into a number of administrative units called sectoral boards which are responsible for the administration of different industrial sectors within an industry. For example, the all-union Ministry of Machine-Tool and Instrument Industry has the following sectoral boards: heavy and custom-built machine tools; automatic lines and universal machine tools; precision machine tools; woodworking equipment; forging, pressing, and foundry equipment; cutting and measuring instruments; technological equipment; abrasive and diamond tools; hydraulic apparatus; general machine parts and items; and casting, forgings, punchings, and welded structures.

In 1973 changes were made in the administrative framework of Soviet industry. Ministries were given less control over Soviet enterprises, with their responsibilities limited to the formulation of overall policy in planning, investment, and technological improvement. More responsibility has been given to production associations, which can be considered as a form of trust that has control over the operations of enterprises in given economic fields. Each association is responsible for fulfilling that part of the economic plan over which it has jurisdiction and for facilitating the implementation of directives from the State Planning Commission and synthesizing recommendations of the individual enterprises under it. An association is also allowed to use part of its own earnings to form its special funds, to finance industrywide investment and research programs, to establish central incentive and bonus funds, and to cover the deficits of

---

[2]In 1978, there were 32 all-union ministeries and 30 union republic ministeries.

its unprofitable subordinates. One major unsolved problem, however, is the exact demarcation of competence between an association and an industrial enterprise.

The Soviet Enterprise

The enterprise is the basic link in the general system of Soviet production management and operates as a legal person engaged in production activity under the national economic plan.[3] It is under an obligation to fulfill its own production plan, which contains certain targets or success indicators that should be attained. It is required to operate under a profit and loss accounting system, and it has fixed and working capital which form the basis of its statutory fund, the size of which is shown on its balance sheet. It can decide how best to use the fixed and working capital assigned to it, providing that each is used for purposes which are stipulated in the production plan. An enterprise also has the right to make capital investments from funds that are set aside for amortization purposes and to fix the prices of its products within the limits set by the economic plan.

The Khosraschet System. Soviet enterprises operate under what is called a *khosraschet* system of organization. This means that they function as autonomous entities with their own profit-and-loss accounts. Operational independence, within established limits, is assigned to khosraschet enterprises. Each enterprise has its own goals to meet and is given a fund consisting of fixed and working capital. There is freedom to utilize this fund within the constraints imposed by the plan. An enterprise is given an account in Gosbank into which proceeds from the sale of its products are deposited and from which payments are made to cover its own expenses. This, of course, means that Gosbank can exercise an important control function by monitoring the accounts of each enterprise.

Enterprises are generally supposed to conduct their operations in such a way that income will cover expenses and leave some profit. Fulfillment of its physical output goal, however, is the prime operational desideratum of an enterprise. Although financial self-sufficiency is desired, most khosraschet enterprises receive some sort of financial support from the state budget, particularly in the financing of capital investment.

Enterprises are supposed to meet their responsibilities in a prescribed manner, and they incur penalties if they do not. For example, fines are imposed by the government for late delivery of products. Reliance on material incentives is another characteristic of the khosraschet enterprise.

---

[3]This means that an enterprise can own property, enter into binding contracts, sue, and be sued.

Funds are set aside to provide bonuses for superior performances on the part of workers. Control by the ruble is exercised by Gosbank over all enterprises. This means that all enterprise transactions in value terms pass through Gosbank, and it can compare actual results with planned targets to see that there is no deviation from the plan.

The Tekhpromfinplan. Each Soviet enterprise has to prepare what is called a *tekhpromfinplan*, which is its operating plan for the year.[4] The tekhpromfinplan is a consolidated plan which includes the financial, output, and investment plans of the enterprise. It is prepared twice. The first is a preliminary draft and the second is a formally approved economic document. It is supposed to be developed within the framework of the long-term or five-year plan, which is not only developed for the economy as a whole, but for each enterprise as well. However, operational targets and the allocation of resources for an enterprise are determined for the most part in the annual plan. The plan also functions on a quarterly and monthly basis.

The tekhpromfinplan contains a number of assigned indexes or success targets which are to be achieved by an enterprise. These indicators are as follows:

1. The volume of output to be produced and sold.
2. The total value of sales.
3. The fulfillment of planned delivery contracts.
4. The amount of profits and level of profitability.
5. Payments to and allocations from the state budget.
6. The amount of funds to be spent on the expansion and improvement of production.
7. The introduction of new techniques and automation.
8. The volume of inputs in the form of material and technical supplies.

In terms of success, an enterprise is judged primarily by the volume of its sales and the amount of its profits, including savings made from economies in production. Constraints are placed on an enterprise in the form of fixed prices of both inputs and outputs and in limitations in the selection of inputs which are allocated to it. All prices, with the exception of those in the free agricultural market, are set by the government. In setting prices, an allowance is made for profits expressed as a percentage of average production cost for an entire industry. Individual enterprises will have differing rates of profits because of differences in production costs. *Profits*, then, can be defined in terms of the Soviet enterprise as the difference between its total income from sales and its cost of production. In its annual operating plan, an enterprise lists its expected or planned

---

[4]Alec Nove, *The Soviet Economic System*, 2nd ed. (London: Allen & Unwin, 1980), pp. 121–23.

profits as a percentage of total production costs. Its planned profits may be more or less than its actual profits. If they are less than actual profits, this is all to the good as far as the enterprise is concerned, for its material incentive fund is increased. On the other hand, an enterprise, or rather its manager, is embarrassed if its planned profits are above its actual profits, or worse, if it operates at a loss. Planned losses can also be made in certain industries, such as coal mining, where it is necessary to set prices below costs to stimulate consumption. These losses are covered by grants from the state budget or by income transfers from other sectors of the economy.

Organization of an Enterprise. In general a Soviet enterprise is organized along the following lines.[5] There is a director who is appointed by the state to run the enterprise. This director is governed from above by directives and rules of behavior which guide all decisions. However, the director is not rigidly circumscribed as to what can be done, but rather is somewhat free to operate in any manner so long as it is within the general framework of the national economic plan and the enterprise's operating plan. The director can influence the contents of the operating plan through familiarity with the resource needs and product specifications of the enterprise. The Soviet planning system, of necessity, has to permit a certain degree of managerial autonomy, for it is impossible to supervise in detail the operation of thousands of enterprises. Caution, rather than risk taking and innovation, appears to be an important characteristic of Soviet enterprise directors because it is easier and safer to work within established production procedures in the fulfillment of the operating plan.

Since the Soviet reward system has favored directors who fulfill or overfulfill their plans, there have been frequent unfavorable results. Directors often have claimed overall plan fulfillment, when in fact the claimed production included subquality output, incomplete items, or an incorrect assortment of goods. To fulfill their plans, directors often have concentrated on goods of high value or items which are easy to produce. This subterfuge is fairly difficult to detect, but the Soviet authorities are aware that it exists. The economic reforms have drastically reduced the number of targets or success indicators with which a director has to contend. Nevertheless, there is a community of interest, which tends to favor plan fulfillment regardless of the method involved, that binds the director and others who are directly associated with the enterprise.

In some respects the functions of a managing director in the Soviet Union are similar to those of an American managerial counterpart; in other respects, they are not. For example, there is a formal chain of com-

---

[5]The Communist Party controls all appointments to important positions through the nomenklatura (patronage) system, meaning appointees have to be either members of the Communist Party or in good standing with the Party.

mand within both the Soviet and American enterprise, and both Soviet and American managing directors would operate through this chain. Also in terms of decisions involving the process of production, that is, quality control standards, budgeting, and production scheduling, there are similarities between Soviet and American managerial responsibilities. There would be similarities with respect to personnel policies involving labor force utilization, promotions, and the development of wage norms.

It is necessary to mention the role that the Communist Party plays in the operation of an enterprise. There is a local unit of the party in all enterprises which is supposed to act as the custodian of the nation's interest as opposed to the more narrowly circumscribed outlook of the industrial manager. Most managers, however, are members of the Communist Party, but, despite this fact, the party maintains its own independent hierarchy in each enterprise. At the head of this hierarchy is the party secretary, who shares responsibility with the director for plan fulfillment. The secretary is also supposed to keep the party informed of any adverse developments in the enterprise. Some ambivalence exists in defining the secretary's relationship with the director and with the party. The secretary can neither exercise excessive interference in the decisions of the director, nor be too lax from the standpoint of control.

However, as mentioned above, there is a mutuality of self-interest on the part of both the director and secretary which often works for collusion with respect to fulfilling the enterprise plan. Since each is judged and rewarded on the basis of the same success criteria, it is to their advantage to secure an easy plan or to produce the things that are easiest to produce to fulfill the plan. Since party and other officials are judged by the performance of enterprises under their jurisdiction, it is often to their advantage simply to stress plan fulfillment, regardless of method. This places the burden of authority and control on agencies and officials at the national level, and pressures for change and innovation often have to emanate from those sources.

The Soviet Reforms and Economic Incentives

A series of economic reforms have been introduced into the Soviet Union in an attempt to improve efficiency in the use of resources and the quality of products. An initial set of reforms, which were developed in 1965, restored the ministerial system of managing industry and called for the merger of industrial enterprises into large associations in order to obtain economies of scale and save on administrative costs.[6] In 1973 further moves toward concentration were expedited by decrees coordinat-

---

[6]Gertrude E. Schroeder, "The Soviet Economy on a Treadmill of Reforms," in *Soviet Economy in a Time of Change*, Vol. 1, Joint Economic Committee, 96th Congress, 1st Session, 1979, pp. 314–16.

ing enterprises into production associations.[7] By 1980 production associations were supposed to account for about three-fourths of total industrial output.[8] The production associations are formed along product or geographic lines or vertical lines combining products and their required material inputs. Plans have also been advanced to form associations for foreign trade and construction.

The economic reforms have also included measures to improve enterprise performance. The 1965 reforms created a system of incentives tied to meeting plans for two basic plan indicators: (1) sales, and (2) profit based on a return on fixed and working capital. Wage and bonus funds were linked to profit. Later these funds were also tied to the fulfillment of plans for labor productivity and for product quality. Then in 1977, rules governing incentive funds were modified in an effort to improve quality and delivery of output. Ministries control the wage and bonus funds and choose the performance indicators. Fulfillment of plans for labor productivity and a specified share of products of highest quality in the total value of output are mandatory.[9] There is the specification that managerial personnel must be deprived of all or part of their bonuses for failure to comply with contractual arrangements for product delivery. Total bonuses for an enterprise are limited to the incentive fund with specific shares being set in annual plans for white-collar and production workers. A ceiling of 50 percent of salary is imposed on the size of bonuses paid for plan fulfillment from the material incentive fund.

The economic reforms have developed a number of flaws. For one thing, they are usually introduced piecemeal, with some enterprises being converted immediately while others are not. Another flaw involves the fact that there is no accompanying program of political reform. In the realm of politics, there is no extension of political autonomy—in short, no real change in the individual's subordination to the state. Soviet bureaucracy is reluctant to relinquish any of its authority so that reforms, even though they may be successful, are regarded with suspicion. As a consequence, centralized planning and administration remain strongly entrenched.

Channels of Distribution

In the Soviet Union the government owns and controls every distribution outlet in the production process. There are two networks through which

---

[7]The extent of industrial concentration is higher in the advanced communist countries than in the capitalist countries. The organization of industry has to be considered a basic part of the economic and political organization of the state. There is a constant effort to combine industrial and agricultural enterprises into a larger units to increase output to support the population and to export to world markets.

[8]Schroeder, *Soviet Economy in a Time of Change*, p. 316.

[9]*Ibid.*, pp. 327–29.

goods move—a material and technical supply network, which is responsible for moving supplies to and from industrial enterprises, and a state trading network through which consumer goods are sold. The key state agencies which are responsible for distribution are Gosplan, Gossnab, and the Ministry of Trade. As far as material and technical supplies are concerned, requirements are written into a plan for material supplies which is a part of the national economic plan. Gosplan is responsible for the development of this plan, and Gossnab (the State Committee of the USSR Council of Ministers for the Supply of Materials to the National Economy) is responsible for carrying out plans for supplying materials and equipment drawn up by Gosplan. Gossnab is also responsible for the distribution of production which is not distributed by Gosplan. What all of this means is that materials and equipment are centrally allocated, and material transfers to enterprises must be authorized by the government and must be accompanied by payment of money on the part of the enterprise.

Figure 14-1 presents the distribution system of the Soviet Union. The important decision-making and distribution units include the Council of Union Ministers, which establishes the priorities in resource allocation. Gosplan is responsible for the development of the annual production–distribution (material balances) plan. It handles goods that are in short supply and the high-priority defense items. Gossnab is responsible for the development of the distribution plans for some 17,500 items. It also controls the distribution of products to consumers and regulates the output of all the plants and enterprises. Soyuzselkhoztekhnika (Union Agricultural Technical Bureau) is responsible for the handling of agricultural machinery and other products. It coordinates material supplies to state farms, collective farms, and other agricultural units. Ministeries have responsibility for allocating funds and exercising control over supplies and materials going to all of their units and enterprises.[10]

A materials supply plan is developed annually to balance production with consumption. The plan is divided into three sections:

1. A materials balance between consumer needs based on the preceding year's supply and the currently available production capacity is prepared. Items covered in this balance are food, shoes, other consumer goods, and appliances. Side by side, a production balance is developed in terms of need versus available capacity of machines, raw materials, and fuel.
2. Distribution plans which show the detailed allocation of each product from production centers to distribution centers are prepared.
3. Interstate and interregional plans specify the volume of production to be obtained within the republic or region, the volume to be provided by other republics or regions to each republic or region, the volume to be

---

[10]Sumer C. Aggarwal, "Managing Material Shortages: The Russian Way," *Columbia Journal of World Business* (Fall 1980), pp. 27–28.

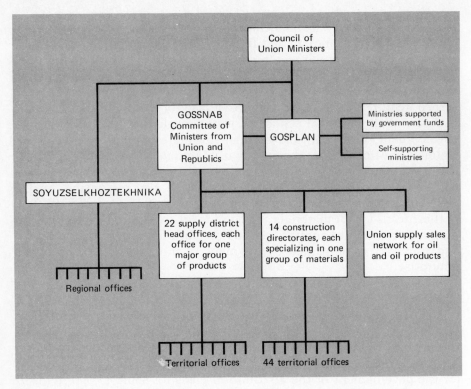

FIGURE 14-1 GENERAL ORGANIZATIONAL LINKAGES OF THE
SUPPLY–DISTRIBUTION SYSTEM IN THE USSR
Source: Reprinted with permission of the author and publisher from "Managing Material Shortages: The Russian Way," by Sumer C. Aggarwal in *Columbia Journal of World Business* (Fall
1980), p. 27.

contributed by each region or republic to national needs, and the volume
needed for exports.[11]

The actual distribution of supplies is carried out by various supply
agencies attached to the ministries. These agencies function at both the
national and republic levels. An enterprise estimates its output targets
and input norms based on its proposed production plan and makes its
requests, called *zaiavki,* for materials to a supply agency (*glavk*) which is
part of the ministry that has ultimate jurisdiction over the enterprise. It is
the responsibility of the glavk to ascertain whether or not the requests of
the enterprise are legitimate, for in many cases enterprises pad their
orders in order to enhance their chances of fulfilling their production
plans. A fact of economic life for the director of a Soviet enterprise has

---

[11]*Ibid.,* pp. 26–27.

been the inadequate provision of resources necessary to fulfill the production plan. An unsteady flow of supplies causes work stoppages and jeopardizes plan fulfillment; the disruptions spread through the economy in a chain reaction. In fact, a weakness in the Soviet economic system is the planning and distribution of supplies, and in spite of the many organizational reforms that have been introduced in the Soviet Union during the last two decades, uncertainty in resource allocation still remains as a critical problem for enterprise managers.

Consumer goods also go through various stages of distribution. At each stage, the characteristics of centralized allocation of resources are all present—estimation of needs, requests by enterprises, determination of delivery orders, and the transfer of funds. It is not until the final stage— retail trade—that goods are freely sold to the consumer. As is also true for the distribution of industrial supplies, planning of consumer goods involves a reconciliation of requests from wholesale or retail organs at the lower levels with the production and distribution plans at the higher levels. For example, a wholesale outlet may receive a request from retail stores for a certain commodity. These requests are transferred to the Ministry of Trade in the republic in which the wholesale and retail outlets are located. These requests eventually are transmitted upward to Gosplan. The allocation of consumer goods is determined in the overall national plan, and the amount of the particular commodity is allocated to the Ministry of Trade in the Republic and also to the republic Gosplan, which are responsible for delivery to the wholesale outlet. It, in turn, is responsible for the final delivery of the commodity to the retail stores.

The Ministry of Trade, which is a union-republic ministry, is at the apex of the consumer trade network. It is responsible for the operation of a network of government stores that are located in urban areas. There is a Ministry of Trade in each republic, which has control over a number of wholesale outlets. Typically, government retail stores are under the control of a local city trade organization called a *torg*. The torg has within it trade departments which are responsible for supplying goods to the city and supervising the operation of the retail store system. Warehouses are also attached to the trade departments.

Retail stores represent the ultimate link with the consumer. Retail prices are, for the most part, fixed by the government at levels which attempt to equate supply with demand. The retail price consists of several elements: production cost, profit of the producer, the turnover tax, and wholesale and retail markups. In other words, it consists of all of the components which make up the price charged by the seller to the retailer plus a retail markup added as the last element of retail price formation.

In addition to the network of government stores, there is a consumer cooperative store network which also has its wholesale and supply system. Consumer cooperatives operate primarily in the rural areas. Like other organizations in the Soviet Union, they are formed in the structure of a pyramid, with local outlets at the base and the decision-making agenices at the republic and all-union levels at the apex. Prices are set by the Ministry of Trade usually at rates higher than those set on consumer goods in the urban areas. This is to compensate in part for higher transportation costs. Wholesaling is performed by government wholesale distributing units, the trade warehouses. Residents of a village or state farm are organized into consumer cooperatives and become shareholders. They are supposed to elect a governing board, a director, and an inspection committee, although actually there is little autonomy granted to local cooperatives.

LABOR UNIONS AND THE SOVIET WORKER

Labor unions exist in the Soviet Union, and workers are not only permitted but are encouraged to belong to them. Unlike their counterparts in the industrial countries of the West, unions do not enjoy a significant sphere of autonomous action. They do not have the right to strike, and decisions on wage rates, output norms, hours of labor, and similar matters are prerogatives of government rather than unions. These decisions are made on a national scale by the State Committee on Labor and Wages, which is a part of the Council of Ministers of the USSR. Such powers that unions do possess in the Soviet Union are in relationship to the operation of an enterprise. Although it was originally intended that important managerial decisions would be made by a troika of management, union, and party representatives, the role of the union declined in importance as the drive for industrial efficiency strengthened managerial authority. It can be said that in terms of a constellation of power, unions rank behind both management and party in an enterprise. They have certain functions which can be enumerated as follows:

1. They have the right to participate with management in the development of the economic plan for an enterprise.
2. They are responsible for the maintenance of worker discipline by discouraging tardiness, absenteeism, and worker turnover and by promoting measures to encourage productivity.
3. Management is required to obtain their permission in assigning workers to wage categories and in introducing regulations on piecework and bonus systems.
4. Unions play an important role in the area of social insurance, and they carry out a variety of activities in connection with vacations, education, recreation and culture. They are responsible for the collection of social security contributions from enterprises and disbursement of cash benefits.
5. They have the right to express opinions on candidates nominated for management positions and to oppose discharges of workers that are initiated by management.

Nevertheless, the basic collective bargaining function, which unions perform in the Western democracies, has been emasculated in the Soviet Union. Unions are supposed to cooperate with management and function in the interest of the state and its national objectives. Although they have specific powers and responsibilities, they are subservient to the interests of the Communist Party.

AGRICULTURE

Russia at the time of the czarist revolution of 1917 was predominantly an agricultural country. In the period immediately prior to World War I, agriculture underwent some dramatic changes. Under the Stolypin reforms of 1906, a large number of peasants were given legal title to the land they worked. The large landowner declined in importance and even disappeared from the economic scene. However, the deep-seated aspirations of the Russian peasantry, the desire to own and manage their own land, was to be thwarted when the Communists came into power. It was inevitable that an effort would be made to socialize agriculture, for many of the Communists believed that communism would never succeed in the Soviet Union as long as agriculture remained a small-scale, capitalistic enterprise.

During the early years of their regime, the Communists were faced with the problem of converting Russian farms into large-scale, efficient units capable of furnishing large surpluses of food for the urban and industrial population and providing large quantities of raw materials for industry. In 1929 the First Five-Year Plan went into effect. Huge state farms were established on old estates, and every effort was made to get individual peasants to pool their holdings and operate them as large, cooperative undertakings.

Initial efforts to collectivize agriculture were not too successful. In the first place, many of the more prosperous peasants refused to cooperate, and the government's relentless persecution of these *kulaks* deprived the collective farms of potential managerial ability. Second, many peasants killed and ate their animals before joining a collective farm, a practice that was encouraged by the fact that the government made heavy grain requisitions which left the peasants short of food and fodder. This heavy grain collection brought a resumption of the old practice, which was prevalent under the czars, of hiding grain and decreasing the areas under cultivation.

By the end of the First Five-Year Plan, the basic structure of Soviet agriculture had been decided upon. This structure was based on two forms of collective enterprises—the state farm and the collective farm. The state farm was (and is) the full property of the Soviet government. It represents the main communist objective for agriculture—the peasants are truly proletarians with no property of their own.[12] The collective farm, as the name implies, was supposed to be a self-governing cooperative made up of peasants who voluntarily pooled their means of production and divided the proceeds. The first collective farms were basically of two types—collectives in which all livestock and implements were held in common by the peasants, who lived in communal buildings; and collectives in which the peasants were allowed to own livestock and a small plot of land as well as live independently of other members of the collective farm. The latter type of collective has become the prevalent form of agricultural unit in the Soviet Union.

Agriculture is controlled by the government through national economic planning. The supply and price of inputs, the share of output marketed, the prices paid for agricultural products, and farm income and expenditures are regulated by the plan. Overall procurement goals are established for agricultural products that are to be delivered to the government. These goals are disseminated downward by Gosplan to the Ministries of Production and Procurements in each republic and to lower administrative units in the provinces and districts. Given the procurement goals, which are supplemented by local requirements, each state farm and collective farm has to formulate a production plan. When this is done, each plan goes up the administrative line—district, province, and republic—to be examined and combined with other plans. Finally, the combined plans reach Gosplan for approval. Gosplan also is responsible for the determination of the production and use of such agricultural inputs as machinery and fertilizer. Material balances, which represent a balance sheet of the supply and demand for various inputs, are used in planning. Separate balance sheets are used for each input, with the left side showing the sources of inputs and the right side its uses.

State Farms

State farms, as mentioned above, are owned by the government and operated as regular industrial establishments with managers and hired workers. Their annual budgets and operating plans are developed by the government, which is also responsible for the determination of wages paid to the workers and for the provision of livestock and equipment.

As originally set up, the state farms were extremely large. They were intended to increase agricultural production by enlarging the land area under cultivation, by utilizing modern, efficient farming techniques, and by serving as experimental stations and model agricultural centers. The

---

[12]According to Marx, the ideal agricultural organization would be state farms where private ownership, no matter how insignificant it might be, could not exist and where all of the workers were to be paid by the government on the same basis as factory workers.

state farm remains today as the highest form of a socialized agricultural unit and enjoys a favored position in Soviet agriculture. In recent years the number of state farms has increased considerably because some collective farms have been converted into state farms. Also, a number of specialized meat, dairy, and vegetable state farms have been created around major urban centers. In terms of physical output, they accounted for one fourth of total agricultural output—an amount which is adversely affected by the fact that many state farms are established in areas of low productivity.

State farms sell their produce to the government for processing and distribution through state stores, for stockpiling, and for export. The arrangement between state farms and the government takes the form of a contract which specifies the price to be paid for the commodity produced and the delivery date. There is usually a basic procurement price, subject to some regional variation, for each commodity. Prices can be used as incentives for changes in production. For example, if an increase in the production of dairy products or meat is desired, prices are raised. In this way, prices perform a function in allocating resources which is similar to their role in a market economy. Prices are also set at levels that reflect, at least in part, differences in average production costs on state farms operating in different areas of the country. Lower prices are paid in better land areas, reflecting the fact that no charge is made for land rent.

State farms are managed by directors who have the right to determine the total number of workers to be used on the farm, the planned production costs, the planned labor productivity, and other general factors of management control. Although this has meant greater independence of state farm management from central control, the basic policies to be followed are determined by the government, and directors must operate according to these policies.

Since state farms are entirely owned and operated by the state, workers are direct employees of the state and are paid a wage. This wage varies according to the type and the quantity of work done. Payments primarily take the form of piece rates that vary according to the classification of the worker. Specialists, such as agronomists, are paid on a monthly basis. Wages are paid from a general wage fund which must be provided for in the development of the state farm's overall operating plan. In addition, a bonus arrangement is provided for out of the material incentives fund which is separate from the wage fund.

The starting point in the distribution of profit is gross sales, which is obtained by multiplying the planned volume of sales per product by the set state price. From gross sales production costs, including the cost of seed and fertilizer and depreciation, are deducted to get gross income. From gross income a deduction is made into the wage fund, and the remainder is called the socially clear income. This income may be considered a residual that is divided between the state farm and the state.

There is a deduction from profit, which also goes to the state. Remaining income is divided into various funds. An example of the utilization of profit of a state farm is as follows:

Total sales		$1,300,000
Less seed, fertilizer, and other costs including depreciation		650,000
Gross income		$ 650,000
Less wage funds		260,000
Social clear income		$ 390,000
Less special costs	$ 65,000	
Less production levy	52,000	117,000
Net profit		$ 273,000
Less profits taxes		52,000
Net profit		$ 221,000
Less investment funds	$104,000	
Less enterprise funds	3,900	
Less social and cultural funds	48,100	156,000
Profit residual		$ 65,000

Collective Farms

The collective farm is the dominant type of agricultural organization in the Soviet Union when measured from the standpoint of number of farm units, share of land area sown, and number of workers employed. It may be defined as a form of agricultural organization in which varying numbers of individual peasants combine their resources and talents and operate on a collective basis. The land occupied by a collective farm is secured to it without payment and without time limit, and the livestock, implements, and public structures in its possession are considered to be its property. Each collective farm household, in addition to its basic interest in the collective property, is entitled to a small plot of land for private cultivation, housing, and such auxiliary items as productive livestock, poultry, and minor agricultural implements.

Differences from State Farms. Members of a collective farm are not paid wages, but share in the income of the individual collective farm. This income depends directly upon the crops which are produced. After certain deductions are made from the harvest, the remainder is distributed in kind among the collective farmers, or is sold for cash, which is then distributed, usually at the end of the year. However, with later agricultural reforms, there was a shift to a regular cash wage which is paid on a monthly basis. This reflects an attempt on the part of the government to use similar methods of wage payments for both collective and state farm workers.

Investment in collective farms is not financed out of the state budget, but from the income of the individual collective farm. From this income, the collective farm must pay an income tax and various current expenses, including those for administration and for educational and cultural purposes. An undivided surplus must also be set up to cover necessary capital expenditures.

Collective farms are also smaller than state farms in terms of size and number of workers employed per farm. In 1978 each collective farm had, on the average, approximately 539 households, 16,302 acres of land, 1,768 cattle, and 1,030 hogs.[13] The number of collective farms in the USSR is growing smaller. In 1940 there were 240,000 collective farms; in 1978 this number had been reduced to 27,700. This reduction can be explained by the fact that in recent years a large number of collective farms have been merged into larger collectives or have been converted into state farms for the purpose of increasing agricultural output.

Distribution of Income and Production. There are three claimants to the income and output of a collective farm—the state, the collective farm itself, and the members of the collective farm. The state has first claim on production. Prior to 1958, collective farms had to deliver to the government at low fixed prices certain specified quantities of crops and animal products. To acquire farm products cheaply had always been one of the main goals of Soviet economic policy. Also, payment in kind of a certain amount of produce had to be made to the Machine Tractor Stations. In 1958, however, the government introduced a single system of procurement prices, and agricultural products are now purchased from collective farms at a basic price for each product. Currently a wide variety of prices exists for most commodities depending on such factors as the type of market, quality, location, and the season when the commodity is marketed.[14]

There are two agricultural marketing systems in the Soviet Union— the state system and the private market system. Under the state system, the state assumes the responsibility for transporting and marketing all products it produces. For example, state-owned processing plants receive raw materials at a specified price, which is established by the government, and deliver the finished products to state stores and other outlets at specified prices, which are also set by the government. These products are then distributed to the consumer through state stores. The state marketing system has proven to be inefficient, so the collective farms are now allowed to deliver their produce to stores and other retail outlets; for their produce they are allowed to receive the retail price less a discount.

After the collective farms deliver procurement quotas of their product to the government, they are free to sell any surplus or remainder in

---

[13]U.S. Department of Agriculture, *Farm Income Statistics,* Statistical Bulletin No. 609 (Washington: U.S. Government Printing Office, 1978), Table 55.

[14]The Russians have been reluctant to publish average prices received by all farms throughout the USSR for individual commodities.

the free market. This produce is usually sold in the immediate local areas because transportation is a problem. In some areas, the collective farm may provide its own facilities for retailing its product. Prices are set by ordinary supply and demand factors operating in the market.

The revenue derived by collective farms from the sale of their produce is used for several purposes. First of all, a number of general expenditures have to be met. These include contributions to a sociocultural fund, production expenses for such items as fuel and fertilizers, insurance which is designed to protect the collective farm from the loss of its physical assets, and contributions to a capital fund for the purpose of acquiring capital goods. Prior to 1965, a standard 12.5 percent tax was levied against the gross income in cash and in kind of collective farms. However, in order to improve production incentives, changes were made in the tax in 1965. The tax is now calculated on the basis of net income, which is the difference between gross income and production costs plus deductions to the social insurance fund. A portion of net income which is equal to a profitability rate of 15 percent is exempt from the tax. The profitability rate is the ratio of net income to total costs. A tax of 12 percent is levied on the remaining net income.[15]

Wages paid to collective farm workers come out of a wage fund. The standard method of payment has involved the use of workdays. The *workday* is an abstract unit which is based on such factors as the quality and quantity of work performed and the type of work involved. Each worker must work a minimum number of workdays a year. The total number of workdays accumulated by a worker is divided into the amount of income available in cash or in kind for distribution at the end of the year. The result is a worker's income for the year. This system has been erratic over the years, and incomes of collective farm workers have lagged behind those of state farm workers. To remedy this defect, measures have been taken to raise incomes of collective farm workers up to a parity with incomes of state farm workers. The guaranteed minimum income, which was 60 rubles or $73.17 a month in 1978, was made applicable to collective farm workers. A monthly wage system has been introduced. This places the worker's claim on a part of the income ahead of the claim of the collective farm instead of the other way around.

Private Plots

Private plots represent the third form of agricultural institution that exists in the Soviet Union. To a certain extent, they are almost an anach-

---

[15]For example, assume a gross income of 2 million rubles and total costs of production plus social insurance contributions of 1.5 million rubles. Net income is 500,000 rubles. The profitability ratio is 33⅓ percent (500,000:1,500,000). Fifteen percent of the profitability ratio is exempt, or 225,000 rubles (225,000:1,500,000). Taxable net income is 500,000 minus 225,000, or 275,000 rubles. The tax is 12 percent of 275,000 rubles, or 33,000 rubles.

ronism in that they represent the only substantial form of private enterprise that exists in the country. However, the fact that they do exist can be attributed to the fact that the Russian peasants have never been completely subverted to the idea that land should belong to the state and not to them. The typical private plot is only two-thirds of an acre in size. Although dwarfed in terms of physical size by the state and collective farms, the private plots account for an inordinately large share of agricultural output. Although private plots and land holdings account for only 3 percent of all of the sown agricultural land, they contribute substantially to the production of livestock, dairy, and truck garden products. The bulk of the products produced on the private plots are high value products. In 1980 the private sector produced 30 percent of the total meat supply, 35 percent of the milk, 35 percent of the eggs, 59 percent of the potatoes, 34 percent of the vegetables, and 44 percent of the fruit in the USSR. Sales of products from private plots represent a substantial amount of the income of collective farms.[16]

The private sector of Russian agriculture can be classified into three categories—private plots which are held and operated by members of collective farms, private plots which are operated by state farm workers and by other state employees, and private land which is held by individual peasants. The last category is rare in the Soviet Union. Individual peasants who own and operate their own farms are located primarily in sparsely populated regions where the formation of collective farms is not economically justifiable. Ownership of private plots on collective farms represents a partial retreat from the complete collectivization attempts of the 1930s which had disastrous results. Although, in general, the attitude of the government toward private farming has ranged from encouragement to hostility, individual ownership and use of farmland is legal according to Articles 7 and 9 of the 1936 Constitution of the Soviet Union, providing it does not involve the use of hired labor. Collective farm private plots are allowed as an entitlement under a 1935 statute.[17] It can be said, however, that the ultimate wish of the government is the elimination of all private holdings.

In addition to their private plot of land, collective farm workers are also allowed to own livestock and farm implements. The amount of livestock which farm workers are permitted to own varies according to the nature of the collective farm. The collective farmer is allowed to sell the produce which he grows on his plot of land. Prior to 1958, there was a compulsory delivery of a certain percentage of this output to the government at a price which was arbitrarily set far below its market price. This compulsory delivery could be regarded as a form of agricultural tax in that

---

[16]Anton F. Malish, "Internal Policy, Decision Making and Food Import Demand in the Soviet Union," unpublished paper (June 1981), p. 7.

[17]The plot is given to the household for its personal use only. It cannot be sold or rented, and, if not used, it is taken away.

the same result is achieved by taking a part of farm produce at an arbitrarily low price as would be achieved by letting the farmers sell their crops for full market value and then taking a portion of their income by means of taxation.[18] In 1958 compulsory deliveries were abolished, and the farmers are now free to sell their surplus produce in the open market. There are also the alternatives of selling the surplus through arrangements with the collective farm or of selling through consumer cooperatives.

State farm workers and other state employees are also allowed to farm private plots of land. The arrangements are similar to those on the collective farms. The private plots represent an entitlement which permits the worker to use the land for farming purposes. Surpluses from the plots can be sold in the free market. However, private farming, in general, has been a thorn in the side of the Soviet agricultural policy makers because many farmers, in pursuing their self-interests, have neglected their collective or state farm work to concentrate on production on their plots, which they can sell in the free market. Attempts to suppress the use of private plots have inevitably led to a decline in initiative on the part of the farm workers and a concomitant decline in productivity. So the private plots remain an anomaly under the Soviet system, an institution tolerated because of its importance in the production of high-quality foodstuffs and because it makes the socialization of agriculture more palatable to the farmers.

---

[18]This reasoning can be explained as follows: In the graph shown, P_2 represents the prices charged by the government to consumers and P_1 represents the price paid to farms for their produce. The shaded area from P_2 to P_1 represents the tax.

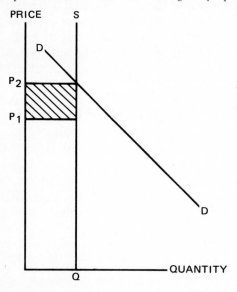

An agricultural tax is paid by collective farm workers who derive income from private plots of land. This tax can be used as a control measure to insure that workers and their families work the prescribed minimum number of workdays. If workers or their families fail to work the minimum number of workdays, the agricultural tax is increased by 50 percent. State farm workers do not pay an agricultural tax on their income from private plots; instead, as regular employees of the state, they are subject to payment of the personal income tax.

Recent Agricultural Reforms

The performance of Soviet agriculture during the regimes of Khrushchev and Brezhnev has been, to say the least, rather poor. To a major extent, agriculture has been the Achilles heel of the Soviet economy. Underinvestment in capital, excessive central planning, and a general lack of economic incentives have contributed to the stagnation of Russian agriculture. It has been evident that the Russians have failed to fulfill the demand for high-quality food products. Increasing incomes in the Soviet Union and fixed prices have greatly increased Soviet consumer's desire to eat more meat, dairy products, fruits, and vegetables.[19] In addition, with relatively few choices of other consumer goods, the income elasticity for quality food products is high. Food shortages, reflected by long lines at state outlets, are a particularly sensitive political issue, since the average Russian citizen uses food availability, in particular meat, as a barometer of economic well-being.

The Soviet draft guidelines for the Eleventh Five-Year Plan (1981–1985) calls for an average annual increase in agricultural output of 12 to 14 percent.[20] To expedite the achievement of this and other agricultural goals, a series of agricultural reforms were promulgated during the period 1977–1981. Private plots, which have long been recognized as the most important source of high-quality food products, have been linked with efforts to increase livestock output. A contractual arrangement has been created between the state sector and the private plot holder which increases the number of animals a private holder can keep. Livestock, poultry, and milk produced on private plots can be sold to state and collective farms, which can count these items as a part of their plan fulfillment. Collective and state farms are supposed to provide private plot holders greater access to pasture land and credits for the acquisition of agricultural equipment. They are also supposed to provide construction materials and fertilizers and to help in transportation.[21]

---

[19]The retail prices of meat and meat products, butter and other dairy products, and eggs have not been changed since 1962.

[20]David M. Schoonover, "Soviet Agricultural Policies," in *Soviet Economy in a Time of Change*, p. 113.

[21]*Ibid.*, pp. 114–15.

Greater initiatives for state farm managers have also been provided. Plan indicators have been reduced. A 50 percent bonus for output in excess of the average level achieved in the Tenth Five-Year Plan is directed at eliminating payments to farms which do not increase production.[22]

Operating Results of Soviet Agriculture

An increase in the population and a rise in per capita income have combined to generate a constantly increasing demand for an improved product mix. However, there have been perennial problems of inefficiency, low labor productivity, and high production costs on both collective and state farms. Despite the fact that agriculture has received priority in the current five-year plan and in the economic reforms, labor productivity lags far behind productivity in the industrial area, as indicated in Table 14-1. To some extent the material incentive system, which is really more oriented toward motivating industrial workers, has failed to elicit a similar response among agricultural workers. The end result of general inefficiency is that Soviet agriculture is one of the most expensive food producers in the world, a fact which redounds to the disadvantage of the consumer because real income is reduced in comparison with that of consumers in other countries.

Comparisons can be made between agriculture in the United States and the Soviet Union. Agriculture contributes about 16 percent of the Soviet gross national product and employs about one-fourth of the labor force. In the United States, agriculture contributes about 3 percent of the GNP and employs 4 percent of the labor force.[23] Net farm output is increasing at a more rapid rate in the Soviet Union than in the United States. However, given the facts that agriculture has a greater impact on the Soviet economy and that the typical Soviet state or collective farm is many times larger than the typical American farm in terms of size and number of workers, performance clearly favors the American farm. For example, farm efficiency, measured in terms of output per unit of input, is substantially higher in the United States than in the Soviet Union. The United States has made more capital inputs and has achieved greater yields. The Soviet Union also lags far behind the United States in use of mineral fertilizers.[24]

---

[22]*Ibid.*

[23]In 1980 the typical U.S. farm averaged 395 acres and employed 1.5 workers; the typical USSR state farm averaged 43,960 acres and employed 588 workers, and the typical collective farm averaged 16,302 acres and employed 539 workers.

[24]Douglas B. Diamond and W. Lee Davis, "Comparative Growth in Output and Productivity in U.S. and USSR Agriculture," in *Soviet Economy in a Time of Change*, pp. 45–54.

TABLE 14-1
SOVIET AGRICULTURAL PRODUCTION, 1961–1980

Year	Percentage Increase or Decrease
1961–1965	3.6
1966–1970	3.9
1971–1975	−0.4
1976–1980	−1.0
1975	−8.8
1976	8.1
1977	4.6
1978	3.3
1979	−5.8
1980	−4.4

Source: Central Intelligence Agency, *Handbook of Economic Statistics* (Washington, 1981), Table 40.

Agricultural reforms introduced by Brezhnev in March 1965 involved an enormous increase in outlays for machinery, construction, fertilizers, and land reclamation. By 1977 the annual Soviet investment in agriculture ran to $78 billion, an amount more than seven times U.S. agricultural investment. Even so, the Russians have developed an agricultural system capable of meeting only the most elementary needs of an industrial society. Grain imports have supplemented the domestic harvest in every year since 1971. Although adverse weather conditions have had some impact on Soviet agricultural production during the 1970s, productivity has not been good. There were numerous shortages during 1980 of meat, milk, sausage, cheese, cooking oil, and specialty items. The Russians have not yet devised a way to assure even the present inadequate levels of agricultural production without infusions of long-range massive investments.[25]

INCOME DISTRIBUTION

In a communist country, income is primarily limited to wages and salaries because, under communist doctrine (which has been subject to question only recently), labor is the only factor of production endowed with the capability of creating value. Therefore, labor should be remunerated to the exclusion of land and capital. The total amount of wages to be

[25]Elizabeth Clayton, "Productivity in Soviet Agriculture," *Slavic Review* (September 1980), pp. 446–58.

paid, and the production counterpart to support wages, depends on the division of socialist national income between accumulation and consumption, and further, of consumption between the social consumption fund and the wage fund.

National Income

National income in a communist economy begins with the concept of the *net material product,* which can be defined either as the net contribution of the productive sectors of the economy (that is, gross production less the value of intermediate products and depreciation charges) or as the total income realized by the productive sectors. To put it more simply, the concept of communist national income is that of national income produced and national income distributed. National income produced covers those activities that create material goods or help in the productive process—for example, gathering raw materials and processing them into finished products. National income distributed refers to the process of primary distribution of the income of the labor force, enterprises, and society by financial flows. This income can be divided into two categories. The first category of income is distributed to individuals and consists of gross money income before taxation of workers employed in the production process, money income and income in kind of farmers, and the value of net production from private activity of a productive character. The second category of national income distributed consists of gross profits before taxation of production enterprises, the turnover tax, and contributions of enterprises to social insurance.

The distribution of national income may be shown as follows:

Primary Incomes of Individuals

1. Wages and salaries of the state sector of productive industries
2. Wages and salaries of producer cooperatives
3. Income of cooperative farmers from cooperative activities
4. Income of cooperative farmers from private plots of land
5. Incomes of individual farmers
6. Incomes, private or otherwise, from other activities of a productive nature

Primary Incomes of the Social Sector

1. Gross profits before taxes of productive enterprises
2. Turnover taxes
3. Contributions of enterprises to health insurance

Communist income accounting differentiates between productive and nonproductive sectors. As these primary incomes of individuals and firms are generated only in the productive sectors, this flow of distribution gives no account of incomes of individuals working in the nonproductive spheres of activity, of unearned incomes of individuals with claims to transfer payments from public funds, and of enterprises operating in the non-productive sectors. All of these incomes are included under the category of personal income, along with the primary incomes of individuals employed in the productive sectors.

Personal Income

The main difference between national income and personal income in a communist system of national income accounts lies in the fact that only incomes of individuals and firms generated in the productive sectors—industry, agriculture, and others—are counted in national income, while personal income takes into account income earned in the non-productive sectors as well. These sectors are education, health, justice, finance, and public administration. These sectors are considered non-productive not because they are not useful, but because they don't contribute directly to the creation of material production. Thus, personal income in a country such as the Soviet Union would consist of wages and salaries of all workers employed in both productive and nonproductive industries, incomes of self-employed persons and independent entrepreneurs, and income from other souces including, for example, the income from the sale of agricultural products grown on private plots of land. Personal income would also include transfer payments of various types—family allowances, old-age pensions, and other types of income transfers.

Personal income can be regarded as income generated in the process of redistributing the communist national income. This process is effected by transfers between the state and society, between different sectors of society, and between different units of a public character. These transfers are realized mainly through the state budget, which is the most important instrument in modifying income flows in a communist economy, and through a system of credits. Many transfers are payments by the state for which no service is provided in return, but which redistribute income to various groups. Examples are old-age pensions and family allowances. Personal outlays include personal consumption of goods and services, taxes, and other payments. The end result is an economic balance that relates total money income of the population to their total outlays. An example of this balance is shown in Table 14-2.

Table 14-3 presents a division of the major components of personal income in the Soviet Union for 1977. Also included in the table are direct taxes levied on the population. In the Soviet Union both taxes and transfer payments have a redistributive effect on income distribution. It is important to point out the fact that the price structure in the Soviet Union, particularly for food and basic services, is maintained at a low

TABLE 14-2
PERSONAL INCOME AND OUTLAYS IN A COMMUNIST ECONOMY

Income	Outlays
Wage fund (wages and salaries)	Consumption goods
Income of cooperatives and individual farmers	Services
Other income from enterprises (supplements)	Consumption of goods in kind
Imputed rent	Consumption of services in kind
Other labor and rental income	Total private consumption
Total income from work and property	Personal contributions
Government transfer payments	Personal tax payments to institutions
Total income	Total outlays

level to favor low-income consumers. The use of subsidies to maintain low prices for certain foodstuffs, transportation, and services is common. The prices charged by the state to consumers bear little relationship to the different production costs or the procurement prices paid to farms. Many consumer goods are priced below costs; on the other hand, prices for such luxury items as coffee and fruit are maintained at high levels. Price subsidies are a factor to consider when income distribution is examined.

TABLE 14-3
PERSONAL INCOME IN THE SOVIET UNION, 1977

Component	Billions of Dollars*
Total personal income	$379.21
Wage and salary payments	$271.46
Collective farm wage payments	23.93
Household income from the sale of farm products	15.06
Profits distributed to cooperative members	.52
Military pay and allowances	5.30
Transfer payments	58.42
Less: Direct taxes (personal income and agricultural taxes)	41.35
Total disposable income	$337.86

*In 1977, 1 ruble = $1.37 [$1 = 0.73 ruble].

Source: M. Elizabeth Denton, "Soviet Consumer Policy: Trends and Prospects," *Soviet Economy in a Time of Change*, pp. 775, 785.

As mentioned before, wages constitute the great bulk of personal income distributed in a communist economic system. Although labor itself enjoys some freedom from central planning, there is a high degree of centralization and control over the determination of wages. The total amount of wages to be paid is set in the wage fund, which provides gross payments for all work done, including basic wage rates, payments based on piece-rate norms, basic salaries, premia and bonuses of all kinds, payments for overtime, and payments for night work and work on Sundays and holidays. The wage fund is linked to private consumption. Consumption, both collective and private, has to be planned in advance because it constitutes an integral part of the national economic plan, which cannot be constructed and balanced unless the size and structure of consumption are laid down. The planning of consumption necessitates the planning of the wage fund.

Wage Determination. Wages are determined by government fiat. In the Soviet Union, there are several state agencies that play a role in wage determination. Within the organizational framework of the Council of Ministers of the USSR, there is the State Committee on Labor and Wages. This committee is responsible for examining prevailing wage structures and practices within the Soviet Union. Within the committee there is the Institute of Labor, which does research on wage questions and policies. The committee takes this information and makes recommendations concerning changes in wages for various occupational groups. Gosplan and the Ministry of Finance also participate in the calculation of wages which are a part of the national economic plan. The total amount of wages for a given industry or enterprise would depend upon changes in the size and composition of the labor force, expected changes in the availability of consumer goods, and output and labor productivity plans. Once the total amount of wages has been determined for a particular industry, it is subdivided among each enterprise on the basis of the criteria mentioned above. Each enterprise, then, has its own wage fund from which it pays the wages of its workers.

Soviet economic reforms have provided a set of incentives to increase worker performance. Worker incomes come from two main sources—the regular wage fund from which wages are paid to all workers and the material incentives fund from which bonuses are paid. Money for the material incentives fund comes out of profits in accordance with standards prescribed by the state. Jurisdiction over bonuses was tightened by the state in 1972 and 1973. The amount of the bonus is set by Gosplan and implemented by ministries responsible for individual enterprises. The planned size of the material incentive fund is fixed for each year. Actual incentive funds may deviate from the planned funds, with the funds increased or decreased based on enterprise performance, which includes, among other things, the quality of the product produced and the production of new products.[26] The incentive funds are also tied to the government's efforts to produce more consumer goods.

Wage Differentials. Wage and salary differentials exist in the Soviet Union to a considerable degree. These differentials are based on several factors.

Within the factories, there are wage differentials which are based upon skills. In most industrial plants, there are six skill grades which are differentiated according to variations in skill from unskilled to highly skilled categories. The requirements for each grade are determined by the State Committee on Wages and the All-Union Central Council of Trade Unions. Differentials between the lowest and highest grade can vary according to the industry. These ratios, however, involve only the basic standard wage rate for each grade and do not take into consideration the fact that the use of piece rates and bonuses can cause considerable differentials in earnings among workers within the same grade.

Wage differentials are also based on conditions of work with hard or hazardous work commanding a higher premium than less arduous work. Within a given skill grade, there may be different gradings based on work conditions. Rates for work under hazardous conditions would carry a premium of as much as 30 percent above the basic wage rate.

The form of wage payment used also is responsible for wage differentials. Piece-rate workers are generally better paid than time-rate workers because under piece rates there is a direct correlation between output and payments.

Regional differentials also exist in terms of wage and salary payments. To attract workers to less desirable areas of the country where labor shortages are endemic, additional payments ranging from 10 to 100 percent of the base wage are added to all grades.[27]

Salary differentials also exist for engineers, economists, and white-collar employees. These differentials are based on the skill requirements of the job, the complexity of work, and the economic importance of the industry. There are various salary categories, which are similar to the wage grades used for the plant workers.

Wage Systems. There are several systems of wage and salary compensation used in the Soviet Union. These systems usually combine time rates or piece rates with bonus payments and cover most industrial wage earners. The rationale of the bonus is to tie personal interests of workers more closely to the interests of production. Bonuses may be awarded on the basis of individual or collective performance. Individual bonuses are based on the performance of each worker as measured against other workers, while

---

[26]In the past, bonus funds encouraged enterprise managers to stress the volume of total output and quality was a neglected factor.

[27]Gertrude E. Schroeder, "Soviet Wage and Income Policies in Regional Perspective," *Association for Comparative Economics Bulletin*, Vol. XVI, No. 2 (Fall 1974), pp. 3–20.

collective bonuses reward a group of workers as a whole and are divided uniformly among the workers. Bonuses, however, are not always tied to the output performance of the enterprise, but may be awarded for other reasons. For example, workers can get bonuses for reducing waste or for coming up with suggestions that contribute to the efficient operations of an enterprise. In 1981 new pay scales were put into effect in a number of industries in order to increase productivity. The pay scales permit wages for outstanding workers to be 50 percent above the average. Those workers who invent new techniques to improve productivity will be given patent royalties that could make some of them millionaires.

The economic reforms have intensified the incentive role of bonuses as a lever for achieving an increase in worker productivity and the rate of economic growth. As it now stands, Soviet workers receive fixed payments according to their grades from the wage fund of an enterprise plus a bonus which can come from the wage fund and from the material incentives fund. Workers could fall under one of three compensation categories:

1. *Time rate plus a bonus.* In this type of compensation system, wages are based on hourly rates which are set for each skill grade. In addition, bonuses are paid on either an individual or collective basis. These bonuses are often related to quantified standards such as output quotas, cost reduction, and material usage. In such cases, workers receive bonuses for the fulfillment and overfulfillment of individual or collective targets.

2. *Piece rate plus a bonus.* The piece rate can be progressive, which means that earnings rise more than in proportion to output above the standard task. However, progressive piece rates have declined in importance and have been replaced primarily by straight piece rates, in which earnings vary in direct proportion to output. Bonuses are paid when an enterprise exceeds planned production targets.

3. *Straight time and piece rates.* Straight time rates, usually monthly, would be paid to professional workers, such as doctors, teachers, and employees of various government agencies. Salaried workers for enterprises, such as engineers, managers, and technicians, are also paid time rates, but receive a bonus as well, provided that the enterprise achieves its targets. Under the reforms, bonuses to salaried workers come from the material incentives fund, the amount of which depends upon the profits an enterprise earns.

Transfer Payments and Special Benefits. Money wages are only one source of a Russian worker's income. When various government expenditures for free subsidized consumer services, such as medical benefits and transfer payments, are taken into consideration, total money and real income can be increased considerably for the average Russian worker. Transfer payments account for around 15 percent of total personal income in the Soviet Union and have increased at a more rapid rate than wages and salaries. In 1977 transfer payments amounted to about $60 billion, compared to personal income of about $380 billion.[28] Consumer welfare has been stressed in recent years. Pensions and welfare grants have been liberalized and collective farms have been brought under social insurance coverage. In addition to transfer payments, Russians gain from subsidies on housing and basic foodstuffs. Russian workers also receive benefits from the sociocultural funds of state enterprises.

The welfare of the consumer is receiving increasing attention in the Soviet Union. Among other things, priority is given in the economic plan to improvements in the quality and selection of consumer goods. Real disposable income of consumers has risen on the average 6.2 percent since 1965, as living standards have shown a marked improvement in recent years. Basic foodstuffs and services are maintained at a low price level to favor low-income consumers. Many consumer goods are priced below costs; on the other hand, prices for luxury goods and various consumer durables including automobiles, are maintained at very high levels. Moreover, disposable income has increased at a rate faster than the state's capacity to produce consumer goods and services, thus necessitating long delays in purchasing on the part of consumers.

Income Inequality

It is rather obvious that a truly egalitarian society does not exist in the Soviet Union, and it is a myth that the worker is first among equals. It is true, however, that income differentials in the Soviet Union have been reduced as the Soviets have raised the incomes of millions of low-income workers. Nevertheless, this point may be misleading, for there are certain privileges expressed in nonmonetary terms that redound to the advantage of the party elite, professional workers such as managers, sport heroes, and members of the intelligentsia. The difference between the income of the average worker and that of the privileged strata is striking and is enlarged by special contributions from the state, including such benefits as private villas, personal limousines, and travel privileges.[29]

AN APPRAISAL OF THE SOVIET ECONOMY

The economic performance of the Soviet economy was generally good during the period 1950–1975. During this period the Soviet leadership

---

[28]M. Elizabeth Denton, "Soviet Consumer Policy Trends and Prospects," in *Soviet Economy in a Time of Change*, p. 785.

[29]Hedrick Smith, *The Russians* (New York: New York Times Book Co., 1976), pp. 25–53.

was able to pursue successfully a policy of guns and butter as well as economic growth. The Soviet Union developed into one of the two major superpowers of the world and proved itself capable of creating a military–industrial complex which rivals that of the United States. In the field of space technology, the Soviet Union has made very important contributions, indicating the ability of the leadership to mobilize resources to accomplish certain objectives. The Soviet Union increased its influence in the international arena and at the same time witnessed the economic and political decline of its chief adversary, the United States. The Soviet leadership dealt successfully with unprecedented dissent movements among the intelligentsia and assured a relatively high degree of political and social stability in the country. It was a period in which the leadership was able to avoid significant crisis within its social and political system.

However, the economy of the Soviet Union has developed its problems. To some extent these problems have to be viewed within a global context. During the latter part of the 1970s and the early 1980s, all major industrial countries, capitalist and communist, experienced a decline in their growth rates. Inflation developed into a worldwide phenomenon, affecting both capitalist and communist countries. Domestic and international conditions and circumstances have changed rapidly as far as the Soviet Union is concerned. Economic performance in the 1980s may create an economic and political crisis in the Soviet Union.

Economic Growth

Table 14-4 presents the growth rate of the Soviet economy for the period 1960–1980. The growth experience of the Soviet Union during the 1960s was generally good, averaging around 5 percent a year. During the 1970s the growth rate exhibited a decline. There are specific reasons for the decline in the Soviet growth rate. Military expenditures absorb resources that could be made available for growth-promoting capital formation. There are resource constraints, both human and material, that inhibit the growth rate. The economic system, with its bureaucratic centralization, has become increasingly cumbersome in running a vast country. Moreover, in the 1980s the Soviet Union will face a growth rate that is projected to increase at an annual average rate of 2.5 percent.[30] There will be an increased sectoral competition for resources. While accustomed to scarcities and shortages, the Soviet system is not accustomed to dealing with prolonged periods of low economic growth.

---

[30]Seweryn Bialer, "The Harsh Decade: Soviet Policies in the 1980's," *Foreign Affairs,* Summer 1981, p. 1005.

TABLE 14-4
AGGREGATE FACTOR PRODUCTIVITY IN THE SOVIET UNION, 1961–1980
(percentage increase or decrease)

| | Gross National Product | Factor Productivity | | |
		Labor	Capital	Land
1961–65	5.0	3.4	−3.4	4.4
1966–70	5.2	3.2	−2.1	5.6
1971–75	3.7	2.0	−3.9	2.9
1975	1.7	0.5	−5.5	1.2
1976	4.8	3.6	−2.3	4.8
1977	3.2	1.7	−3.5	3.4
1978	3.4	1.7	−3.3	3.4
1979	0.8	0.7	−5.6	0.8
1980	1.4	0.2	−4.8	1.4

Source: Central Intelligence Agency, *Handbook of Economic Statistics* (Washington, 1981), Table 45.

Consumption

As Table 14-5 indicates, consumption is given a lower priority in the Soviet Union than it enjoys in capitalist countries. In the United States, for example, consumption expenditures constitute around 70 percent of gross national product; the percentage for the Soviet Union is much lower. This can be attributed to the fact that in the Soviet Union investment priorities have favored heavy industry and defense. These priorities, coupled with a rigid and cumbersome system of distribution, have created a consumer sector which lags far behind not only the Western countries but most of the Eastern European satellite countries as well. Low-quality goods and services, queues, and shortages have become a way of life to Soviet consumers. Although there has been an upward trend in the well-being of the Russian consumer, expectations of more have been built into the Soviet system. In view of other claims on resource allocation, it may be difficult for the Soviet leaders to continue a policy of consumption growth during the 1980s, particularly with a decline in the growth rate.[31]

There is a considerable gap between consumption levels in the United States and the Soviet Union. The biggest gap is in the consumption of durable goods and consumer services. Per capita consumption of con-

---

[31]The Eleventh Five-Year Plan, 1981–1985, calls for a lower rate of increase in consumption than did the previous five-year plan.

TABLE 14-5
PERCENTAGE OF SOVIET
GROSS NATIONAL PRODUCT ALLOCATED TO
CONSUMPTION, INVESTMENT, AND DEFENSE

	1960	1970	1980
Gross national product	100	100	100
Consumption	58	54	53
Fixed investment	20	23	26
Other investment	4	5	7
Defense	18	18	14

Source: Central Intelligence Agency, *Handbook of Economic Statistics*, 1981, Table 37.

sumer services in the Soviet Union was one-fifth of that for the United States in 1976.[32] The gap is even greater in the consumption of such durable goods as automobiles. For the consumption of food the gap narrows considerably, with the Soviet Union equaling or exceeding the United States in the consumption of starchy goods—potatoes, bread, cereals, and sugar and confectionaries.[33] In contrast, Soviet consumption of fats and oils, meat, fruits, and vegetables is far below the U.S. level. In comparison to the United States, the Soviet Union fares least well in the provision of housing. Urban housing is in short supply, crowded, of poor quality, and badly maintained. An estimated 30 percent of the urban population still live either communally or in crowded factory dormitories.[34] Although housing has been given high priority in the state allocation of resources, the rate of construction still lags behind the demand for dwellings.[35] Consumption differences between the United States and the Soviet Union in education and medical care are not as pronounced.

SUMMARY

The cornerstone of the Soviet economy is the industrial enterprise. It operates on the basis of an annual production plan which is integrated into the national economic plan. Its performance is based on a series of success indicators. Enterprises operate

---

[32]Joint Economic Committee, *Consumption in the USSR: An International Comparison*, 97th Congress, 1st Session, 1981, pp. 5–6.

[33]*Ibid.*, p. 7.

[34]Henry W. Morton, "The Soviet Quest for Housing—An Impossible Dream?" in *Soviet Economy in a Time of Change*, pp. 790–808.

[35]Most newlyweds are compelled to live with their parents for many years before receiving an apartment of their own.

under a profit-and-loss accounting system, and their success is supposed to be judged primarily by the volume of their sales and profits. Each enterprise is run by a director or manager whose responsibilities are similar to those of managers of American enterprises. However, the government prescribes the policies all enterprises are to follow in the national economic plan, and managers are confined by the targets and resource limits prescribed in it. There is a government and party hierarchy which plans and administers Soviet industry and, for that matter, the entire economy.

Agriculture has long been a problem in the Soviet Union. It has suffered because of underinvestment, excessive central direction, and lack of incentives. In terms of production and performance, it lags well behind agriculture in the United States. The United States uses more capital to achieve a greater output. Most equipment used on Soviet state and collective farms is not used at an optimum level because there is a chronic shortage of technical personnel. There has been a large-scale migration of younger workers, especially those who are trained, from the rural to urban areas. To arrest this urban migration and to promote greater efficiency in agriculture, economic reforms were introduced which have as their objectives the raising of rural incomes and living standards and the increasing of capital investment. Guaranteed minimum monthly payments to collective farmers have been introduced, and state farm workers have been put on the same wage system used for industrial workers. Although managers of state and collective farms have been given more autonomy, pricing of farm products remains in the government's domain.

Under the Soviet system, wages are regarded as remuneration for work in proportion to its quantity and quality. Incentives, both material and nonmaterial, are used to motivate workers to produce with optimal efficiency. Reliance is placed on a bonus system which is tied to the level of enterprise profits, and wage payments to the majority of Soviet industrial workers can take the form of either piece or time rates plus a bonus. In addition to their regular monetary income, Soviet workers receive other benefits, such as free medical care and family allowances, which can raise total income by a considerable amount.

REVIEW QUESTIONS

1. Distinguish between Gosplan and Gossnab.
2. Discuss the supply system of the Soviet Union.
3. Distinguish between state farms and collective farms.
4. How are state farms financed?
5. What are the functions of labor unions in the Soviet Union?
6. Income distribution in the Soviet Union is, theoretically, based on the Marxist concept of "from each according to his ability to each according to his need." Do you agree? Explain.
7. What is the role of the manager in the Soviet enterprise?
8. Why have the Soviet economic reforms failed to accomplish their objectives?
9. As you see it, what are the strong and weak points in the Soviet economic and political system?
10. Discuss the problems of the Soviet Union in the 1980s.

RECOMMENDED READINGS

Abouchar, Alan. *Economic Evaluation of Soviet Socialism.* New York: Pergamon Press, 1979.

Clayton, Elizabeth. "Productivity in Soviet Agriculture." *Slavic Review* (September 1980), pp. 446–58..

Malish, Anton, and Yuri Markish. "New Directions in Soviet Agricultural Policy." In *Agricultural Situation USSR: Review of 1980 and Outlook for 1981.* Washington: U.S. Department of Agriculture, 1981.

Miller, Robert F. "Whither the Soviet System?" *Foreign Affairs* (Fall 1981), pp. 1115–45.

Newsweek. "A System that Doesn't Work." April 12, 1982, pp. 36–44.

U.S. Joint Economic Committee. *Consumption in the USSR: An International Comparison.* 97th Congress, 1st Session, 1981.

———. *Allocation of Resources in the Soviet Union and China—1980,* Part 6. 96th Congress, 2nd Session, 1980.

Valkenier, Elizabeth K. *Soviet–Third World Relations: The Economic Bind.* Washington: National Council for Soviet and East European Economic Research, 1981.

Woodrow Wilson International Center for Scholars. "The Soviet Future." *Wilson Quarterly,* Vol. 5, No. 1 (Winter 1981), pp. 116–51.

15

The People's Republic of China

INTRODUCTION

China is the largest country in the world from the standpoint of population and third in terms of land size. The population is estimated to be around one billion—a factor that presents both a blessing and a dilemma in terms of world geopolitics. The land area, however, presents a serious problem in that less than 15 percent of it is arable, with the result that millions of Chinese depend upon small allotments of land for their subsistence.

From the year 1949, which marked the downfall of the Nationlist Chinese government, to the present, the Communists have worked to transform China into a communist economic system. Industrialization has been the primary economic goal. Economic policy has been directed toward the expansion of productive capacity in basic industrial commodities such as steel, coal, and petroleum. Agriculture has been put under state control and assigned the task of supplying raw materials to industry as well as feeding the population. During the earlier part of the development of the economic system, the Chinese looked to the Russians to provide the expertise and guidance necessary to transform China into a planned economy along Soviet lines. This approach, however, was discarded in 1958 in favor of the use of idealistic extremism to develop the economy. By the early 1970s, more moderate thinking and planning again prevailed.

DEVELOPMENT OF THE ECONOMIC SYSTEM

At the end of World War II, China was split into two factions, both of which had resisted Japanese incursions since the beginning of the Sino–Japanese War, which started in 1937. These factions were the Nationalists and Communists. Japan's defeat set up a struggle for control of occupied China extending from Manchuria in the north to Canton in the south. Although mediation was attempted by the United States, and a tripartite committee consisting of Nationalists, Communists, and the United States was set up to work out conditions for a coalition government, these efforts proved short-lived and a civil war broke out which lasted from 1946 to 1949. The initial advantage possessed by the Nationalists in terms of territory and logistics was lost, and the Nationalist government was driven from the Chinese mainland to Taiwan by the Communists, who, by 1949, had become masters of the country.

The development of the Chinese economic system has gone through several stages during the period from 1949 to the present. The first stage, which lasted from the latter part of 1949 to 1952, was a period of consolidation during which the Communists laid the foundation for a national government. The second stage was the period of the First Five-Year Plan, which lasted from 1953 to 1957. This stage, which borrowed heavily from Soviet economic planning, marked the beginning of forced-draft industrialization along Soviet lines. The third stage was the Great Leap Forward, which lasted from 1958 to 1960. The rationale of the Great Leap Forward was the use of indigenous Chinese resources, particularly labor of which China had plenty, to drive the economy ahead at a faster pace. Russian-style planning was abandoned in favor of this new approach toward industrial development. The fourth stage involved a return to economic planning after the collapse of the Great Leap Forward. This stage, which lasted from 1961 to 1965, involved the adoption of more rational economic policies toward industry and agriculture. The fifth stage, lasting from 1966 to 1969, was the Proletarian Cultural Revolution. In essence, the Revolution represented a regression to the political idea that only Mao Tse-tung had the answer for everything. The period from 1970 to 1976 marked a resumption of economic growth except for some political interruptions, and the period after Mao's death in 1976 to the present has been an attempt to restore orderly growth.

The Period of Consolidation, 1949–1952

When the Communists formally announced the creation of the Chinese People's Republic on October 1, 1949, they were able to begin the consolidation of power and the development of a new type of economic system. Certainly the task was not easy. Years of fighting and inflation had debilitated the economy. Widespread corruption had been rampant under the Nationalist government. The masses of the people were agrarian and illiterate and had to be trained and educated to fit into an industrial base which was to be the fountainhead for the development of the communist economic system.

Upon gaining control of the country, the communist regime stamped its imprimatur upon society through a series of nationwide reforms which attempted to refashion nearly every aspect of Chinese life. Of paramount importance was the redistribution of land to the peasants and the elimination of landlords as an economic class. This marked the first step toward *collectivization*. Then followed a series of organizational reforms beginning with the simplest form of social enterprise, the *mutual aid team*, and progressing through successive stages of so-called producer cooperatives to complete collectivization of the farms in 1957, during which time the peasant lost title to the land.

The First Five-Year Plan, 1953–1957

The First Five-Year Plan marked the second stage in the economic development of the People's Republic of China. To implement the plan, the Chinese relied heavily on Russian expertise because planning had been used to develop the Russian economy and the Chinese wanted a model to follow. Soviet technicians were imported to develop the plan and to run the factories. Agreements were reached providing for Russian aid in building or expanding electric power plants and in the supply of agricultural, mining, and chemical equipment. Russian financial aid took the form of low-interest loans. The Russians also contracted for the construction of factories producing a wide variety of products including chemicals, synthetic fibers and plastics, liquid fuel, and machine tools. The Soviets also built modern iron and steel complexes, nonferrous metallurgical plants, refineries, and power stations, and they trained Chinese technicians to operate them. Sets of blueprints and related materials giving directions for plant layouts were also provided for the Chinese.

The Great Leap Forward, 1958–1960

In 1958 the Chinese decided to depart from the pattern of economic development set by the First Five-Year Plan and to use a new approach which relied on the idealistic fervor of the masses of workers and peasants to drive the economy ahead at a much faster rate. This approach was called the *Great Leap Forward*. It represented an example of idealistic extremism which substituted zeal for the material incentives developed under the First Five-Year Plan. China's enormous population was to be regarded as an economic asset and not a liability—the more people, the more hands to build communism. Emphasis was placed on indigenous methods of production and the development of labor-intensive invest- ment projects. National output in industry and agriculture was to be doubled and redoubled in a few short years, and hated imperialist powers, such as Great Britain, were to be surpassed in production. To put the basic objective of the Great Leap Forward simply, the population was to be harnessed to increase production and make China a great power.

Agriculture. In agriculture, economic policy involved the formation of communes. The communes marked the final stage in the transition of agriculture from private enterprise, which had existed during the first years of communist rule. Under communal organization, all vestiges of private property were eliminated. The peasants were not only deprived of the private plots, livestock, and implements which had been left to them by the previous collectivization, they also had to surrender their homes, and it was part of the idea of the commune that they should be rehoused in some kind of communal building. The purpose was to turn the peas- ants into mobile workers ready for any task in any area to which they might be assigned.

Industry. In industry, economic policy placed emphasis on the utiliza- tion of labor to create thousands of tiny industrial units throughout the country. This has been called facetiously "the steel mill in every back- yard" policy. Again, the Communists planned to capitalize on the pres- ence of a large labor surplus to accomplish rapid industrialization, partic- ularly in the rural areas. During that part of the year when the rural population was underemployed, labor could be used for useful output. Small indigenous industrial plants were created to harness the energies of the labor force. These plants included handicraft workshops, iron and steel foundries, fertilizer plants, oil extraction, machine shops, cement manufacture, coal and iron ore mining, and food processing. The capital used to build the small plants came from the local communes and from taxes on state enterprises. Labor, however, was the key factor employed in the development of local industry.

Top priority was given by the Communists to the iron and steel industry. This was to be the key to industrial success that would enable China to overtake Great Britain in industrial production in 15 years. Lack of technology and equipment was to be replaced by mass fervor. Some 80 million persons were involved in an attempt to create a do-it-yourself steel industry. Two million backyard furnaces developed throughout China. Many millions of Chinese worked day and night turning out steel, while millions of others labored with the extraction of iron ore and coal. The result was the development of a labor-intensive, small-scale steel producing unit with a low capital-output ratio. Although the output of iron and steel was increased by the backyard furnace method, much of it was of poor quality, reflecting the absence of quality-control standards and the necessary technical expertise. Production in other areas suffered as well because more than one-tenth of the population was diverted from other pursuits, such as farm production, into the production of steel.

Failure of the Great Leap Forward. The Great Leap Forward was not a success. Although industrial and agricultural output rose sharply in 1958, much of the gain was spurious. As mentioned above, the quality of the steel produced by the backyard furnaces left much to be desired. The products of many small plants were of such poor quality that most of them had to be scrapped. Production costs were high for many plants, reflecting an indiscriminate development of small plants in almost all industries. There was also a disregard for cost considerations at the local plant level because the most important success indicator was the degree to which the local cadre or leaders could fulfill or overfulfill quotas. This output was maximized at the expense of quality and cost, even though in many cases the quantity produced exceeded the quantity needed, and inputs of labor and raw materials could have been more effectively employed elsewhere. Also, a shortage of fuels and raw materials caused by the wastage involved in the backyard furnace method of production and by lack of adequate transportation facilities was responsible for the demise of many plants.

Sino–Russian Relations. The Great Leap Forward also caused a rift in the relationship between the Chinese and the Russian advisers and technicians that had been sent to help them. In essence, the Russian blueprints for making China a self-sufficient world power had been ignored in favor of a development program that made little economic sense. The Russians believed that the communes would not work and that they had developed a program for agriculture that would work. The Chinese persisted in ignoring the advice of their Russian technicians despite the fact that Russia intimated that support would be withdrawn unless the Great Leap Forward was discontinued. In 1960 the Soviet technicians were withdrawn from China, and with them went the equipment, financial aid, and blueprints that had played the paramount role in the development of the Chinese economy during the First Five-Year Plan. This en masse departure of the technicians had a deleterious effect on the Chinese because they could not supply the expertise to replace them.

Economic and Social Readjustment Phase, 1961–1965

The period 1961–1965 marked a return to more orthodox economic and social policies. Economic planning, which was largely superseded by the Great Leap Forward, was resumed, and agricultural policy was modified to include smaller production units. For all practical purposes the commune was abandoned. Various forms of material incentives were restored, and farmers were again able to have private plots of land for their own use. Agriculture was given increased priority in terms of investment, while overall industrial investment suffered a retrenchment in favor of certain high-priority industries, in particular those that contributed to the development of agriculture. Foreign trade, which had been previously tied to the Soviet Union, involved an exchange of basic raw materials for Western and Japanese machinery, technology, and grain in order to supplement domestic production.

Proletarian Cultural Revolution, 1966–1969

The Third Five-Year Plan was eclipsed by a political aberration of the first magnitude called the *Proletarian Cultural Revolution*. It was an attempt by Mao Tse-tung to mold Chinese society into his prescribed pattern. It placed primacy on ideological cant over scientific expertise and reverted back to the Great Leap Forward period in its attempt to replace material incentives with political ideology and also to denigrate any emphasis on technical excellence.[1] It aimed at annihilating, throughout China and particularly in the universities, any tendency toward a moderate or revisionist viewpoint concerning the role of communism in world affairs. Intransigence toward the Western countries in general and the United States in particular was to be maintained until Western influence was eliminated from Asia. The Russians also did not escape the general opprobrium that the Chinese engendered toward the West, because Mao was furious with them for drawing back from war and subversion in the interest of coexistence; and, with respect to the building of socialism, Mao deplored the use in Soviet economic practice of material incentives for the workers. He contemptuously referred to this practice as an example of *goulash communism*.

The rationale of the Proletarian Revolution was political as well as economic. It involved in part an attempt by Mao to develop a new socialist morality that would place the public interest above private individualism. He believed that Stalin had permitted the development of a new class structure in the form of a state bureaucracy which differed little from a capitalist class structure. What this had done is to separate Soviet claims of egalitarianism from the facts of special privileges for a small bureaucratic and technical elite. Moreover, Mao believed that Russia and other communist countries had moved further away from the utopian ideal of a perfectly egalitarian society by introducing material incentives

---

[1]A poster in a Peking park proclaimed, "We do not need brains! Our heads are armed with the ideas of Mao Tse-tung."

and bonuses, which in themselves tend to differentiate among workers. An ethical revolution was needed, for people had to be changed in order to create a new order of society.

The Proletarian Cultural Revolution represented a step backward in terms of economic growth. In the wake of its destabilizing conflicts, the regime faced the task of rebuilding a stable institutional structure and working out a new pattern of relationships between various groups. During the Cultural Revolution there was less physical damage to capital equipment than there was disruption of production and transportation which reduced current output, but averted long-term damage to the economy. The average annual rate of growth of gross national product during the period 1966–1968 was −2.5 percent, reflecting a general decline in industrial output of around 15 to 20 percent in 1967. More important, the Cultural Revolution encouraged an ideological polarization within the regime and weakened consensus on the nation's fundamental values and priorities.

The Post–Cultural Revolution Period, 1970–1976

The end of the Cultural Revolution ushered in another stage of Chinese economic development. For one thing, systematic economic planning in the form of the Fourth Five-Year Plan was reintroduced. Both the Second and Third Five-Year Plans were largely shunted aside by sudden shifts in Chinese political and economic policies—the former by the Great Leap Forward and the latter by the Proletarian Cultural Revolution. The Third Five-Year Plan (1966–1970) was designed to make China safe from external aggression and internal subversion. It proposed to secure minimum food needs by placing controls over farm development and population growth. Another objective was to secure a modern industrial base by stressing the development of technological growth industries.

The Fourth Five-Year Plan (1971–1975) had several objectives. In the area of industrial development, priority was to be given to the production of sophisticated electronic instruments, including computers. Continued effort was to be given to increase the output of heavy industry, particularly iron and steel, hydrocarbons, and chemical fertilizers. Agriculture, however, still remained the basis of the economy, and agricultural policy under the plan aimed at making rural areas more self-sustaining. Investment was to be increased in various water conservation programs, including the construction of dams, dikes, storage reservoirs, and irrigation canals.

However, there were more political interruptions during this period. There was a jockeying for power as it became evident that both Chairman Mao and Premier Chou En-lai were in failing health. Radical elements in the Communist Party wanted to continue the Cultural Revolution: They denounced material incentives, orderly economic planning, reliance on foreign technology, and they brought disorder into production by opposing rules and regulations. Toward the end of 1975 and the beginning of 1976, the radicals increased their attacks on government bureaucrats and party leaders who were in favor of economic modernization. Serious riots occurred in some of the larger Chinese cities.

Post-Mao Developments

The year 1976 was a momentous one as far as China was concerned. Premier Chou died in February and Chairman Mao died in September. With the death of the two major leaders, a struggle for succession developed. (After more than two years, Teng Hsiao-ping was finally chosen party leader.) Mao's death was also followed by the arrest of his wife and three other supporters of the Cultural Revolution.[2]

An economic development program begun by Chou in 1975 was enacted as China's prevailing policy and became known as the "Four Modernizations Program." The objective of this program was to turn China into a modern nation by the end of this century through emphasis on the four major economic sectors: agriculture, industry, science and technology, and national defense. During the spring of 1978, the Four Modernizations Program was promoted into a new Ten-Year Plan covering 1976 to 1985. The goals of this plan call for rapid and substantial increases in grain output, steel production, and capital construction through the purchase of foreign plants and technology. In 1979 there was a reordering of China's modernization policies within a framework of what was called the "readjustment policy," the centerpiece of which was a shift in emphasis from heavy energy-consuming industry to agriculture and light energy-conserving industry.

THE ECONOMIC SYSTEM

The institutional arrangements of China are basically the same as those of the Soviet Union. There is, of course, the Communist Party hierarchy and its all pervasive influence at all levels of economic and political activity. The state prescribes the ultimate objectives to be followed by all Chinese. Society is controlled for the purpose of accomplishing specific economic and social goals. Unlike a capitalistic system where resource allocation is determined by price interaction in the marketplace, economic questions of what to produce, how much to produce, and for

---

[2]They were called the "Gang of Four" and were the alleged leaders of the radical group. In a showcase trial in 1978, they were found guilty and imprisoned.

whom to produce are resolved by the state through comprehensive economic planning. Market forces have been replaced by state action developed by bureaucrats which involves plans, exhortation, rules of social behavior, and reliance on both material and nonmaterial incentives.

Economic Planning

The Chinese have developed six formal five-year plans. The First Five-Year Plan (1953–1957) was patterned after the Russian plans and was developed with Russian assistance. State investment played a crucial role during the operation of the plan. From the standpoint of resource allocation, capital investment went into industry and transportation. The First Five-Year Plan set very high goals for industrial expansion. It called for the expansion of the gross value of output of producer goods by 128 percent over the 1952 level. It planned to produce 4 million tons of steel by 1957 and to raise cement production by 110 percent over the 1952 level. In agriculture, the plan set as a target an increase in the gross value of production of 23 percent in five years.[3]

The Second and Third Five-Year Plans also set goals for industry and agriculture to attain—goals that were superseded by the Great Leap Forward and the Proletarian Cultural Revolution. The Fourth Five-Year Plan (1971–1975) placed priority on the development of heavy industry. The Fifth Five-Year Plan (1976–1980) was absorbed into the Ten-Year Plan (1976–1985) which aimed to increase agricultural and industrial output through the acquisition of foreign technology. The Sixth Five-Year Plan (1981–1985) and a new Ten-Year Plan (1981–1990) have also been formulated. Both reflect policies of retrenchment and readjustment in the Chinese economy.[4] Investment is to be cut back and shifted more to agriculture and light industry. There is recognition that future economic growth will be more difficult and that energy shortages and insufficient consumer goods have created immediate problems that need to be resolved.

Chinese economic plans are similar in their functional character to the plans developed in other communist countries. There are the physical output plans, which involve production, distribution, and investment goals, and financial plans, which are derivatives of these plans. Then, too, plans differ in terms of time limits. There are long-range plans, which may extend to 30 years, and which usually deal with a particular aspect of the economy. Then there are the medium-term plans, which usually cover a period of five years and which develop targets or goals to be

---

[3]Arthur G. Ashbrook, Jr., "China: Shift of Economic Gears in Mid 1970's," in *Chinese Economy Post-Mao*, Vol. 1, Joint Economic Committee, 95th Congress, 2nd Session, 1978, pp. 205–8.

[4]Joint Economic Committee, *Allocation of Resources in the Soviet Union and China, 1981*, 96th Congress, 2nd Session, 1981, p. 106.

accomplished during this time. The normal frame of reference when one thinks of planning is the five-year plan. There are also annual or operating plans that involve production and distribution goals to be followed by Chinese enterprises and other organizational units during the year. Annual plans can be broken down into quarterly or monthly periods.

Formulation of Economic Plans

The national plan is a composite of a number of sectoral plans. There is a sectoral plan for industry which indicates what and how much individual enterprises should produce. This plan is subdivided into two parts—one for heavy industry and one for light industry. The plan also specifies the amount of producer goods and consumer goods that should be produced.

Plans are also developed for agriculture and transportation. In agriculture, specific goals are set for consumption within the agricultural sector and for distribution to other sectors. The plan also covers all facets of agricultural production including crop rotation techniques and anticipated harvests. In transportation, the plan covers the construction of facilities, with particular emphasis placed on the development of the railways system. It also covers the anticipated volume of passenger and industrial traffic to be carried by the various transportation systems.

Another plan covers capital formation for individual economic sectors and is concerned with resource allocation as an end use. The plan includes a listing of the objectives of each capital project.

Other plans include a labor plan which involves the allocation of labor inputs in the various sectors of the economy. This includes providing an adequate supply of labor to meet anticipated demands. There are also plans which involve the allocation of materials consistent with the output plans of the industrial, agricultural, and transportation sectors, and the flow of products for consumption by the workers in agriculture and industry. The latter plan is subdivided into parts which involve the production of final products for wholesale and retail trade. These parts are further subdivided on the basis of geographic areas and trading companies.

There is also a cost plan which specifies relationships between wages and productivity as well as setting cost standards for enterprises to follow in each sector of the economy. It also provides for cost reduction goals. A plan for technology covers the provision of the latest developments in science and technology, including those from abroad, to the various sectors of the economy.

Plans for foreign trade, social and cultural development, and regional development also exist. The foreign trade plan covers export and import commodity targets and foreign exchange. The social and cultural plan covers education, public health, and housing. It also includes the training of Communist Party cadre. Regional development plans involve the development of areas of specialization and enterprise within various regions.

Finally, a set of financial plans controls government income and expenditures with the objective of regulating resource allocation between consumption and investment and regulating the flow of credit from the banking system. There is also control over the financial plans of government ministries, enterprises, and communes.

Public Finance

Taxes in China reflect the relationship of the state to state-owned enterprises. The function of taxes is to ensure control through the state budget over a part of the incomes of state enterprises as well as over the financial and economic activities. The state budget itself is very important to the national economy, for virtually all economic sectors are owned by the state, and a very large part of all investment is undertaken with funds that are allocated by the budget. In addition, such normal government expenditures as national defense and social services are financed through it.

Government Revenues. Total budgetary revenue is obtained from both tax and nontax sources. In the tax revenue category, industrial and commercial and agricultural taxes comprise the bulk of tax receipts. Taxes are collected at various levels of government by a system of collection agencies and are paid into the People's Bank of China. In the nontax revenue category, profits from state enterprises, which are considered to be state property anyway, comprise the most important revenue source. Depreciation reserves and other income from state enterprises also constitute an important source of nontax revenue. Nontax revenue has increased in importance as a source of income for the national budget.

The Turnover Tax. This form of revenue, which is common to all communist countries, represents the difference between the producers' and the retail price, excluding the wholesale and retail margins for trading enterprises. These taxes apply mostly to consumer goods and some consumer services. The government imposes a turnover tax to separate retail prices from producer prices, and so is in fact redistributing nominal money incomes. Some consumer goods, such as foodstuffs directly sold by peasants to consumers, are free from turnover taxes. Whatever the basis of fixing this tax, the effective rates are highly differentiated. In a sense, the size of the turnover tax does not determine the level of retail prices—on the contrary, the magnitude of these taxes depends upon the predetermined price level.

Agricultural Taxes. Agricultural taxes are usually levied in kind rather than in monetary amounts. One reason for this type of levy is that a problem which has faced the Chinese government is not a lack of adequate revenue, but rather a lack of an adequate supply of marketable agricultural products. The tax is levied on the most important crop in each region—usually a grain crop, such as wheat or rice. Payment is made in grain, or if the predominant crop is not grain, it is converted into grain measurements to determine the amount of tax payable. When the grain or other agricultural produce is transferred by the collection agencies to the state trading companies for general sale, the amount is converted into cash and entered into the national budget as such. In addition to the agricultural tax on grain and other commodities, a pastoral tax, which takes the form of a capital levy, is levied on livestock. There are also a number of minor taxes levied by local units of government on the sales of various types of agricultural produce.

Receipts from State Enterprises. The most important source of revenue for the national budget comes from a nontax source—receipts from state enterprises. A certain percentage of profits has to be remitted to the national government by each enterprise. Enterprises are also allowed to retain a certain percentage of profits as retained earnings to be used for working capital and capital investments. Profits, as defined previously, usually are the difference between the proceeds that each enterprise obtains by selling its products at state regulated prices and production costs and tax payments. Since the Chinese attach no significance to the capitalistic viewpoints on profits and their relationship to invested capital, the concept can be considered more in terms of a residual which belongs to the state after each enterprise has fulfilled the objectives set forth in national planning.

Depreciation Reserves. A second important source of budgetary revenue is depreciation reserves for the amortization of fixed assets. Depreciation is charged only on the amount of fixed assets actually used in the production process. The Chinese feel that since capital is provided by the state to individual enterprises to be used, the depreciation reserve that is set aside to compensate for the wear of capital rightly belongs to the state.

Government Expenditures. The items of expenditure in the Chinese state budget are arranged according to their role in the creation of national income. More than one-half of total expenditures is devoted to the financing of material production. Expenditures under this category would include allocations to state enterprises for capital investment and for working capital. Capital goods and construction industries are the major recipients of budget funds for investment purposes. Appropriations from the state budget are also used to finance the construction of transportation facilities, investment in state farms and housing construction. The provision of finance for stocks and reserves of materials and of subsidies to loss-incurring enterprises is also classified as productive expenditure. The financing of material production comes largely from two revenue items, deductions from profits of state enterprises and depreciation reserves. This means that although state enterprises remit most of their profits, they are returned in the form of capital investment expenditures.

Social security benefits consist of old-age and invalidity pensions, sickness and maternity benefits, and work injury compensation. The benefits are administered by the Ministry of Labor and are paid by employers. Coverage includes workers in factories, mines, and transportation, communication, construction, and public service.

Banking

The banking system in the People's Republic of China represents a financial control mechanism for carrying out economic planning. All state enterprises and cooperatives have accounts with the banks, and control can be exercised since most transactions are in terms of money through bank transfers. Purchases and sales of goods by each enterprise can be matched against authorized payments and receipts. Government control over income and expenditures is also expedited through the credit and cash plans of the banking system as well as through the national budget.

The People's Bank of China. The People's Bank of China is the major banking institution and was formed in 1959 as the central bank of the country. It is under the administrational jurisdiction of the Staff Office for Finance and Trade and is responsible for the supervision of the financial transactions which correspond to the physical production plans. It is also an important control device which exercises a very important influence on the national economy. All state enterprises have accounts in branch banks under its direct jurisdiction. In this way, the People's Bank can exercise control because all expenditures and transfers made by the enterprises come under its scrutiny.

The People's Bank, as the central bank of China, has the following functions:

1. It is responsible for the issuance of Chinese currency.
2. It is responsible for the financing of credit to state enterprises. Funds to support credit expansion are obtained from the national budget, from retained profits, and from customer deposits.
3. It is responsible for the supervision of expenditures of state enterprises to see that they conform with national planning objectives.
4. It is responsible for the development of the Credit Plan and the Cash Plan, which are financial counterparts of the physical economic plans.
5. It is expected to monitor the performance of state enterprises.

The Credit Plan. The Credit Plan involves the amount of short- and medium-term credit which is to be given to all state enterprises and agricultural communes by the People's Bank. The plan involves a balance sheet statement showing sources of funds and uses of funds. Sources of funds emanate primarily from one source—appropriations from the national budget which are obtained primarily from the earnings of state enterprises. Other, lesser sources of funds are from increases in savings deposits, and government deposits, and deposit balances of communes. Use of funds include increases in loans to industry, commercial organizations, and agricultural communes and cooperatives. The statement should balance, and funds can be allocated only for purposes that conform to the national plan.

The Cash Plan. The Cash Plan is designed to maintain control over currency circulation, with the People's Bank responsible for the issuance of currency and the receipt of cash from state enterprises, communes, and government administrative units at all levels. This means that the People's Bank has control over the amount of money in circulation because it is both a starting point and a finishing point in the flow of currency throughout the system.

The Cash Plan consists of a set of cash inflows and cash outflows essentially in the form of a balance statement. Cash inflows include such items as retail sales receipts, savings deposit receipts, repayment of agricultural loans, deposits of communes, and public utility receipts. The total represents an injection of currency into circulation. Cash outflows represent a net withdrawal of currency and consist of wage payments by state enterprises and communes, government purchases of industrial and agricultural products, government administrative expenses, payments by the state to the individuals, management expenditures of state enterprises, new loans to agriculture, and withdrawals of savings deposits.

The Credit and Cash Plans have to be coordinated with the physical production plans. A function of these financial plans is to provide financing for expenditures required by the production plans. This means that the People's Bank can supervise the operations of state enterprises to enforce conformance with production plans since purchase and sales of goods can be matched against authorized payments and receipts.

Other Financial Institutions. There are several specialized financial agencies which also provide money to finance the transactions of enterprises in a specialized area of production. These specialized financial institutions, like the People's Bank, do not allocate funds independently of national planning objectives and thus have no influence on resource allocation as they would in a market economy.

The Agricultural Bank has as its functions the provision of agricultural loans and control over the mobilization of rural savings to provide a source of credit to the rural credit cooperatives which are responsible for the provision of credit to communes and to individual members of communes. Loans are also made by the rural credit cooperatives to individuals for sideline undertakings involving private plots of land. The Agricultural Bank is under the jurisdiction of the State Council and is operated independently of the People's Bank. It has provincial branches and also branches which operate at the municipal, or *hsien*, level of administration.

There are also several banks which are under the jurisdiction of the Ministry of Finance. One bank, the People's Construction Bank, is responsible for providing investment funds to enterprises. These funds are obtained from the national budget and do not have to be repaid. It is also responsible for providing short-term loans to enterprises for capital construction projects. Another bank, the Bank of Communications, is responsible for the distribution of nonrepayable funds from the national budget to state enterprises.

Interest has no significant role in resource allocation in the Chinese economic system. However, interest rates are charged on all loans by the banks to industrial enterprises, communes, and individuals, but the rates are far below the rates that would prevail under a system of free markets. Grants provided by the People's Bank to enterprises for capital investment are interest-free, but interest is charged on working capital loans to enterprises. However, interest charges are mostly paid by the state through a reduction in the profit tax liability.

Organization of Industry

Although agriculture, providing the raw material for industry and food for a growing population, remains the foundation of the Chinese economy, any meaningful claim to a great power status must be based on the development of industry. The process of industrialization has been difficult, and the Chinese people have paid a price in terms of resources sacrificed to achieve this end. At the present the Chinese have a long way to go before they can match the industrial potential of the Soviet Union or any of the major Western industrial nations. Even within their own sphere of influence, the Chinese do not rival the industrial base of Japan, which today remains the major industrialized nation in Asia.

Government Control of Industry. A number of ministries have been created as both departments of government and of economic activity. These ministries are in charge of industrial production for a whole group of related industries or a single industry. They do not produce anything but are merely control groups or administrative agencies. Within the ministries are a number of subdepartments or control groups that are responsible for the activities of a single industry, for data collection, for implementation of planning, for supervision of accounting methods, and for the development of new production facilities.

Industrial Chain of Command. The designation of authority is vertical. Between the ministries at the top and the enterprises at the bottom there is, as a matter of necessity, a chain of command which is responsible for the execution of national plans. Each ministry and subdepartment within it has a counterpart at the provincial and municipal levels. The span of control is direct in that the branch offices are responsible only to the ministry and, in turn, direct the units of production under their jurisdiction. This means that a large, intermediate, bureaucratic structure has been erected between the ministries and the local enterprises. Some degree of decentralization exists in that provincial and municipal administrative units have control over a number of industries, such as light industry and nonstrategic industrial enterprises, and they also have some control over resource allocation among enterprises. Managers of enterprises are permitted flexibility in terms of product mix planning.

There is another link in the chain of command between ministries and enterprises in the form of an industrial corporation which is either under the jurisdiction of municipal industrial branch offices or directly under the national ministries. The industrial corporation is responsible for the operation of a number of enterprises producing a homogeneous product.

Some enterprises are directly under municipal authority, particularly if they produce a product that is used primarily in the local area. Other enterprises are directly under the national ministries. This occurs when an enterprise is producing a product which is of national importance or which is used for national defense purposes. Enterprises that use a new production process or that are established with foreign support and assistance are also under national ministerial control.

Ministerial relations with most enterprises, however, are indirect and are confined to the following functions:

1. Disseminating the details of the national plan as it would affect individual enterprises
2. Allocating investment funds
3. Planning and designing important capital investment projects
4. Designing and developing important new products
5. Training high-level personnel for the enterprises

Industry—Party Relationship. A dual relationship exists in the organization of Chinese industry in that parallel Communist Party committees exist at all levels of industry. Party committees exist at the provincial and municipal branch levels of the various industrial ministries and also at the local enterprise level. The main purpose for this dual role

between professional managers and bureaucrats and the party committees is the coordination of national objectives. This is an attempt by the
party to insure that enterprises and regional administrative offices do not
stray from policy goals.

Price Determination. In setting prices, one element used by the state is
productive costs, based on the average cost per product for enterprises in a
particular industry. Another element is average profit for each product for
these enterprises. Prices then should cover average costs plus an average
profit for all enterprises within an industry. Taxes and the costs of distribution could also be added to give a final price which an enterprise can
set for its product. Prices, then, should cover costs of production, which
include labor, raw materials, and depreciation; profits, which can be expressed as a rate of return over cost; and taxes, such as the turnover tax.

There are different sets of prices which cover the production and
consumption of commodities. There are procurement prices which cover
the acquisition of agricultural products, and ex-factory prices for industrial commodities, wholesale prices which involve the intermediate
transfer of commodities from the production to the retail level, and retail
prices which are charged to the ultimate consumer. There are also prices,
called allocation prices, which determine the relationship of exchange
between various enterprises producing different commodities. These
prices are determined in different ways. For example, ex-factory prices are
determined by using average cost of production, taxes, and a margin for
profits, and wholesale prices are comprised of ex-factory prices and the
expenses and profits of wholesaling. Allocation prices of industrial commodities include ex-factory prices and various distribution expenses.[5]

In a country as large as China with a poor transportation system and a
diverse industrial base, diffusion of responsibility for price determination
is necessary. Decentralization has occurred in the setting of prices as well
as in the control of industry. Local price variations exist and they are set
by provincial and municipal governments. Apparently a dichotomy of
responsibility exists between the national governments and local governments. Of this number, the prices of five items were controlled by the
central government and the remainder were controlled by the provincial
governments. The actual mechanics of price determination are the responsibility of the various ministries or bureaus, depending on the level
of government, that maintain control over a particular industry.

Although the prices of most commodities are set by state agencies,
managers of enterprises have some control over the setting of prices under certain conditions. For example, price changes can be proposed for
products which are not standardized and for changes in design and prod-

---

[5]Barry M. Richmond, *Industrial Society in Communist China* (Cambridge: Harvard
University Press, 1969), pp. 62–68.

uct specification. Managers can also establish cost plus prices for minor subcontracting services—with the prices often providing for a profit margin of 15 to 20 percent to encourage product innovation. In some cases, formal approval from a state agency is necessary for price setting; in other cases, approval is not needed.

Organization of Agriculture

Agriculture, since time immemorial, has been the foundation of the Chinese economy. It provides a living for at least 80 percent of the population and furnishes the raw material base necessary for the performance of the planned economy. Unfortunately for the Chinese, most of the land area is not conducive to the production of agricultural products. Much of China is mountainous and dry, and unfavorable soil and climate conditions inhibit agricultural development in other areas of the country. In addition, there is a very large ratio of population to cultivable land, which reduces efficiency in production. This has meant that the country has had to operate at a margin which is very close to a minimum subsistence level. It has also meant that the Communists have had to face the problem of a growing population and a relatively small and technically backward agricultural base while at the same time trying to build up an adequate industrial base in order to become a major world power.

The Collectivization of Agriculture. Agriculture went through several distinct phases of collectivization since the Communists came to power in 1949. At that time the peasant farms were privately owned either by landlords or by peasant owners. To win the support of the masses of the peasants, landless or otherwise, the Communists redistributed millions of acres of land and eliminated landlords as a class. Once the land was redistributed, peasants were allowed to operate the land as private owners. However, the peasants were not long left undisturbed. The Communists were merely marking time until economic control had been established over the other sectors of the economy.[6]

Producers' Cooperatives. Agricultural producers' cooperatives were established in 1955. Farmers were organized into these cooperatives and had to pool their lands for cultivation. The land, however, was still held privately, and rent was paid by the cooperatives for its use. The cooperatives were run by central committees and were divided into production teams. The product was distributed by the cooperatives and the peasants compensated on the basis of labor contributed. Although land, animals,

---

[6]Marion B. Larsen, "China's Agriculture under Communism," in *An Economic Profile of Mainland China*, Vol. 1, Joint Economic Committee, 90th Congress, First session, 1967, pp. 212–18.

and implements, for the most part, were still privately owned, there was the continued trend toward the centralization of farm management.

Collective Farms. The next stage in the socialization of agriculture occurred in 1956.[7] The agricultural producers' cooperatives, which had retained many of the elements of private property ownership, were consolidated into collective farms. On these collective farms the peasants were supposed to pool their land, animals, and livestock. Land now was no longer to be privately owned; it was to be collective property. However, the peasants were permitted to own small plots of land to be used for their own purposes. They could produce and sell products from these plots. Similarly, domestic livestock and small farm implements were left in private hands. The peasants were formed into brigades, with brigade leaders given the responsibility for assigning workers their tasks. Income depended directly upon the crops that were produced, and workers were compensated on the basis of labor days contributed. The compensation was net of compulsory deliveries to the government of a certain percentage of the crop produced and deductions of taxes paid to the government. The collective farms were also required to set aside reserves for contingencies.

Communes. In 1958 the communes replaced the collective farms. A commune was designed as a multipurpose unit which would perform administrative as well as economic functions. The *hsiang*, or local government administrative unit, was merged with the commune. The commune was responsible for both agriculture and industrial production. It was considerably larger than the collective farm in terms of area and households. The typical commune contained around 24,000 people. The transition to the commune was rapid. The decision to form communes was announced in August 1958, and by the end of the year, some 750,000 collective farms representing virtually all of the peasant households had been formed into 26,578 communes. All vestiges of private property ownership were removed. The peasants were organized into production brigades and teams. The latter was the basic work unit and was given responsibility for the use of labor, land, animals, tools, and equipment. Living was communal. The peasants ate in mess halls, and the distribution of food was based in part on the needs of individuals and in part on work performed. Workers had to perform tasks that were by no means limited to agriculture, such as producing steel and mining coal.

However, by the end of the Great Leap Forward there was a shift in agricultural policies with respect to the communes. The complete collectivization of nearly all production and consumption in the communes did not achieve the desired results. Production fell and China became a net importer of grain. Private plots of land were restored to the peasants, and

---

[7]*Ibid.*, pp. 218–20.

the free market was permitted in which the peasants were free to sell their produce for income. Pigs, which were in short supply as a result of Great Leap Forward mismanagement, were returned to private ownership, and peasants were given incentives to raise pigs for sale to the government. There was also a shift away from communal living, with a restoration of the family unit.

The communes remain as the highest level of collective organization in China. There are about 50,000 rural communes in China, each with about 15,000 inhabitants.[8] Communes operate industries and handicrafts and provide individual benefits, including education and health facilities and other services. Most factors of production are owned jointly by the members of the commune rather than by the state. The communes are responsible to county government units for the fulfillment of agricultural plans. County governments decide on the allocation of agricultural inputs such as fertilizer, and plan the procurement and disposition of output, in accordance with the plans of the higher state levels to which they are subordinate, including prefectures, provinces, and the national Ministry of Agriculture and Forestry, which has the ultimate responsibility for planning and organizing agricultural production in China.

Production Brigades and Teams. There has been a shifting of control over production downward from the communes to production brigades and teams, with the brigade consisting of usually several villages and the team consisting of one village or 20 or 30 households. The important social and production unit is the team. It is the basic accounting unit in Chinese agriculture, and it takes care of day-to-day farm management.[9] The production team divides its collective incomes—the proceeds of the sale of crops and other products, less the cost of inputs such as seed, fertilizer, and farm tools, as well as funds for investment—among its members on the basis of the number of work points each has accumulated during the year.[10] It also has to contribute a certain percentage of its product to the brigade, and the brigade contributes a percentage to the commune.

The "Learn from Tachai" Policy. Chinese agricultural policy has come to include what is called the "Learn from Tachai" policy. In 1960 a production team leader from the village of Tachai informed his superiors that his group had increased agricultural production to high levels through a new kind of team spirit and cooperation. The team had organized farmers to work without pay to build earth dams in ravines to

---

[8]Henry J. Groen and James A. Kilpatrick, "China's Agricultural Production," in *Chinese Economy Post-Mao*, p. 618.

[9]However, the Chinese leadership appear to be moving the basic accounting unit up to the brigade level.

[10]A healthy male can usually earn 10 points for a full day's work. Those with a "bad class background" or the "wrong political viewpoint" may receive fewer points.

prevent water runoff and to reclaim more land. In this way the village expanded its cultivated land and water supply. The villagers refused state assistance when a rainstorm destroyed the dams, rebuilt them, and increased food and grain yields. The new income generated by these harvests enabled the production team to rebuild the village. This spirit, which involved overcoming natural disasters while scorning state aid, caught the attention of Mao and convinced him and subsequent leaders to recommend that the Tachai policy be adopted by all production teams.

State Farms. State farms are another type of agricultural organization that exists in China. All the land, building, machinery, and productive equipment in general are owned by the government, and the farms are managed by government-appointed directors. The employees of the state farm are wage earners who have no more direct interest in the farms than industrial workers have in their factories, and they have no claim on the products of the state farms. The state farms typically specialize in the production of a single commodity, and they are mechanized to a much greater degree than the communes. Workers on the state farms are usually paid on a standard wage basis plus piece rates for exceeding a norm and are permitted to own small numbers of domestic animals. There are some 2,000 state farms in China, and they occupy less than 5 percent of the country's cultivated land. There are located most often in frontier areas.

Private Plots. Just as in the Soviet Union, private plots have come to play an important role in Chinese agricultural production. Private plots are guaranteed in the constitution and serve an important role in the economy by providing most of the poultry, pigs, and vegetables consumed in China. Private plots are in many ways the most productive tracts of land in China. This may be attributed in part to the fact that farmers are strongly motivated to maximize output in order to increase family income.[11] From the point of view of the state, while these activities do not have a central place in agricultural production, they are a practical way of obtaining the intensive use of peasant labor for the production of some high-value items. Chinese leaders have emphasized in recent years the need for free markets and private plots and there has been an increase in private trade in agricultural products.[12]

Incentives and Income Distribution

The Chinese have oscillated between reliance on material incentives and nonmaterial incentives to motivate people. The former relies on

---

[11]It is estimated that 35 percent of peasant farm income is derived from family plots.
[12]A. Doak Barnett, *China's Economy in a Global Perspective* (Washington: Brookings Institution, 1981), p. 341.

some form of income payment to motivate people to work; the latter relies on some form of external approval (prestige, power, public honors, and acclaim) to provide the motivation. Under the Proletarian Cultural Revolution there was an attempt to eliminate class distinctions based on wage differentials and occupational status. Educators and bureaucrats were required to work side by side with peasants, and managers were required to spend at least part of their time working alongside the workers on the production line. The Chinese perhaps felt that an individual would not mind being poor or moderately poor if there were no prosperous persons to whom he could compare himself unfavorably. They felt that income differentials which were often as low as 2 to 1 between skilled and unskilled workers coupled with nonmaterial incentives would prove adequate to provide incentives for all. Time and experience proved them to be wrong.

Material Incentives. Economic incentives which involve wage and bonus payments are used in China. During the First Five-Year Plan the Russians introduced a wage system which tied rewards to performance. Income differentials existed between the engineers and technicians and the workers in the factories. During the Great Leap Forward, income incentives were criticized as being an example of right-wing communist revisionism, and income differentials were reduced. After the Great Leap Forward, there was a reversion to the type of incentives that existed during the First Five-Year Plan. Reliance was placed on piece rates to motivate increased productivity on the part of the workers. The enthusiasm engendered by the Great Leap Forward had palled by 1960, and performance on the part of workers and farmers declined, so material incentives linked to performance were utilized more and more. This continued until 1966 when the Proletarian Cultural Revolution occurred, and then material incentives were denounced as being capitalistic. Production, as a matter of economic policy, was to be achieved through reliance upon ideological motivation. It is apparent that the Chinese Communists have used economic incentives to accomplish specific economic policy goals in industry and agriculture; when these goals were accomplished, then ideology replaced material incentives in importance.

The Chinese have maintained the eight-wage classification system for both production and white-collar workers which they borrowed from the Soviet Union. Classes 1 and 2 are for unskilled and part-time workers; classes 3 and 4 are for semiskilled workers; class 5 is for skilled workers who have passed a special examination, but who have no work experience; classes 6 and 7 are for skilled workers with work experience; and class 8 is for workers with extensive specialized knowledge. Thus, Chinese industrial workers are paid according to variations in skill from unskilled to highly skilled workers. There are also wage scales within classes. Wage scales by classes are also differentiated by industrial branch in line with the Chinese regime's priorities for differential industrial development. Class 8 industrial workers receive wages from three to five times higher than Class 1 workers.[13]

There are also income differentials based on occupation. Managerial, professional, technial, and political cadres also receive income payments which can result in a differential of 10 to 1 between top and bottom income earners in China. Moreover, party and government officials enjoy many perquisites not included in their regular salaries. Senior party cadres starting at rank 13 for heads of counties and running up through rank 1 have special access to cars and limousines graded by make, color, and curtains.[14] They have special rooms, and sometimes whole wings, reserved for them in hospitals. Privileges may also extend to getting special treatment for family and relatives in school admissions, employment, and the ability to go abroad.[15]

However, health services for workers are free and are provided for their dependents at nominal rates. All necessities are priced at very low levels and, as a result, consumption is subsidized by the state, while luxury goods are priced very high. Housing rentals are very low in China, averaging from 2 to 4 percent of monthly incomes. The price structure has built into it certain elements of progressivity that tend to narrow the real purchasing power differential between the top and the bottom of the income scale in China. There are few luxury items available for consumption in China, and conspicuous consumption is frowned upon since the days of the Cultural Revolution. Thus the possession of various goods that would normally incite envy in Western countries is limited by production in China. There is also rationing of some basic consumer goods so that higher-income groups cannot bid them away.

Wide disparities in income distribution have existed between urban and rural areas as well as between different provinces and regions, and efforts are being made to narrow the gap. In the rural areas agricultural prices paid to the communes have been increased to raise farm incomes. Also, more incentives have been provided to farm the private plots and to participate in rural free markets—insofar, of course, as this does not involve speculative behavior or cut into work obligations on the communes. The government is also encouraging the development of crops with the highest commerical advantage, increasing investment in agriculture, and promoting the development of rural industry in order to narrow the urban–rural gap in incomes.

---

[13]Alexander Eckstein, "The Chinese Development Model," in *Chinese Economy Post-Mao*, pp. 98–100.

[14]William L. Parish, "Egalitarianism in Chinese Society," *Problems of Communism*, Vol. 30 (January–February 1981), pp. 42–43.

[15]Traveling abroad is one of the most important privileges afforded to party officials and other elites in most communist countries. The traveler has the opportunity to bring hard currency and goods back to the home country. There is also status to be gained from traveling to Western countries.

Nonmaterial Incentives. Individual nonmaterial incentives stress altruistic motivation. There is use of honors and symbols, such as titles, medals, and certificates of merit, to inspire greater effort on the part of the individual. With these honors go such perquisites as extra paid vacations, opportunities for advancement, and the chance to join the Communist Party. In one program, called the "five good workers," workers were selected for an award if they performed well on their job, improved their skills through study, helped other workers with their jobs, engaged in political study, and helped other workers to accomplish ideological self-improvement. Medals and titles were given to those who merited the "five good workers" award. This was supposed to encourage other workers to emulate the accomplishments of the "good workers." In fact, the key motivating force in the use of nonmaterial incentives is emulation: the desire to emulate some standard or individual and thus gain recognition and esteem by one's peer group. Special titles, such as *labor hero*, are given to workers who turn in performances in the Stakhanovite pattern—performances that are not easily duplicated and are to serve as an inspirational example to other workers.[16] Exceptional performances may win workers the opportunity to travel to Peking and perhaps meet one of the party officials.

Income Distribution and Consumer Sovereignty. Land, labor, and capital are the three factors of production, and rent, wages, and interest are payments for their use. Of these payments, only wages have any real significance in China. The role of rent and interest in resource allocation is minor. As mentioned previously, interest is charged on certain types of loans by the banks. Interest is also paid by the state to former capitalists for properties which were expropriated. Rent is paid for housing, but like interest, is set at rates which are too low to perform any allocative function pertaining to housing and capital. Property income is nonexistent, for the land of the country is owned by the state and there is no separate class of people who, as landowners, receive rent as private income.

Wages, then, are left as the major factor payment, and these wages are determined by government action rather than by the free play of market forces. Wages are determined, in conformance with planning objectives, by the Ministry of Labor and by other ministries responsible for a particular area of production. That is, the economic plan specifies a certain total sum or fund which is to be used for wage payments in a given year and indicates how this fund is to be allocated among the different industries and enterprises in the country. Each industry and each enterprise thus knows in advance how much money it may pay out in wages during each

---

[16]The Russian coal miner Alexei Stakhanov was reported to have mined 102 tons of coal in 6 hours. As a result, he was lionized by the Soviet press, and countless honors were bestowed upon him. Other workers were urged to emulate his accomplishments—hence the "Stakhanovite" movement.

year. This amount governs the number of workers an enterprise can hire and the wages it can pay.

Wages in the Chinese and Russian economic system have performed similar functions. They have constituted a device for evoking among the various occupations and industries of each country the distribution of labor which is appropriate for the carrying out of the economic plans. They have also provided a reward for accomplishment in production and an incentive to continued productive activity.

The Chinese have generally followed a low-wage policy to make possible rapid capital accumulation. In general, wages have been set at a rate which has been considerably less than labor productivity. Another objective of the low-wage policy has been to minimize inflationary pressures in the consumer goods market by keeping demand in urban areas in balance with the limited supply of consumer goods. This has been done through control over the urban wage bill rather than through the use of general fiscal and monetary controls. The wage bill, which includes all wages, bonuses, and subsidies which an enterprise can pay, is set by the national planning authorities.

In a capitalistic market economy, consumer preference, which is expressed through the price mechanism, determines what is to be produced, at what quality, and in what quantities. In the People's Republic of China, consumer preference or sovereignty does not exist in the sense that the consumer is able to influence, by his spending actions, the allocation of resources among various types of consumer goods. The production of consumer goods and services is determined by the state. However, consumers have freedom to choose among the various goods and services that are produced. In the absence of a market economy, it is difficult to relate consumer wants to what is being produced by the state. This problem is circumvented in part by having retail outlets and other commercial organs report to the planners the needs and requirements of the consumers. It is reported that the Chinese have considered the use of consumer surveys to find out what consumers really need.

Freedom of choice does not necessarily redound to the advantage of all Chinese consumers. Even though a person may have the wherewithal to purchase a consumer good, such as an automobile, he may find that it is available only to the party elite. With disparities in income existing, although reduced during the Cultural Revolution, a rationing function is performed in that various desirable goods go to those who can afford to pay for them. With wages kept low as a matter of public policy, many consumers cannot afford most of the goods that are being produced.

AN APPRAISAL OF THE CHINESE ECONOMY

Change and the impermanence of any particular form of economic and social organization have been the dominant features and realities of

Chinese life since 1949. There has been a struggle between two factions—between "reds" and "experts"—which has involved debate over whether to stress economics or politics, professional competence or egalitarian goals, material or ideological incentives, orderly incremental changes or sudden dramatic leaps. The "reds" measure costs and gains in ideological terms; their goal is the transformation of the Chinese soul, and they lean toward the drama of struggle as the preferred engine of rapid social change.[17] Conversely, the "experts" favor expertise over ideology. They prefer that an educated elite maintain control of the process of change, in which compromise rather than struggle results in evolutionary, not revolutionary, change. At the risk of delaying rewards for the masses, they prefer to concentrate limited resources for planned economic and political development.

The contrast between the two factions can be made by comparing the goals of the Proletarian Cultural Revolution of 1966–1969 and the Four Modernizations Program of 1978. In the Cultural Revolution, political objectives were given greater prominence than economic objectives. One goal was to destroy the elitism of the bureaucracy and the technicians by, among other things, making them work on the farms. This would cure them of any elitist impulses. Higher education was denigrated because it supposedly created technicians who were above the masses. Enrollment in colleges was sharply curtailed and some colleges were closed. Material incentives were rejected in favor of nonmaterial incentives. Managers in factories were replaced by revolutionary cadres whose idea of running factories was to read quotes from Mao Tse-tung. The Cultural Revolution aimed at mass participation in the political and economic process. Americans were excoriated as foreign imperialist devils.

The Four Modernizations Program had diametrically opposite goals.[18] Introduced by Premier Teng Hsiao-ping, the program involved a commitment toward modern economic growth. Schools and universities closed since the Cultural Revolution were reopened in order to produce a large supply of technocrats, scientists, and managers. Academic excellence, which was considered elitist in the Cultural Revolution, was reinstated along with entrance exams as performance criteria. There was an attempt to link effort and reward by reliance on material incentives. China also began to purchase more plants and equipment from Western countries, with particular leanings toward Japan and the United States for technology, credit, and trade.[19] By obtaining foreign capital and technol-

---

[17]William W. Whitson, "The Political Dynamics of the People's Republic of China," in *Chinese Economy Post-Mao*, pp. 68–70.

[18]Ramon H. Myers, *The Chinese Economy Past and Present* (Belmont, Calif.: Wadsworth, 1981), p. 245.

[19]Coca-Cola and China concluded an agreement in 1979 which allowed for the production and distribution of the drink in China. Reynolds Industries opened a plant to manufacture cigarettes.

ogy from the West, the Chinese hoped to revitalize their economy.[20] Many Chinese students were also sent abroad to learn foreign technology, even from the former American "devils."

As mentioned previously, a period of retrenchment occurred in 1980 as the Chinese realized that modernization of the economy would take longer than anticipated. As is true in the Soviet Union and the United States, future economic growth will be more difficult and at least for the immediate future will be lower than the rate for the 1970s. China is presently at a watershed in its economic development, and its near-term ability to overcome its economic problems will effectively dictate its options available for the future. The various reforms and policy shifts will not, however, be sufficient to rapidly improve China's modernization. During the 1980s, China can benefit significantly from external support, particularly from Japan.

Economic Growth

The annual growth of China's gross national product has been around 6 to 7 percent throughout the nation's 30-year history of Communist rule.[21] The Communists took over an essentially agrarian society and built a substantial industrial foundation. During the period 1952–1977 the rate of annual economic growth averaged 5.7 percent, with wide swings occurring in individual years. The rate of growth was rapid in the 1950s, averaging 8.8 percent a year for the period 1952–1958. Then there was a negative rate of growth for 1960–1961, reflecting the excesses of the Great Leap Forward. This was followed by a rapid rate of economic growth, which averaged 12 percent for the period 1962–1966. Then for the years 1967 and 1968 there was a negative rate of growth due to the effects of the Cultural Revolution. Toward the end of the Revolution the growth rate began to increase. During the period 1968–1975 the rate of economic growth averaged 8.5 percent.[22] The growth rate for the years 1970–1981 is presented in Table 15-1.

In many respects the performance of the Chinese economy has been good despite an erratic rate of growth. Rural and urban poverty has been eliminated and, although consumption levels and living standards are low by Western standards, goods have been distributed in a relatively equitable manner. The education of the populace has been improved. An industrial base has been created in a society that was mainly agrarian before the Communist takeover in 1949. Unlike the Soviet Union and its

---

[20]Purchases from the the United States increased from $1.7 billion in 1979 to $3.8 billion in 1981.

[21]U.S. Joint Economic Committee, *Allocation of Resources in the Soviet Union and China, 1981*, p. 112.

[22]Barnett, *China's Economy in a Global Perspective*, pp. 17–18.

TABLE 15-1
REAL ANNUAL INCREASE IN CHINA'S
GROSS NATIONAL PRODUCT, 1970–1981

Year	Percentage Annual Increase
1970	13.5
1971	6.8
1972	4.6
1973	12.9
1974	3.6
1975	7.0
1976	0
1977	8.1
1978	11.6
1979	5.4
1980	2.8
1981 (est.)	2.1

Source: Central Intelligence Agency, *Handbook of Economic Statistics*, 1981, Table 59.

Eastern European satellites, China has avoided excessive foreign debt. There has been a positive rate of growth in agriculture in a country where famines were not at all uncommon.[23] Inflation has been kept under control, and unemployment, at least until recently, has generally been kept low.[24] The primary causes of economic decline in the past have been short-term and political in character, but the post-Mao leadership has given high priority to economic modernization, professionalism, and incentive systems in planning and management. Moreover, China's potential for long-run economic development is enhanced by large reserves of almost all strategic raw materials.

However, the Chinese economy is by no means free from problems. It is highly unlikely that high growth rates can be achieved in the foreseeable future—growth rates of 2 to 3 percent are much more likely. The transportation system leaves a lot to be desired, which works against the development of natural resources. Technical training can be expected to grow as the process of industrialization becomes more complex, but much of the educational system was shut down during the Cultural Revolution. Thus, the educational system has had to be reorganized and revitalized, and the Chinese start from behind in technical training. Consumer aspirations can also create problems. Will increased production be

---

[23]In one famine in the 1930s an estimated 30 million Chinese died of starvation.
[24]It was reported that unemployment among urban youths was as high as 20 percent in some cities in 1981.

translated into increased consumer appetites, or can consumerism be contained and the spirit of frugality preserved? In industry bottlenecks and uneven growth have occurred despite the fact that industrial production increases at a rate of 10 percent a year during the 1970s. Finally, there is always the possibility of another policital upheaval similar to the Cultural Revolution that would cause economic hardships.

Agricultural Performance

Agriculture is the mainstay of the Chinese economy, employing around 80 percent of the population. Success in agricultural production determines the country's prospects for industrialization and long-term industrial development. Agriculture serves many purposes in the Chinese economy. It is needed to feed the people and to provide raw materials for industry. In addition, the Chinese agricultural goods that are used as export commodities are extremely valuable as a source of hard currency. Without these earnings, the Chinese would not be able to buy much of the Western equipment and technology that are needed for economic modernization. For example, in 1980 agricultural goods accounted for 30 percent of total exports. Thus, the state emphasizes the rural sector as the primary factor in the process of modernization.

As Table 15-2 indicates, Chinese agricultural output levels have been characterized by periods of growth interspersed with periods of stagnation. The technical transformation of agricultural which has begun in China still has far to go. Weather is a big determinant of agricultural output. There is the need to feed a population which has grown at a rate of 15 million persons a year, which means that there is not much of a margin above subsistence. There are few areas that have not been untouched by the push for agricultural modernization. But in most areas, modernization has not proceeded very far, and it remains a potential rather than an actual accomplishment.

Industrial Production

Years of political upheaval have resulted in erratic industrial development in China.[25] This fact can be illustrated by examining Table 15-3, which provides percentage changes in industrial production for the period 1970–1980. The rate of growth has also varied between industries, and many enterprises are run at a loss. The chairman of the Communist Party, Hua Kuo-feng, admitted problems in industrial production when

---

[25]Robert Michael Field, Kathleen M. McGlynn, and William B. Abnett, "Political Conflict and Industrial Growth in China, 1965–1977," in *Chinese Economy Post-Mao*, pp. 240–45.

TABLE 15-2
AGRICULTURAL PRODUCTION
IN CHINA, 1970–1980

Year	Grain Production (million metric tons)
1970	243
1971	246
1972	240
1973	266
1974	275
1975	284
1976	285
1977	286
1978	305
1979	332
1980	338

Source: *Allocation of Resources in the Soviet Union and China, 1981*, p. 71.

TABLE 15-3
PERCENTAGE CHANGE
IN INDUSTRIAL PRODUCTION,
1970–1980

Year	Percent
1970	22.2
1971	11.2
1972	9.2
1973	11.6
1974	1.8
1975	15.1
1976	−.3
1977	14.1
1978	13.7
1979	7.8
1980	3.2

Source: *Allocation of Resources in the Soviet Union and China, 1981*, p. 108.

he stated that many products of the light and textile industries were insufficient in quantity, poor in quality, and limited in variety. He also stated that output in the coal, petroleum, and power industries lagged behind the requirements of an expanding economy.[26]

To improve quality and to increase the quantity of industrial production, the Chinese made a number of changes in the late 1970s. There was a shift away from ideology to an increase in the importance of enterprise management by professional managers. There was also a consolidation of enterprises into combines in order to achieve a new level of efficiency and productivity in key fields. Large-scale combines were created in the petroleum and agricultural machinery industries. It is hoped that substantial benefits will flow from new economies of scale and from a combination of increased specialization and improved coordination of related activities. To promote efficiency, more emphasis is placed on profits and quality of products, and prices must be based on realistic calculations of cost. Successful enterprises will be allowed to keep a part of profits, either to expand production or to improve workers' welfare.

SUMMARY

In many respects the institutional arrangements of China are similar to those of the Soviet Union. The Communist Party is the dominant form of political organization and has control over political and economic activities. There is reliance on economic planning, and the function of banking is the same as it is in the Soviet Union. However, agriculture is organized differently, with the commune, production brigades, and production teams replacing the collective farms. There also have been much wider swings in the internal politics of China, which have had a deleterious impact on the economy. However, the current Chinese leaders are much more flexible and eclectic than their Russian counterparts, and are borrowing from the experiences of a wide variety of countries. Renewed emphasis has been placed on improved management of state enterprises and communes. There is also emphasis on the need for greater specialization throughout the economy in order to raise technical levels and operational efficiency. More reliance has been placed in material incentives to increase productivity.

REVIEW QUESTIONS

1. What were the objectives of the First Five-Year Plan?
2. Discuss agricultural policy during the Great Leap Forward.
3. What is the difference between a production brigade and a production team?
4. It has been said that Chinese economic policy between 1949 and the present has oscillated between economic rationality and idealistic extremism. Discuss.

---

[26]Barnett, *China's Economy in a Global Perspective*, p. 91.

5. What was the purpose of the Proletarian Cultural Revolution?
6. Discuss the functions of the People's Bank of China.
7. The state budget is an important control mechanism in the Chinese economic system. Discuss.
8. In what ways is the Chinese agricultural system similar to that of the Russians? In what ways is it different?
9. What are the differences between material incentives and nonmaterial incentives?
10. Evaluate the performance of the Chinese economy in terms of living standards and economic growth.

RECOMMENDED READINGS

Barnett, Doak A. *China's Economy in a Global Perspective.* Washington: Brookings Institution, 1981.

Bernstein, Richard. *From the Center of the Earth: The Search for the Truth About China.* Boston: Little, Brown, 1982.

Butterfield, Fox. *China: Alive in the Bitter Sea.* New York: Times Books, 1982.

"China's Creeping Capitalism." *Fortune,* December 12, 1981, pp. 91–98.

Copper, John F. *China's Global Role.* Stanford, Calif.: Hoover Institution Press, Stanford University, 1980.

DePauw, John W. *U.S.–Chinese Trade Negotiations.* New York: Praeger, 1980.

Dernberger, Robert F., ed. *China's Development Experience in Comparative Perspective.* Cambridge: Harvard University Press, 1980.

Dreyer, June T. "Limits of the Permissible in China." *Problems of Communism,* Vol. XXIX (November–December 1980), pp. 48–65.

Eckstein, Alexander, ed. *Quantitative Measures of China's Economic Output.* Ann Arbor: University of Michigan Press, 1980.

Myers, Ramon H. *The Chinese Economy, Past and Present.* Belmont, Calif.: Wadsworth, 1980.

Parish, William L. "Egalitarianism in Chinese Society." *Problems of Communism,* Vol. XXX (January–February 1981), pp. 22–36.

Rawski, Thomas G. *China's Transition to Industrialism.* Ann Arbor: University of Michigan Press, 1980.

U.S. Joint Economic Committee, *Allocation of Resources in the Soviet Union and China, 1981.* 96th Congress, 2nd Session, 1981.

16

Yugoslavia

INTRODUCTION

The Federal Republic of Yugoslavia represents a rather distinct brand of communism which is different from that prevailing in the rest of Eastern Europe and the Soviet Union. The economy has been called a synthesis of state economic planning and a market economy. It contains many features of a market economy, including the decentralization of management, the provision of credit for small-scale private enterprises, the formation of advertising associations to promote the distribution of products, and the use of personal incentives to accomplish desired economic objectives. There is also a constitutional guarantee of private peasant landholdings of up to 25 acres of arable land. There is a decentralization of economic decision making and a virtually complete autonomy of individual producing units, which indicates that the term *decentralized socialism* describes the goal of Yugoslavia.

Economic planning is far less imperative than it is in other communist countries. The national five-year plan contains general sectoral targets which are not binding on enterprises. The plan is designed to guide each enterprise in the formulation of business decisions. Indirect policy instruments, such as taxation and bank credit, are used to implement the plan's objectives. The banking system, for example, can influence compliance with its targets by allocation of investment funds for capital formation.

Yugoslavia was formed in 1918 out of the countries of Serbia and

Montenegro. With the dissolution of the Austro-Hungarian Empire, it included five Slavic groups—Serbians, Croats, Slovenes, Macedonians, and Bosnians—as well as Hungarians and Albanians. A centralized monarchy was created with the support of the dominant Serbian elements in the population and against the wishes of the Croats, who wanted a federal system of government that granted a certain amount of regional and ethnic autonomy. Antagonism between the Serbs and Croats characterized the internal history of Yugoslavia between the two world wars. Although considerable autonomy was given to the Croats by the time of World War II, rivalries existed between Serbs and Croats which even today the present government finds difficult to sublimate.

During World War II, Yugoslavia was occupied by the Germans. Resistance forces were split into two groups—the Chetniks, representing the exiled government of King Peter, and the Partisans, who were led by Tito and the Communist party.[1] The Partisans emerged as the stronger of the two groups and received the bulk of Allied military support. Those forces that had identified with Tito formed an independent base for the establishment of a communist regime at Belgrade at the end of the war. Since the liberation of Yugoslavia owed nothing to the Russian army but much to Tito and his supporters, there was no reason to be grateful or subservient to Moscow. For this reason, Tito could assert the independence of his regime from Russian domination. In 1948 Yugoslavia was expelled from the Soviet-dominated Cominform for pursuing policies independently of Moscow's influence in both domestic and foreign affairs.

After the split with Moscow, Yugoslavia effected a rapprochement with the Western countries based on trade and aid and the desire to secure an alliance in the event of Russian aggression. However, in terms of foreign policy, it has pursued an independent line between East and West and has attempted to project itself as the leader of nonaligned nations, eschewing proximity to neither the Eastern nor Western military bloc. Although relations with the Russians have improved since the hardline Stalinist days, Yugoslavia's economic ties are essentially with the West, and there is participation in such Western economic organizations as the Organization for Economic Cooperation and Development and the European Economic Community.

The latest of several Constitutions was drafted in 1974. It retained the features of a federal system, with six republics and two autonomous regions. A problem confronting the drafters of the Constitution was how to reconcile the national differences and desire for autonomy on the part

---

[1]The *Chetniks* were Serbian nationalists who desired an independent Serbia. The *Partisans* were primarily Croats and were led by Josip Broz (Tito), a Croat and also a Communist. Although Communists controlled at the top, considerable support was obtained from persons and groups of differing political opinions, who believed in Tito's call for national unity.

of the Croatian and Serbian republics. Another problem in drafting the Constitution was the replacement of Tito when he died. In 1971 a collective presidency was established as an amendment to the 1963 constitution. The collective presidency consisted of 23 members, including three from each republic, two from each autonomous region, and Tito as chairman. In the 1974 constitution the number of members was reduced to nine—one from each republic and autonomous region and Tito. In the event of Tito's death or retirement, it was intended that these representatives would take turns in acting as chairman of the collective presidency. There has been a conflict between those persons who want more centralized control and those who want further decentralization.

Administratively, Yugoslavia has a president and legislative and judicial units. The Federal Assembly is the supreme organ of authority. It decides on changes in the Constitution, passes the federal laws, adopts the economic plans, and approves the federal budget. It also determines foreign policy and elects the president. There is also a Federal Executive Council which is responsible for the implementation of economic policy decided upon by the Federal Assembly.

There are the six republics and two autonomous regions. Each has a president, republic assemblies, and numerous specialized administrative agencies. Greater authority has been given to republics, as the federal government has sought to decentralize decision making and to encourage wider popular participation in economic affairs.

The commune (which has nothing in common with the Chinese institution of the same name) is a local government unit which forms the basic self-governing entity in Yugoslavia. It would roughly correspond to a small city or county in the United States, and has three basic responsibilities: guiding economic affairs, including planning, investment, and supervision of enterprises; providing municipal services; and managing various social welfare activities.

Yugoslavia is a communist country, and the Communist Party (League of Communists of Yugoslavia, LCY) is the only political party. It should be emphasized that despite the institutional arrangement of the Yugoslav economic and political system, the LCY is the final authority over and above all other decision makers, and what it gives it can also take away. It participates directly in the institutions of the state and of self-management, all the way down to the lowest level of enterprise organization. In these respects the LCY is no different from Communist Parties in the Soviet Union and the People's Republic of China.

THE ECONOMIC SYSTEM

Yugoslavia possesses a unique, complex economic system, which combines elements of both a centrally planned and free market economy.

One unique feature of the Yugoslav economy is the workers' council, which is elected by all workers in each enterprise. The workers' council has extensive management powers concerning the operation of an enterprise. It approves the production plan, the hiring and firing of workers, the distribution of income to workers, and the annual financial statement. It also has control over the diversion of production and the use of investment funds from outside sources. The workers' council functions through a management board, which it elects from its members to perform the necessary decisions involving the day-to-day operations of an enterprise.

Another unique characteristic of the Yugoslav economic system is a reliance on decentralization of economic decision making and a dependence on the free market to accomplish the allocation of resources. Autonomy has been given to enterprises with regard to price and production policies and to the distribution of their incomes between wages and investment. Enterprises are legally independent in that their property is not owned by the government, but the property is held in trust by the enterprises for society as a whole. Within the limits dictated by national and international competition, they are free to set prices, to decide what and how much to produce, and to distribute income from sales from their products.

Economic Reforms

Economic reform in Yugoslavia has been developed beyond the direct influence of Soviet military power, and the country has been able to move farther and farther away from the Soviet model of economic and political development. The purpose of the Yugoslav economic reforms has been the development of a decentralized economic system, in part for political reasons and in part to promote economic efficiency. The reforms have reflected a need on the part of the government to press for changes in resource allocation and administration in order to promote economic performance, while recognizing the interests of various nationalist groups within the country.

Minor economic reforms were initiated following Yugoslavia's expulsion from the Cominform in 1948. A major reform was carried out in 1952 when detailed annual plans were discontinued, substantial independence was granted to state enterprises, a greater role was assigned to the price mechanism, and a decollectivization of land was permitted. In 1953 the attempt to collectivize agriculture was abandoned. Further reforms were implemented in 1954 when centrally imposed output goals for enterprises were eliminated.

Steps to decentralize the economy and establish the socialist market system were intensified in the 1960s as economic problems, quantitatively expressed by an erratic growth rate and decreasing factor efficiency, developed. Moreover, given the fact that Yugoslavia had limited domestic markets and resources, foreign trade became an indispensible avenue for promoting technological progress. However, dependence on imports of raw materials and machinery created large deficits in the balance of payments. Given recurring crises in the economy, the government constantly had to intervene in the economy.

1965 Reform. The economic reforms of 1965 accelerated the decentralization of economic management. Administrative elements of control were greatly reduced and transformed in terms of content and in terms of methods of intervention. It was felt that greater autonomy on the part of state enterprises would improve efficiency. There were two basic objectives of the reforms: improvement of the productivity of capital and labor, and a more balanced rate of economic growth. The reforms ushered in a phase in Yugoslavia's economic development referred to as *market socialism*. The price system was reformed with the objective of eventually allowing the free determination of prices by market forces. Prices of goods and services were raised to bring them into harmony with those that prevailed in the international markets and also to use them as instruments of development policy.[2]

A major reform involved the decentralization of the fiscal system. Several national taxes were eliminated. Major elements of public finance were transferred from the national government to the republics, districts, and communes. Responsibility for resource allocation was transferred from the state to economic enterprises and banks. Banks were organized into three broad areas of specialization—investment banking, commerical banking, and mixed banks. (The areas of specialization were changed again in 1977.) Banks were freed from direct government control, and their existence came to depend upon funds provided by enterprises.[3]

Reforms of the 1970s. The 1965 reforms had some adverse effects on the economy. Under decentralization of state control, some of the state's effective policy instruments were dismantled—notably those for fiscal policy, resource allocation, and the compulsive coordination and implementation of plans. Policy making was regionalized, but there was no attempt to introduce alternative mechanisms for coordinating diverse economic objectives. In the opinion of many political and economic leaders, the market system failed to live up to anticipations: growth over the 1965–1970 period was disappointing, and inefficiencies in the use of capital and labor remained. In addition, there was an increase in the rate of

---

[2]Martin Schrenk, Cyrus Ardalan, and Nawal El Tatawy, *Yugoslavia: Self-Management Socialism, and the Challenge of Development* (Baltimore: Johns Hopkins University Press, 1979), pp. 26–28.
[3]*Ibid.*

inflation and a perceived concentration of power in the hands of the financial institutions, a managerial elite, and wholesale, retail, and foreign trade enterprises.[4]

New institutional reforms were introduced in the 1970s. Small self-management units each called a Basic Organization of Associated Labor (BOAL) were created within existing enterprises. The BOAL is the locus of all economic decision making and is an autonomous legal entity having its own income statement and balance sheet.[5] Within an enterprise, the BOAL is the smallest technological entity producing a marketable product. By law, a BOAL can be established for any group of workers whose work results can be evaluated independently of the results of other workers. The rules of enterprise behavior are set down by bargaining among BOALs, each of which has its own workers council, its own assets, and its own income which it distributes as it sees fit. The 1965 reforms emphasized the autonomy of enterprises by shifting decision-making power from state organs to enterprise management; the creation of BOALs carried decentralization one step further by making them the principal decision-making unit. They are building blocks of all other economic units.[6]

Yugoslavia's fourth Constitution was instituted in 1974. It was designed to provide a firm legal basis for self-management.[7] The area of self-management was extended to the social services, with the idea of encouraging more independent activity by citizens, not only as producers, but also as consumers. Social compacts and self-management agreements became basic instruments of economic management. *Social compacts* are agreements concluded between any political or economic unit concerning planning, pricing, income distribution, international trade, and employment. They are used in lieu of state laws to regulate economic activity in these areas. *Self-management agreements* are contracts that cover almost all transactions within and between enterprises. The Constitution also made important concessions to regional government units by setting limits on the power and authority of the national government.[8]

Economic Planning

Yugoslavia has moved from a centralized planning procedure that copied that of the Russians to a decentralized form of planning. This

[4]Laura D'Andrea Tyson and Gabriel Eichler, "Continuity and Change in the Yugoslav Economy in the 1970's and 1980's," in *East European Economic Assessment*, Part 1, Joint Economic Committee, 97th Congress, 1st Session, 1981, pp. 141–43.

[5]Duncan Wilson, *Tito's Yugoslavia* (Cambridge: Cambridge University Press, 1979), p. 216.

[6]*Ibid.*, p. 217.

[7]Steven L. Burg, "Decision-Making in Yugoslavia," *Problems of Communism*, Vol. 29 (March–April 1980), p. 14.

[8]*Ibid.*, p. 15.

process of decentralization was developed at the time of the political split with Russia and has continued to the present. Whereas the early economic plans gave definite instructions to each Yugoslav enterprise pertaining to the methods and scope of production and distribution, the relationship between the most current economic plan and the enterprises and other units is totally different. The plan contains a statement of economic and political objectives and a definition of the basic economic changes to be accomplished. It provides for certain measures designed to control the distribution of enterprises and cooperatives. With the plan framework, the federal government uses methods which rely on the individual interests of the workers and the enterprises to produce in terms of the desired social product and national income. The federal government does not make detailed decisions concerning production, but leaves them to the various production units to make. The economic plan serves as a guide for the production and distribution decisions of enterprises.[9]

Current economic planning in Yugoslavia is the result of a process of decentralization which has been going on for 30 years. During the First Five-Year Plan (1947–1951), the Yugoslav economic system was based on completely centralized management by the state and on government planning as the basic method for the allocation of goods and services. At that time the dominant theme was the liquidation of the market system and its replacement by a system of economic planning.[10] Subsequent economic plans shifted from a centralized command procedural arrangement to a more decentralized form of planning which came to resemble French economic planning more than Russian economic planning. The system of fixed production quotas and prices was abandoned, and a devolution of planning controls occurred. Enterprises were given more latitude in price setting and in the distribution of income. However, during the 1970s the need for more conscious direction of the economy became essential and more state direction developed.

The Five-Year Social Plan (1976–1980). Under the Five-Year Social Plan of 1980, enterprises had to coordinate their programs horizontally at the republic and autonomous province level and to reconcile them vertically with other independent enterprises at regional levels. Implementation of the plan is reviewed by *Communities of Interest* formed in major industrial sectors. These consist of representatives of enterprises and citizens represented in their capacity as consumers. The Communities of Interest regulate all matters concerning short-term and long-term supply and demand. They thus transcend both the market mechanism and the state as

---

[9]There are annual and middle-term (five-year) plans, and also a ten-year plan. The fundamental elements of the policy of Yugoslav development are expressed in the five-year plans.

[10]Albert Waterston, *Planning in Yugoslavia* (Baltimore: Johns Hopkins Press, 1962).

regulators.[11] The self-management agreements and social contracts, which contain information about major investment projects, physical output, and financing, form the operational part of the plan. The agreements and contracts are legally binding unless renegotiated.

The Yugoslav Five-Year Plan for 1976–1980 emphasized economic growth through the increase of labor force, the return of migrant workers from West Germany, and the development of those sectors which could make the country more independent of imports.[12] Also emphasized was a reduction in income disparities between regions. To reduce problems associated with unemployment, the plan encouraged the development of labor-intensive and small-scale industries. The plan placed emphasis on transferring resources (both financial and managerial) from the more developed regions to the less developed regions. The plan identified priority sectors that were to receive special encouragement during the plan period and have first claims on investment resources—coal, transport, shipbuilding, basic chemicals, production of nonmetallic minerals, and electrical power generation and transmission.[13] There was a shift in emphasis from sectors producing consumer goods to those producing intermediate and capital goods.

A Ten-Year Plan (1976–1985) was also created. It had long-term objectives that were to be considered in the annual and five-year plans. It addressed itself to six fundamental problems that need to be resolved. The problems and goals are as follows:[14]

1. The stabilization of the economy to avoid inflation, unemployment, and continued wide variation in the level of economic activity.
2. The reduction of income disparities between regions.
3. Improvement of external economic relations which have been marked by large and increasing deficits in the balance of payments.
4. Mobilization of resources to correct fluctuations in their distribution between final demand (personal and government consumption) and investment and savings.
5. A more efficient allocation of resources between sectors of the economy. One purpose is to reduce inefficiencies in production characterized by low growth of labor productivity, insufficient modernization of facilities, unsatisfactory capacity use in some sectors, and a lack of coordination in the expansion of facilities.
6. There is a need to generate employment in excess of the natural increase

---

[11] A Community of Interest is organized on the smallest regional scale possible. It is an institution unique to Yugoslavia. To some extent it is participatory democracy at the local level.

[12] The development of priority projects required the increase of imports beyond the country's ability to pay, while exports remained below targets.

[13] Schrenk, Ardalan, and El Tatawy, *Yugoslavia: Self-Management Socialism*, pp. 89–91.

[14] *Ibid.*, pp. 86–87.

in the labor force and also provide domestic employment for workers who had jobs in other countries.[15]

The Five-Year Social Plan, 1981–1985. The current five-year plan is characterized by lowered expectations in terms of growth and industrial development. Two major objectives of the plan are to reduce inflation and a chronic deficit in the balance of payments. Target goals, which are presented in Table 16-1, were reduced in comparison to the 1976–1980 plan, which did not live up to its objectives. As the table indicates, priority is given to an increase in exports in order to reduce balance-of-payments deficits. Fixed investment in low-priority areas is to be reduced.

TABLE 16-1
PLANNED ANNUAL GROWTH RATES
IN THE YUGOSLAV FIVE-YEAR PLAN, 1981–1985

Areas	Growth Rate
Social product	4.5%
Industrial production	5.0
Agricultural output	4.5
Employment	2.5
Labor productivity	2.0
Standard of living	7.0
Exports of goods and services	8.0
Imports of goods and services	1.1
Investments in economically productive projects	1.1
Investments in noneconomically productive projects	0.1

Source: The Economist Intelligence Unit, *Yugoslavia: Annual Supplement, 1981* (London, 1982), p. 6.

Formulation and Implementation of Yugoslav Plans. There are actually three sets of plans in Yugoslavia—national, republic, and commune plans. The Yugoslav national plan lays down the basic guidelines, targets, and aims of economic policy. Within the guidelines and objectives determined by the national plan and plans of the republics and communes, Yugoslav enterprises and other economic organizations are free to formulate their own production plans. This is in keeping with the decentralization policies of the government and reflects the view in Yugoslavia that it is necessary to turn more and more authority in the sphere of economics from the government to the enterprises and communes. It also reflects the view that the workers, rather than the state, must decide on the allocation and use of the goods which they produce. This is done, as will

---

[15]*Ibid.*, p. 88.

be discussed later in the chapter, through the election of workers' councils who have vested control over the operations of all enterprises. Worker self-management fits in with the process of decentralized planning.

The national plan is prepared by the Federal Planning Institute and is approved by the Federal Assembly. The Federal Planning Institute consists of a number of technical divisions, each of which is responsible for the preparation of a certain part of the plan. These divisions include agriculture; forestry; transportation and communication; regional development; personal consumption and social welfare; investment; domestic trade and tourism; industry, power, and mining; and social product and national income.

The republic plans set for the republics the same objectives embodied in the national plan, allowing for special features of the republic economies. Republic plans refer only to segments of the economy, and do not involve such subjects as foreign trade or balance of payments. The republics are free to set goals that go beyond the scope of the federal plan and are under no legal obligations to harmonize their plans with the federal plan. However, as the commune has emerged as the basic unit of government, republic plans have come to play a more limited role.

After the republic plans are completed, the communes prepare plans. The plans of the communes are more comprehensive and detailed than the republic plans and are prepared after consultations with various workers' organizations. They encompass such activities as planned tax policies and social welfare services. The communes, as well as the federal government, can influence compliance with planning objectives through control over policy instruments in the fields of credit, finance, and taxation. Neither the republic nor the commune plans must harmonize in detail with the national plan; nevertheless, these lower administrative units have to consider the overall frame of reference which is provided by the national plan.

The plans of the communes are worked out by the communal assemblies. Special committees within the assemblies are responsible for preparing the commune plans, and these committees work in conjunction with local enterprises and other organizations in developing recommendations. Public discussions are also held, and a preliminary draft is developed.

Public Finance

During the first part of the post–World War II period the state was preeminent in all economic activities. All phases—production distribution, exchange, and consumption—were included in government planning. Of all instruments of control available to the state during this period, the general state budget was the most important. It was composed of the federal budget, the budgets of the national republics, and local budgets. The general state budget was, for all practical purposes, one unitary fund, established by one authority, the national government. The general state budget served as the main distribution of investment funds. Its main sources of revenue were the sales tax, a form of profits tax from the socialist sector, and an income tax collected from the private sector.

The 1965 economic reforms had their effect on the public finance system of Yugoslavia. The first important change took place in 1964, when the investment funds were abolished and their resources were transferred to corresponding banks for investment, agriculture, and foreign trade, which at the same time took over the responsibility for the success of investment projects already begun. The basic goal of the 1965 tax reforms was to modify the scale and structure of taxation on Yugoslav enterprises in order to provide them with more financial resources. The process of decentralizing economic decision making and establishing a market mechanism system, which was the nexus of the 1965 reforms, carried over into taxation and expenditures of the national government. The producer's turnover tax, the business net profits tax, and the general turnover tax, all of which were major national taxes, were eliminated.

Government Revenues. Currently government units in Yugoslavia rely on several types of taxes as revenue sources. The sales tax is an important source of revenue for the operating budget of the federal government. A general tax rate of 14 percent is normally charged at the time of purchase on all items bought at the retail level. Special taxes on luxury goods can range up to 100 percent of the purchase price, while some essential goods are not subject to taxation. Communes and republics also levy sales taxes. The sales tax imposed by both types of administrative units is confined to retail trade, is uniform within each territorial district, and has the maximum limit prescribed by federal regulation.

There are also fixed capital and income taxes. The *fixed capital tax* is levied on the fixed assets and buildings owned by an enterprise. The federal government is the sole recipient of revenue from this tax source and uses the revenue to finance economic development in the less developed areas of the country and to finance infrastructure investments that benefit the nation as a whole. *Income taxes* are levied by the federal government and shared with the communes and republics. The range of tax rates vary, with the average Yugoslav worker paying a rate of 12 percent and private enterprises paying as high as 35 percent.[16] Foreign firms, which are allowed to conclude joint ventures with Yugoslav enter-

---

[16]Private enterprise is permitted in Yugoslavia. Business owners are allowed to employ up to five workers. Private enterprise is important in the service areas—restaurants, dry cleaning, and hotels. There are also craftsmen.

prises, are also subject to a 35 percent federal income tax. The rate is reduced to 10 percent if the money is reinvested in Yugoslavia.

Government Expenditures. A characteristic of the Yugoslav budgetary system is that it is decentralized. Jurisdiction has been transferred from higher to lower administrative units, and the growth of the budgets of the communes has been increased. All sociopolitical units, with the exception of the autonomous provinces and districts, are independent in determining their revenues from taxes and contributions and determining the rates. Outside of the budget system is a payment of interest by all Yugoslav enterprises on their business funds.

Social welfare expenditures are also excluded from budgetary accounts and are collected and distributed by the communes and districts. Yugoslav workers have to pay various social security taxes, which average about 25 percent of their gross income. The social security system itself includes old-age and survivors pensions, sickness and maternity benefits, unemployment compensation, work injury and disability benefits, and family allowances. All wage and salary earners are eligible for full coverage under the social security system, while limited benefits are available to the remainder of the population. Although private farmers, craftsmen, and shopkeepers are eligible for health and old-age benefits, they are not eligible for family allowances.

The Banking System

Banking laws passed in 1976 and 1977 applied the provisions of the 1974 Constitution to the banking system. The current system includes the National Bank, which is responsible for general central banking operations, regular banks, and specialized banks. Regular and specialized banks are not intended to function as profit-making institutions, nor are they instruments of the state. Accordingly, banks may be funded by enterprises, self-management Communities of Interest, and other legal entities, but not by local governments or government agencies. Each organization or member associated with a bank has a delegate in the bank's assembly. Management of the bank is entrusted to the bank assembly. Apart from participating in the bank management, the members also have the right to share in any profits of the bank. The members also jointly carry the liability for all bank obligations.

The National Bank of Yugoslavia (Narodna Bank Jugoslavije). The National Bank is the central bank of Yugoslavia. It has branches in the republics and autonomous provinces, and governors of these banks constitute the Board of Governors of the National Bank. In addition to issuance of bank notes as legal tender, it is also responsible for the monetary policy of Yugoslavia. The National Bank is authorized to regulate the money supply by using minimum reserve ratios and by conducting open market operations in treasury and commerical bills. It utilizes instruments of qualitative credit control, such as rediscounting, to exert a selective influence on the structure of short-term investments by basic and associated banks. However, it cannot extend long-term loans, except to the national government to finance budget deficits, or to guarantee foreign loans.

Regular Banks. There are three kinds of regular banks: internal, basic, and associated. *Internal banks* are established by groups of enterprises for their own use and do not serve the general public. They can perform all banking transactions for their members. Since they do not deal with the general public, they do not create money and are not subject to monetary regulation. Their main function is to facilitate pooling of resources among the member enterprises. *Basic banks* are conventional commerical banks which can be created by enterprises, Communities of Interest, and other social legal entities. They are all-purpose banks largely carrying over the activities of the former commercial banks which were replaced by the new banks laws.[17]

Associated banks are formed by basic banks for tasks which exceed their own possibilities and are authorized to engage in foreign exchange operations. They specialize in foreign trade investment in particular sectors such as manufacturing or mining. Interest rates on loans extended by the associated banks are determined by self-management agreements with the borrowers, while interest rates on deposits are determined by interbank agreements. Each republic and autonomous region also has its own associated bank.[18]

Specialized Banks. In addition to the main banking system, there are three specialized financial institutions. The Yugoslav Foreign Trade Bank (Jugobanka) is responsible for the holding of foreign exchange and the provision of long- and short-term foreign exchange credits. The United Agricultural Bank (Jugoslovenska Poljoprivredna Banka) is responsible for extending long-term agricultural loans. The Yugoslav Bank for International Economic Cooperation is authorized to finance exports of capital goods as well as the construction of overseas products, to provide export insurance against noncommerical risks, and to promote cooperation between Yugoslav and foreign firms in third markets. The bank's operations are financed by other banks and enterprises, but not by the federal government.[19]

The Role of Interest. Under a capitalistic system, when quantities of

---

[17]Schrenk, Ardalan, and El Tatawy, *Yugoslavia: Self-Management Socialism,* pp. 140–41.
[18]*Ibid.*
[19]Unclassified data provided by the U.S. Embassy in Belgrade, Yugoslavia, April 1982.

capital funds are available for investment, the question of how they should be allocated is determined by the amounts of interest which firms in various fields of production are willing to pay for their use. The rate of interest will be determined in the market by the forces of supply and demand, and the rate plays the role of an allocator of resources. The underlying assumption is that if an economic entity is willing to pay more for the use of capital resources, the productivity of that entity is expected to be higher.

In Yugoslavia interest is also used as a device to allocate investment funds. Enterprises have to pay interest on borrowed funds and on their fixed and turnover capital. Since almost all of real capital is owned by society and since enterprises are entrusted with the use of this real capital, it is to the benefit of society to accomplish full and efficient utilization of these resources. This is ensured by charging interest for the use of fixed and working capital, the idea being that those who have no use for the capital will hesitate to hold it if theyhave to pay a certain price for its use. By granting loans to those who are willing to pay the highest rate for the privilege, the rate of interest plays the role of an allocator of financial resources. This rate of interest is not only applicable at the enterprise level, but also at the personal level, that is, the interest rate payable on consumer credit and on personal savings.

Agriculture

Agriculture in Yugoslavia (and Poland) departs from the typical pattern found in the Soviet Union and its Eastern European satellites. The ownership and management of farms in Yugoslavia continues overwhelmingly in private hands, organized in many small family farm units. State farms and collective farms, which are the dominant forms of agricultural production in the Soviet Union, control only about 16 percent of the productive farm land in Yugoslavia.[20] The Yugoslav government has actively supported private farming by providing a number of incentives to stimulate the expansion of farm output:

1. Increasing prices paid by government to farmers for their products
2. Expanding agricultural loans to private farmers on favorable terms
3. Increasing imports of animal feed and protein meal, sold to private farmers to enhance output of meat and dairy products
4. Greatly expanding the use of fertilizers by private farmers
5. Encouraging specialization and interfarm cooperation in the use of machinery
6. Abstaining from further forced collectivization of agriculture[21]

---

[20]Gregor Lazarcik, "Comparative Growth, Structure, and Levels of Agricultural Output, Inputs, and Productivity in Eastern Europe, 1965–1979," in *East European Economic Assessment, Part 2,* pp. 587–628.

[21]*Ibid.,* p. 590.

There are also state farms in Yugoslavia where the emphasis is placed on the large-scale production of grains and potatoes. Both state-supported and private agricultural sectors can be regarded as largely complementary: the state sector produces the bulk of industrial crops and grains, while the private sector produces most of the vegetables, fruits, and meat products that supply the population with food. The private sector is important during the current plan period because of the continuing emphasis on livestock breeding to achieve both domestic diet and export goals. According to the plan, national diets are to shift away from cereals toward higher-quality foodstuffs, especially meat. In the state sector, which accounts for around 25 percent of real agricultural social product, more intensive efforts are to be placed on the production of grain.

Land on the collective farms is state owned and is worked by the farmers in common. The produce is distributed according to the contribution of each member. In terms of its functions and operations it is similar to the Russian collective farm. The government encourages cooperation between the collective farms and private farmers; in some instances, private farms are worked by a collective farm on a sharecrop or cash basis. In this way farmers may retain possession of their land and benefit from the use of agricultural machinery, fertilizer, and farming techniques which are provided by the collective farm.

There are also general agricultural cooperatives which are jointly managed by the farmers and their own employees. The land is owned by the cooperatives and is farmed by private farmers who are paid in cash. The cooperatives provide the machines, implements, seed, and fertilizer. The cooperatives are also responsible for the marketing and sale of farm produce. The private farmers neither subscribe to business shares in a cooperative nor are they liable for its debts. Cooperatives and individual farmers may produce jointly, with profits shared in proportion to the contribution made by each partner, or the cooperatives may be responsible only for participation in the production process—furnishing services and equipment—and, in return, receive a fixed share of the profits of the farmers. In most cases, the cooperatives and the private farmers conclude, in advance, contracts on production and the purchase of farm produce at fixed prices or at prices found on the market at the date of delivery.

The Yugoslav agricultural sector is caught in a bind because productivity is lower than it would be with larger-scale operations. Ideology and inheritance customs in the country have caused private farm holdings to be too small to effect economies of scale. Private farms are limited by law to 10 hectares (24 acres), but most private farms are smaller. Farmers have subdivided their farmland between their heirs, constricting the size of private farm holdings. Also, private enterprise, including private farms, is constrained by rules limiting the number of hired workers they may employ. Attempts by the state to encourage the movement of farmers from their private holdings into labor-managed collective farms have failed. The difference in ownership rights evidently has discouraged many farmers from leaving their own farms, no matter how small they are.

The Yugoslav Enterprise

The Yugoslav enterprise is the basic economic unit and may be started or expanded in several ways:

1. It may be formed by any governmental unit—commune, republic, or the national government.
2. It may be formed by individuals who have pooled their assets. However, at least five persons must be involved.
3. It may be formed by the division of an existing enterprise, or by the merger of two or more enterprises.

When the enterprise starts operation, it acquires an independent status even though its sponsors have committed considerable resources to its formation. Its assets become social property and the people which it employs have the right to self-government and to participate in the income of the enterprise on the basis of work done. It may merge with another enterprise provided that a majority of workers in both enterprises approve the merger. As a matter of economic policy, mergers have been encouraged in order to improve productivity and make Yugoslav firms more competitive in the international markets.

Yugoslav enterprises possess certain similarities to their American counterparts. Profit is the basic criterion of success for enterprises in each country, and each enterprise is independent in the pursuit of its business and development policies. Each can determine the volume and assortment of production according to its assessment of the market and each can determine its pricing policies. Although economic planning exists in Yugoslavia, the government does not direct that specified quantities of products have to be provided by each enterprise, but instead relies on more indirect controls, including a reliance on pecuniary measures, to encourage compliance with national economic objectives.

Management of an Enterprise. A law concerning economic organizations was passed in 1950 which stated that the management of all enterprises would be given to their workers. That is, all factories, mines, and other enterprises which had been under state ownership since the coming to power of the Communist Party in Yugoslavia were turned over to the workers of these enterprises to manage. The ownership passed from the state to society in general. Enterprises were defined, not as state property, but as social property, and workers were given the right to manage them, but not to own them. The key instrument through which this management would be accomplished was the workers' council, which in essence became the trustee of social wealth and the provider of self-management for an enterprise. Through the system of workers' councils, the workers, in principle, exercise ultimate control over economic policy, including the formulation of economic plans.

Workers' Councils. Workers' councils are comprised of delegates elected by secret ballot from within the work organization and from a list of candidates prepared by unions.[22] The authority of workers' councils is substantial. Within the limits set by the government, they have the right to decide what to produce and in what quantity, and they are also responsible for the setting of prices, the determination of wages, and the distribution of profits. The last responsibility is one of their most important functions. They distribute enterprise profits in the form of wage bonuses to the various investment and social welfare funds of the enterprises. They also choose a management committee, which is their executive organ. The management committee is responsible for the development of the production plans of the enterprise, the appointment of workers to important administrative positions, the specification of wage and production norms, and the development of methods designed to increase productivity.[23]

Basic Organization of Associated Labor (BOAL). Workers' councils are elected in each technologically identifiable unit which produces an article or renders a service of marketable value. This unit, as mentioned previously, is called a Basic Organization of Associated Labor (BOAL). Most enterprises are constituted by several BOALs. For example, an integrated textile mill could be divided into a BOAL each for spinning, weaving, finishing, final processing, and retail outlets. Each BOAL is a self-management unit within the enterprise and represents workers linked by a common working interest. BOALs associated with an enterprise share risks, gains, and losses. To be valid, the plan of each enterprise must be accepted by all constituent BOALs. Profit to be distributed is computed for each BOAL on the basis of internal prices determined by self-management agreements between BOALs, by the business success of the whole enterprise, and by the contribution of each BOAL.

Enterprise Managers. Administration and management of the enterprise is the responsibility of the manager (or management board), who is appointed by the workers' council and the people's committee of the local commune. Management positions must be publically advertised, and the manager (or management board) is appointed on the basis of a competitive examination. Friction between the workers' council and the

---

[22]The Communist Party is heavily represented on each workers' council.

[23]John H. Moore, "Self-Management in Yugoslavia," in *East European Economic Assessment, Part 1*, p. 217.

management often arises over the distribution of profits, with the workers' council tending to favor higher wages out of profits, while the manager or board strives for increased investment. Management is responsible for carrying out the decisions of the workers' council and for handling the day-to-day affairs of the enterprise according to its plan and business policy. Management is subject to recall at any time by either the workers' council or the assembly of the local commune. It is excluded from personnel relations in that it does not have the right to hire or fire workers, take disciplinary action, or determine the internal distribution of income.

Control of Enterprises. The Yugoslav enterprise operates within a different institutional framework than its American counterpart and is subject to more constraints. For example, the enterprise must coordinate its plan of production with the general development policies of the commune, republic, and federal government.

Economic Chamber. The enterprise is required to join a semigovernmental organization that enters into some phases of its business affairs. This institution is called the Economic Chamber and is set up at the federal, republic, and commune levels. The major administrative tasks with which the chamber is charged are the allocation of foreign exchange quotas and the supervision of producer–consumer agreements for price increases. Another of its functions is to bring continuously to the attention of the managers of enterprises the current economic goals which have been established by the various levels of government.

Relationship to the Commune. There is also an important relationship between the commune and the enterprise. The commune can provide financial support for an enterprise, and it can supervise the distribution of profits and audit the accounts of the enterprise. Through the people's committee, the communes can regulate various activities of an enterprise. As mentioned previously, the people's committee participates with the workers' council in the hiring and dismissal of the director. It can also participate in the setting of wages. The commune has some control over the provision of credit by the banking system to an enterprise in that it can underwrite or guarantee loans. The commune also has the responsibility for coordinating the production plans of all enterprises under its jurisdiction with its own plan. Although compliance on the part of an enterprise is not mandatory, continued failures to meet planning objectives can bring about the dissolution of the workers' council by the commune. Mismanagement of an enterprise can also bring about a dissolution of the workers' council by the commune.

Social Compacts. Enterprises are supposed to operate within the framework of *social compacts* which regulate rights and obligations affecting broad economic issues and policies. The social compact is designed to substitute for the direct coordination of economic policy by government agencies.[24] It has been accorded an important role in the planning process in that plans are now required to be drawn up by enterprises and government agencies, with mutual consultation on the part of everyone involved. The new planning process begins with an obligatory exchange of information by all enterprises and government agencies on their prospective plans based on a list of plan indicators. All parties then seek to realize a set of mutually consistent and acceptable plans. Social compacts can regulate such things as policies for prices and employment and the distribution of income between personal incomes and capital accumulation. They can lay down ground rules for self-management agreements. Compacts can be concluded at several different levels: enterprise to enterprise, enterprise to commune, and republic to republic. Once concluded, social compacts have, for practical purposes, the force of law.[25]

The Operation of an Enterprise. The process of decentralizing economic decision making and establishing the market mechanism, which has taken place in Yugoslavia, has an effect on the operations of an enterprise. An enterprise can draw up its own plans for production independent of the national plan, but within limits prescribed by the plan of the commune. The production plan is approved by the workers' council after being put forward by the management committee of the enterprise. Once passed, the plan may be amended by the workers' council. Usually the enterprise is free to make its decisions pertaining to what to purchase and what to sell, and it can establish prices for its products unless they are subject to some form of price control. Distribution is not regulated, and an enterprise can bring out its goods in a comparatively free market which is guided by commerical principles.

The value of goods and services sold constitutes the gross or total income of an enterprise. The deduction of operating costs—excluding labor income, which is treated as a claim on income arising from current output and is not treated as a cost—leaves the net income of the enterprise. Operating costs cover outlays for the purchase of raw materials, depreciation, overhead costs, maintenance of fixed assets, research and development, insurance, interest on fixed and working capital, and payment of membership dues.

The income statement of a Yugoslav enterprise does not show wages as a cost of production; instead, after operating expenses are deducted, the net income is divided between an appropriation for personal income and for reinvestment. The workers have the right to participate in the income of the enterprise on the basis of work done, and the workers' council

[24]Laura D'Andrea Tyson, *The Yugoslav Economic System and Its Performance in the 1970's*, Research Monograph No. 44 (Berkeley: University of California, Institute of International Studies, 1980), pp. 3–12.

[25]*Ibid.*, p. 13.

decides on the amount to be paid out in terms of base pay and supplements. Income is set aside in a wage fund and is shared among the workers in accordance with a wage schedule adopted by the workers' council. To start with, a guaranteed minimum wage is assured all workers, and no worker can be paid less than this amount. Actual earnings, however, exceed the guaranteed minimum by a substantial amount, and the minimum assumes importance only when it cannot be covered out of the earnings of an enterprise. If this situation occurs, then the commune is required to make up the difference between the actual wage and the guaranteed minimum wage.

AN APPRAISAL OF THE YUGOSLAV ECONOMY

Yugoslav communism is unquestionably more liberal and humane than the communism of the Soviet Union and its satellites. The reforms and the general attitude of the government indicate a flexibility and a willingness to experiment that is lacking in other communist countries. In order to honor promises to workers and to stimulate production, the government has decentralized management and has introduced workers' councils in economic enterprises. There are, however, certain problems which confront the Yugoslav economy.

From the beginning of its history, Yugoslavia has been confronted by a seemingly insoluble nationality problem. It is really a confederation of rather diverse ethnic groups which are difficult to weld into a homogeneous unit. Rivalries exist between regions and are exacerbated by the fact that economic development is extremely uneven between regions. The hope that surplus capital would flow more to the less developed regions of the country has not been realized. Neither Croatia nor Slovenia, which are among the most developed and richest republics of Yugoslavia, have shown much interest in investing in the underdeveloped areas of the south. Chauvinistic sentiment must be considered to be a key deterrent to the free flow of capital between regions.

The death of Tito in 1980 could eventually intensify regional rivalries which appear to be an ineradicable feature of the Yugoslav political and economic system. Much of Yugoslavia's success over the last several decades was derived from the unifying force of President Tito's leadership. Tito's charisma helped prevent the country's political disintegration into a number of regional special-interest groups.[26] The problems the current leaders of Yugoslavia have are to prevent a recrudescence of regional nationalism and separatism and to create a viable economy that continues to increase living standards and reduces income disparities between prosperous and less prosperous republics. Antagonisms, ethnic

---

[26]Burg, "Decision-Making in Yugoslavia," p. 16.

differences, and other sources of discord in Yugoslavia are likely to continue in the future because even adherence to communism as a unifying factor has not united the people of Yugoslavia.

Economic Problems

The economic problems of Yugoslavia are similar to those present in capitalist, socialist, and other communist countries in the early 1980s. There is a low rate of economic growth, productivity has declined, and there is a marked variation in the regional rate of development within the country. Import restrictions imposed in 1981 to conserve hard currency resulted in a shortage to consumers of many food products and food prices increased by as much as 40 percent. Agricultural production increased by only 1 percent during 1981, a rate well below the 4 percent annual increase projected in the 1981–1985 plan. The economic growth rate for 1981 was 2.0 percent, and the forecast for 1982 is 2.5 percent.[27] These rates impact more heavily upon the poorer regions of the south than the more wealthy northern republics.

Unemployment. Unemployment has been a problem which has confronted Yugoslavia. The transition from an agricultural to an industrial economy has not been smooth, with the result that many workers migrated to jobs in more advanced industrial countries in Western Europe.[28] However, as economic growth slowed and the rate of unemployment increased in Western Europe, Yugoslav and other foreign workers were the first to be laid off. The phenomenon of foreign employment of Yugoslav workers cut both ways. The emigration eased unemployment problems in Yugoslavia, and hard currency earnings of the workers were remitted home, which had a favorable impact on the Yugoslav balance of payments.[29] However, the social and political attitudes of Yugoslav workers were affected by foreign employment, making them less patient with economic and political conditions at home. The return home of many Yugoslav workers has contributed to an unemployment rate which was 12.2 percent in February 1982.[30]

Inflation. Probably the most important problem confronting the Yugoslav economy is inflation. The period since the reforms of 1965 have been highly inflationary as a result of the gradual lessening of control

---

[27]Data provided by the United States Embassy in Belgrade.

[28]These workers, called *Gastarbeiter* (guest workers) in West Germany, were an important addition to the West German labor force. In the middle 1970s, as many as 500,000 Yugoslavs worked in West Germany.

[29]Hard currency is simply convertible currency. Sending deutsche marks back to Yugoslavia (where they are exchanged for dinar) enables the Yugoslav government to use this currency to buy from West Germany.

[30]Data supplied by the United States Embassy in Belgrade.

over the economy and the move to a freer price structure. During the period 1967–1975, consumer prices increased at an annual average rate of 10 percent in spite of the imposition of wage and price controls and attempts to limit the money supply. In 1978 and 1979 inflation increased at a rate of close to 20 percent. In June 1980 the government announced a price freeze in an effort to reduce inflation, but the measure was largely unsuccessful. In 1981 the rate of inflation, as reflected by the consumer price index, registered an increase of 43 percent, leading to a further price freeze and the reduction of subsidies on food. For the third year in a row, real income of Yugoslav workers showed a decline.[31]

Industrial Growth. It can be said that the Yugoslav economy is one of contrasts. With a mixture of a planned and market economy and a policy of accelerated industrialization, the government has transformed Yugoslavia from an agrarian society to a position just short of the less developed Western European countries. However, there have been variations in the rate of industrial growth. In 1974 the rate of industrial growth was 10.9 percent. It fell to 3.3 percent in 1976, but increased to 9.5 percent in 1977 and 3.7 percent in 1978.[32] By 1980 the rate of industrial growth had decreased to 5.0 percent and 4.2 percent in 1981.[33] Yugoslav industry has suffered chronically from low-capacity utilization, inefficient resource allocation, and a shortage of skilled labor. At times, gains in industrial production have been achieved through an increase in employment rather than through higher productivity. Industrialization has required some sacrifices on the part of consumers. Although productivity has increased, it has not kept pace with consumption demands, and this has caused some discontent.

Comparisons with Other Countries

Comparisons of Yugoslavia with other communist countries in Eastern Europe are difficult to make. For one thing, there are differences in the kind of economic development and resource availability. Moreover, some countries were more adversely affected by World War II than others. East Germany had a pre–World War II industrial base on which to rebuild its economy. Czechoslovakia was also an advanced country, particularly in comparison to Bulgaria and Romania.

There is also an exogenous, namely Soviet, influence on the economic process that affects comparisons of countries. Soviet control and influence over industrialization policies tend to fall more heavily on

---

[31]*Ibid.*

[32]*Statistical Yearbook of Yugoslavia* (Belgrade: Federal Institute of Statistics, 1980), p. 34.

[33]Data supplied by the United States Embassy in Belgrade.

countries that are closer to its sphere of influence. Additionally, comparisons are difficult because a comparatively good performance in one area of the economy may be achieved at the expense of a concurrent or postponed weaker performance in some other area.

Table 16-2 presents a comparison of annual average growth of per capita net material product for Yugoslavia and other Eastern European countries for the period 1965–1979. Net material product excludes service sectors that are included in gross national product. These services are regarded as nonmaterial or nonproductive. The value of material production less depreciation and other costs represents net material product.

TABLE 16-2
PERCENTAGE CHANGES IN NET MATERIAL PRODUCT
FOR YUGOSLAVIA AND OTHER EASTERN EUROPEAN COUNTRIES,
1965–1979

Country	1965–1970	1970–1975	1976	1977	1978	1979
Romania	6.2%	10.1%	10.4%	7.7%	6.4%	5.3%
Poland	5.2	9.0	5.8	4.0	3.2	−2.7
Bulgaria	7.8	7.2	6.0	5.7	5.4	6.4
Hungary	6.4	6.0	2.5	7.5	3.5	1.3
East Germany	5.2	5.7	4.0	5.2	3.9	4.0
Czechoslovakia	6.5	5.0	2.7	3.9	3.4	2.1
Yugoslavia	4.8	4.9	2.9	7.3	5.8	6.0

Source: Paul Marer, "Economic Performance and Prospects in Eastern Europe: Analytical Summary and Interpretation of Findings," in *East European Economic Assessment, Part 2,* p. 36.

SUMMARY

The fundamental feature of the Yugoslav economic system is not state ownership of the means of production, but the self-management by workers and other direct producers of the operation of all economic organizations. The Yugoslav concept of communism is that society is a community of working people who create material wealth through their work. Thus, it is these working people who must decide on the allocation and use of the goods they produce. If working people are the leading social group, then the basic question concerns the construction of an economic system in which the active role of the producers and their associations will be strengthened and the economic and social role of the state will decrease and gradually disappear. According to the Yugoslav concept, the state, with its bureaucratic organization, represents an obstacle to progress, for it encroaches on the rights of workers to distribute income and to participate in the operation of the economy. The state is simply an institution which has replaced private capitalism in the communist countries, but it imposes a new set of constraints upon the working people so that true communism is never achieved.

A Yugoslav enterprise is managed by its workers through a managerial body called the workers' council. Workers' self-government and social management are supposed to encourage initiative and bring about a combination of centralized and decentralized decision making. The workers' council is responsible for the development of the plan and work schedule of an enterprise. It also makes decisions concerning basic matters of business policy and the use of the resources and funds of the enterprise. The workers' council selects a management board, which has the responsibility for enforcing decisions made by the council. Every enterprise also has a managing director who executes the decisions of the workers' council and the management board. The manager is elected by the workers' council on the basis of public competition and is responsible to the council and to the management board for the performance of specific duties.

As for economic planning, the Yugoslav type of plan differs considerably from the centralized command plans of the Soviet Union and other communist countries. Actually, it is closer to the French type of planning in that it does not contain rigid targets for industries to attain. To the contrary, it specifies only general goals for the economy. Republics and communes possess considerable flexibility in the development of their plans.

REVIEW QUESTIONS

1. Compare the role of economic planning in Yugoslavia and the Soviet Union.
2. What is a BOAL?
3. What are the responsibilities of a workers' council?
4. Discuss the operation of the Bank of Yugoslavia in the monetary system.
5. What is the purpose of a social compact?
6. Describe the Yugoslav system of self-management.
7. What is the role of the commune in the Yugoslav economic and political system?
8. What were the objectives of the Five-Year Social Plan for 1976–1980?
9. What is the philosophy that explains the relevance on worker self-management of Yugoslav enterprises?

RECOMMENDED READINGS

Burg, Steven L. "Decision Making in Yugoslavia," *Problems of Communism.* Vol. XXIX (March–April 1980), pp. 1–20.

Comisso, Ellen. *Workers' Control under Plan and Market.* New Haven: Yale University Press, 1979.

Doder, Dusko. *The Yugoslavs.* New York: Random House, 1978.

Moore, John H. *Growth with Self-Management: Yugoslav Industrialization, 1952–1975.* Stanford, Calif.: Hoover Institution Press, 1980.

Sapir, A. "Economic Growth and Factor Substitution: What Happened to the Yugoslav Miracle?" *Economic Journal,* Vol. 90 (June 1980), pp. 194–213.

Schrenk, Martin, Cyrus Ardelan, and Nawal El Tataway. *Yugoslavia: Self-Manage-*

ment Socialism and the Challenge of Development. Baltimore: Johns Hopkins University Press, 1979.

Sirc, Ljubo. *The Yugoslav Economy under Self-Management.* London: Macmillan, 1979.

Stankovic, Slobodan. *End of the Tito Era: Yugoslavia's Dilemmas.* Stanford, Calif.: Hoover Institution Press, Stanford University, 1981.

Tyson, Laura D'Andrea, and Gabriel Eichler. "Continuity and Change in the Yugoslav Economy in the 1970's and 1980's." In *East European Economic Assessment,* Part 1, Joint Economic Committee, 97th Congress, 1st session, 1981, pp. 139–214.

Wilson, Duncan. *Tito's Yugoslavia.* Cambridge: Cambridge University Press, 1979.

17

Poland

INTRODUCTION

"The Winter is yours, the Spring belongs to us."[1]

In December 1981 the Polish government, under pressure from the Soviet Union, imposed martial law on Polish society. Thousands of workers, intellectuals, and dissidents were arrested and the independent Solidarity union was dissolved. The government was put in the anomalous position of repressing the very workers it claimed to represent. Tanks ringed factories and mines, and soldiers and police used force to clear out resisting workers. In the coal-mining area of Katowice, workers who resisted were killed or injured. The lesson that can be learned is the last thing a communist state would tolerate is any move that would cause its decline or that would mitigate the dictatorship of the Communist Party. Lenin once reduced the past and future alike to two pronouns and a question mark: "Who—whom?" It meant: Who would prevail over whom? To the Soviets the answer was never in doubt: Lenin and those who have followed him in the Soviet Union would prevail over "whom"—whoever they were.

The tragedy of Poland is its geographic location. Poland has had the unique misfortune of being located between Germany and the Soviet Union. A historian once wrote: "It is easier to lecture the Poles than to live their lives between Berlin and Moscow."[2] However, long before Ger-

[1]Sign in the Lenin Shipyard in Gdansk.
[2]Salvador de Madariaga, *Victors Beware* (London: Jonathan Cape, 1946), p. 214.

many and the Soviet Union became nation-states, Poland was a common battleground for invaders ranging from the Mongol hordes of Genghis Khan to the Magyars and Swedes. In addition to suffering repeated foreign invasions, Poland was partitioned in the 18th century and eliminated as a polity until 1918. From 1918 to 1939 Poland was recreated as a country out of territory that had been taken in the partitions by Germany, Austria, and Russia. During World War II Poland was again partitioned between Germany and the Soviet Union. When Germany invaded the Soviet Union in 1941, much of the early fighting was done on Polish territory held by the Soviet Union. During the German retreat from the Soviet Union in 1944, many battles were again fought in Poland. Some 6 million Poles were killed in World War II, the highest casualty rate for any country involved in the war.[3]

Successive occupations have given the Poles a deep-seated resentment of foreign-imposed rule of any form. The Poles developed early a sense of national unity tinged with romantic fatalism. Poles have revolted countless times against their oppressors, these revolts usually ending in failure. In 1978 the election of the first Polish pope, John Paul II, helped to create a psychological climate which eventually resulted in the creation of an independent labor movement which challenged the existence of the communist state.

This chapter will break somewhat from the form followed in the previous chapters which involved individual countries. Sections covering banking, public finance, and central planning are not included because Poland follows the same procedures as the Soviet Union in these areas. The historical background and events leading to the current instability in Poland are explored as an example of problems faced by command economies.

RELIGION, HISTORY, AND ECONOMICS

Modern Poland was created as a result of agreements reached at the Yalta conference of 1945. At the end of World War II there were two rival factions in Poland, both of which were resistance groups during the German occupation. One faction was the so-called National Army of Liberation, and the other was the Communist People's Army.[4] The agreements of the Yalta conference allowed the Soviet Union to extend its sphere of influence over Poland. Although free elections were called for, the Soviet

---

[3]Poland at that time had a population of 30 million.

[4]The National Army of Liberation was a part of the Free Polish group that was based in London during World War II. During the Warsaw uprising against the Nazis in 1944, the Russian army did nothing to help the Poles even though it was across the Vistula river from Warsaw.

Union had already created a provisional government, and it was only a matter of time before Communist Party influence was firmly established. When free elections were finally held in 1946, the outcome was preordained. The Communist Party and its affiliated groups received 89.8 percent of the vote. Members of the National Army groups were either eliminated or left the country. In 1949 the Communist Party became the only political party in Poland, and in 1952 a Constitution based on the Soviet Constitution was promulgated.

After the war, the immediate need was to reconstruct the Polish economy, which had largely been destroyed.[5] The institutions of a Soviet command economy were introduced by degrees. During the period 1945–1948, industry, trade, and finance were nationalized and a two-year plan aimed at reconstruction of the economy was introduced. The direction and structure of the Polish economy was designed primarily to accord with Soviet economic and strategic priorities at considerable cost to Poland's own economic development.

Consumption was given short shrift. In the late 1940s the Polish regime, under strict Soviet tutelage, began trying to control consumption through detailed planning and administrative rationing in order to hasten the building of an industrial state. Once adequate supplies of basic necessities had been restored, the expansion of heavy industry took precedence over further increases in consumption. The distribution of food and housing was governed by administrative rationing. Prices were relied upon to govern the distribution of meager supplies of food, clothing, and consumer durables, but these prices were held below equilibrium levels with the result that shortages and queues (waiting lines) were commonplace.

Certain contradictions developed in the Polish economy and society despite attempts to impose the Soviet-type economic and social model. In the Soviet model, agriculture is collectivized, management and labor relations are controlled by the state, and resources are allocated on the basis of centralized economic planning. Religion was regarded by Marx as the opiate of the masses, so it would be eliminated (or at least severely discouraged). The application of the Soviet model was more difficult to implement in Poland than in the other Eastern European countries. For one thing, Poland was a larger country from the standpoint of both population and geography. Poland was a Roman Catholic country, with strong attachments to the Church that went back a thousand years. The tradition of Polish agriculture ran counter to the establishment of collectivized agriculture. The Polish farmer has a deep-rooted sense of private property, individual freedom, religious feeling, and family farming. Attempts by the state to alter these institutions were not successful.

---

[5]Warsaw was 95 percent destroyed by the end of the war.

Religion

The Catholic Church has been an integral part of Polish life ever since the baptism in 966 of the nation's first ruler, Prince Mieszko I. It helped to keep the Polish language and culture alive during periods of occupation. After the communist takeover of Poland in 1945, religion remained largely untouched. The Roman Catholic Church was too much a part of Polish history and a repository of its culture for the state to eliminate. A policy of accommodation developed between Church and state in Poland. The Church did not criticize the communist regime directly, and the regime ignored the Church as best it could. The primate of Poland from 1948 to his recent death, Stefan Cardinal Wyszynski, set Church policy, which was based on moral criticism and ethical guidance to the faithful. The essence of the Church was its religious mission. It would not identify itself directly with any opposition movement, but would also defend every persecuted opposition movement. However, the Church was not submissive to the state. Bishop Karol Wojtyla, who would later become Pope John Paul II, was a critic of the temporal power of the state. The viability of the Catholic Church is evidenced by the fact that 88 percent of the population of Poland are communicants today.

Poland from 1950 to 1970

Aside from religion and agriculture, the Polish socioeconomic system is similar to the Soviet Union's, even the standing in line. What makes Poland unique are the people and their state under communist misrule. The three main social classes are the intelligentsia, the workers, and the peasants. Real political power is exercised by the top leadership of the Communist Party. In times of stress such as in 1956, 1970, and 1981, the party merely reshuffles the leadership and demotes a few bureaucrats. The Poles are adept, through long years of experience with foreign rule, at frustrating the objectives of any authority. When denied other means of political opposition, they withdraw into tight circles based on family and friends and there preserve their own traditional system of values.

The 1956 Revolt. In 1956 an event of historic significance broke down the pretense of worker support for the communist regime. Industrial workers of the city of Poznan went on strike, demanding bread, freedom, free elections, and the departure of the Russians. The strike escalated into armed attacks on police headquarters; it was suppressed with much bloodshed by the army and punished by massive arrests. Threatened Soviet intervention led to worker and student demonstrations throughout much of Poland. Various factions in the Communist Party blamed each other for the riots. The Stalinist faction wanted tighter controls placed on the press, intellectuals, and workers, but also wanted to increase workers' wages as a palliative for their discontent. Another faction wanted to implement economic and political reforms. Wladyslaw Gomulka, who was not identified with either faction, became party boss.

The Gomulka Period, 1956–1970. Gomulka enjoyed tremendous initial support because he was never identified with the pro-Russian faction. His immediate task was the restoration of order in the country. Anti-Soviet feeling was high, and political activity threatened to vote the Communists out in a general election, which would have meant immediate Soviet intervention. Gomulka made a number of concessions to workers, farmers, intellectuals, and the Catholic Church to lessen discontent. He succeeded in reestablishing Communist Party rule over the country, but his popularity within the country began to decline as he began to eliminate workers' councils and other forms of democratic self-expression. A closer working relationship with the Soviet Union also caused him to lose popularity within the country. Tensions also developed with the Church, the intellectuals, and students at Warsaw University. Student demonstrations in 1968 led to arrests and an attempt by the party to blame the unrest on the Jews.[6]

Gomulka's economic policies were based on a continuation of industrialization based on the Soviet industrial model. Resources were directed to such industries as iron and steel, heavy machinery, and chemicals—industries that are typical of 19th-century industrialization and sensitive to technological change. The development strategy was wrong for Poland because it is totally different from the Soviet Union in resources and size. Profitable industries had to subsidize unprofitable ones, and high operating costs made many plants and industries unprofitable. The consumer and agricultural sectors, whose resources went into the forced draft industrialization policy, suffered accordingly, and by 1968 the Polish economy was stagnant.

Poland in the 1970s

After riots in 1970, Gomulka was replaced by Edward Gierek as party secretary. He faced several major economic problems, the most important of which was a high level of consumer unrest, which was attributed to chronic shortages of meat and quality consumer goods. Gierek promised dramatic gains in the nation's standard of living, mainly through a massive influx of foreign investment. Poland imported large amounts of new capital goods from the West, which was paid for with Western credit. The Poles expected to pay off their debt with expanded exports to the West in the form of goods produced by their new technology. Industrial

---

[6]Poland has never been a model of religious tolerance. Anti-Semitism runs deep in Polish history.

cooperation agreements involving a considerable amount of money were concluded with Western firms. For the most part, these agreements accomplished little or nothing in terms of enhancing the ability of the Poles to earn hard currency in order to finance Polish debt payments to the Western banks.

RCA–Corning Agreement. One of the largest industrial cooperation agreements concluded in Poland involved the United States firms Corning and RCA and UNITRA, the Polish foreign trade organization that is responsible for the development of the state electronics industry. The agreement, which was supported by financing by the U.S. Export–Import Bank (a U.S. government agency), was designed to provide the construction of a plant complex that would produce 21-inch, in-line color television picture tubes. The facility is comprised of a tube assembly plant and production lines for deflector components, electric guns, and phosphors. The plant complex was supposed to turn out 600,000 color television sets by 1981, and the Poles created a state enterprise, Polidor, to sell the color television sets in Poland and the rest of Eastern Europe. The total cost of this plant complex was about $250 million, but in 1981 only 50,000 sets were produced as a result of bad management and a shortage of parts.

Problems of Agriculture. Poor agricultural harvests and government inefficiency played havoc with agricultural production in one of the premier agricultural countries in Europe. Meat consumption, a critical element of the Polish diet, declined to the point where rationing was imposed as early as 1977. Meat exports to the West, which were an important source of hard currency earnings, declined to the point where meat eventually had to be imported. A shortfall in the potato crop, a major source of feed for hogs, forced farmers to purchase livestock feed from the state. This resulted in an increase in Polish grain imports, which impacted heavily on the trade deficit with Western countries. The cost of the grain imports was passed on to farmers, but it was not matched by higher prices for livestock.

The state's pricing system, designed to hold down food costs to consumers, was an invitation to disaster. The state was paying farmers 10 zlotys for a liter of milk that it sold in the store for 4 zlotys.[7] Live hogs were bought from farmers at 130 zlotys per kilogram and sold as butchered pork for 70 zlotys per kilogram. Farmers bought bread and fed it to their livestock because it was cheaper than the wheat from which it was made. The state began to lose in two ways. First, price subsidies began to absorb more and more of national budget expenditures. Second, farmers felt that prices offered by the state for meat and other food products were too low. They began to withhold meat and other products from state

---

[7]The zloty exchanged at 19 for $1 in 1981. It is not convertible outside Poland.

buyers, preferring to sell them in private markets or use them for personal consumption. To compound his errors, Gierek was allowing wages to rise 40 percent from 1970 to 1975, while keeping consumer prices artificially low. When it became necessary to raise food prices to prevent a continuing drain on the state budget, major riots occurred in Poland. To make matters worse, poor harvests from 1974 to 1980 hurt agriculture, which Gierek had ignored in favor of industrial development.

There was the need on the part of the authorities to respond to increasing consumer unrest. The 1976–1980 economic plan had to be revised to placate consumers, with increased priority attached to an increase in investments in the food, housing, and commercial service areas. An important aspect of the revised plan was the placing of more reliance on the Polish economy's private sector to stimulate an increase in the output of consumer goods and services. Many concessions were made to private enterprises, including reduced taxes on private businesses and raising the tax-free limit on private service income by 500 percent. Credit was increased to private enterprises, private artisans, and private craftsmen. Efforts were made to attract foreign investments of the type that would improve the service sector in order to attract foreign tourists with their hard currencies.

The Increase in the Polish Foreign Debt. The growth of exports to the West did not keep pace with the growth in imports and the increase in the hard currency debt. As borrowing increased, Poland became more and more dependent on private credit from Western commercial banks. In 1970 debt to Western commerical banks and governments amounted to $1.3 billion; by 1981 the amount of debt owed to Western commercial banks and governments had increased to $25.5 billion.[8] Serving and repaying the loans consumed all of Poland's hard currency export earnings, estimated at $6.5 billion in 1981.[9] The increase in debt service payments, which resulted from a rising debt, forced Poland to seek easier credit terms in the West and to appeal to the Soviet Union for financial assistance. Soviet aid took the form of financial loans, shipments of grain and crude oil, and the provision of certain consumer goods. But this assistance, by itself, was not sufficient to solve Poland's balance-of-payments problems and debts to the West, nor did it resolve consumer unrest.

The significance of the Polish debt to the West is reflected in the comparison of debt services to exports. A debt service to export ratio of 0.25 is considered by bankers as a signal for lending caution. The ratio for Poland reached 0.81 in 1980, which means simply for every $1.00 earned

---

[8]*Time*, January 4, 1982, p. 69.
[9]U.S. banks have made about $1.8 billion worth of loans to Poland. West German banks have been the largest lenders to Poland, with $2.7 billion in loans as of 1981.

from exports, $.81 is paid out in debt service payments. The Polish capacity for handling the debt is exacerbated by agricultural problems which require an increase in the imports of food products. Overemployment, generally low productivity in most industries, and an emphasis upon meeting quantity output plans as expressed in the economic plan also worked against Poland's capacity to increase its exports.

The debt has placed Western banks and the Soviet Union in a dilemma. The banks are reluctant to lend money to a country which could default on its loans. Yet at the same time, the banks would lose billions of dollars if Poland defaulted on existing loans. A Polish default would have an impact on Western lending to other Eastern European countries and the Soviet Union. Both Eastern Europe and the Soviet Union are dependent upon Western banks to finance projects like the new $15 billion Siberian natural gas pipeline. The Russians then may be put in the position of having to pay off the Polish debt in order to keep their own lines of credit open in the West. To do this would require the Soviet Union to sell off some of its gold reserves and to recommit its financial resources away from other uses.

Extraneous Factors. There were also factors over which Poland had no control that contributed to the decline of the Polish economy. One such factor was a decrease in the demand for Polish coal. The importance of coal as an export commodity rests on Poland's vast reserves, whose development has been steadily maintained. Poland is the second largest coal-exporting country in the world; half of Poland's coal shipments go to hard currency countries. During the latter part of the 1970s, a lessening of coal demand in the West, which resulted from a slowdown in economic activity, worked to the detriment of Polish exports of coal. In addition, rapidly rising domestic demand made it difficult for Poland to boost coal exports, given the long lead times needed to construct new mines. The growth in hard currency earnings from the export of coal became highly dependent on world economic recovery and increases in world coal prices.

Table 17-1 presents the performance of the Polish economy during the 1970s as measured by industrial and agricultural output and by an increase in gross national product. The results for the first half of the 1970s were impressive and were based to a large extent on Gierek's development strategy which was to increase both investment and consumption by modernizing the economy through utilizing a large-scale transfer of Western technology. The development strategy began to collapse around 1976 in part because of poor investment decisions and an inability to sell the produced output to the West to earn hard currency.[10]

---

[10]Gary R. Teske, "Poland's Trade with the Industrialized West: Performance, Problems, and Prospects," in *East European Economic Assessment, Part 1*, Joint Economic Committee, 97th Congress, 1st Session, pp. 83–85.

TABLE 17-1
INCREASE IN POLISH TOTAL GNP,
INDUSTRY, AND AGRICULTURE, 1970–1979
(1965 = 100 percent)

Year	GNP	Industry	Agriculture
1970	121.7	135.4	99.3
1971	130.4	144.2	107.3
1972	139.9	155.8	112.8
1973	150.2	168.0	116.7
1974	159.1	179.6	114.2
1975	166.6	195.0	104.7
1976	173.5	203.6	106.4
1977	178.3	213.1	106.9
1978	185.3	220.7	116.0
1979	185.3	222.2	114.8

Source: Zbigniew M. Fallenbuchl, "The Polish Economy at the Beginning of the 1980's," in *East European Economic Assessment, Part 1*, Joint Economic Committee, 97th Congress, 1st Session, 1981, p. 68.

AGRICULTURE

Poland is the only centrally planned economy that relies principally on private farming.[11] Unlike any other Eastern European country, the Communists never succeeded in collectivizing the bulk of its agriculture; even at the outset of Communist Party rule, its hold on the allegiance of the people, especially in the heavily Catholic countryside, was simply too tenuous. It is not as though the Communists didn't try. It has been pointed out that some 17,000 people, including many members of the Polish Communist Party who had been active in the underground movement against the Nazis, were killed during the immediate postwar years.[12] A number of those who were killed were victims of the communist effort to collectivize all forms of agriculture against the often armed opposition of the farmers. In 1956 the government formally postponed the political efforts required to enforce the collectivization of agriculture. The result is that today approximately 75 percent of the country's arable

---

[11]Yugoslavia also has private ownership of agriculture, but it does not fall within the mold of the centrally planned economy.

[12]Thomas T. Hammond, ed., *The Anatomy of Communist Takeovers* (New Haven: Yale University Press, 1975), p. 341.

land is farmed by more than 3 million independent small farmers, who account for 75 percent of the country's agricultural output.

Table 17-2 presents the share of net agricultural production provided by the state and private farms for the period 1960–1978. The state sector, as represented by state and collective farms, had increased its share of total net agricultural production. The main reason for this is an outmigration of labor from the farms to the cities. Rural youths do not want to work on the farms left to them by their parents, so they sell them to the state. Most private farms are less than 10 hectares in size, and upon the death of the farm owner, these farms become more fragmented in size.[13] Government policy has focused on reducing the number of small marginal farms by persuading older farmers to turn their land over to the state.

TABLE 17-2
SHARES OF NET AGRICULTURAL PRODUCTION:
STATE AND PRIVATE IN POLAND, 1960–1978
(in percent)

	1960	1965	1970	1975	1976	1977	1978
Agricultural output	100	100	100	100	100	100	100
State	12	14	16	23	25	26	26
Private	88	86	84	77	75	74	74
Crop production	100	100	100	100	100	100	100
State	15	17	21	28	27	29	27
Private	85	83	79	72	73	71	73
Livestock production	100	100	100	100	100	100	100
State	10	12	14	21	24	25	25
Private	90	88	86	79	76	75	75

Source: William J. Newcomb, "Polish Agriculture: Policy and Performance," in *East European Economic Assessment, Part 1*, p. 102.

Poland, along with France, was considered the breadbasket of Europe before World War II. By 1980 it was no longer self-sufficient and was forced to import food. There are two factors responsible for the generally erratic performance of Polish agriculture. First, most private farms are too small to achieve economies of scale. Incomes are too low on a large number of the smallest farms to afford investment in equipment for mechanizing seasonal farm tasks, and peasant farming continues to be

---

[13]In 1956 the Polish government passed a law limiting the size of private farms to a maximum of 50 hectares (123.5 acres). In 1976 the government increased the permissible size of 100 hectares (247 acres). The purpose of the law was to encourage efficient private farmers to enlarge their holdings. However, only 14 percent of all Polish farms are larger than 10 hectares (24.7 acres).

labor-intensive. Typically, farmers continue to depend on horses for trac-tive power. Second, government policy toward agriculture has not been a model of consistency. The government has subsidized consumers at the expense of farm income. Investments in agriculture have generally been low, as the government has favored the development of the industrial sector. From time to time there have been efforts by the government to take over more private farms by denying them such resources as fertil-izers and tractors. For years, private farming suffered from neglect and government policies had discouraged expansion and limited growth in productivity. Discrimination against the relatively more efficient private sector reduced agricultural exports and made imports of grain necessary.

GOVERNMENT AND LABOR RELATIONS

In 1980 the most important development since the beginning of the modern communist state in the 1917 Bolshevik Revolution in Russia occurred in Poland with the formation of the Solidarity union and its subsequent challenge to state authority. Unions heretofore were state-controlled organs which were little more than passive organs of the state. Workers were forbidden to strike, for to do so would be striking against the instrument that claimed to be the representative of the proletariat. Therefore, workers would be striking against themselves. Solidarity, which was formed in the Lenin Shipyard in Gdansk, was more than a union. It became a national movement representing workers and intellec-tuals, and at its peak claimed 10 million members.

Factors Responsible for the Rise of Solidarity

The spark that united the Solidarity movement was a government decree that raised meat prices in 1980. However, forces were already at work to create worker discontent. These forces were built into the expec-tations of workers as to how their economic system should function. There were major differences between promises and performance. Since 1945 the workers had been promised a communist paradise of milk and honey, but the paradise had not arrived. As one teacher said, she got tired of being told how good she had it and how bad off the capitalist countries were.[14] Visits to the West had convinced her otherwise. There was much in evidence to convince even the most gullible Polish workers that the economy was not functioning the way it should.

Standing in Line. Standing in line (queueing up) to buy things is very much a way of life in Poland. For that matter, it is also a way of life in the

---

[14]Conversation with a Polish professor.

Soviet Union, but the Soviet citizen is more malleable and has been doing it longer than his or her Polish counterpart. It is often necessary to stand in several lines in order to get meat at a meat market, bread at another store, and milk at still a third store. Many important products are in short supply. Soap, for example, has become largely unobtainable in the larger Polish cities. To make matters worse, there are several types of retail outlets. The first type of outlet is the PEWEX store, which sells imported goods for hard currency. Although Poles may shop there, provided they have hard currency, this type of store is designed for the foreign visitor.[15] Then there is the state store, which is characterized by low prices, negligible stocks of goods, and standing in line.[16] Finally, there are the open markets, which are usually on the periphery of a city, where almost anything can be obtained for a price. There are also barter arrangements where, for example, a pair of leather boots can be exchanged for a sack of potatoes.

The Nomenklatura System. There is a famous quotation from George Orwell's classic *Animal Farm:* "All animals are equal, but some are more equal than others."[17] Supposedly workers are "first among equals" in Poland and in other communist countries, but this is hardly the case. There is an ideological imperative which is simply that party bosses maintain a monopoly of political, ideological, and economic power. Their attitude toward the workers is pragmatic and paternalistic. Force will be resorted to only if the masses do not understand that the bosses know best and are merely trying to insure that the masses are brought to salvation despite their regrettable contrariness.

Nomenklatura is simply patronage. It means that if you want to get ahead, enjoy the best things in life, and travel to Paris or New York, join the Communist Party. Promotions and rewards in the system are more than likely attached to party membership than to merit.[18] Party hacks often run the show, while initiative and new ideas are discouraged. The best and the brightest workers are often barred from advancement because they are not ideologically pure. Practicing Catholics, for example, cannot join the Communist Party and therefore cannot rise to policy-making positions in the Polish government. It is not uncommon for a Catholic to provide the managerial skill which makes an enterprise suc-

---

[15]Almost anything can be bought at these special stores. The author once bought a box of Kellogg Cornflakes.

[16]A verse popular in Poland in 1978 ran as follows: "One Pole is pope of Rome. / Another helps run Carter's show. / Some kneel in homage to Uncle Brezhnev. / The rest queue in sunshine, rain, and snow."

[17]George Orwell, *Animal Farm,* Chapter 10.

[18]This is also likely to hold true in the United States. The political machines in large cities always have given political plums to the party faithful. However, U.S. political parties do not control every phase of life.

cessful, but, solely on the basis of religion, be effectively barred from rising to head it.

Solidarity and Lech Walesa

Shakespeare wrote, "There is a tide in the affairs of men, which taken at the flood, leads on to fortune."[19] The tide was flowing in July 1980 when workers in the Lenin Shipyard in Gdansk walked out in protest of the government's decision to raise meat prices. The protest appeared to be going nowhere when an unemployed electrician named Lech Walesa, who had been fired for trying to create an independent union, climbed over the shipyard fence and became the catalyst in a labor movement that was to shake Poland and the world. That he was able to do what he did in a shipyard named for one of the saints of communism has some irony, for the last thing in the world that Lenin wanted, or would tolerate, was any move that would cause the state to wither away or that would mitigate the dictatorship of the Communist Party.

Walesa assumed control over the protesting shipyard workers and the protest movement began to spread to other parts of Poland. A link was formed between intellectuals and workers which led to the creation of Solidarity.[20] The Lenin Shipyard became the focal point of the Solidarity movement; and in August, Walesa and other Solidarity officers met with members of the Gierek government to hammer out the Gdansk agreement. The government agreed to allow the workers the right to strike—something unheard of in a communist state where Marxist theory holds that in a system of public ownership of the means of production there are no contradictory class interests to cause labor conflicts. Workers were also given the right to form their own unions. Censorship was reduced and access to the state broadcasting networks was given to the unions and the Church.

After the Gdansk agreement, the Solidarity movement spread like wildfire across Poland. Solidarity evolved into a loose-knit federation of labor to which some 10 million Poles belonged. Everyone from coal miner to college professor belonged to Solidarity, which was divided into 38 semiautonomous regional chapters throughout Poland. Problems of policy and strategy developed because some members wanted a union federation concerned with labor goals, while other members wanted to mount opposition to the state. Cross-currents were at work in Solidarity, and the federation was increasingly forced into the path of contentious political activism by its various factions. Elements within Solidarity

---

[19]*Julius Caesar*, Act V, Scene III.
[20]The Committee for Social Self-Defense was a precursor of Solidarity. It was formed by dissident intellectuals to oppose political oppression.

eventually gave the government the excuse it was looking for when they called for a national referendum on the future of the communist government in Poland and reexamination of Polish military ties with the Soviet Union. In December 1981, martial law was declared in Poland and Lech Walesa and thousands of other Poles were arrested.

Goals of Solidarity

During its brief existence Solidarity accomplished a number of things which may now be abrogated by the state. It is necessary to remember that the root causes of the upheaval which created Solidarity were economic. The Communist Party and the government had fallen into a state of near-terminal paralysis. But Solidarity was also concerned with political goals as well as economic ones. It wanted a democratization of the political process. The goals and accomplishments of Solidarity are briefly summarized here.

Work Week. Solidarity won a concession from the government for a five-day workweek after decades of a six-day workweek. This concession was a mixed blessing. Although the workers gained in terms of leisure time, the economy incurred a loss in production, particularly in the output of coal. In 1979 total coal production in Poland amounted to 240 million tons; in 1981 coal production had decreased to 168 million tons.[21] In 1979 Poland exported 40 million tons, yielding a hard currency profit of $3 billion. In 1981 exports of coal dropped to an estimated 10 million tons. The government offered coal miners triple pay to work on Saturdays; the workers refused because there was nothing to buy in the shops. Poland lacked the hard currency to import consumer goods and food from the West.

Nomenklatura. Solidarity mounted an attack on nomenklatura, the system whereby the Communist Party exercises the right to appoint bureaucrats, administrators, and managers in Poland. Nomenklatura in Poland and the other communist countries really involves a position of privilege which is attained on the basis of nepotism,[22] favoritism, service to the Communist Party, and other factors that have little to do with merit. Most galling to many Poles were the special privileges that accrue to those who were a part of the nomenklatura system—villas, yachts, special stores—privileges that were handed down by the ruling elite to their

---

[21]Lawrence Weschler, "A Reporter in Poland," Part II, *New Yorker*, November 16, 1981, p. 199.
[22]Nepotism is rampant in the communist countries. The premier of Romania, Nikolae Ceausescu, has appointed many members of his family to key positions in the government.

families and cronies.[23] Solidarity wanted the complete elimination of the nomenklatura system.

Workers' Councils. Solidarity wanted to create workers' councils similar to those that exist in Yugoslavia. These councils would appoint managers on the basis of their skills, not on their loyalty to the party, and the managers would be subject to worker recall. The state would exercise a normative influence through setting regulations and pollution standards, and an economic influence through the use of monetary and fiscal policies. There would be reliance on free markets to allocate resources. Free unions would represent workers.[24]

Censorship. Solidarity wanted a relaxation of press censorship and more free expression on television and in the theatres.[25] It wanted history books to reflect true Polish history, not a distortion of it. An example of distortion was the claim that only Communists were a part of the underground movement during World War II.

THE POLISH ECONOMY: POST-SOLIDARITY

The Polish economy in early 1982 was in a state of chaos. Communist Party leaders blamed this chaos on Solidarity, but Solidarity was the result, not the cause, of the problem. The simple fact is that after 36 years with a monopoly on power, the communist regime has not been able to fulfill its economic promises to the people of Poland. On numerous occasions it has had to use force on the very workers it claims to represent. It has demonstrated that it will not tolerate free elections, human rights, and economic and social reforms that might in any way compromise its privileged position. The communist ideology contains imperatives which, although they render impossible the solution of important problems, the regime cannot discard. At its back are the Soviet leaders, whose concern above all is that Poland and the other Eastern European countries be ruled by a party of the Leninist–Stalinist type. This means that parties must maintain a monopoly of political, ideological, and economic power,

---

[23]The author has seen the villas, yachts, and special stores. A member of Solidarity told the author that what was so bad about nomenklatura were the special privileges. She would stand in line for meat that was rarely available, and then see party favorites and their friends come out of the special stores with plenty of meat.

[24]There are some contradictions. Why would unions be necessary since workers would perform the functions of both labor and management? Workers' councils were introduced in a few enterprises before martial law was proclaimed by the government.

[25]It should be emphasized again that Solidarity was a broad-based movement, including workers, intellectuals, and many members of the Communist Party who were disillusioned with the system.

i.e., central planning, centralized control of industrial production, and the elimination of beliefs which compete with Marxism–Leninism.

Poland from 1976 to 1981

Table 17-3 presents the performance of the Polish economy from 1976 to 1981. It was evident that the economy was headed toward a major crisis long before Solidarity was created. The Polish debt and debt service payments to the West more than doubled during the period. Drastic shortages of consumer goods were being experienced. In 1977 Poles had to forego the consumption of meat one day a week. There was a decline in capital productivity and the rate of growth of domestic net material product declined to 3.0 percent in 1978 and −2.3 percent in 1979. Capital and labor productivity also showed sharp declines. Exports, which are the source of foreign currency earnings, declined at a rate of −4.3 percent in 1980, while hard currency indebtedness to the West increased. The crisis of 1980 led to a downward revision of the annual plan, and an attempt was made to enforce an improvement in the balance of trade.

TABLE 17-3
THE PERFORMANCE OF THE POLISH ECONOMY, 1976–1981
(percentage annual growth, in constant prices)

	1976	1977	1978	1979	1980	1981*
Domestic net material product	6.8	5.0	3.0	−2.3	−5.4	−14.5
Industry	9.3	7.7	2.5	−1.7	−3.0	−18.7
Construction	2.5	1.0	−0.3	−6.2	−10.5	−19.8
Agriculture	1.1	−0.2	8.5	−3.2	−14.0	−4.2
National net material product	7.0	2.7	0.7	−3.4	−5.9	−13.4
Expenditure on consumption	8.7	6.6	1.0	3.2	6.4	−6.0
Investment	3.7	−5.3	−1.4	−18.0	−37.0	−56.0
Foreign trade						
Exports	4.4	8.0	5.7	6.8	−4.3	−13.5
Imports	9.6	−0.1	1.8	−0.9	−2.8	−8.2
Capital–labor ratio	7.1	9.4	10.6	9.7	9.5	8.0
Productivity of capital	1.0	−1.1	−2.6	−4.3	−5.6	−11.0
Productivity of labor	8.2	8.3	7.7	5.0	3.3	−4.0

*Estimate
Source: Zbigniew M. Fallenbuchl, "Poland's Economic Crisis," *Problems of Communism*, Vol. 31 (March–April 1982), p. 6.

The Future Direction of the Polish Economy

As of June 1982 General Wojciech Jaruzelski and his military junta remained in control of Poland. There continue to be demonstrations of protest, overt and covert, and the eventual direction the economy will take appears difficult to ascertain. Workers can be forced, under martial law, to report to work, but that does not guarantee work will be done properly. The problems still remain; it is estimated that for 1982 industrial production will continue to show a negative rate of growth, and that shortages, particularly of intermediate goods and spare parts, will continue to get worse.[26] Farmers are reportedly holding agricultural goods off of the market. Obviously, the military solution cannot guarantee satisfactory results.

The military authorities have made some attempts to establish an economic policy. They have declared that they will not change policies toward agriculture, although Rural Solidarity, the farmers' adjunct of Solidarity, has been dissolved. They have also stated that they will accept the private sector as a permanent feature of the agricultural economy and will not discriminate against it in the future. But this, in itself, has not reassured the farmers, nor has it accomplished any gain in output. If compulsory deliveries, which have been used in the past, are reintroduced by the government, trouble may well result. Since consumer goods are in short supply, farmers are going to be less likely to sell their produce for money that won't buy anything, even though the military authorities have introduced higher prices for farm products. A shortage of parts for farm equipment has also created production problems.[27]

The annual plan for 1982 has been abandoned and quarterly plans substituted in its place. The first-quarter plan projected a decline in industrial production of 8 to 10 percent. This was revised downward in February to 10 to 11 percent. An objective of the quarterly plan was to increase the output of oil refineries. There is also a strategy to increase coal production by increasing the number of miners. This may not work because of resentment of repressive measures used by the government to put down coal miners' strikes in December 1981. The plan goals are also inhibited by a lack of inputs from outside the economy, specifically, raw materials, machine components, and intermediate goods which are imported from the capitalist countries. There is an absence of hard currency with which to buy these goods.

There are several directions in which Poland could go. There could be a somewhat modified return to conditions that existed before martial law

---

[26]Zbigniew M. Fallenbuchl, "Poland's Economic Crisis," *Problems of Communism*, Vol. 31 (March–April 1981), p. 9.

[27]*Ibid.*, p. 18.

was imposed where freedom within state-determined limits would be permitted. There could be the adoption of more oppressive state control of the type that exists in Czechoslovakia and East Germany. Finally, there could be the adoption of a more flexible economic policy that is used in Hungary. However, it is necessary to point out that reforms in Hungary exist only within narrowly circumscribed limits. Regardless of the approach, the government has to convince the Poles that it is capable of improving their economic lot.[28] That is rather difficult to do, for efforts to redress economic imbalances by raising the price of food and basic staples have only reduced standards of living and increased popular resentment.

Oppressed people often protest their condition through songs of protest, verse, and graffiti scribbled on the walls of buildings. The Poles are no exception. There is one verse of a song that was sung after the Gdansk riots of 1970 that is as appropriate in 1982 as it was in 1970. It is as follows:

Oh, People's Poland, what was it all for?
Why, long years after the war, still so poor?
Prices are rising, while wages go down.
The rest of the world thinks the Poles are all clowns.[29]

SUMMARY

Joseph Stalin once said that it is easier to saddle a cow than it is to impose communism on Poland. Although Stalin has been dead for many years, subsequent events have proved him to be right. There are several reasons why the Poles have proved to be so intractable. First, Poland had no tradition of communism before World War II. In East Germany and Hungary, there were well-established Communist Parties during the period between World Wars I and II.[30] Second, Poland has been occupied by foreign powers throughout much of its history. There is a resentment of the Soviet Union. Third, the Roman Catholic Church has always been a viable part of the life of Poland and a bulwark against repression. Finally, there is the Polish national character itself—a romantic fatalism which has been created by many centuries of being the battleground for neighboring powers.

A Soviet command economy was implanted in Poland in the late 1940s and early 1950s. The implant did not take well. One feature of the command economy is overcentralization, which works against efficiency. A second feature has been the imposition of the Soviet industrial model, with its required imports, when no export sector had been developed. The agricultural and consumer sectors have largely been ignored. A third feature of the economic system has been the reorientation of

---

[28]General Jaruzelski announced in April that any substantial improvement in the Polish economy was unlikely until 1990.

[29]Cited in *Problems of Communism*, Vol. XX (July–August 1970), p. 64.

[30]After World War I and before Hitler became dictator of Germany, the Communist Party was a large political party in Germany, with most of its strength concentrated in Berlin and the current area of East Germany.

Poland's foreign trade toward the Soviet Union and its isolation from the world economy. Development strategy was based on tying growth rates to increases in the quantity, as opposed to the productivity, of inputs. This did not help when it became necessary to export more goods to the West.

REVIEW QUESTIONS

1. What were some of the factors contributing to the decline of the Polish economy?
2. Discuss the system of nomenklatura.
3. What were the goals of Solidarity?
4. Discuss the Gierek program designed to increase Polish living standards. Why did it fail?
5. What is the significance of the Polish debt to the West?
6. What role has religion played in the life and history of Poland?
7. Discuss the problems of Polish agriculture.
8. Why did the revolt against the communist system occur in Poland?

RECOMMENDED READINGS

Ascherson, Neil. *The Polish August*. New York: Viking Press, 1982.

Blazynski, George. *Flashpoint Poland*. New York: Pergamon Press, 1979.

Connor, Walter D. "Dissent in Eastern Europe: A New Coalition?" *Problems of Communism,* Vol. XXIX, January–February 1980, pp. 1–17.

Fallenbuchl, Zbigniew M. "Poland's Economic Crisis." *Problems of Communism,* Vol. XXXI, March–April 1982.

_____. "The Polish Economy at the Beginning of the 1980's." In *East European Economic Assessment,* Part I. Washington: Joint Economic Committee, 97th Congress, 1981, pp. 33–71.

Schoepflin, George. *Poland: A Society in Crisis*. London: Institute for Study of Conflict, 1979.

Wanless, P. T. "Economic Reform in Poland 1973–79." *Soviet Studies,* Vol. 32, No. 4 (1980), pp. 28–57.

Weschler, Lawrence. "A Reporter in Poland." *New Yorker,* Part I, November 9, 1981, pp. 59–153; Part II, November 16, 1981, pp. 188–222.

de Weydenthal, Jan B. "Workers and Party in Poland." *Problems of Communism,* November–December 1980, pp. 1–22.

_____. *Poland: Communism Adrift*. Washington: Georgetown University Center for Strategic and International Studies, 1979.

PART 5
CONCLUSION

18

The Economic Systems: Evaluation of Goal Fulfillment

INTRODUCTION

Full employment, price stability, and economic growth are basic goals of any economic system. To these goals, a fourth goal, an equitable distribution of income, may also be added. The results of production must be shared among members of society in such a way that it is felt to be just and equitable. However, there is no absolute standard of income distribution that can satisfy everyone. It is also necessary to mention the fact that noneconomic goals, such as the political freedoms of the individual in society, are very important. Recent events in Poland illustrate the fact that to many people individual freedom is at least as important as full employment and a high rate of economic growth, and should be factored into any comparison of economic systems.

Governments in Western countries and Japan have come to play a very important role in the attainment of economic goals. This role has taken two basic forms which have been mentioned repeatedly: (1) Changes in taxation and government spending have influenced output, prices, and employment. Moreover, progressive income taxation and transfer payments have been used in most countries to create a more equitable redistribution of income. (2) Governments have also come to serve as a powerful force in the determination of productive capacity. There is public ownership of certain key industries, and there is also direct participation in the formation of capital. Government expenditures have also contributed to the health, education, and training of the labor force, and hence to productive capacity.

There are several variants of communism today. The first is Soviet communism, which involves a highly centralized command economy under which party officials and government bureaucrats in Moscow determine such details as how many millions of zippers will be produced. One advantage of a command economy is that resources can be concentrated in areas which are assigned growth priority; one disadvantage is inefficiency built into a centralized bureaucratic system. A second is Yugoslav communism, which offers a striking contrast to the Soviet variant. It is a style of communism in which the Communist Party guides but does not command the operation of the economy. The third variant is Chinese communism, which, at least in the early 1980s, combines ideology and pragmatism. As one Chinese leader has said, "It makes no difference what color the cat is, as long as it catches mice."

THE WESTERN WORLD: GOAL FULFILLMENT

As of June 1982 an economic malaise gripped both capitalist and communist countries alike. The ailment, which has all but stopped global economic growth, can be attributed to a number of factors. For the economy of the United States, the long trend of good performance since the end of World War II ended in the 1970s when three major sets of problems matured and converged: the problem of inflation, the energy problem and its consequences, and finally the problem of a government increasingly incapable of controlling its own budget as entitlement after entitlement was built into the spending mechanism. By the end of 1980 the United States reached a major turning point in economic policy, with new policy measures designed to bring about a change in the performance of the economy. It remains to be seen whether this policy is successful or whether there will be a replay of what happened during the 1970s.

Factors Contributing to a Decline in Performance

High interest rates and a redoubling of oil prices in 1979 are two factors that have had an adverse impact on the global economy. High interest rates are intended to slow inflation, but at the same time they constrict buying and investment, putting a break on expansion. The rapid rise in oil prices worsened the rate of inflation in all countries.[1] The outbreak of war between Iran and Iraq in 1980 led to a substantial cut in oil exports from Iraq, which just prior to that war had ranked as OPEC's second largest producer.[2] Increases in the price of oil marked an immediate, sharp check to the growth of consumption and buying power. Different countries reacted in different ways, but Japan came out of the oil price increases performing better than any other industrial power, including the United States and Germany. Living standards and consumption were sacrificed to investment, which has paid off in a redirection of Japanese industry away from its dependence on oil.

There are other factors contributing to the slowdown in the world economy that have little to do with high interest rates and rising oil prices. In the communist countries bureaucratic centralization and rigidities in the planning mechanism have contributed to a declining rate of economic growth; in the capitalist countries, a lack of direction and the inability of special-interest groups to compromise are factors. As economies become more service-oriented, there also can be a factor contributing to declining productivity. There is a tendency to think of economic growth in terms of investment and new products, but disinvestment is also a necessary precondition. To have the labor and capital to move into new areas, it is necessary to be able to withdraw labor and capital from old, low-productivity areas. But every disinvestment represents a threat to someone.

The 1982 Economic Scenario

The economic scenario as of the middle of 1982 can be presented for each of the Western countries used in the textbook. World production, which increased at an annual rate of 2.2 percent for the period 1979–1981, is projected to increase at an annual rate of less than 2 percent for 1982.[3] There is worse unemployment in Western Europe, where the rate has hit double-digit figures, than in the United States, where the rate is around 9 percent.

United States. As of May 1982 the unemployment rate in the United States was 9.4 percent, the highest rate since the Depression of the 1930s. Conversely, the rate of inflation was down to 0.3 percent for the month, or 4.5 percent when projected out for 1982. The rate of economic growth

---

[1]During the first quarter of 1980 the average price of oil imported into the United States rose to $30 a barrel, double the $15 a barrel price paid during the first quarter of 1979.

[2]However, Saudi Arabia stepped up its production of oil in order to maintain supply to Iraq's former customers.

[3]*Washington Post,* May 16, 1982, Section F, p. 1.

for the first quarter of 1982 was −3.9 percent. The U.S. economy continued in a recession, with few bright spots to project when it would end, and the deficit in the federal budget was around $100 billion. Neither major political party seemed capable of providing solutions to the problems of the 1980s, because both are locked into the shibboleths of the past.

France. One year after the election of a socialist government and president, the French economy suffers from an inflation rate of 14 percent and an unemployment rate greater than 8 percent. The Mitterand government has pursued expansionary fiscal and monetary policy measures to stimulate the French economy.[4] It raised the minimum wage by nearly 10 percent and increased the minimum old-age pension from $250 to $333 a month.[5] It reduced the workweek from 40 hours to 39 hours and granted all workers a fifth week of paid vacations. The government also levied a 10 percent surcharge on the income taxes of those who paid more than $4,000 in 1981. It levied a tax on expense accounts and increased the estate and inheritance taxes on wealth. There has been a narrowing of the scope of the nationalization program which has been an integral part of the socialist program. Certain French subsidiaries of large foreign firms, such as ITT and Honeywell Bull, have been allowed to retain their foreign participation.

Japan. The Japanese economy is still the best-performing economy in the world. However, the state of the world economy has had some effect on an export-oriented country such as Japan. In the final quarter of 1981, Japanese gross national product decreased at a rate of 1 percent—the first decline in 6 years.[6] Industries that once flourished on cheap oil, such as steelmaking, are in trouble. Automobile exports, an economic cornerstone of the Japanese economy, were down 11 percent in the first quarter of 1982 from the same period a year previously. The unemployment rate is far and away the lowest for all major industrial countries. It has held steady at 2 percent through April 1982, largely because of the reluctance on the part of many Japanese companies to lay off workers. Instead, thousands of Japanese workers have been put on reduced schedules at reduced pay. The rate of inflation has also increased and is projected to be around 7 percent for 1982.

United Kingdom. Prime Minister Margaret Thatcher was having economic problems before the Argentine seizure of the Falkland Islands. The British unemployment rate in early 1982 was 12.6 percent—the highest rate since the Depression of the 1930s.[7] Prime Minister Thatcher's aus-

---

[4]In 1982 the deficit in the French budget is projected at $15–31 billion.
[5]*Newsweek*, May 10, 1982, pp. 57–58.
[6]Bank of Japan, "Monthly Economic Statistics," April 1982, p. 4.
[7]*Lloyds Bank Review*, March 1982, p. 1.

terity measures have had an important impact on the economy. Interest rates are high, and the Confederation of British industry reported that in February 1982, 57 percent of British firms had cut their work force in the previous four months. British economic policy has attached overriding importance to the reduction of inflation, with reliance on monetary policy to achieve this goal. The transitional consequences of Mrs. Thatcher's policy have been quite painful, as is evident by the high rate of unemployment that prevails in the economy. It remains to be seen whether the austerity measures will rehabilitate the British economy.

West Germany. The West German economy, which has been one of the strongest in the world, has developed some of its own problems. The unemployment rate was 7.6 percent in March 1982—the highest rate since 1949 and a rate not all that far below the unemployment rate that prevailed in 1933 when Hitler came to power. The gross national product for the first quarter of 1982 increased at a rate of 0.75 percent.[8] The federal government approved measures designed to stimulate investment by providing a 10 percent subsidy for capital spending and the granting of low-cost loans for certain types of investments. To compensate for the loss of revenue, the government plans to increase the value-added tax by 1 percent. There is a planned shift from direct to indirect taxes, with planned reductions to occur in both the individual and corporate income taxes.

Western Governments and Rising Expectations

The role of government has become a key factor in the economies of all the Western countries. Gone are the days of laissez-faire, with its idea of limited government. Keynesian economic policies, which place government at the fulcrum of economic activity, has dominated Western government economic policy for 30 years.[9] This policy has been accompanied by a shift of resources away from some groups and to other groups. These shifts have included a redistribution of resources from the private to the public sector, from workers to nonworkers, from the young to the old, and from risk takers to bureaucrats. In addition, there has been a collective shift from market processes to political processes, from investment to consumption, and from the growth of income to the distribution of income.

Governments could afford these shifts as long as productivity was expanding rapidly and prosperity continued. But prosperity led governments to try to do more and more of the things that generate political

---

[8]Deutsches Bundesbank, *Monthly Report*, March 1982, p. 1.
[9]The United States and West Germany were the last Western countries to adopt Keynesian economic policy measures.

popularity, such as a redistribution of income, increased social services and benefits, and greater regulation of industry. These have had the effect of destroying the link between work and consumption and rewards that accrue to success and penalties that accrue to failure, both of which are relevant to a market system. Economic policies have been largely inflationary in the interest of pushing the pace of economic growth and the redistribution of income. These policies set in motion forces that have led to the acceleration of inflation in the Western industrialized world. Prosperity had also been fueled by the existence of cheap sources of energy, particularly oil. Oil price increases in the 1970s changed the relationship of energy to the production process.[10] The industrial economies will have to adjust to a lower capacity to grow during the 1980s.

Slower growth will create problems because in the last two decades economic growth has been tied to various social objectives, the chief of which has been full employment and a steady increase in consumption. In sum, government policies of Keynesian demand management have created a powerful and irreversible revolution in social expectations.[11] Governments will have a difficult time controlling those expectations. The furor over social security in the United States is a case in point. As long as the country was prosperous and the rate of growth was increasing, politicians expanded the coverage and benefits of social security almost at will, particularly during election years. The question is whether the economy can be disciplined—and the master has to be the government— to live within the actual cash flows available.

THE COMMUNIST COUNTRIES: GOAL FULFILLMENT

The economies of the Soviet Union, China, and Eastern Europe also face a period of crisis. Soviet industrial growth fell short of the plan target during the first three months of 1982. Figures released by Tass, the official news agency of the Soviet Union, showed industrial production in the critical oil, coal, and steel sectors remained level or fell from the first quarter of 1981.[12] Declines were also experienced in the ferrous metal industry, the building materials sector, light industry, meat and milk production, and other areas. Similar patterns prevail in the Eastern European countries. The proliferation of claimants for East European goods and services runs well ahead of the ability to increase output to satisfy their demands. The options for improved performances are especially limited, and there is a technology lag in comparison with the Western

---

[10]Ezra Solomon, *Beyond the Turning Point* (San Francisco: Freeman, 1982), pp. 25–27.
[11]Daniel Bell, *The Cultural Contradictions of Capitalism* (New York: Basic Books, 1976), p. 244.
[12]*New York Times*, May 3, 1982, p. 2.

countries at a time when there is a revolution in rising consumer expectations.

To some extent the problems of the capitalist and communist countries are interrelated. The slowdown in the world economy affects both. The communist countries depend on exports to the West in order to earn hard currency. When the West is in a recession, imports from the communist countries decline, with a resultant decline in hard currency earnings. Without hard currency it becomes increasingly difficult for the communist countries to import goods from the West to satisfy consumer demand. Poland's development strategy during the early 1970s was to import Western technology to modernize its industrial base and thus to increase its exports to the West. This strategy failed for several reasons, not the least of which was a recession in the West, which had the effect of reducing Polish exports.

High interest rates in the West during the early 1980s also have had a deleterious impact on the economies of the communist countries. Inflation became the major economic problem in the West, beginning around 1975. The root cause, allowing for the oil price increases in 1973–1974 and 1979–1980, was that political imperatives forced central banks to sacrifice the proper objective of monetary policy, control over the money supply for the purpose of providing price stability, in favor of other objectives.[13] The rate of inflation increased in the late 1970s, prompting central banks to pursue a tight money policy. Interest rates increased to record highs in the United States. It was a factor that attracted other currencies to the dollar and thus drove up the dollar's exchange rate. In order to counter the rising dollar, other countries had to take steps to increase their own interest rates toward the level prevailing in the United States. Rising interest rates in Western Europe exacerbated a recession that began in 1979. As the recession increased, Western European exports from Eastern Europe and the Soviet Union declined.

Factors Contributing to a Decline in Performance

Communist command economies have several advantages over capitalist economies. They can enforce a high degree of mobilization of resources; they can ensure full utilization of those resources; and they can direct the allocation of these resources toward the fulfillment of selected quantitative resources. Given these advantages, there is one thing the command economies do not do well; namely, they cannot ensure efficiency in the operation of their system. There is overcentralization at the

---

[13]A good example was President Lyndon Johnson's insistence on a policy of "guns, butter, and the Great Society," all with no increases in taxes to offset the inevitable increase in total spending which that package of policies ensured.

top, with decisions filtering down through a bureaucratic hierarchy which is intent on preserving its own interests. In the absence of a market price mechanism, no rational and workable pricing system has been devised. Prices do not fully reflect factor costs, as rent and interest are not fully accounted for in them; furthermore, different criteria for price setting are used for different categories of products. As a result, prices do not, and cannot, perform a rational allocative function.

For a considerable period of time, industrial development policy emphasized the growth of a self-sufficient industrial base. Development strategy concentrated on branches of industry that produced producer goods required for domestic investment. Priority industries were all capital-, energy-, and material-intensive, which required imports. Virtual insulation from world market prices worked against the development of viable export industries. Consumer goods industries and agriculture have been relegated to second place. Industrial development has been broad, but superficial and insufficiently specialized. Stress was placed on import substitution rather than on the promotion of manufacture based upon comparative advantage and efficient resource allocation. This approach slowed the evolution of domestic industry founded upon rational economic specialization and did not permit the early maturing of large-scale exports of specialized industrial production. The lack of an adequate export base is a factor which has contributed to an increase in the hard currency debt.

External Debt

Mounting problems in the economies of the communist countries exacerbated many economic deficiencies. One deficiency has been that economic development has been inhibited by a lack of sophisticated technology in most industrial fields. Imports of technology, consumer goods, and agricultural products have placed a heavy burden on the economies of the Eastern European countries and, indirectly, the Soviet Union, a burden that has been compounded by a limited access to hard currency. In many situations this inability to earn hard currency is attributable to the fact that most state enterprises are unable to offer products or services that are up to the quality standards found in the highly competitive world markets. The disintegration of stable world markets and prices has hampered the communist economies. This has assumed critical proportions as the higher import prices they are forced to pay are not duplicated in their export prices because of their marginal position in the world markets.

Table 18-1 presents the hard currency debt of the Soviet Union and the Eastern European countries for 1980. Even allowing for inflation, the

TABLE 18-1
SOVIET UNION
AND EASTERN EUROPEAN
HARD CURRENCY DEBT
TO THE WEST, 1980
(billions of dollars)

Poland	24.5
USSR	11.5
East Germany	9.7
Romania	8.6
Hungary	7.1
Czechoslovakia	3.3
Bulgaria	3.0

Source: Central Intelligence Agency, National Foreign Assessment Center, *Handbook of Economic Statistics* (Washington, 1981), p. 22.

increase in the hard currency debt is phenomenal. In 1970 the hard currency debt of East Germany was $1.2 billion; by 1980 the East German debt had increased to $9.7 billion. The Polish debt to the West increased from around $1 billion in 1970 to $24.5 billion in 1980. Moreover, the amount of debt increased from around $67 billion in 1980 to $80 billion by 1981. The Polish debt to the West is projected to increase to $30 billion by the end of 1982. China's debt to the West is not included in the figures, but the Chinese have been much more circumspect in their borrowing from the West. The estimated Chinese hard currency debt is in excess of $3 billion. Yugoslavia, with its ease of access to Western hard currency, does not have the same debt problems.

The debt presents a problem for the communist countries. In order to keep new borrowing down, they will have to monitor imports from the West while attempting to maximize exports. The latter will prove difficult to do. Exports from the communist countries to the West are either raw materials or low-technology manufacturing goods. There continue to be problems in the marketing and quality of goods for export as well as certain deficiencies in domestic production. Internal domestic prices have virtually no relation to production costs and to demand factors that determine domestic prices in market economy countries. With the exception of the Soviet Union, the other countries are resource-poor and have little to export. There are also indications that the Soviet Union is running short in certain resources. Energy output in the 1980s may present economic and policy problems for the Soviet Union.[14] Some estimates of Soviet oil production indicate that it will decline to the point where the USSR will no longer be capable of exporting oil. The Soviet Union currently derives about half of its hard currency earnings from the export of oil and natural gas.

Efficiency and the Need for Reforms

For the most part, the economic systems of the communist countries are notoriously inefficient when it comes to delivering most goods and services. Most consumer goods are of poor quality, and there is a lack of coordination between production and distribution. Maintaining a modicum of growth in consumer welfare will be necessary in order to minimize consumer discontent. Standing in line, waiting years for apartments and cars, searching the shops for scarce products, and bribing the butcher and repairman are a way of life for consumers. As a result of agricultural inefficiency which has made the communist countries high-cost food producers, real consumer income has been reduced in comparison with that of other countries. There have been meat shortages in Poland and the Soviet Union.

Inefficiency, however, is by no means limited to consumer goods. There is also a need to reform planning and management in order to stimulate productivity and the quality of output. It is necessary to increase incentives to managers, workers, and peasants to increase production and to promote productivity. Few economic plans are completely fulfilled; most are modified along the way. However, reforms and reorganization in planning, management, and incentives threaten various groups who are interested in maintaining the status quo. There are certain institutions that are held to be basic to the economic development of the communist countries. Party involvement in the economy is one of them. The point was made in the chapter on the People's Republic of China that there has been a long-standing conflict between technicians and "reds." Increasing the role of the technician professional threatens the traditional role of the party apparatus.

There are other inhibiting factors that tend to contribute to inefficiency. One factor is the guarantee of full employment, which leads to the creation of a number of make-work jobs and to much underemployment of labor resources. This also tends to create dissatisfaction with the job and perhaps may explain in part the high degree of alcoholism in the Soviet Union.[15] Workers also are very rarely fired. Wages are the same in

---

[14]Joint Economic Committee, Subcommittee on International Trade, *Energy in Soviet Policy*, 97th Congress, 1st Session, 1981, pp. 1–17.

[15]Andrea Lee, *Russian Journal* (New York: Random House, 1982), pp. 54–64. This book provides an excellent insight into the lives of ordinary Soviet citizens.

related state enterprises, and since there is no distinction made between good and bad workers, there is no incentive to work hard. The lack of wage differentiation inhibits labor productivity and an efficient allocation of manpower. There is, however, not only a gross absence of correlation between productivity and wages, but a lack of effective means to induce labor to work intensively. Earning a higher income offers little incentive to workers because there is a lack of consumer goods on which wages can be spent.

A COMPARISON OF ECONOMIC SYSTEMS

In the remainder of this chapter, various measures will be used to compare the operating results of some of the major capitalist and communist countries. Comparisons can be made of income, consumption, and economic growth. Economic systems can be judged on the basis of how well they channel the energies of their producers and meet the needs of their consumers. There is one difference between the systems which is very important. Communist leaders have made power politics both paramount and as independent as possible from those concerns that govern the welfare of society. Capitalism and socialism are economic systems that are free to succeed or fail on how well they solve such problems of today as inflation, recession, unemployment, and poverty, and must suffer any political side effects. Communism, by contrast, is not attached to a political superstructure: it *is* that superstructure.

Income Comparisons

Table 18-2 presents a comparison of per capita income and average annual real per capita income growth rates for major capitalist and communist countries. The per capita incomes for the capitalist countries are well in excess of those for the communist countries. The People's Republic of China is a special case and perhaps should not be compared to the more industrialized countries. It is one of the world's underdeveloped countries, with agriculture the most important component of the economy. China also has the largest population of any country in the world, a factor which compels the Chinese to emphasize the agricultural sector as the primary factor in the rural modernization program. In all likelihood, agricultural success will determine the country's prospects for industrialization and long-term economic development. Without the hard currency earnings from agricultural exports, the Chinese would not be able to buy much of the Western equipment and technology that is needed for industrial development.

At the other end of the communist spectrum is East Germany, with a 1980 per capita income of $7,180, which ranks it first among all commu-

TABLE 18-2
A COMPARISON OF PER CAPITA INCOME
AND AVERAGE ANNUAL GROWTH RATES
FOR CAPITALIST AND COMMUNIST COUNTRIES

	Per Capita Income, 1980	Percentage Change in Real per Capita Income, 1970–1979
Capitalist		
Canada	$10,130	2.9%
France*	11,730	3.0
Japan	9,890	3.9
Sweden	13,520	1.1
United Kingdom	7,920	1.9
United States	11,360	2.2
West Germany	13,590	2.6
Communist		
China	290	2.8
Czechoslovakia	5,820	4.1
East Germany	7,180	4.7
Hungary	4,180	4.8
Poland	3,900	5.2
USSR	4,550	4.1
Yugoslavia	2,620	5.4

*France, although a socialist country, is included with the capitalist countries.
Source: World Bank, *1981 World Bank Atlas* (Washington, 1982), pp. 10–20.

nist countries and 19th among all countries. There is no question but what East Germany is the most successful of all communist countries. It has the highest standard of living of the Eastern European countries and a highly developed industrial economy. There are, however, some extenuating circumstances that have helped contribute to the East German success. Although separated from West Germany ideologically and by physical barriers, East Germany has received various types of financial support from West Germany. There are special trade considerations that have been given the East Germans. The sale of West German agricultural products to East Germany is subsidized, and trade between East and West Germany is treated as free commerce and is not subject to a tariff. Hard currency payments are made to East Germany. An example is payments made for the release of East German political prisoners.

As Table 18-2 indicates, growth in real per capita income was higher for the communist countries than for the capitalist countries during the 1970–1979 period. This can be attributed in part to the fact that real incomes in the communist countries were far lower to begin with, and any significant gain would show up in a higher percentage gain in real per capita income. Nevertheless, the economies of the communist countries did register considerable advances, particularly during the early 1970s. The economies of both the capitalist and communist countries began to slow down after 1975, in part as a result of the oil price increases that had an adverse impact on both East and West. Modernization, the raising of efficiency in production, and quality of supply close to that of the advanced Western countries have become imperative to support needed trade and to provide an opportunity for sustaining economic growth. In the 1980s growth rates may continue to slow in both the capitalist and communist countries.

Consumption Comparisons

A prime measure of economic performance is to compare living standards of the capitalist and communist countries. The Soviet Union once claimed that its people would have the highest living standards in the world by 1980. That is hardly the case, for events have turned out quite differently. Instead of gaining on its capitalist rivals, the gap in living standards has been widened, with real per capita consumption in the Soviet Union running at less than a third of that in the United States. Moreover, living standards in most of the Eastern European satellite countries are much higher than those of the Soviet Union. Even Poland, which suffers by comparison with the West and with its neighbors Czechoslovakia and East Germany, has living standards that are higher than those that prevail in the Soviet Union. In the 1980s, living standards in the Soviet Union are likely to improve much more slowly than in the past because of the projected constraints on economic growth.

Table 18-3 presents a comparison of living standards for selected countries. There is a sizable gap between levels of living in the Soviet Union and in other countries, both East and West. Meat consumption in the Soviet Union is far below the levels that prevail in the United States, France, and West Germany. The Soviet position is better with respect to the number of television sets, although the quality is inferior to Western sets. In contrast, the Soviet Union is the leader in the number of doctors and hospital beds per 100,000 people. Health care services in the Soviet Union are extensive and available to everyone free of charge, but the same is true of countries such as West Germany. There is also a question of the quality of both doctors and medical services in the Soviet Union. Clinics and hospitals are crowded, often dirty, and poorly equipped; queues for the best doctors and hospitals are long. Payments "under the table" to obtain desired services are quite common. In contrast, a network of special private clinics and hospitals exist for the party elite.

The Soviet Union and other communist countries lag behind the

TABLE 18-3
PER CAPITA INDICATORS OF LIVING STANDARDS IN PHYSICAL UNITS, 1976

Source	Unit	USSR	U.S.	West Germany	France	Italy	United Kingdom	Japan	Poland	Czechoslovakia	Hungary
Meat	Kilograms per year	46	118	92	102	67	70	26	70	81	68
Potatoes and grain products	Kilograms per year	166	66	84	92	134	90	126	159	128	134
Television receivers	Units per 1,000 persons	223	571	305	235	213	315	233	198	253	233
Telephones in use	Units per 1,000 persons	66	695	317	262	259	379	405	108	NA	NA
Passenger cars	Persons per car	46	2	2	3	4	4	6	27	9	14
Health services	Per 100,000 persons										
Doctors		297	159	199	147	206	134	118	222	282	262
Pharmacists		20	68	41	58	69	31	69	NA	NA	NA
Hospital beds		1,164	670	1,155	1,024	1,053	895	1,287	NA	NA	850

NA: not available.
Source: U.S. Joint Economic Committee, *Consumption in the USSR: An International Comparison*, 97th Congress, 1st Session, 1981, Table 10, p. 22.

West in the production of housing. Although the supply of housing has been much improved during the 1970s through large investments in construction of new apartments, the quality is low by Western standards.[16] Many urban dwellers live in dull, drab apartment complexes that look alike. Apartments are small, and renters are fortunate to get one with more than two rooms plus a bathroom. Some apartments are shared with more than one family unit. There are apartments that are luxurious by Western standards, but they are reserved for party officials or those persons who have the right connections. Rents are maintained at artificially low rates, but have begun to move up as efforts are made to upgrade the supply of housing. Many adjustments in the basic rate of rent are made to include such factors as location, age and state of repair of the buildings, income of the occupants, and special amenities such as services provided to the occupants.

Anyone who has had to shop in the Soviet Union is familiar with the poor quality of service and a lack of variety in style and design in the products. The same holds true in varying degrees in the other communist countries. There is narrowness of the range of choice[17] available to consumers that rises in part from the fact that planners' choice rather than consumer preferences determine the diversity of product mix, and in part because producers, in response to the incentives facing them, have shown a persistent preference for quantity production of a few standardized items. Clerks are often surly and unresponsive, reflecting the lower wages that are paid to them and the "second-class" status assigned to the distribution and service sectors in the governments' scheme of things.

Economic Growth Comparisons

Table 18-4 presents the average annual rates of growth of real gross national product measured on a per capita and a per employed worker basis for two time periods, 1956 to 1978 and 1971 to 1978. Seven major industrial countries, including the Soviet Union, are used. As the table indicates, Japan was the best performer for both time periods. The performance of the Soviet Union was superior to that of the United States for both periods, but inferior to France, West Germany, and Japan. A feature of Soviet economic growth has been a prodigious growth in the labor force relative to the other countries. This growth, however, has slowed down in recent years.

---

[16]The author, who has been in several apartments in Poland, found them to range in size from small to rather opulent, depending on the status of the occupant. For a good description of typical apartments in the Soviet Union see Lee's *Russian Journal.*

[17]The author shopped for a warmup suit in the industrial city of Jelenia Gora near the Czech border. The suit came in three sizes, small, medium, and large, and in one color, brown; the same was true for women's warmup suits. Running shoes were also all brown.

TABLE 18-4
AVERAGE ANNUAL RATES OF GROWTH
OF REAL NATIONAL PRODUCT PER CAPITA
AND PER WORKER, SELECTED COUNTRIES

	Real Gross National Product	
	Per Capita	Per Employed Worker
1971–1978		
United States	2.5%	0.9%
France	3.3	3.4
West Germany	2.6	3.6
United Kingdom	2.0	1.8
Italy	2.0	1.8
Japan	4.3	4.5
USSR	2.8	2.4
1956–1978		
United States	2.2%	1.5%
France	3.9	4.4
West Germany	4.2	4.2
United Kingdom	2.0	2.1
Italy	3.8	4.3
Japan	7.5	7.3
USSR	3.6	3.2

Source: U.S. Joint Economic Committee, *Consumption in the USSR: An International Comparison*, 97th Congress, 1st Session, 1981, Table 16, p. 27.

Disastrous agricultural results could be a harbinger of worse things to come for the Soviet economy. A study prepared for the top Soviet leadership and released in May 1982 outlined a precipitous decline in the Soviet Union's ability to feed itself.[18] The study provided figures that showed a ten-fold increase in Soviet food imports over the preceding decade, mishandling of agricultural equipment, and direct losses of harvested crops due to negligence. It is estimated that one-fifth of the grain harvest and one-third of the potato harvest is lost each year because of an inefficient distribution system and a lack of storage facilities. As a result, the average Soviet citizen is poorly fed, consuming 54 pounds of meat per year less than required by Western medical standards.[19] The study concludes

---

[18]*Washington Post*, May 23, 1982, pp. 1, 24.
[19]A pound of meat, when available in state stores, costs $1.40. The state buys the meat from collective farms for $4.00 a pound. The market price in Moscow's open markets is around $6.00 a pound.

by stating that the existing economic mechanism does not provide the necessary economic incentives for production increases and fuller use of the potentially available land. Demands and expectations have risen dramatically to make the issue of food a critical problem for the Soviet leaders in the current decade.[20]

The capitalist countries cannot, however, take comfort in the misfortunes of Poland and the Soviet Union. There are indeed many inefficiencies built into the command economies. It is also not helpful to be locked into an obsolete ideology that is responsible for most of the deficiencies. But the capitalist countries are also having their own set of problems, which few of them have solved. In the United States and Western Europe, the rate of unemployment is high and the rate of economic growth is low. Inflation is still a problem in some countries, notably France and the United Kingdom. Western economies have still not resolved the inflation–unemployment dilemma. Although the rate of inflation has gone down in the United States, the rate of unemployment has increased. Income distribution still remains an important economic and political issue.

SUMMARY

Economic systems can be compared on the basis of how well they satisfy various performance criteria: employment, price stability, economic growth, and an equitable distribution of income. In recent years there has been a breakdown in the performance of both the capitalist and communist countries, in part for similar reasons and in part for different reasons. All countries were adversely affected by the increase in world oil prices during the 1970s. High interest rates in the United States have also had an adverse impact on the economies of Western Europe. But there are other factors that have contributed to the slowdown. For the capitalist countries, it is difficult to match the performance standards of the post–World War II period, and for the communist countries, inefficiencies built into the system have caught up with it.

REVIEW QUESTIONS

1. What are some of the factors contributing to the declining performance of both the capitalist and communist countries during the early part of the 1980s?
2. What impact do Soviet military expenditures have on the consumer sector of the economy?
3. Compare consumer living standards in the capitalist and communist countries.

---

[20]It is estimated that the Soviet Union will have to import 45 million tons of grain in 1982. Total food imports for 1982 are estimated to be three times higher than total food imports for the period 1966–1970.

4. Why are some of the Eastern European countries able to perform much better than the Soviet Union?
5. Compare the performances of the Soviet Union and the United States in terms of economic growth and income distribution.
6. France and the United States have taken diametrically opposite approaches to solving similar economic problems. Discuss.
7. The poor performance of Soviet agriculture could well have an inhibiting effect on the Soviet economy during the 1980s. Discuss.
8. Why has Japan had the best overall performance of all major countries?

RECOMMENDED READINGS

Feldstein, Martin, ed. *The American Economy in Transition*. Chicago: University of Chicago Press, 1980.

Heilbroner, Robert, and Lester Thurow. *Five Economic Challenges*. Englewood Cliffs, N.J.: Prentice-Hall, 1981.

Levine, Charles H., ed. *Managing Fiscal Stress: The Crisis in the Public Sector*. Chatham, N.J.: Chatham House, 1980.

O'Toole, James. *Making America Work: Productivity and Responsibility*. New York: Continuum Press, 1981.

Pechman, Joseph A. *Setting National Priorities, Agenda for the 1980's*. Washington: Brookings Institution, 1980.

Rostow, Walt W. *The World Economy: History and Prospect*. Austin: University of Texas Press, 1978.

Servan-Schreiber, Jean-Jacques. *The World Challenge*. New York: Simon and Schuster, 1981.

Solomon, Ezra. *Beyond the Turning Point*. San Francisco: Freeman, 1981.

U.S. Joint Economic Committee. *Consumption in the USSR: An International Comparison*, 97th Congress, 1st Session, 1981.

_____. *The Political Economy of the Western Hemisphere: Selected Issues for U.S. Policy*, 97th Congress, 1st Session, 1981.

Index